Cavan County Library
Withdrawn Stock

D1465503

Hamlyn Illustrated History

ASTON VILLA

1874—1998

Hamlyn Illustrated History

ASTON VILLA

1874—1998

Graham McColl

HAMLYN

Acknowledgments

The author would like to thank the following representatives of Aston Villa for giving so much of their time and help in interviews: Charlie Aitken, Gordon Cowans, Dennis Mortimer, Peter McParland and Nigel Spink. Thanks also to Neil Rioch of Aston Villa Old Stars. I would also like to thank Reg Thacker, the Aston Villa archivist and a true gentleman, for his unfailing friendliness and help, and for providing his expertise in reading and checking the manuscript and page proofs, providing statistics and for supplying match programmes from his collection. Many thanks also to Abdul Rashid, commercial manager at Villa Park, for his ongoing help with the project and for providing access to the club.

I would also like to thank Wilson Design Associates for their design work and Brenda Clynch for picture research. Thanks also to Rab MacWilliam of Sport and Leisure Books Ltd and Adam Ward of Reed International Books Ltd for commissioning me for this project and for their help and humour over the months it took to bring all the strands together.

The newspaper archives of the Central Reference Library in Birmingham proved to be an invaluable source of information. Back numbers of the following newspapers and magazine helped greatly in my research: The Birmingham Mail, The Sports Argus, The Birmingham Post, The Independent, The Daily Telegraph, The Sunday Times, World Soccer.

The following books also proved extremely useful in my research:

Aston Villa. The First 100 Years by Peter Morris (Centenary edition published by Aston Villa Football Club Limited, 1974); **The Great Years of Aston Villa** by David Goodyear (Published by David Goodyear, 1982); **Triumphs of the Football Field**, narrated by Archie Hunter, the Famous Villa Captain (First published by the Birmingham Weekly Mercury (1890) Re-published in 1997 by Sports Projects Ltd, Warley, West Midlands); **Aston Villa: A Complete Record 1874-1992** by David Goodyear & Tony Matthews (The Breedon Books Publishing Company Ltd, Derby, 1992); **The Villa Park Encyclopedia** by Dean Hayes (Mainstream Publishing, Edinburgh, 1997); **Villa Park – 100 Years** by Simon Inglis (Sports Projects Ltd, 1997).

Produced for Hamlyn by Sport and Leisure Books Ltd.

First published in Great Britain in 1998
by Hamlyn, an imprint of Reed Consumer Books Limited
Michelin House, 81 Fulham Road, London SW3 6RB
and Auckland, Melbourne, Singapore and Toronto

Copyright ©1998 Reed Consumer Books Limited

ISBN 0 600 59529 3

CAVAN COUNTY LIBRARY
ACC. No. C178093
CLASS No. 796.334
INVOICE NO. 4018
PRICE 17.99

All rights reserved. No part of this publication may be reproduced, stored in a retrieval system, or transmitted in any form or by any means, mechanical, photocopying, recording or otherwise, without the permission of the copyright holders.

A catalogue record for this book is available from the British Library

Printed by Mladinska knjiga

Picture Acknowledgements
Aston Villa Football Club 18, 20, 25, 33 top, 35, 36, 37 top
Colorsport 8, 15, 16, 26-27, 28, 30-31, 32-33, 37 below, 38, 40, 42, 43, 44 top, 44 below, 45, 46, 47, 48, 49 top left, 49 top right, 50, 51, 52, 54, 56, 58 top left, 58 below right, 59, 60, 62 below left, 62 below right, 63 top, 63 below, 64, 66, 68, 69, 71, 76, 80, 82, 84, 86, 87, 88, 89, 90, 91, 93, 94, 96, 97, 98, 101, 103, 104, 106, 108, 110, 111, 112, 113 top, 113 below, 114, 117, 120, 121, 122, 123 top, 123 below, 124, 125, 126 below left, 126-127 below centre, 127 top left, 128, 129, 130, 132, 133, 135, 137, 140, 142, 143, 144 top left, 144 top right, 145 below left, 146, 147, 149, 150, 151, 152, 153, 154, 155, 156, 157, 158, 159, 160
News Team 72, 74, 75, 78, 79, 81, 85
Sport and Leisure Books Ltd. 10, 12, 138, 139, 141 top left, 141 top right, 141 below left, 145 centre left

We are grateful to Aston Villa for permission to reproduce their programmes and match tickets and for providing their statistical information, to Coca-Cola for the use of their programmes and to Dawn Cover Productions for use of their cover images. Other programmes used with kind permission of Wembley Stadium Ltd. Every effort has been made to trace copyright-holders but if errors or omissions are brought to our attention we shall be pleased to correct them in future editions of the book.

Contents

FOREWORD
by Dennis Mortimer

Before joining Aston Villa I knew very little about the club. The only two stories about Villa that did stick in my mind revolved around Tommy Docherty. One was about him having a carpet of astro-turf laid in his office, the other was him making Jimmy Brown the youngest captain of Aston Villa at the age of 16. That was the extent of my knowledge about Aston Villa, so I will always remember my first game for the club, when we won 4-1 against West Ham United on Boxing Day 1975. There were 52,000 inside Villa Park that day and the excitement generated by the crowd was powerful enough to blow you over. That immediately made me realise the stature of the club I had just joined.

I played in many impressive stadiums during my career but few matched Villa Park for a combination of grandeur and atmosphere. It was particularly inspirational to have the Holte End willing you forward or to be aiming to score in front of them and then see the fans' tumultuous celebrations on that massive terracing. The grand nature of the ground, particularly that of the Trinity Road stand, also provided a constant reminder of the strong traditions that were expected to be upheld by those who wear the claret and blue.

It was therefore a source of great satisfaction to I and my team-mates that the football we played during our time at Aston Villa not only brought us victories but was also in the finest Villa tradition. I was fortunate to be part of the greatest decade that Aston Villa have enjoyed in modern times. During those exciting years, the club swiftly re-established itself among the leading names in Britain and, for the first time, as the champions of Europe.

Winning the League Championship in 1981 was a special achievement, particularly as the club and its supporters had waited so long for the League title to return to Villa Park. Then, when we won the European Cup the following year, the feeling of holding that trophy was, and remains, indescribable. One of the benefits of being a captain is that you are the first member of the team to hold a trophy! The run to the final was equally memorable – we defeated some of Europe's leading clubs, clubs that were brimful with talent. We played the game at a tremendous pace but always with a great degree of skill. The hallmark of the great Villa sides during the early years of the club had been teamwork allied with a highly entertaining passing game. We were proud that our style of play maintained those standards, while we played at a speed commensurate with that required for the modern game. Combining both of those elements is one of the most difficult tasks in football but we managed to do so with considerable success.

It was a great honour to have played for Aston Villa and to have been captain of the side in their finest hours. Many captains before me will have felt very proud to have led Aston Villa to success. Those after me would also have felt the same. This book shows in detail how the club has become one of the greatest names in world football and why Aston Villa remains special to those fortunate to have become part of the club and its history.

From the very beginning, Aston Villa were ambitious. The early years saw the Midlands club quickly develop into a professional outfit capable of challenging the top teams in the country.

1 Seeds of Success: 1874–87

Aston Villa football club was built on a sublime synthesis of hard work, football skill and style, the qualities which have defined the Villa tradition. In its formative years the club enjoyed extreme good fortune – another quality that no successful club can be without. Fate was firmly on the side of Villa as they developed into the premier side in England in the final two decades of the 19th century. Most notably it was by sheer chance that both George Ramsay and Archie Hunter arrived at Villa. Those two men would do most to develop the club on and off the pitch during its earliest years.

Ramsay, a Scotsman, had arrived in Birmingham from his native land to start a new job. He was out for a stroll one day in 1876 when he saw the Villa players practising their skills. Ramsay, then 21 years old, asked if he could join in and immediately impressed the Villa lads through his exceptional ability with a football. They asked him if he would like to join their club, which was then just two years old. He would play for Villa for four years, becoming captain in 1878. As secretary, he would make an even bigger impact, securing the club their first home. He remained in that post until 1926 when he became vice-president of Villa until his death in 1935. 'I helped to plant the seed,' Ramsay would say, 'and I have seen a strong oak grow.'

Archie Hunter was an even luckier find. Another Scot, he had also come to Birmingham for work, in 1878, from his native Ayrshire. He had heard about Calthorpe FC (formerly Birmingham Clerks), Birmingham's premier team at the time, and intended to join them. Unluckily for Calthorpe, Hunter was tipped off by an acquaintance at his workplace that a fellow Scot called Ramsay was doing great things at a club called Aston Villa. Hunter went along to Villa and became the club's first star player.

Equally significantly, Villa had the good fortune to be unhampered by restrictions when, in 1885, their committee decided it was time to switch from amateur to professional status. The lease on their then ground, at Perry Barr, placed no restrictions on the club charging spectators for admission. During the early years of the game, such details could mean the difference between survival and extinction. When Villa's major rivals, Calthorpe, were unable to charge entry money because of the terms of their lease they fell behind Aston Villa forever.

The first game: 15-a-side

By the mid-1880s, Aston Villa had grown considerably since its birth in 1874. The club had been formed at the start of that year by members of the Villa Cross Wesleyan Chapel in Lozells Road. Having enjoyed the companionship and exercise afforded by cricket during the summer months, they sought a more vigorous sport for the colder, shorter days of winter and decided on football.

In March 1874, they played their first match, against Aston Brook St Mary's, a rugby club, at a ground on Wilson Road, Birchfield. In the first half, the game was to be played under the rules of rugby, in the second half under the rules of football. Nevertheless, the teams were 15-a-side for the entire match. The first Aston Villa side

Aston Villa in 1880 with the club's first trophy, the Birmingham Cup. George Ramsay, the team captain, holds the ball.

to enter the field of play was: W. Scattergood, W. Weiss, W. H. Price, F. Knight, E. Lee, G. Matthews, H. Matthews, C. Midgley, J. Hughes, W. Such, H. Whateley, G. Page, A. Robbins, W. B. Mason and W. Sothers. In the first half, under rugby rules, Villa held St Mary's to 0–0. When the codes changed to football in the second half Villa deployed half of their 14 outfield players in attack and came out on top, winning 1–0, courtesy of a Jack Hughes goal midway through the half. The only goal of the game was scored with a football that Villa had hired at the cost of one shilling and sixpence (7½ pence).

In their first full season of existence, 1874–75, the club gradually felt its way into competitive football, playing friendlies against other clubs in the Birmingham area who were seeking to establish themselves. Villa played their home matches on Aston Grounds or Aston Lower Grounds Meadow. In 1878, two years after joining the club, George Ramsay was made captain. While out for a walk one day that year,

Ramsay came across a piece of land at Wellington Road, Perry Barr, that looked perfect for football and arrangements were quickly made for its rental. The Old Crown and Cushion, a pub on the corner of Aston Lane and Wellington Lane, became the club's administrative headquarters. The players used a blacksmith's hut opposite the ground for their changing-rooms. The first match at their new ground was watched by 21 people, who paid threepence (1¼ pence) a head.

Initially, the rent of the Perry Barr ground was £7 10 shillings (£7.50) but when the landlord, a butcher, saw Villa's growing success he decided their rent should rise commensurately. In the following year the rent increased to £15 then to £20. Villa were then told that the landlord planned to sell the land to allow building to take place on it. To prevent this, Villa agreed a seven-year lease for the ground at £100 per year. Their landlord's increasingly excessive demands would later lead to Villa becoming their own landlords.

The Crown and Cushion, Perry Barr, stands on the site of the Old Crown and Cushion. The pub was used by Aston Villa as a changing room for home games from the 1870s until the 1890s. The pub was also a meeting place where players could discuss tactics. The committee would hold meetings there. The presence of club officials and players attracted many supporters to the premises, where they could mingle freely with representatives of Aston Villa FC.

The influence of Ramsay, then Hunter, led Villa to develop an intricate passing game, a revolutionary move for an English club in the late 1870s. It was a style of play modelled on that which was prevalent in Scotland at the time and which had been pioneered by Queen's Park, the Glasgow side. This type of sophisticated teamwork had rarely been employed in England. Instead, individuals would try to take the ball as far as they could on their own until stopped by an opponent.

William McGregor, a fellow Scot and committee member of Aston Villa, remembered Ramsay the player: 'I can see now the little dapper, well-built laddie, with a black-and-red striped cap, red-and-blue hooped jersey, and the same coloured stockings, getting hold of the ball on the extreme wing, well within his own territory, and going off like streaked lightning, wiggling, waggling past opponents one after another and finally landing the ball between the sticks.'

Quest for the Cup

One indicator of Villa's rapidly increasing status came in season 1879–80. Aston Villa took part in the FA Cup – then the only major competition for English clubs – for the first time. They were drawn away to Stafford Road Railway Works, a team from Wolverhampton. The first game ended 1–1 and Villa won 1–0 in the replay. Another away draw followed, at Oxford University. In those days of amateur football, the students had been winners of the Cup in 1874 and twice finalists, in 1873 and 1877. The draw brought a strange response from the Villa committee. For reasons never fully explained, they decided to withdraw from that year's tournament.

Archie Hunter took over from Ramsay as team captain on his countryman's retirement as a player in 1880. The Scottish influence remained strong, however, with Villa adopting the Scots' national symbol of a Lion Rampant as the club badge on the advice of director William McGregor. As the 1880s progressed, Aston Villa became a well-known Cup name. Villa twice reached the quarter-finals, in 1883 and 1884. Drawn away to Notts County in the last eight in 1883, Villa drew back to

3–3 after being 3–0 down but a late County goal ended that year's FA Cup affair. The following season, a 6–1 quarter-final defeat by Queen's Park at Titwood Park, Glasgow, put a dampener on Villa's budding romance with the Cup.

Three years later, however, a match between Aston Villa and Wolves in the FA Cup did much to endear the tournament to Midlanders' hearts. At that time, each club started playing Cup ties at the beginning of the season and in the autumn of 1886 Villa began with a local derby, against Wednesbury Old Athletic. Villa, now wearing new striped jerseys, won 13–0 then beat Derby Midland 6–1 in the next round. Villa remained in the Midlands for the third round, against Wolves. This tie would fan enthusiasm for football in the region like no other event up until that point.

The first match, at Perry Barr in early December 1886, ended 2–2. The replay at Wolverhampton was postponed several times because the Wolves' pitch was unplayable. It eventually took place on 15 January. Even then, hundreds of tons of snow had to be removed from the pitch in the preceding week. Around one thousand Villa fans took the train to Wolverhampton for the match, watched by a crowd of 6,000 at the Dudley Road ground, which was Wolves' then home.

On inspecting the pitch, the teams discovered that a thin layer of ice topped its surface. Both sides played under protest at the conditions. 'The Astonians displayed a cautious and scientific mode of aggression which at times completely puzzled their opponents,' reported *The Birmingham Daily Post*. 'Their neat and accurate passes and effective combination runs would have told well in their favour under more advantageous circumstances.' The teams ended level at 1–1. On consideration of the two sides' protests, however, the FA refused to recognise that first replay and ordered it to be played again at Wolverhampton.

That replayed replay, on 22 January, also resulted in a draw, 3–3, after 90 minutes. At the end of the match, Mr McIntyre, the referee, suggested that the teams play an extra half-hour. Villa, however, did not come to an agreement with him. Instead of playing extra time, a third replay between the two clubs was agreed and scheduled for Birmingham a week later.

The three previous instalments of this tie had stirred up tremendous excitement among local fans. Villa, in anticipation of a big crowd, erected an extra stand and extra entrances at Perry Barr to accommodate the expected numbers. On the day, brakes (supporters' horse-drawn carriages) and buses lined the sides of the playing field. Other fans watched proceedings from the trees that surrounded the ground. There was also a tram depot situated beside the ground and some fans decided to watch the match from the roofs of the tram sheds. Just before the anticipated 3.00pm kick-off, however, some tram workers, unhappy with this encroachment on to their territory, turned hoses on the spectators on the roof. Those drenched didn't much like it, but the rest of the spectators thoroughly enjoyed this unexpected addition to the afternoon's entertainment.

The 12,000 crowd – the highest attendance yet seen at Perry Barr – needed the pre-match diversion. They had been in place by 2.45pm but the match was delayed because of the late arrival of referee McIntyre's train. Conditions for spectators and players alike were uncomfortable – the match taking place in a fierce late-January gale. Eventually, at 3.20pm, Mr McIntyre took the field and the match kicked off.

A storming performance saw Villa forwards swarming all over the Wolves penalty area. Goals from Freddy Dawson and Archie Hunter had Villa 2–0 ahead at half-time. The scoreline remained the same at the end of the match – although it should have been more – and Villa went through deservedly.

Aston Villa were then given a bye into the fifth round to meet Horncastle, a team from Lincolnshire. The time-eating replays with Wolves meant that this match would take place just a week later, on 5 February. After the struggles against Wolves, this match was expected to be straightforward. So it proved. A 5,000 crowd at Perry Barr saw Villa ease to a 5–0 win. It was the first time Villa had gone beyond five rounds of the Cup.

The following week, Villa's rapid run through the rounds continued with their

The Villa Cross Wesleyan Chapel, on Lozells Road, which was built in the 1860s. When, in 1874, some of its members decided to form a football team they were, to some extent, following fashion. The new game and the new team would, however, engender feelings among aficionados that guaranteed that both would survive and thrive longer and more successfully than the founders could have imagined.

quarter-final at Perry Barr. It was the fifth successive Saturday on which Villa had played a Cup-tie. Their opponents were Darwen, a Lancashire side. The crowd was almost as big as the one for the third replay with Wolves. Villa bamboozled their visitors with their close-passing game and were 3–0 ahead by half-time. During the break, Mr Amos Roe, president of Moseley Rugby Football Club, displayed the Midland Counties Challenge Cup, which his club had recently won, and filled it with champagne. The players of Aston Villa and Darwen were then invited to drink their fill from the cup, which they duly did. Shortly after half-time, Jimmy Warner, the Villa goalkeeper, went to kick clear but missed the ball entirely to concede a soft goal. Another miskick, by Villa right-half Burton, presented Darwen with their second goal. Villa held on, however, to reach the semi-final.

The FA Cup had grown continually in prestige and excitement since its establishment in 1872. In the 1886–87 season, the tournament had attracted the biggest entry yet of 132 clubs, including representatives from Scotland, Wales and Ireland. Villa's opponents in their semi-final at Crewe on 5 March would be the last non-English team left in that year's competition, Glasgow Rangers. In 1884 and 1885, Rangers' Glasgow rivals Queen's Park had reached the FA Cup final. In an attempt to emulate them, Rangers co-opted players from all the leading Scottish clubs – such as Dumbarton, Queen's Park, Renton and Hibernian – for the tie against Villa. By the time of the Villa match, the Rangers team was comprised entirely of Scottish internationals.

Villa had prepared for the match with a week's retreat at Holt Fleet, deep in the countryside to the south of Birmingham and close to the village of Ombersley. There they had trained and taken relaxation in brine baths.

The match at Crewe attracted 4,000 Villa fans in a crowd of 10,000. The locals were also on Villa's side, sporting 'Play up, Villa' cards which they stuck in their hatbands. Archie Hunter gave Villa an early lead but Rangers equalised before half-time. In the second half, Albert Brown got Villa's second and Hunter a third. By the end, Villa were well on top and unlucky not

to add further goals to their tally. Rangers' only response was to increase the emphasis on physical strength but their clumsy fouling did little to deter a nimble Villa side. Despite Rangers' attraction of the best Scottish players the sum of the parts was greater than the whole. Villa had beaten the Scots with their own game – teamwork.

Aston Villa had now scored 39 goals on their way to the final. Parallel to their progress in the FA Cup they had also played numerous friendlies in the 1886–87 season. Among their opponents had been Sheffield Wednesday, Middlesbrough, Welsh Druids, London Caledonians, a team from Scotland called Cowlairs and Stafford Rangers. The highlight was Villa's match against Hibernian on New Year's Day 1887. That visit to Edinburgh resulted in an 8–3 win over the home side, who would be the winners of the Scottish Cup that year.

Final at the Oval

Villa's opponents in the 1887 FA Cup final would be West Bromwich Albion, the beaten finalists in 1886. The match would be played at the Oval cricket ground in Kennington, south London. Albion were reported as being so confident of victory that they had made plans to transport the Cup back to West Bromwich via Kidderminster to avoid transporting it through Birmingham (their players and supporters bridled at any suggestion that West Bromwich was part of Birmingham). WBA had knocked Villa out of the Cup in 1885 and they had reason to believe that they could repeat the feat in 1887. In a friendly that season, Villa had drawn 1–1 with WBA a week before Christmas. Villa had also lost a Birmingham Cup tie against the same club by a goal to nil. Albion were also fresh from a notable semi-final victory over Preston North End, nicknamed 'The Invincibles' and regarded as England's premier team.

Before the final, Villa again sought peace and quiet at Holt Fleet where they trained on ground overlooking the River Severn. Additional to the usual football training, some players rowed on the river or took lengthy walks in the surrounding countryside. Howard Vaughton, the inside-left, and the only amateur in the Villa side, was unable to join his team-mates in seclusion but he would be in the side for the final. The Villa team to face Albion would be: Warner, Coulton, Simmonds, Yates, Dawson, Burton, Davis, Brown, Hunter, Vaughton and Hodgetts.

The Oval's playing surface was of an average size. That was foremost in Archie Hunter's thoughts as he took time out at Holt Fleet to look forward to the match. 'I think a big ground gives the Villa a big advantage,' he said. 'Our style of play is suited to a big ground, and the Albion with their long passing have the advantage on a small field. On the Oval we both shall have an equal chance, and where things are equal the short passing game is always the best. These are my reasons for thinking we will win on Saturday.

'We have had many a hard struggle in the English Cup competition, we have been fancied more than once, but up till now we have had a rough time of it. We have had to play hard matches early in the competition, and were done up and beaten because of that when we had got half through. We are fresh and fit now, and in the final. You may depend on it we will make a hard fight of it to win.'

The Football Association had made arrangements to defray the costs of supporters who travelled from Birmingham and District to the Oval for the final. On production of their railway ticket, which cost seven shillings (35 pence), at the gate they would gain entry at half-price: sixpence (2½ pence) instead of one shilling (5 pence). Regardless of this concession, the railway companies estimated that only 1,500 supporters of Villa or WBA travelled on the special trains that were laid on for the final. A visit to London was a major excursion. There were, however, many exiled Brummies at the game, including a number of servicemen stationed in the South; in particular, red-coated guardsmen stood out in the crowd.

Hodgetts the hero

At breakfast-time on the day of the game, London endured a snap snowstorm. By kick-off that afternoon the sun was shining but the playing surface at the Oval, which wasn't in particularly good condition anyway, was now muddy. The conditions hampered Villa's slick, accurate, ground-based game. A strong wind gave Albion an added advantage in the first half and Villa faced almost incessant Albion pressure. It put great stress on the Villa backs but they stood up to it manfully. Frank Coulton, the sturdy Villa right-back, and goalkeeper Jimmy Warner were particularly impressive in dealing with the WBA attacks.

One save from Warner had the crowd of 15,334 gasping with disbelief. A low, hard shot from Albion's Perry looked a certain goal but Warner dived, got to the ball on his line and scooped it over the bar. Later in the half, a magnificent overhead kick from Albion's Green was going wide until a sudden gust of wind re-directed it towards the Villa goal. Warner managed to stretch for the ball and tip it round his post. As he did so, he was clobbered by the inrushing Albion forward Pearson. Another scoring effort from Albion was headed off the Villa goal-line by Coulton.

It was unusual for Villa, habitually an attacking side, to be relying so heavily on defence – a defence that was showing hidden depths. For most of the first half, Villa were dangerous only on the break. In the second, with the wind at their backs, they got the breakthrough. Rich Davis, the Villa outside-right, made speedy progress down his wing. His cross fell nicely for Dennis Hodgetts to move in from the opposite wing and sidefoot sharply between the WBA posts (goal nets would not be seen in an FA Cup final until 1892). WBA players darted in the direction of the referee, claiming that Hodgetts had been offside. The referee, Major Marindin, who was also President of the FA, refused to change his mind. Villa were 1–0 ahead.

With a minute remaining, Archie Hunter cut through the Albion defence. He appeared to have pushed the ball too far ahead of him as Roberts dashed from goal to make a challenge. Hunter, stretching to the full, managed to get one final touch on the ball. As he and Roberts collided, the ball skidded under the WBA man for Villa's decisive second goal.

Back in Birmingham the public houses had been packed with Villa fans all afternoon, waiting eagerly to hear the latest news from London. They kept abreast of the score through a series of telegrams sent on the instructions of those who were at the game. Enterprising businessmen posted telegrams in their windows, updating the news with each fresh telegram – one shop displayed 12 successive telegrams that afternoon. In Summer Lane, a vast crowd stood outside the shop window of William McGregor's draper's shop to keep up with the news. When the final result was known, thousands of Villa supporters took to the streets in celebration. The crowds were at their most dense in the Lozells and Aston New Town.

The Aston Villa players took the 11.20pm train from Euston and arrived at New Street shortly after 3am on the Sunday morning where they were greeted by an exuberant crowd that packed the platforms. The following day, Villa fans celebrated with Archie Hunter at the Bell Inn, where he lived. By early afternoon the place was packed and proceedings became frenzied when the pub's landlord returned from a visit to Mr Kynoch, the club president, with the FA Cup. It was the first time the major-

ity of those present had seen what the FA Cup looked like. The Villa captain, looking back on the Cup final, said: 'The fact is, being such near neighbours, and being engaged in such a tremendously important fight, we all felt too excited to play well. It was not as good a match as the one you will see on Saturday.' That match at Perry Barr lived up to Hunter's promise. Villa defeated Hibernian, the 1887 Scottish Cup holders, 3–0.

The first all-Midland final had ensured that the centre of football was now in the Midlands rather than in Lancashire. Aston Villa's progress over the season, culminating in the FA Cup victory, had established them as the leading team in Britain. Excitement for football among their supporters and in the city of Birmingham had never been greater. The Villa players had been unmatched in initiative but the next momentous move on the part of the club would be made away from the field of play. That step would change the nature of football in England, Scotland and around the world, forever.

The Aston Villa players who brought the FA Cup to Birmingham for the first time, by defeating West Bromwich Albion 2–0 at The Oval on 2 April 1887. The players standing are (left to right): Coulton, Warner, Dawson, Simmonds, Allen (reserve). Seated in the middle row are (left to right): Davies, Brown, Hunter, Vaughton, Hodgetts. Seated are: Yates, Burton.

The 1880s saw Aston Villa play a key role in the development of the new Football League. On the pitch Villa continued their success story and in 1897 they won the double to become England's premier team.

2 Glorious Home-coming: 1887–99

A struggle for the 'championship of England and the world' was one newspaper's billing for the 1888 FA Cup tie between Villa, the holders, and Preston North End, the team with the best all-round record in England. The seriousness of the struggle was emphasised when Preston sent out a second eleven for their friendly fixture with Cowlairs the week before the tie. Preston's top men were in intensive training for the match with Villa, which took place at Perry Barr on 7 January 1888.

Press reporters from all over Britain were gathered at the game. In Birmingham, supporters started taking trams to Perry Barr at 11.00am – the kick-off was at 2.15pm. From noon, all roads seemed to lead to Perry Barr as crowds of people, carriages and cabs swarmed towards Villa's ground. At the ground, enterprising cart-owners charged for access to their vehicles and an elevated view of the game. The match produced a record crowd for a football match in England, estimated at between 20,000 and 30,000. Every place had been taken an hour before the match was due to begin. Only 50 policemen were on duty, assisted by two helpers on shire-horses.

Kick-off had to be delayed until the crowd had retreated far enough to make the touchlines visible. Villa held their own in the first half and at half-time the score was 1–1. In the second period, Preston, tutored by their imported 'Scotch professors', got into the groove of their superior passing game. Villa couldn't cope and the Lancashire side ended well-deserved 3–1 winners. In those early days, the game was constantly changing and the slightest innovation could provide a team with the edge over their opponents. One tactical modification employed by Preston gave them a distinct advantage over Villa: instead of running alongside the man from whom a pass was anticipated, Preston's players would run ahead of him.

Four times during the match the crowd had spilled on to the pitch and after Villa's goal Preston had protested. The referee had declared that the match would not be considered as a Cup tie; the rest of the game would played as a friendly. After their victory, however, Preston claimed the tie. At a meeting of the FA Council the following Saturday morning, it was decided that as Villa were responsible for the crowd so the result should stand. This seemed patently unfair as Villa had played much of the game in a friendly fashion.

A competitive League

Local interest in football had reached a peak with the Preston game, yet Villa's matches in national competition were now over until the following autumn. They would focus their attention on the Birmingham Cup and friendly matches. One man on the Villa committee, William McGregor, was dissatisfied with this situation. He wanted matches such as the one with Preston to become a perennial feature of the footballing calendar. There were fears at the time that without proper organisation football might lose its grip on the public imagination. Football supporters were becoming more choosy about which matches to attend; the attraction of friendlies had begun to fade. The crowds for such matches were much lower than those for competitive cup ties. The growth of professionalism also meant that clubs needed steady, guaranteed income to

Aston Villa's 1895 FA Cup winners pose with the Cup. Bob Chatt, the goalscorer in the final, is third left in the front row.

pay their staff. Income was erratic because many friendlies were cancelled at the last minute. McGregor proposed a means for the top professional clubs to meet regularly.

On the Friday evening of 23 March 1888, the eve of Preston playing WBA in the FA Cup final, McGregor and other representatives of the most progressive clubs in English football met at Anderton's Hotel in London. They were there to discuss a union of the leading 12 clubs in the country under a league system. That meeting had been called at the instigation of William McGregor. Three weeks earlier he had written to several clubs proposing the get-together. 'Every year it is becoming more and more difficult for football clubs of any standing to meet their friendly engagements, and even arrange friendly matches,' he wrote. 'The consequence is at the last moment, through Cup tie interference, clubs are compelled to take on teams who will not attract the public.

'I beg to tender the following suggestion as a means of getting over the difficulty. That ten or twelve of the most prominent clubs in England combine to arrange home-and-away fixtures each season, the said fixtures to be arranged at a friendly conference about the same time as the International Conference...My object in writing to you at present is merely to draw your attention to the subject, and to suggest a friendly conference to discuss the matter more fully. I would take it as a favour if you would kindly think the matter over, and make whatever suggestions you may deem necessary. I am only writing to the following: Blackburn Rovers, Bolton Wanderers, Preston North End, West Bromwich Albion and Aston Villa, and should like to hear what other clubs you would suggest.'

On 17 April, the formation of the Football League was announced. Initially the League would comprise Accrington, Aston Villa, Blackburn Rovers, Bolton Wanderers, Burnley, Derby County, Everton, Notts County, Preston North End, Stoke, West Bromwich Albion and Wolverhampton Wanderers. Teams would play matches on a home-and-away basis, loosely modelled on the system used in the county cricket leagues. Four of the 12 would be subject to annual re-election. At the beginning of May 1888, in Birmingham, a League committee met to arrange the first season's fixtures. It

Charlie Athersmith was Villa's regular outside-right from 1891 to 1901. One of the quickest wingers in Britain, he also possessed a strong shot, which brought him 85 goals in 308 League games. Athersmith and Villa captain John Devey made their international debuts on the same day, representing England in the 2–0 victory over Ireland on 5 March 1892. Athersmith went on to win 12 England caps.

was agreed that teams would be awarded two points for a win and one point for a draw.

Aston Villa's first League match took place on 8 September 1888, away to Wolves. In front of 3,000 spectators, Wolves took the lead in the first half but shortly before half-time Tom Green, Villa's inside-right, scored the club's first League goal. The score remained 1–1 at the end of the match. The Villa team was: Warner, Cox, Coulton, Yates, Devey, Dawson, Brown, Green, Allen, Garvey, Hodgetts. The following Saturday, with 4,000 watching at Perry Barr, Villa lit a fire under their League campaign, beating Stoke 5–1.

North End challenge

By mid-November 1888, Villa were in second place in the new 12-team League. Preston were top with eight wins and a draw from nine games. Villa had lost one of their nine – 2–0 at Everton – and had drawn twice, at Stoke and Wolverhampton. It meant that

Villa were three points behind the leaders prior to the top of the table clash at Preston on 10 November The match attracted a record crowd of 10,000 to North End's Deepdale ground.

Preston went ahead after only two minutes when Villa goalkeeper Warner had been unsighted by one of his defenders. In the second half of a wide-open, fast-flowing game, both sides created a cornucopia of chances – football in the 1880s was geared toward attacking play. Archie Hunter came close to an equaliser with a shot that slithered just wide of the Preston goal. With two minutes remaining, Archie Goodall crossed into the middle and Green shovelled the ball over the Preston goal-line.

The good work of that afternoon was, however, undone the following week when Villa went down 5–1 away to Blackburn Rovers. A month previously, Villa had beaten Blackburn 6–1 at Perry Barr. On the first Saturday of January 1889, Archie Hunter failed to turn up for the match at Burnley. Hunter frequently had to race away from work at the last minute on a Saturday morning to make the Villa match. Indeed, the entire Villa party were late in arriving at the ground, so much so that Villa began the match with only eight players on the pitch. Two latecomers took the field after five minutes. Villa, with only ten men, lost 4–0. That afternoon, leaders Preston defeated Notts County 4–1. It left Villa 11 points behind with five games to play. Preston were champions.

Fittingly, the final home match of that first season was between Villa and Preston at Perry Barr. Villa knew beforehand that they would finish second in the League regardless of the result. Again they matched the masters in the first half but in the second they were thoroughly outplayed, losing 2–0.

Friendlies kept Villa in trim as they prepared for their next big test, an FA Cup tie at Blackburn Rovers in early March. For the first time, the Cup included preliminary rounds, which whittled the original entry of 151 down to 32 by the time Villa entered the competition. The match with Blackburn brought Villa's season crashing to a sudden end. Four Villa men – Devey, Burton, Yates and Hunter – were visibly struggling with injuries and lack of fitness throughout the game. It was a massive problem in an era long before substitutes were allowed. Villa were 3–0 down at half-time and beaten 8–1

by the end, the club's worst defeat in any competition. Only a stunning performance from Warner in goal had kept Blackburn's scoring in single figures.

Hard times

The match at Blackburn signalled the start of a grim time for Villa. There was a perceived lack of discipline at the club. The late 1880s and early 1890s brought rumours of easy living among the Villa players. Several members of the Villa team had been installed as pub landlords by the club as a perk. There was concern that these players were sampling their own establishments' products and that this was consequently affecting their performances.

A letter in *The Birmingham Daily Mail* of 6 January 1890 from 'A Member' and entitled 'Aston Villa Football Club' read:

'I notice that they have won two matches since the commencement of November – one a very fluky win, and the other against the weakest team in the League, and they have now started the month in January with a nice defeat of seven goals to none. My object in writing this letter is to see if the members cannot do something to alter this state of things, and I would suggest that they call a meeting to see what steps the committee have taken to obtain better players and, if a satisfactory explanation is not forthcoming, to, if possible, elect a committee who understand something about football, as the present committee seem to know very little. No doubt many of the followers of the club will agree with me that if other clubs can afford to obtain good players, surely Aston Villa ought to be in a position to do so… they certainly ought to be able to compete with any other club in the kingdom as regards finance.'

The Villa committee would survive – for the moment – but the club's perilous situation had been aggravated severely in that opening week of the 1890s. At half-time in the away match with Everton at Anfield Road, Liverpool, on 4 January Archie Hunter collapsed into a pool of water on the pitch. Initially it was suspected he had suffered an epileptic fit. The player had, however, felt one side of his body become paralysed; he had, in fact, suffered a stroke. Medical advice was that he should never play again.

Archie Hunter had been a mixture of toughness and cleverness at centre-forward. Known as 'the Old War Horse', he had been the first truly talismanic player Villa had fielded, a man who allied the delicate, crafty touches of the Scottish game with the physical strength needed for English football. He was also a superb dribbler, specialising in running at defences from deep in his own half. As centre-forward he linked up well with players on both wings and, to cap it all, possessed fierce shooting power. At the time of his sudden departure from the game he was 30 years old. He would be sorely missed on the playing side but remained at the club in an administrative capacity. Three weeks after his collapse Hunter was back at Perry Barr, running the touchline as an umpire (in the 1890s the clubs supplied linesmen). It was a brave and quick recovery at a time when medical care was, at best, rudimentary. In late November 1894, however, Archie, whose health had remained fragile after his stroke, died at the tragically early age of 35.

In the 1889–90 season Villa finished eighth in the First Division and were knocked out of the FA Cup in the second round. The following season, they fell to ninth in the First Division and again lost in the second round of the Cup. Villa, as one of the bottom four, faced a fight for re-election. Fortunately, they were saved this embarrassment when the League was expanded to 14 clubs.

Cup controversy

The 1892 FA Cup resurrected Villa's reputation. A Dennis Hodgetts hat-trick pushed Villa to a 4–1 home win in their opening tie with Heanor Town. They were next drawn against Darwen, one of Villa's victims in the Cup-winning year of 1887. A week was spent at Holt Fleet in preparation for this tie but Villa looked out of sorts on the afternoon of the match. Their performance was so disappointing that the Perry Barr crowd began to urge on the visitors during the second half. Villa still managed a 2–0 win.

Another of the clubs Villa had faced in 1887, Wolves, would be their next opponents. Again Villa passed the week before the tie at Holt Fleet, while Wolves spent it at a retreat in Arley. On the Saturday morning of the match, both teams shared a train from Droitwich to Wolverhampton. A record attendance for Wolves of 25,000 saw the home side take the lead. A slick overhead kick from Louis Campbell, Villa's inside-left, made for a stunning equaliser and, inspired by that, Villa ran out 3–1 winners. In the semi-final, at Bramall Lane, Sheffield, a 25,000 crowd saw Villa outplay Sunderland to win 4–1. Sunderland were then third in the League but would go on to win that year's championship.

A strong sense of déjà vu had been cast over much of that FA Cup campaign and it would be nowhere stronger than at the final itself. Again the venue would be Kennington Oval and again Villa would face their Midlands neighbours WBA. Villa would travel to London after a week's preparation at Holt Fleet. Unlike 1887, however, the League table could now be scoured for form. Villa were fourth; Albion were third from bottom.

The Saturday prior to the final, Villa flashed a warning to their rivals by setting a new goalscoring record for the four-year-old League. A 12–2 defeat of Accrington superseded the previous record of 10–1 held by Preston for three years. An exquisite blend of passing and shooting had seen John Devey, the Villa inside-right, hit four goals and Louis Campbell and Billy Dickson, the centre-forward, both score hat-tricks.

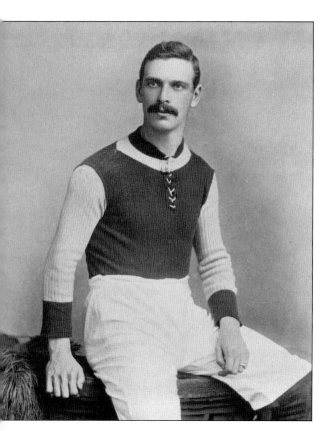

John Devey was captain of Villa during their great triumphs of the 1890s. Birmingham-born Devey was a standout as an inside-forward, his intelligent, stylish play bringing him 187 goals in 306 games. He won five First Division championship medals and two FA Cup winners' medals during his ten-year career at the club. He became a Villa director when he ceased playing, in 1902, and served on the board until 1934.

On 19 March, the day of the final, Villa appeared set on another afternoon of high-scoring activity. From kick-off a swift Villa move ended with Devey's header skirting the crossbar. Then WBA goalkeeper Reader had to make two sharp saves, one from Dickson and one from Devey. After four minutes, Albion broke quickly from defence and Villa goalkeeper Warner was beaten by a soft shot from winger Jasper Geddes. Villa pushed hard for an equaliser. Hodgetts struck the bar and Cowan had a low, hard shot saved by Reader.

After a quarter of an hour Albion made a second decisive breakaway. Geddes crossed for Nicholls and the ball bounced between the Albion forward and Warner. It should have been the keeper's ball but he hesitated and the Albion man nicked it past him. From then on, Albion dominated and ten minutes after half-time Jack Reynolds got a third goal for WBA with a long-range shot that Warner should have saved. By the end Villa were well beaten, with right-half James Cowan their only success on the day. The Villa team had been: Warner, Evans, Cox, Cowan, H. Devey, Baird, Athersmith, J. Devey, Dickson, Campbell, Hodgetts.

Rumours abounded in Birmingham that Jimmy Warner had 'sold' the game after betting against his own team. Warner, who ran a public house, defended himself on the Monday after the game, saying: 'I wouldn't do such a thing for £1,000. I bet £18 to £12 against Albion winning and I even bet an even £1 that they would not score against me…The fact is, the Villa team thought they only had to go on the field to bring the Cup away. I told them not to be so sure but start in the same way as we did against Wanderers and Sunderland. So sure were the men of winning that they began to talk about who should engrave their names on the medals.

'They say the first Albion goal broke up the Villa forwards, but everyone knows that the Villa play up better after the first reverse. Look at the Wanderers and Sunderland matches. It was not my fault at all. Evans left his wing and Geddes got the ball with no one in front of him but me. The goal is a big gap and a schoolboy can get a ball past a goalkeeper if the backs don't interfere with him. Baird was always too slow for Bassett and he did just what he liked. Groves bottled up Devey and Athersmith and the forwards never settled down.

'Soon after the match was over, someone came into my house and commenced to blackguard my wife and asked her what she thought of her beautiful husband now. Yesterday, as soon as the house was opened, a mob came in and began hissing me. These allegations are most hurtful to me and I can't stand them much longer. I know I am innocent, and if the remarks are repeated the one who does it will either have to thrash me or else I'll thrash him, and soundly too.'

Warner had been seen receiving money after the match from a character whom the Villa committee regarded as disreputable. The goalkeeper claimed, however, that he had been borrowing 'a couple of pounds' to tide him over until he returned to Birmingham. George Ramsay defended Warner against the accusations, although solely on the basis that none of his accusers had produced proof of any wrongdoing. It then emerged that Warner's conduct had been entirely unsatisfactory during Villa's preparations for the match. Warner had refused to do the same training as the other members of the team at Holt Fleet. He had also insulted some members of the committee. At Holt Fleet, against the express wishes of the committee, his guest was the same man he was seen receiving money from after the final. In London, before the match, he had been ordered by members of the committee to leave a railway carriage after persistently using foul language.

At a meeting of the committee on the Wednesday after the Cup final, it was decided to drop the player for the following Saturday's game at Sunderland. It was the end of Jimmy Warner's days at Aston Villa. Despite the inglorious conclusion of his time at the club, he had been Villa's first outstanding goalkeeper.

Rinder takes charge

Bill Dunning replaced Jimmy Warner as Villa's regular goalkeeper for the 1892–93 season, during which Villa again finished fourth in the League and lost 5–4 to Darwen in the first round of the Cup. The season had been more notable for off-field events. Frederick Rinder, a Villa club member since 1881, had called a special meeting that was held at the New Gallery on Barwick Street on a Friday evening, 24 February 1893.

Rinder was applauded enthusiastically as he mounted the platform to address the assembled members, many of whom were still aggrieved at losing the 1892 Cup final to the patently inferior WBA. He asserted that there was something rotten in the affairs of the club and that the committee members had brought the wrong players to Aston Villa. The Team and Match Committee had also, in his opinion, consistently failed to select the correct players for the first team.

Rinder alleged that players were known to neglect training in favour of drinking and that on one occasion police had been called to the clubhouse at 3.00am on a Saturday morning to break up a boisterous drinking session. The team had been due to assemble at 9.00am at New Street that morning to travel to Liverpool for a League match with Everton. Rinder finished his speech with the following motion: 'That the members of the club, having lost all confidence in the majority of the present committee, hereby require the honorary treasurer and honorary secretary and other members thereof to at once resign their respective offices.' This motion set off further raucous cheering in Rinder's favour.

Various members of the committee offered defences on behalf of themselves and their colleagues. The most amusing offering came from Archie Hunter, by then an advisor to the committee on the playing side. He reminded Mr Rinder that, despite some players' unusual means of preparation, the Villa team had won the match at Everton on the afternoon following their visit from the police. Any defence, however, was unlikely to stand in the way of the vast majority of those present. They had decided they wanted change. The motion was carried by a considerable majority, inspired by Rinder's fiery denunciation of the committee's incompetence. Rinder, as the financial secretary on the new committee, would from then on introduce a series of measures to put the club's finances on a more secure footing.

New Villa romp to title

Prior to the 1893–94 season, Villa signed Willie Groves, a left-half, and Jack Reynolds, a right-half, from WBA. Both players had been members of the team who had defeated Villa in the 1892 final. Under the rule of the new committee, Villa were now much more cautious in their transfer dealings, making detailed assessments of potential signings before bidding for them. The club was also carefully encouraging local talent. The Villa committee had strengthened the club by creating a reserve squad of around 20 'colts', these young players representing the finest talent in the Birmingham area.

Having strengthened the side, Villa were now ready to challenge for the League title. In November 1893, champions Sunderland visited Perry Barr. Goalkeeper Dunning looked shaky but Villa still managed to eke out a somewhat lucky 2–1 win. At the start of December, Villa visited Derby County, at whose ground they had never won. On a hard, icy surface both sides struggled initially to retain control of both the ball and their footing. Soon, however, Villa players were moving with surefooted stealth, finishing 3–0 winners.

The strength of this Villa side was in the half-back line. James Cowan, at centre-half, had been signed by George Ramsay in 1889, moving to Villa from Vale of Leven, a top Scottish club at the time. Cowan was a man who mixed imagination with discipline to great effect. His passing could look flamboyant but it was always safe; he would have measured all the angles before permitting the ball to leave his boot. He was also gifted with a stunning turn of pace. Allied to his more eye-catching skills with the ball was his strong sense of competitiveness both in his tackling and in urging his team-mates to give of their best. Alongside Cowan on that day at Derby, Groves, a fellow-Scot, and Reynolds, an Anglo-Irishman, were immense. With the passing game now established as the model for the best League clubs, it was vital to have expert exponents of that style of play in midfield.

With their talented half-back line supplying the forwards, Villa powered to the top of the First Division table. On Boxing Day 1893, 14,000 people were in the meadow at Perry Barr to see Darwen beaten 9–0. That gave Villa a six-point lead over second-placed Burnley as the year ended. Through the late winter and early spring Villa maintained their lead at the top. On Easter Monday, 26 March, Villa drew with Wolves at Perry Barr. They were still six points clear of second-placed Sunderland who had just three matches left to play. At Burnley on 7 April, Villa won 6–3 to take the title. On the following Monday, 4,000 were at Perry Barr to see Villa defeat Celtic, the Scottish champions, 3–2.

Cowan had been the only ever-present in all 30 League games. John Devey, a signing from Mitchell St George's in 1891, had been top scorer in the League with 20 goals. Villa's two wingers, Dennis Hodgetts and Charlie Athersmith, had been next highest scorers; Hodgetts with 12 goals, Athersmith with 11. The 1893–94 title triumph was a significant step for Villa, but to the fans the new competition was second-best to the FA Cup. The feat of maintaining consistently good form for seven solid months could not capture their imaginations in the same way as the instantaneous excitement of the Cup.

Villa's average home gate in the League had been around 10,000 and a crowd of 18,000 for the match with Blackburn at Perry Barr on 24 March was the club's highest League attendance. Yet 25,000 had been attracted to Villa's second round FA Cup replay with Sunderland at Perry Barr. All four of Villa's Cup ties that season had attracted crowds of more than 20,000.

Shares in success

Willie Groves had been the first player to be transferred for a fee of £100 when he joined Villa from WBA. His contribution to the Villa half-back line was vital in that title-winning season but in the summer of 1894 he contracted tuberculosis. While the rest of the Villa players prepared for the start of the 1894–95 season, Groves was taking the sea air in Bournemouth. In November 1894 he was told he should never play football again. With their half-back line severely weakened, Villa finished third in the League in 1894–95. They had better luck in the Cup. The draw provided them with three consecutive ties at home. Derby County, Newcastle United and Nottingham Forest were all defeated in straightforward fashion, Villa scoring 15 goals in total and conceding just three. The semi-final produced a 2–1 win over Sunderland, that year's champions, at Bramall Lane. In the final, Villa would again take part in a moveable Midlands feast and again their opponents would be West Bromwich Albion. As in 1892, Villa were fourth in the League, WBA third-bottom.

The 1895 final, played on 20 April, would see the opening of the the new sporting arena at Crystal Palace, which was part of a complex that also included a fairground.

The final would be played out with a big dipper in the background. Entrance to the Crystal Palace gave access not only to the Cup final but also to the funfair. So although 42,560 passed through the turnstiles on the day, a couple of thousand were estimated to have headed straight for the shooting stalls, ghost train and other amusements.

The game kicked off at 3.30pm on a warm spring afternoon. WBA captain Billy Bassett won the toss and decided to make the Villa players spend the first half with the sun in their eyes. From kick-off, Devey passed to Hodgetts and he and Steve Smith whipped the ball up the left wing. It was then switched to Athersmith on the right wing. He passed to Bob Chatt, the Villa inside-right, who met the ball on the turn. His shot struck the legs of WBA goalkeeper Reader and went spinning into goal. Thirty-nine seconds had expired. After scoring from their first opening, Villa made and missed a host of others. After 90 minutes, the score remained the same as it had after the first minute: 1–0 to Villa. The Villa team was: Wilkes, Spencer, Welford, Reynolds, Cowan, Russell, Athersmith, Chatt, Devey, Hodgetts, Smith.

The Villa players arrived back at Snow Hill station in Birmingham at lunchtime on the Monday. A band playing *See the Conquering Hero Comes* was waiting to greet the team. John Devey, clutching the Cup, led the team to a charabanc decorated in Villa colours on which they toured the streets of the city. The players were then driven to a reception at the club's headquarters in Albert Road.

Following that victory, Frederick Rinder decided Villa should capitalise on their success and in January 1896 they became a limited company with four directors: Rinder, Charles Johnstone, Joshua Margoschis and James Lees. On Monday 20 January, the most prominent advertisement on the front page of *The Birmingham Daily Post* read:

The SUBSCRIPTION LIST will be opened THIS DAY (Monday), the 20th January, and CLOSED on MONDAY NEXT, THE 27TH JANUARY. THE ASTON VILLA FOOTBALL CLUB (LIMITED) ABRIDGED PROSPECTUS
Share Capital £10,000, in 2,000 shares of £5 each, payable 10s. on application, 10s. on allotment and the balance by collections not exceeding 10s. per Share at intervals of not less than three months.

The invitation to the public to subscribe to Villa was a well-timed one. The team had just gone top of the First Division. The purpose of the share issue was to construct a stadium that would be a fitting home for the club. Villa had now outgrown the ground capacity and facilities at Perry Barr. The directors, led by Fred Rinder, planned a move to the club's nominal home in Aston, at the Lower Grounds. The share issue was a success and the committee applied their minds to the new venture.

FA Cup stolen

Villa began the defence of the FA Cup away to Derby County on 1 February 1896 but they were now playing for a new trophy. After their victory in the final at the Oval in April 1895, Villa had kept the FA Cup in a safe in Birmingham. In late August, Mr William Shillcock, a boot and shoe manufacturer, was given permission by the Villa committee to display the trophy in his shop window in Newtown Row. Shillcock, a friend of William McGregor, manufactured, among other things, football boots, footballs and cricket equipment. He would also, for many years, supply the 'McGregor ball' for the FA Cup final. On the morning of 12 September, at 8.00am, Shillcock opened his shop as usual. At first he saw nothing amiss then noticed that a cash box had been removed from its place and emptied. On going through to the front of his shop he discovered a pile of rubble on the floor, a hole in the roof and the FA Cup missing from his window display. Police investigations discovered evidence of entry from the roof, while a stepladder appeared to have been used to exit the shop. Shillcock offered a reward of £10 for information about the robbery but the Cup was never recovered. The contract to create a new trophy went to Vaughton & Sons Limited of Birmingham, the family firm of the former Villa forward Howard Vaughton.

The Cup match with Derby in February 1896 was a meeting of the top two in the League. A crowd of 27,000 – the biggest on the day – paid a total of £1,254 to see the match, which ended in a 4–2 defeat for Villa. The following week Villa were back at the Baseball Ground for a League match in which they went 2–0 down in the first-half. John

Cowan, James' brother, brought it back to 2–1 just before half-time then late in the game Athersmith scored an equaliser.

As in 1893–94, the half-back line remained the rock on which the Villa team was built. At the centre of that mobile edifice, James Cowan was still the cornerstone of the team. At Derby, he had played one of his most outstanding games for the club. The club prized his talents highly – just how highly had been clearly illustrated a few weeks earlier. Cowan had been allowed to return home to Dunbartonshire during the closing weeks of 1895 to recover and rest from an injury. However, while in Scotland he had entered the Powderhall Sprint, a race with considerable prize money that took place in Edinburgh every New Year's Day. Cowan won the race but had failed to inform the Villa committee of his entry. On his return to Birmingham on 3 January he was suspended by the club. A meeting to consider a suitable punishment was to take place on 9 January. However, with Villa in contention for the League title, their decision was to fine Cowan four weeks' wages and lift the suspension. The centre-half's return to the side that January coincided with a run of form that brought the championship to Birmingham for a second time.

Cowan still had Jack Reynolds on his right with either Frank Burton or Jimmy Crabtree on his left. Crabtree had been signed from Burnley at the start of the 1895–96 season as a left-back but was so versatile that he was playing as an inside-forward as Villa ended their fixtures. During the 1896–97 season he would settle at half-back, the position for the most complete footballer in any side. Villa also had a new centre-forward in the 1895–96 season, Johnny Campbell, who had been lured south from Celtic in the summer of 1895. He had played on the left wing for Celtic but the Villa committee were persuaded of his talents as a centre-forward. Their judgement was quickly vindicated. Campbell ended the 1895–96 season as Villa's top scorer with 27 goals.

Claret and blue double

After that match at the Baseball Ground in February 1896, Villa had strode on to the title, finishing the season four points ahead of Derby. With the Villa side remaining

Johnny Campbell was 22 when Aston Villa signed him from Celtic in 1895. He had been a key member of the Celtic team that had won the Scottish Cup in 1892 and the Scottish League title in 1893 and 1894. His experience and skill helped Villa become Football League champions in 1896 and double winners in 1897. Campbell's 27 goals in the 1895–96 season made him the top scorer in Britain.

together for the following season, there appeared a strong prospect of them repeating the achievement in 1896–97. In February of 1897, as Villa prepared for their second round FA Cup tie with Notts County, captain John Devey was setting his sights even higher. 'I don't see why we should not bring off the double event in winning the League trophy and the English Cup,' he said. 'It has been done before and it will be done again – and we were very near it in 1893–94.

'I should think 42 points will win us the League championship. I have an idea that in the eight matches we have yet to play we ought to make 14 points so that if we only drop four points it will be a very good performance. That would bring us up to 44 points. But even if we lose six points I think we shall win.'

In the event, there was no need for Villa to worry about margins of error. The team

powered on to finish the season with 47 points, 11 clear of joint second-placed Sheffield United and Derby County. Reynolds, Cowan and Crabtree were the half-backs, supporting Athersmith and Devey on the right wing. Campbell was still centre-forward. Freddie Wheldon, a £100 signing from Small Heath in the summer of 1896, and John Cowan, James' brother, were the left-wing partnership. Tom Wilkes was in goal with tough-tackling full-backs Albert Evans and Howard Spencer in front of him. Wheldon was top scorer in the League with 18 goals and Devey was close behind on 17. Campbell had scored 13 times.

Having built up an unassailable points lead in the League, Villa were able to concentrate fully on each Cup tie as and when it came round. A home tie with Newcastle United resulted in a 5–0 win on the final Saturday in January. Notts County were also beaten at Perry Barr, 2–1, but Preston North End offered stronger resistance. After a second replay, at Bramall Lane, Villa won 3–2. The same venue saw a 3–0 Villa victory over Liverpool. In their fourth FA Cup final Villa would face Everton on 10 April 1897.

In the late 19th century, most workers had to perform a shift on a Saturday morning. On the Saturday of the 1897 Cup final, however, several factories in Birmingham were forced to close because so many key workers had made it clear they would be on their way to London. A crowd of 65,891, including 10,000 Villa supporters, attended the match at Crystal Palace. It was the biggest crowd for any football match and it generated record receipts for the FA of £2,875.

The Saturday prior to the final, Villa team-mates James Cowan and Reynolds had faced each other at Crystal Palace in the annual encounter between Scotland and England. Villa's other half-back, Crabtree, had been in danger of missing the final through injury but in the week before the match he was passed fit. On the afternoon of 10 April, Derby County lost to Bury, confirming Villa as League champions. If Villa defeated Everton, both legs of the double would be completed on the same afternoon.

Villa won the toss and captain John Devey elected for Villa to play with the wind at their backs. After 15 minutes, Johnny Campbell's hard, accurate drive from 25 yards slapped into the Everton net to give Villa the lead. But two quick goals from Everton put them in the lead before half an hour had passed. In the 34th minute Crabtree's free-kick sat up nicely for Wheldon to bring the scores level. Two minutes later, Reynolds' corner was headed into the Everton net by Wheldon to make it 3–2 to Villa. After that flurry of action, the game settled down into a less frantic but equally fascinating joust. The tempo increased again in the final 10 minutes as Everton, roared on by their considerable support, engineered a coruscating climax to the match. Villa's defence showed great strength to hold out and Devey once again got his hands on the Cup. It had been the most entertaining FA Cup final up to that point.

The Villa team was: Whitehouse, Spencer, Evans, Reynolds, James Cowan, Crabtree, Athersmith, Devey, Campbell, Wheldon, John Cowan. It had been a victory inspired once again by Villa's half-back line. All three players had assisted in attack and defence in equal measure. Athersmith and Devey had worked well together on the right wing. Campbell again emphasised that he was the best centre-forward in the country. Amidst a plethora of exceptional displays from players on both sides, however, it was James Cowan who was the finest performer on the day.

A new home at Villa Park

Almost as if part of some predestined scheme of things, Villa's first match as holders of the double would be played at their new ground, a League fixture against Blackburn Rovers on 17 April 1897. To have such a special team allied to a magnificent new stadium bore testimony to the hard work, willpower and sharpness of judgement shown by Frederick Rinder and his fellow members of the committee since they had taken control of the club in 1893.

On the Witton Lane side of the ground, a claret and blue grandstand would hold 5,500 seated fans, but it was incomplete on that opening day. The roof of the grandstand extended to form a covered, standing enclosure for 4,500 spectators. Another 8,000 could find shelter under a free-standing covered enclosure on the Trinity Road side of the ground, opposite the grandstand. Although most of the new ground was uncovered it was still an improvement on Perry Barr, where only the well-heeled had been under cover.

A cycling track separated the terraces from the pitch. The playing surface measured 70 yards by 110 yards. Villa had taken advice on how to lay the turf from John Bates, groundsman at Warwickshire County Cricket Club. The turf in the centre of the pitch was laid on a slightly higher level than that around the edges of the pitch, sloping very gently down to provide drainage.

The ground was estimated to have a capacity of 70,000–80,000, but it would be a case of trial and error to see exactly how many it could hold. It was a bold move on the Villa committee's part to envisage a time when such numbers would wish to attend matches at Villa Park. In 1896–97 the average attendance for Villa's matches had been 13,500, including the final two matches played at the Aston Lower Grounds. The committee's ambition had also proved expensive in the short term – the total cost of construction was approximately £20,000, double the amount that had been raised to build the stadium through the share issue.

Against Blackburn, Villa fielded their Cup-winning side but with the double already won most supporters were attending Villa Park out of curiosity to see the new ground. The covered sections had been designed particularly to encourage attendance on wet days and they received their first test on that opening occasion, when the heaviest of April showers fell on Birmingham throughout the morning and afternoon. Around 15,000 spectators still turned up for Villa's first match at the new park. It was a much bigger crowd than would normally have been expected. Crowds in those times would not normally turn out for a match to celebrate past achievements, even those of only a week before. The celebrations for the double had been carried out in numerous street parties the previous Monday when Villa had returned from London with the Cup.

Johnny Campbell scored the opening goal at Villa Park, a goal worthy of the occasion, dribbling through the Blackburn defence before shooting firmly past the goalkeeper. Villa went on to win 3–0. Two days later, on Easter Monday, another home match kicked off at 5.00pm. Wolves were the visitors and the match, in conjunction with an attractive cycling meeting, drew 35,000, the biggest crowd to have watched a football match in Birmingham. It inspired Villa to a

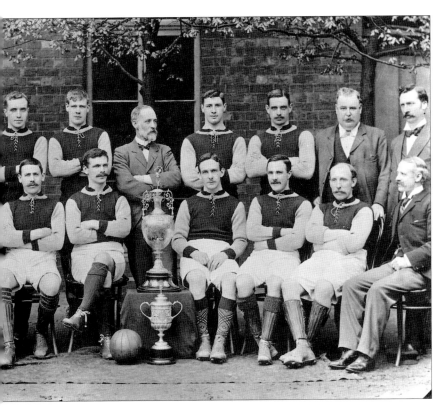

The Aston Villa side that clinched the FA Cup and League championship double on the same afternoon in April 1897. Standing, from left to right, are: G. Ramsay (secretary), J. Grierson (trainer), H. Spencer, J. Whitehouse, J. Margoschis (chairman), A. Evans, J. Crabtree, J. Lees (director), C. Johnstone (director). Seated, from left to right, are: V. Jones (director), J. Cowan, C. Athersmith, J. Campbell, J. Devey, F. Wheldon, J. Cowan, J. Reynolds, F. Rinder (Honorary Treasurer). The FA Cup sits beneath the League Championship trophy.

5–0 win, the team playing as if the destination of the double depended on Villa obtaining a commanding victory.

The committee were given little time to sit back and enjoy the afterglow of that magnificent season. They were soon faced with new problems. Campbell's goal against Blackburn had been his final significant act for the club. A fortnight later, he was tempted back to Celtic, whose representatives were even more predatory than George Ramsay when it came to snatching players away from other clubs. Reynolds, too, moved to Celtic Park, leaving two gaping wounds in the body of the side that had won the double for Villa. Consequently, they missed out on both League championship and Cup the following season.

Last day drama

Villa had recovered sufficiently in 1898–99 to play a leading role in an exceptionally tight race for the title. On the penultimate Saturday of the League season, Villa won 6–1 at home to Notts County. That left Villa two points behind leaders Liverpool but with a game in hand. Villa had two games remaining, the first of which saw them

defeat WBA 7–1 at home on the Monday evening. It teed up a tremendous finish to the season; Liverpool were due at Villa Park for both sides' final League fixture. It was the first time the top two in the First Division had met on the final day of the season to decide the First Division championship.

Villa's goal-heavy win over WBA meant they jumped ahead of Liverpool on goal average so a draw would bring the title to Birmingham for a fourth time. Unbeaten at home over the season, Villa approached the match as strong favourites to get the required result. The Villa team prepared as for a Cup final, training at Holt Fleet in the days preceding the match. They lunched in Droitwich on the Saturday then took the train to New Street, arriving at 2.24pm, from where they were driven to the ground at Aston. Liverpool had arrived in Birmingham on the Friday evening, staying overnight in the Colonnade Hotel in New Street.

Ticket prices had been increased for the decider but that did little to deter the 41,000 who made it to the match to see who would win the final major trophy of the 19th century. After four minutes' play, Steve Smith's cross was headed into the Liverpool net by Devey. A quarter of an hour later, with Villa dominating, the same two players repeated their performance and Villa were two ahead. Then, in a five-minute spell between the 34th and 39th minutes, Fred Wheldon directed the ball into the Liverpool net three times to give Villa a 5–0 half-time lead, which they were happy to sit on until the final whistle.

Liverpool had been outmanoeuvred in every part of the pitch. The trickery of the Villa forwards confused their defenders. The solidity of Villa's backs blocked every venture Liverpool made forward. Billy George in the Villa goal made just one save in the entire match. Villa had heavily underlined their right to be First Division champions and had taken the title in the style to which their supporters had gradually become accustomed over the preceding decade. It was their sixth piece of silverware in the 1890s and their seventh overall, making them by far the most successful English club. Aston Villa were also the best supported club in England with an average crowd of 22,000 at Villa Park over the 1898–99 season. There was nothing to suggest that the forthcoming century would bring anything other than sustained success to Aston Villa.

The new century brought yet more trophies and success to Villa Park, as the team continued to contest football's top honours. New players arrived and established stars faded but the quality of football did not diminish.

3 Winning Ways Continue: 1900–14

Money troubles weighed heavily on Aston Villa as the club prepared for the season that would take them into the 20th century. In the summer of 1899, James Cowan had held out for an improved wage before signing with the club for another season. No sooner had he been placated than James Crabtree refused to re-sign for the club unless financial terms were improved.

One bone of contention among the players was that Frederick Rinder, who had been elected chairman in 1896, had withdrawn the traditional annual re-signing bonus despite the team having won the League championship. Rinder, however, stressed that no player would be on lesser terms than he had enjoyed the previous year. The majority of the Villa squad earned £4 10 shillings (£4.50) per week although bonuses could bring that figure up to £5 10 shillings per week (£5.50). Crabtree, however, was aware that two others (most likely Cowan and Devey) were on £6 per week. Eventually, Crabtree signed up for the 1899–1900 season when he was brought in line financially with the two other top earners. These re-signings were essential – the players involved were the glue that held the Villa team together.

Devey and Cowan were now in their early thirties but they were both as strong as ever. Devey remained the craftiest of inside-forwards. He was equally at ease shimmying away from defenders and linking up with Athersmith, his wing-partner, as he was putting the ball in the net himself. Devey had been top scorer in the 1898–99 season with 21 League goals. Cowan had missed just one League game out of the 35 games played by the club over that season.

Formidable start to the century

After those brief financial worries, Villa moved steadily into the new century. The only fresh face in the Villa line-up for the season that straddled the centuries was Billy Garraty, a centre-forward. He had been with the club since 1897 but had broken through to the first team only at the end of the 1898–99 season. He had made a sizeable impact, scoring six goals in the run-in to the title, including a hat-trick in the 7–1 win over WBA. It appeared as though Villa might at last have replaced Johnny Campbell. The club had struggled to fill his shooting boots since his departure in 1897. James Fisher, a 22-year-old from the St Bernards club in Scotland, had been brought south in the summer of 1897 but had failed to hold down a place in the Villa front line. George Johnson, another forward, had also been signed in 1897. He had scored ten goals in the 1898–99 season but it was the more familiar figures such as Athersmith, Devey, Spencer and Cowan who had been the key players in that title triumph.

Villa were in a stable condition during the early months of the 1899–1900 season. They were rarely spectacular although they did come close to matching their record 12–2 victory when they defeated Glossop North End 9–0 in September. As they began the 1900s they were six points behind leaders, Sheffield United in the First Division but with a game in hand. The Villa had left the 1800s on a high, with a 4–2 home win over Sunderland. Garraty got the show on the road with two choice, crisp shots, both hit from considerable distance. Now a regular

A 28,000 crowd follows the action inside Villa Park on 30 March 1907 as the home side defeat Liverpool 4–0 in a First Division match.

goalscorer, he was also proving adept at combining with his wing-forwards. Cowan remained in stunning form at centre-half, although there were occasionally signs that he was slowing up with age. He had been out of action through injury in the weeks prior to the Sunderland game. Now, rested and refreshed, he was ready to give of his best to propel Villa up the First Division table. He was aided by Bowman at right-half and Crabtree on his left, although Crabtree was having a difficult season and struggling to match his own previous high standards.

Howard Spencer, at right-back, and Albert Evans, at left-back, remained iron-hard performers. Both backs were tough in the tackle but possessed the ability to distribute the ball smoothly, a rare quality in full-backs at the turn of the century. They had been with Villa since the early 1890s. Goalkeeper Billy George had replaced Whitehouse in goal in 1897. At 6ft 2ins and 16 stone, he was an equally powerful presence behind the backs. The strength of their rear division had never been so important to Villa. This was a team that relied heavily on experience to pull through situations that a younger side might have struggled to cope with. The Villa team of 1899–1900 would simply tough out many games, earning points the hard way with their rugged defending.

By the beginning of February, Villa were just one point behind Sheffield United. It was United, however, who now had a game in hand. The month started with Derby County visiting Villa. With five minutes remaining, Derby were 2–1 ahead. At the final whistle, Villa were 3–2 winners. Fred Wheldon had headed the third goal with seconds remaining. On the terraces, hats, sticks and umbrellas were thrown in the air to celebrate the winner.

Notts County visited Villa in mid-February and Garraty and Athersmith hit them hard early on, each scoring in the opening two minutes. Cowan, up with the attack, volleyed Villa's third to make it 3–2 before half-time. In the second-half, Villa were excellent, their three half-backs dovetailing seamlessly with the five forwards. When Villa attacked, they did so with eight men working together. Three further goals were the reward for Villa's substantial style. It was one of Villa's finest displays of the season and, fittingly, the 6–2 rout took them to the top of the table.

That set Villa up nicely for their next match, a home game against Sheffield United. The battle between the First Division's top two was watched by 50,000, another record-breaking attendance for Villa. There was so much interest in the match that it was given the rare honour of being filmed by a cinematographic company and shown at Birmingham's Theatre Royal the following Monday evening. Temporary stands were erected on the cycle track behind each goal. Both stands, however, snapped beneath the weight of their assembled throngs, sending fans scrambling on to the track. Only luck prevented a major tragedy.

Shortly before half-time, Sheffield United went 1–0 ahead. During the interval, the Blackpool Lifeboat Band played Rule Britannia, with the vast majority of the 50,000 joining in. In the second half, Villa equalised from a corner when Garraty beat United's Billy 'Fatty' Foulke after the goalkeeper had twice used his considerable bulk to block Villa scoring efforts. Villa had several other chances to score during the match but it remained 1–1 at the end. United were now a point behind Villa but with two games in hand.

Villa show off the championship trophy in 1899–1900. The players are, back row, left to right: Moon, Bowman, Crabtree, George, Spencer, Evans. Front row: Wilkes, Cowan, Wheldon, Devey, Athersmith, Garraty, Smith, Templeton.

There was disquieting news for Villa supporters in the aftermath of this match. It was revealed that a Birmingham detective had been employed by the committee to keep a private eye on the social habits of the players. In the week before the Sheffield United game he had gathered evidence that three players had been drinking and partying excessively. Cowan, Crabtree and Wheldon were dropped for Villa's next match, on the Monday after the Sheffield United game. This was a second replay of an FA Cup tie with Millwall Athletic of the Southern League at the neutral venue of Reading. Villa lost the tie – the first time they had been victims of a major Cup shock.

Cowan and Wheldon were recalled the following Saturday for a League match at Newcastle, but Villa suffered a potentially harmful 3–2 defeat. Luckily, Sheffield United also lost, 2–1 at home to Liverpool. The Blades then collapsed 4–0 at Nottingham Forest, while a Villa side weakened by injuries beat Burnley 2–1 away. The initiative was now with Villa. United had gone stale. Villa's final match saw them achieve a 1–0 win at Wolves. The decisive goal was a cross-shot from Bobby Templeton, an outside-right signed from Hibernian in early 1899. He had attained a regular place in the Villa side during the second half of the 1899–1900 season. The win was just enough for Villa, who won the title and ended the season two points ahead of Sheffield United. Over the season, Villa's home League games had been watched by an average crowd of around 20,000.

Villa fans prove hard to please

It had been a peculiar season. Perhaps because of the high standards set by the club in the 1890s, Villa's admirers had widely construed that this was an inferior Villa side to those of past seasons. The facts and figures do not bear this out. Villa had lost just six and drawn six of their 34 fixtures in the 18-team League. It was a superior record to the one they had established in the 1898–99 season and bore close comparison to the club's record in their other three championship-winning seasons.

The Villa players had used all of their experience and drawn on their knowledge of the game to win through. Garraty, at centre-forward, had been a vital addition to the side. The youngster's enthusiasm and willingness to work had been crucial to the title success. He had scored 30 goals – 27 in the League, three in the Cup – over the season. Wheldon and Templeton had also added youthful vigour to Villa; their skilful play pepping up the attack. The old heads had provided the platform for the younger players to display their talents and in return, the new boys had done much running of which the older players were no longer quite so capable. Aston Villa's tight-knit passing style remained intact and their teamwork was as good as ever.

Howard Spencer had been outstanding throughout the 1899–1900 season. Since his debut in 1893–94, Villa had never failed to win a trophy with Spencer as their regular right-back. In trophyless 1897–98 he had been missing with an injured knee. Prior to his benefit match against Sheffield United on Boxing Day 1900, Spencer looked back on his years at Villa since joining from Birchfield Trinity Unity in 1893. 'I have been lucky in generally having a splendid half in front of me,' he said. 'You don't know how it lightens your work and the sense of comforts it gives you. John Reynolds was a splendid half. He was always worrying the man, and yet, in a way, he was a slow man. That made his play all the more astonishing…

'I am as fond of the game as ever I was: I quite look forward to my football match weekly. And I have had a most kind, considerate and sportsmanlike set of colleagues. I have always been proud to be a member of Aston Villa. But I sometimes feel that I am not the player I was; that I am not doing myself justice. I cannot meet the ball with my left foot as I once did; it is still weak. I feel bad, it affects my play and I don't like it. I sometimes feel I shall have to give it up.'

Despite his own forebodings, Spencer was still in the Villa side in 1905 as they made their next serious bid for a trophy – their fourth FA Cup. Spencer, goalkeeper Billy George and Billy Garraty were the only members of the 1900 title-winning side still at Villa Park. The club's best performances in the FA Cup since winning it in 1897 had been to reach the semi-finals in 1901 and again in 1903. They had lost 3–0 on both occasions; to Sheffield United in 1901 and Bury in 1903.

The First Division title had proved as elusive as the Cup in that first decade of the new century. The triumph of 1900 had been the last hurrah for players such as the great John Devey and James Cowan. Villa had plummeted to 15th in the League in 1900–01. That summer, Jimmy Crabtree, Charlie Athersmith and Steve Smith had left the club. In 1902 James Cowan retired after 13 years at Villa.

Eighth position was attained in 1901–02 but in 1902–03, Villa were 13th in the First Division table at Christmas after an opening half of the season in which they had been at best mediocre. They then finished the season with a flourish, taking 24 points from the available 30 to finish just one point below champions Sheffield Wednesday, who had remained tantalisingly out of reach in the dying days of the season. Villa would remain one of the strongest teams in the League in the first ten seasons of the 20th century. They never finished out of the top half of the table, but failed to repeat their 1899–1900 title win.

The 1905 Cup run had begun in February with a 5–1 home win over Leicester Fosse. A fortnight later, on a windswept afternoon at Villa Park, 40,000 saw an engaging Cup-tie with Bury end 3–2 in Villa's favour. The draw for the quarter-finals brought Southern League side Fulham to Villa Park and 47,000 saw Villa glide to a 5–0 win. In the semi-finals, Villa were drawn against League leaders Everton. After a 1–1 draw played at Stoke, Villa won 2–1 in the replay at Nottingham to reach their fifth final. Almost 60,000 had watched Villa negotiate the semi-final matches.

Final date with the champions

Aston Villa were now mixing up their short passing game with the long, accurate ball. and it was proving highly effective. Since November 1904, Villa had suffered only one defeat – 2–0 in a League match at St James' Park, Newcastle, on 5 April, ten days before the 1905 Cup final. Villa had been weakened by injuries at Newcastle and that defeat had ended their hopes of winning the First Division. They finished the League season in fourth position, six points behind champions Newcastle, who were to be Villa's opponents in the Cup final on 15 April.

Prior to every match in that year's FA Cup, the Villa team had spent a week in seclusion at the Marine Hydro Hotel, Rhyl, on the north coast of Wales, and they did the same for the Cup final. At midday on Friday 14 April they began their five-hour journey to South London. There they stayed overnight at the Railway Hotel, Beckenham Junction, near Crystal Palace, which was again the venue for the FA Cup final. At 7.30am, the entrances to the Palace were opened to allow spectators access for the final. By the 3.30pm kick-off time on that hot afternoon, there were 101,117 present to see Howard Spencer lead the following Villa side onto the field: George, Spencer, Miles, Pearson, Leake, Windmill, Brawn, Garraty, Hampton, Bache, Hall.

Photographs were taken of the two teams before proceedings began. Newcastle won the toss and yet again in a Cup final Villa found themselves staring into the sun. Harry Hampton, who had displaced Garraty as centre-forward during that season, kicked off. Two and a half minutes later, Hampton collected an anaemic clearance from a Newcastle back and made a clever, disguised pass that veered left to Joe Bache on the wing. He delivered a quick cross and Hampton, who had scored five goals in Villa's run to the final, edged the ball into the Newcastle net.

Villa's tactic of hitting high, swinging passes from one wing to the other proved enormously effective. Albert Hall and Billy Brawn, on either wing, were vitally quick to control these long passes before accelerating off with the ball. Newcastle could not equal the dynamism of the Villa forwards. When Newcastle did reach deep into Villa territory they discovered Spencer at his imperious best. After 75 minutes, however, Villa had been unable to add to their opener and the game appeared set to become a close copy of Villa's encounter with WBA a decade earlier. Then Hall swivelled through the Newcastle defence for a shot that goalkeeper Lawrence parried but could not hold. Hampton swept the rebound past him to make it 2–0 to Villa.

Twenty thousand Villa fans had been at the final and thousands more packed the platforms at New Street to welcome the team home on the Monday evening. On seeing the Villa train, those inside the station let out a huge roar which was carried on by the people in the streets above. Another great cheer

Villa's 1905 Cup winners take time out for a team picture inside the grounds of Villa Park. Back row, left to right: G. Ramsay (secretary), F. Miles, H. Toney (director), H. Spencer, F. Rinder (chairman), W. George, J. Devey (director), J. Grierson (trainer). Middle row: V. Jones (director), W. Brawn, W. Garraty, H. Hampton, J. Bache, A. Hall, J. Lees (director). Seated on ground: J. Pearson, A. Leake, J. Windmill.

The ball flies away from the Newcastle goal after one of Villa's many attacking moves during the 1905 FA Cup final.

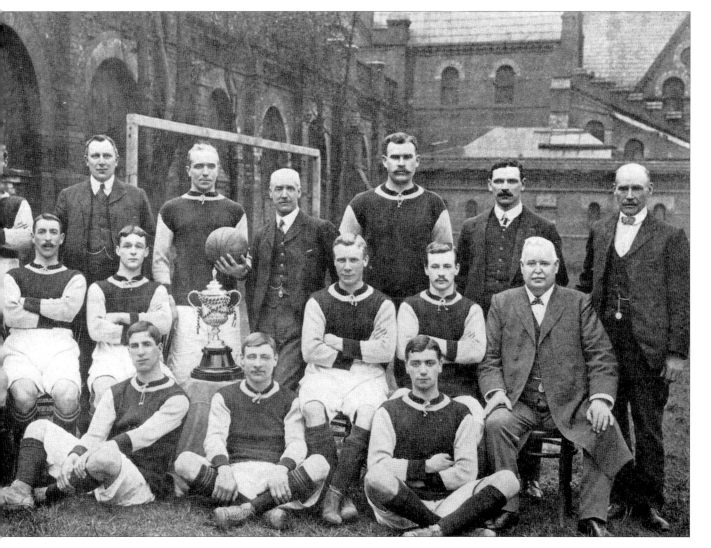

arose with the sight of the Cup, decorated in Villa's colours and with violets attached to each handle. At Rhyl the staff of the hydro had presented the players with violets before each Cup game and the flower had become their lucky symbol. The Cup was paraded through the streets to the Holte Hotel, situated behind the south terracing at Villa Park, where a celebratory reception was held.

A record breaking season

In 1908 Villa finished second to Manchester United in the First Division although nine points separated the clubs in the final reckoning. Two years later, in February 1910, United, who were rapidly becoming one of the great football forces in Lancashire, visited Villa Park for a League match. Villa were in second place in the First Division but had been knocked out of the FA Cup by Manchester City the previous week. In the opening minute Villa left-back Freddy Miles broke up a United attack and propelled the ball forward to outside-left Eyre. He swerved past three tough challenges and crossed for Gerrish to shoot Villa into the lead. By half-time it was 4–0; by full-time 7–1. Consequently, Villa jumped a point ahead of Notts County, who had been beaten 2–0 at Bristol City that afternoon.

Harry Hampton remained at centre-forward. A charismatic powerhouse who had been signed from Wellington Town, he was known to the Villa fans as "'Appy 'Arry" or 'The Wellington Whirlwind'. Opposing fans called him other names because of the full use he made of his weight in charging defenders and, especially, goalkeepers. That was part of the game in the early 20th century – Harry was simply expert at throwing his weight around to best effect. He was fearless in his pursuit of goals, frequently risking serious injury in doing so. Hampton turned out to be a superb investment for Villa – he amassed a record number of League goals for the club, having scored 215 by the time he ended his 16-year association with the club in 1920. His overall total of 242 makes him the second-highest goalscorer in the club's history.

Villa were a lively, exciting team during the 1909–1910 season. Hampton was flanked by nippy forwards: Joey Walters and Eyre on the left wing and Charlie Wallace

and Billy Gerrish on the right. Joe Bache also remained on call. After that momentous win over United, Villa did not look back. On 12 March, Sheffield Wednesday visited Villa Park. They managed to keep the score down to 0–0 at half-time, but by full-time it was 5–0 to Villa. Wednesday's Irish centre-half McConnell was seen with his arms folded in the latter stages, apparently having given up any hope of stopping the Villa forwards.

'Against the Villa it was like this,' McConnell explained, 'I went all out for an hour but I had no luck at all. The Villa forwards were too clever for us. They danced and jigged around us – made us regular laughing stocks at times – and I am blessed if I could get near the ball, however hard I tried. For one thing, it was very light and lively. At half-time I asked the others in joke how it felt to kick the ball. The Villa forwards are a wonderful lot and the marvel to me is that they hadn't scored five times before half-time. They deserved to. I tried as long as I felt there was any hope. But when they had scored twice and were still keeping the ball among themselves – well I really lost heart.'

On 16 April Villa won their sixth championship with a 3–2 win away to Notts County. Villa had been 2–0 down at half-time. Their 53 points equalled the record for a title-winning side. Their 84 goals equalled their own record total of 1893–94 and was the third-highest total to have been recorded in the First Division's 22-year history.

The team had been watched by an average 22,150 in their matches at Villa Park. Villa's two home FA Cup ties, against Derby County and Manchester City, had each drawn crowds of 45,000, the club's two biggest attendances during that title-winning season. Such attendances could be matched in the League – but only when a decisive clash took place.

In that era fans could make a decision on whether to attend a match right up until kick-off time. Season-ticket holders were in the minority and all-ticket games were a rarity. Fans could wait and see what the weather was like if they wished, then roll up at the turnstile with their cash at the ready. Only the most important games were sure to draw a giant crowd. It was a situation that remained the norm in British football until the 1990s when the construction of all-seater stadiums produced a preponderance of season ticket holders.

Supporters could share in the 1909–1910 title win by wearing Villa jerseys, which were available at 26 shillings (£1.30) per dozen from Quaife Brothers and Lilly of 313 Broad Street. Such shirts would be worn only by players in amateur teams – it was unheard of for supporters to wear the team's shirts as a leisure item. Those players could also use 'The Villa', a perfect round ball with 'sections cut from specially tanned leather'. It was available in three different sizes from Clapshaw and Cleave of 11 & 13 Edmund Street, ranging in price from seven shillings and sixpence (37 ½ pence) to nine shillings and sixpence (47 ½ pence).

A valiant defence

In 1910–11 Villa made a strong title defence. At the start of April 1911 they were two points behind leaders Manchester United with a game in hand. A 2–0 defeat at home to Preston on 8 April was their first League defeat at Villa Park since April 1909, a setback as unexpected as it was unsettling. Hampton had been man-marked that afternoon and after Preston scored early in the second half an out-of-kilter Villa side missed several chances. Preston scored the clincher in the final seconds of the match.

It looked like the end of Villa's title hopes but Manchester United also began to falter. On 22 April, a crowd of 47,190 at Villa Park saw Bache and Hampton give Villa a 2–1 half-time lead over United. Henshall and Wallace chipped in to make the score 4–2 to Villa by the end. Villa were now top of the First Division courtesy of a superior goal average to United, who had just one fixture remaining. Villa had two League games left to play. Wallace, Bache and Hampton had been in fiery form in the forward line that afternoon.

Two days later Villa travelled to Ewood Park, Blackburn. The Manchester United team watched this match from the stands. A fast, highly competitive match had failed to yield any goals when, late in the second half, Charlie Wallace was tripped inside the Blackburn penalty area. Wallace himself took the resultant penalty but Ashcroft, the Blackburn goalkeeper, saved it. Villa went to Liverpool for their final match of the season but despite a fighting performance lost 3–1. Liverpool had given it everything and their players celebrated their win long and hard at the end. A victory over Aston Villa remained a prize among First Division clubs. Meanwhile, Manchester United were facing Sunderland. The Wearsiders were in third place in the First Division but they had just returned from a taxing tour of Scotland. They lost 5–1 to United who thus finished the season as League champions, a point ahead of Villa.

Sunderland keeper Butler saves from Harry Hampton (extreme right of picture) during the 1913 FA Cup final at Crystal Palace. Those in the tightly packed crowd of almost 122,000 barely had space to put their hands together in applause. Other branches of the support could sway dangerously with excitement in the trees behind the terracing.

Several people are injured as a refreshment stand, in the grounds of Crystal Palace, collapses during the 1913 Cup final. Supporters had climbed on top of its canvas awning to try to obtain a view of the match after failing to gain admission to the game.

The road to Crystal Palace

After winning the FA Cup in 1905, Villa's record in that tournament had been poor. For eight seasons after that win, they failed to go further than three rounds in any year. Villa's lack of Cup luck continued in 1913 when they were drawn away from home to a strong Derby County side in their opening match of that year's tournament. After an enervating first 45 minutes played in a snowstorm the sides were level at 1–1. At the interval the referee decided to abandon the match because the pitch markings had been obscured. Villa completed the job the following Wednesday, winning the tie 3–1. In the next two rounds, Villa defeated West Ham United and Crystal Palace, 5–0 on each occasion. Those ties, both at Villa Park, were watched by a total of 96,000 supporters. Villa triumphed over Bradford City by the same score in the quarter-final, despite the game being at Valley Parade. In the semifinal a Clem Stephenson goal made for a 1–0 win over Oldham Athletic at Blackburn.

For their sixth FA Cup final, Villa departed from tradition, training at home rather than seeking seclusion. The club used Sutton Park for outdoor practice and the gymnasium at Villa Park for indoor conditioning work. On the evening before the final, the players left for London where they stayed in Beckenham. Sunderland, Villa's opponents in the final, were the League leaders. Villa were joint-second with Sheffield Wednesday and Villa's previous finals in the capital had made them popular with Londoners. A large crowd was thus anticipated for the final but the eventual attendance exceeded all expectations. The crowd of 121,919 was a record gate and represented an increase of more than 10,000 on the previous highest attendance, set in 1901. On the day, the terraces at the Crystal Palace were uncomfortably packed. Trees and buildings close to the ground were busy with onlookers.

Triumph in adversity

After a cagey opening stage, Joe Bache slipped the ball to Stephenson inside the penalty area. He was immediately upended by Gladwin, the Sunderland right-back, and Mr Adams, the referee, awarded a penalty. Wallace stepped up to slide the ball well wide of goal. Midway through the half, Hampton had a goal disallowed for offside. Those two setbacks were compounded by a more serious blow. Sam Hardy, the Villa goalkeeper, had to leave the pitch in the 55th minute after a collision with Sunderland outside-left Harry Martin. Harrop replaced him in goal and Hampton dropped back to centre-half.

Harrop made some impressive saves early in his goalkeeping stint, but he twice needed to rely on a goalpost to keep out shots from Sunderland winger Martin. Harrop was also

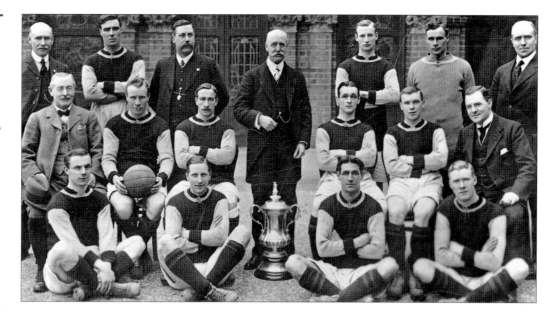

Fred Rinder, the Villa chairman (centre), and his fellow directors again have the pleasure of joining the Villa players for a team picture after the 1913 Cup triumph. Left to right are: J. Grierson (trainer), A. Lyons, P. Bate (director), Rinder, T. Weston, S. Hardy, H. Spencer (director). Middle row: G. Ramsay (secretary), J. Bache, H. Halse, H. Hampton, C. Stephenson, J. Jones (vice chairman). Front row: C. Wallace, T. Barber, J. Harrop, J. Leach.

The cycling track is removed from Villa Park in the summer of 1914. The alterations would bring spectators closer to the pitch, heightening the atmosphere inside the ground.

beaten by Sunderland inside-left George Holley, who rounded him and sent a shot careering towards the Villa goal. Tom Lyons, Villa's left-back, raced back to clear off the line. After an eight-minute absence, Hardy returned with his leg heavily bandaged. Villa now forced the pace.

With 15 minutes remaining, a highly accurate corner from Wallace was met by Tommy Barber, Villa's right-half, for a natty header that gave Villa the only goal of the game and the FA Cup for the fifth time. The Villa team had been: Hardy, Lyons, Weston, Barber, Harrop, Leach, Wallace, Halse, Hampton, Stephenson, Bache.

Double chance

The Villa party stayed in London over the weekend, returning to Birmingham on the Monday evening. Jubilant fans greeted them at New Street and lined the streets to see the Cup. For the players, however, the celebrations had to be of the watered-down variety. Two days later they were due to face Sunderland in a League match that would be crucial in deciding the destination of the title. A record crowd of almost 60,000 saw Villa's Cup-winning team take the field, with the exception of the injured Hardy. Before kick-off, the Cup was paraded around the track.

It was, like the final, a fast-paced game throughout. Sunderland took the lead before half-time but Villa equalised on the hour, Harold Halse depositing Joe Bache's cross in the Sunderland net. Villa worked hard for a second goal but when it failed to arrive they knew their chance of the double had disappeared. They ended the season in second place, four points behind Sunderland.

The following two seasons proved barren for Villa. They did reach an FA Cup semi-final in 1913–14, losing 2–0 to Liverpool, and finished the season in second place in the League, seven points behind Blackburn Rovers. In 1914–15, however, Villa finished in the lower half of the First Division for the first time since 1901 and made little impact in the FA Cup. They would appear in the next FA Cup final but it would be at a new venue, in a much-changed world.

The inter-war years were filled with drama at Villa Park. A first Wembley final, the arrival of prolific goalscorer Pongo Waring, the appointment of the club's first manager and a murder all helped keep Villa in the news.

4 A Time of Change: 1914–39

Football became an irrelevance when set beside the horrors of the First World War and the Football League and FA Cup competitions were discontinued between 1915 and 1919. Hostilities ceased in November 1918 and, in a reflection of society's relief at a return to normal life, people began flocking back to football in massive numbers. The professional game resumed League competition in the late summer of 1919.

Slow start to the season

Villa proved more than a tad ring-rusty after their lengthy competitive lay-off. They suffered their worst start to any season, losing six and drawing one of their opening seven League matches. The team revived during November and December 1919 but they were set firmly in mid-table as 1920 began. In the opening week of that year, Harry Hampton played his last match for Villa, a subdued performance against Burnley.

The following Saturday, for the first time since 1905, Villa began an FA Cup competition without Hampton. He had appeared irreplaceable but that day a youngster named Billy Walker made his debut in the Villa forward line. It proved a seamless transfer of power. The new man scored a goal in each half as Villa defeated Queens Park Rangers 2–1.

For that match, Villa had prepared in Birmingham, making only a brief excursion to Droitwich for a dip in the brine baths. The club's traditional practice of preparing for Cup matches together, then travelling to the game in a group had been discontinued. Villa, after four years of inactivity, were now deeply in debt and could barely afford such extravagances. At the end of the war Villa had had an overdraft of £2,726 due to loss of income from gate receipts. For their next tie, away to Manchester United, the club again eschewed special preparation. This appeared non-problematic until the day of the game when, with 15 minutes remaining before kick-off, Sam Hardy and Frank Barson, Villa's new centre-half, had not turned up. Both men lived in Sheffield and had been due to travel to the match together from that city.

With minutes to go before the game started, they arrived. Their train from Sheffield had been indefinitely delayed at an obscure railway outpost called Dinting Junction. With time rapidly expiring, the two players had disembarked, then run cross-country, through farmers' fields, to the town of Stalybridge, seven miles from where their train had halted. From there they were transported to Manchester. It was an unusual means of preparation for a crucial tie, played in front of 47,500 fans. The aftermath of the match was more relaxed, Villa having produced an impressive performance to win the game 2–1. Walker had scored the winning goal and, despite his pre-match preparation, Barson had done a superb job of marshalling the men around him.

Tough Cup draws continued to come Villa's way. Sunderland, third in the First Division, were their next FA Cup opponents, at Villa Park. There was enormous anticipation for this match in Birmingham so the directors decided to increase admission prices. At 1.00pm on the day of the

Aston Villa captain Andy Ducat receives the FA Cup from Prince Henry after Villa's victory over Huddersfield Town in the 1920 final.

game, a virulent rumour swept the city that the crowd at Villa Park was already so great that the gates had been closed. Many people decided not to venture to Aston. The rumour was a false one but its effect, combined with increased prices, was that only 32,000 attended. That was half the expected crowd. On the field, matters proceeded more smoothly. Andy Ducat, Frank Barson and Jimmy Harrop, the Villa halfbacks, ensured that Villa controlled the game from start to finish. Clem Stephenson, Villa's inside-left, scored the only goal of the game but Villa's dominance had deserved a much greater winning margin.

The quarter-final draw took Villa to White Hart Lane, North London, to face the Second Division champions-elect, Tottenham Hotspur. A crowd of 52,179 saw Spurs' Clay put the ball into his own net after six minutes. Villa faced a rigorous test of their defensive powers for the next 84 minutes but held on to their lucky lead. Another London side, Chelsea, now stood between Villa and their first postwar final. The semi-final was played at Bramall Lane, Sheffield. Five minutes before halftime, Billy Walker slipped away from a couple of Chelsea challenges to pass to Wallace on the wing. A cross from Wallace was met by Walker, still running, and he sent a powerful header into the Chelsea net. Villa eased on to a 3–1 win and were in the final for the seventh time, an unequalled record.

Billy Walker, a native of Wednesbury, scored 244 goals in 531 appearances for Villa between 1920 and 1933. His quickness and exceptional control saw him capped 18 times for England. After his playing career, he enjoyed success as a manager, winning the FA Cup with Sheffield Wednesday and with Nottingham Forest.

The seventh Cup final

The 1920 final would be held at Chelsea's home, Stamford Bridge, on 24 April. The FA had failed to come to agreement with the owners of the Crystal Palace over holding the final there. Villa's opponents would be Huddersfield Town. Unbeaten in 15 games, they had just won promotion from the Second Division. The Stamford Bridge stand had been sold out weeks before the final and a crowd of 80,000 was expected to watch the game. On the day, however, there was a strangely subdued atmosphere as a crowd of just 50,018 attended. It was an occasion symptomatic of recession-hit postwar Britain. Increased fares and the railway companies' unwillingness to run extra trains for a football match – as they had done for pre-war finals – reduced the numbers of fans travelling south from Huddersfield and Birmingham. Londoners had been put off by constant rain in the days leading up to the final and playing the game at a club ground rather than the Crystal Palace made it seem less of a special event. The Villa party journeyed south only on the morning of the match.

Villa were the classier side throughout the final but, on a slippery surface, their forwards struggled to get a grip on their shooting. With the score at 0–0 after 90 minutes it became the first Cup final to go to extra time. After seven minutes of the additional period of play, Huddersfield's Wilson, under pressure in the air from Villa inside-right Billy Kirton, sent the ball past his own goalkeeper. It was all Villa needed to take the Cup. The Villa team was: Hardy, Smart, Weston, Ducat, Barson, Moss, Wallace, Kirton, Walker, Stephenson, Dorrell. 'Perhaps we were a bit lucky in regard to the winning goal,' said Billy Walker, 'but to the end of my life I shall always maintain that on the play we deserved the cup and medals. It was a happy day for all of us.'

Villa arrived back in Birmingham at 4pm on the Monday afternoon. Players, officials and the FA Cup were crammed into a fleet of taxis which made slow progress through the streets which were crowded with supporters. Eventually, the Villa representatives reached the Holte Hotel, situated behind the south terracing at Villa Park. After tea, the players got stripped for a League match with Manchester City. With 45,000 looking on, Ducat, who had captained the Cup-winning team in the absence of the injured Harrop, led the team on to the field with the Cup. Villa lost 1–0.

Frank Barson, the centre-half in Villa's Cup-winning side, had done much to inspire the victory in 1920. He was an abrasive player and opponents regularly complained to officials that his vigorous approach to the physical side of the game infringed the rules. Barson, who was 5ft 11ins and weighed 12st 4lb, also enjoyed a good brawl on the pitch. His team-mates and Villa's supporters were simply grateful that he was on their side. He was a good talker, constantly capable of geeing up his team-mates.

In 1922, Barson was transferred to Manchester United. He had refused to accept the Villa committee's residential rule: players had to live in the Birmingham area. Barson had remained in Sheffield since signing from Barnsley in late 1919. Four other key Villa players – Clem Stephenson, Sam Hardy, Jimmy Harrop and Andy Ducat – had all left the club in 1921 because of this rule. The loss of such steady, influential talents within such a short space of time had a lasting impact on the club.

Billy Walker, in his 13-year career with Villa, would eventually become the club's record scorer with 244 goals. Such a creatively talented individual might appear to have little in common with a man like Barson. Yet in looking back on his earliest years at the club, Walker explained the importance of Barson to the team: 'Much of my success has been due to him. When he was at Villa Park he was ever ready with his advice and encouragement. His passes up the middle to me were real beauties and times out of number I was given credit for work which he accomplished. A man who could not play with Frank Barson behind him would be a very poor fish indeed. Frank used to spoonfeed some of our younger Villa players. He was the greatest centre-half-back I have ever seen.'

Ball shot dead

Villa would remain an entertaining side, capable of matching the best teams in England on their day. In the first nine seasons after the First World War, however, they failed to challenge for the First Division championship. Nor did they come close to the dangers of relegation. Throughout the 1920s they became a model mid-table team.

Barson was replaced at centre-half by Tommy Ball, a 23-year-old Durham man who had been spotted by a Villa scout while playing for Felling Colliery in 1920. Ball had joined as a left-back but took over at centre-half on Barson's departure. On 10 November 1923, he turned in a steady performance in a routine League match against Notts County. In the evening he returned to his home in Perry Barr and went out for a few drinks with his wife. At 10.30pm the couple went back to their cottage and Ball took his dog for a walk. Within minutes, he had been shot dead by his neighbour and landlord George Stagg.

In a statement to police, Stagg said he had heard a disturbance and had gone out to investigate. Stagg stated: 'Mr Hall was under the influence of drink. He shouted to me, "Go in and go to bed. I will bash your brains out."' According to Stagg, Ball then shouted to Mrs Stagg, at her window: 'I will bash your ****** brains out.' At that, Stagg, a former detective and soldier, had fetched his rifle. He claimed that he fired a warning shot past Ball and that the two men then began wrestling for possession of the gun. It accidentally went off, claimed Stagg, wounding Ball. According to one witness, it left a 'wound the size of a half-crown in his chest'. Stagg carried Ball's body into Ball's house where he died almost immediately. At his trial, Stagg was found guilty of 'wilful murder' and sentenced to death. This was later commuted to life imprisonment.

Villa's first Wembley final

Despite the tragic loss of their team-mate, the Villa players managed to make progress in that season's FA Cup. Dr Victor Milne, a player from Aberdeen who had a degree in medicine, replaced Tommy Ball at centre-half. The club had done poorly in the competition since winning it in 1920 but they were back in the final in 1924. This match was to be the second final played at the new Wembley Stadium and the first played before an all-ticket crowd. Villa had conceded just one goal on their Wembley way, as they defeated Ashington, Swansea Town, Leeds United, WBA and Burnley. Fred Rinder proudly led the Villa team on to the Wembley turf.

Villa dominated the game from the start, the forwards attacking with flair, but the Newcastle backs held firm. After 85 minutes Newcastle broke their defensive chains to leap into attack. Harris, their centre-forward, shot, Villa goalkeeper Jackson parried and Cowan, the Newcastle inside-right, pushed the rebound into the net. Kirton almost equalised within a minute but his header went over the Newcastle bar. Two minutes after the opening goal, Newcastle's Seymour made it 2–0.

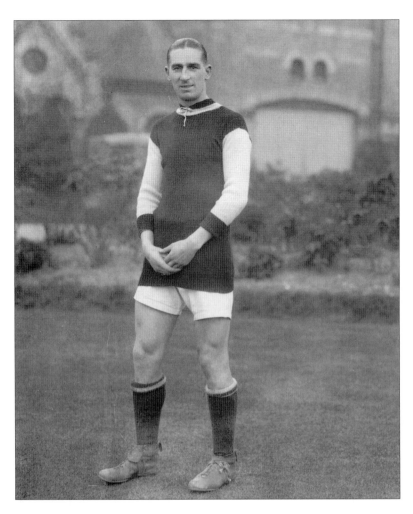

Frank Barson's performances at centre-half bolstered an ailing Aston Villa defence during the early 1920s. He returned to Villa as trainer in 1935, remaining with the club until the Second World War.

A goalkeeper of great grace and excellent positioning skills, Sam Hardy was Villa's undisputed number one during his time at Villa Park. He was with Villa between 1912 and 1921 and, in common with several club-mates, missed out on four seasons through the interruption of the First World War.

Frank Moss, the Villa captain, commented: 'We had 20 chances; they had two. They accepted theirs. We missed ours.'

Villa's record of winning six FA Cups in eight finals had made them by far England's most successful Cup side. It was a tradition that the club would now struggle to uphold. After reaching the final in 1924, Villa were knocked out in the early rounds in every season until 1929.

A new rule and goals galore

Each new season in League and Cup during the 1920s began with Villa supporters buoyant in their anticipation of good things to come. Villa may not have been winning trophies but the team retained their entertaining style of play. One detailed change in the rules of football, made in 1925, looked sure to assist Aston Villa. In that year, the International Board altered the offside rule. For a forward to be offside only two defenders had to stand between him and the opposition's goal-line instead of the previous three. The new rule was expected to bring more goals for teams with attacking flair, such as Aston Villa.

A crowd of 60,000 turned up at Villa Park for the first match of the 1925–26 season. The atmosphere at the ground had become better than ever, the cycling track having been removed in 1914. Spectators were closer to the action with all four sides of the ground now hemming in the pitch. Those at the front of the terraces were almost on top of the players. A stunning new stand on the Trinity Road side of the ground had been opened in 1922, with room for 6,500 seats and an enclosure holding 11,000 situated in front. Those drawn to that Burnley game in expectation of seeing the ball hitting the net a few times were not to be disappointed. In pre-season training, Villa had been working on using the new offside law to best advantage. Wingers Dicky York and Arthur Dorrell and forwards Billy Walker and Len Capewell had planned ways to make speedier than ever switches into attack. Their flair for the unexpected carved out a stunning win. From Burnley's kick-off Walker intercepted the ball and whisked it forward to Dorrell. His cross was angled into the Burnley net by Capewell who scored four more times as Villa raced to a 10–0 win. It proved another false start to a season that eventually came to nothing, but it was an enjoyable one nonetheless.

Rinder resigns

Off the field, there was a good deal of dissatisfaction among the Villa shareholders. The total cost of constructing the Trinity Road stand and carrying out the improvements to the ground had been close to £90,000, considerably more than had been planned. It left the club deeply in debt. Fred Rinder, as chairman, had authorised the extra spending. He would pay heavily for his actions. The extravagances that had seen the club's debts to architect Archibald Leitch tot up considerably were the ornate, decorative elements in the Trinity Road stand that make it such a work of art and

Len Capewell chal-
lenges West
Bromwich Albion
goalkeeper Ashmore
during a derby in the
1920s. Capewell, a
clever inside-forward,
got a round century
of goals in 156
appearances during
that decade.

give Villa Park much of its mystique. After
two meetings at which the overspending
was criticised in detail by the shareholders,
Rinder offered to resign. His resignation
was accepted but he retained the one thing
he treasured more than anything else. He
was still a Villa supporter, albeit one who
could look around his club's home with
even more pride and affection than his fellow fans.

In a bold parting speech at a meeting of
the shareholders and their new committee
on 25 September 1925, Rinder was unre-
pentant with regard to the extra expenses
he had incurred. He maintained that his
pursuit of beauty in creating a genuinely
grand stand had a practical purpose. 'I am
not concerned with the differences of the
shareholders and the directors, but I am
deeply concerned for the future success of
Aston Villa. We have been told that the
finances of the club are in a parlous state.
Don't believe it. The club is in a better

Fred Rinder (right),
the Villa chairman,
welcomes the Duke of
York (centre) to Villa
Park in 1924 for the
official opening of the
new Trinity Road
stand.

position today than it was 12 months ago.
What is the amount of money which you
owe? £55,000. That £55,000 which you
owe, has, during the past two seasons
earned you, after paying all expenses, a net
income of £5,000 and no-one can hope to
receive money unless they spend money
first. You have the best ground in the kingdom and you have got a good team. You

A happy flat-capped crowd on the Villa Park terraces awaiting the action before a match in 1925. A smart suit, shirt and tie were de rigeur for football fans in the inter-war years. Villa Park hosted healthy crowds throughout the 1920s and 1930s. The average League crowd was always in the vicinity of 30,000 until the late 1930s, when it climbed close to 40,000.

have got a better team than you think you have got…

'The directors have never given me an opportunity of discussing the amended accounts in any shape or form. Your directors have ignored me since the last meeting. They have not had so much as the common courtesy to offer me a seat in your enclosure or invite me to the match. Notwithstanding that, I say sink your differences, give them a chance, help them all you possibly can. The success of Aston Villa in the future should be as great as it has been in the past, and I hope sincerely you will do your part to see that is so.' After 33 years on the board and 29 years as chairman, so departed the man whose mind had shaped and sculpted Villa Park.

One of the ways in which the Villa board had planned to recoup their outlay in constructing Villa Park was to have international matches played there. Three internationals had been played at the ground by the time England met Scotland there in April 1922. Three Villa players were in the England team – Dicky York, Billy Walker and Frank Moss. Despite the attraction of seeing some of their own players in the national team,

only 30,000 Brummies turned up for the match, which Scotland won 1–0. It was for FA Cup semi-finals, however, that the ground would become most frequently used as a neutral venue. Birmingham was ideally suited for such purposes and Villa Park, thanks to Rinder, possessed the grandeur required of such occasions.

Villa themselves reached the semi-final in the 1928–29 season, meeting Portsmouth at Highbury Stadium in London. That season also saw the club sustain a realistic challenge for the League title. Speaking before the semi-final, Billy Walker, now Villa's captain, said: 'I think the present Villa side the best that have carried the colours during the time I have been connected with the club. And, what is perhaps more important, they are the happiest set of comrades I have ever known.'

At the beginning of March, a 2–1 derby defeat at Birmingham City appeared to end Villa's title hopes for the 1920s. It left them eight points behind leaders Sheffield Wednesday. In the FA Cup semi-final on 29 March, Villa lost 1–0 to a highly dubious penalty when Teddy Bowen, the Villa right-back, was adjudged to have handled inside the penalty area. A point-blank shot had struck him on the chest and had then flown off the top of his right arm. The referee stunned the Villa players by awarding a spot-kick.

In the weeks either side of that match, Villa made an impressive late climb up the First Division table, but a 3–0 defeat at Manchester City on the penultimate Saturday of the season ended their hopes of finishing the decade as League champions. It was especially disappointing as champions-elect Sheffield Wednesday visited Villa Park for their final fixture of the season and Villa defeated them 4–1 to finish just two points adrift in third place.

Pongo Waring arrives

Villa had scored more goals – 98 – and won more games – 23 from 42 – than any other team in the division. An equally rich seam of goals would be chipped away from rock-

Tom 'Pongo' Waring signed for Villa from Tranmere Rovers, his local club, for a fee of £4,700 in 1928. He went on to score 167 goals in 226 games for Villa. Fifty of those goals came in the 1930–31 season; 49 in the League, one in the FA Cup. He hit the net in 30 of the 39 League games in which he appeared for Villa and on three occasions scored four goals in a match. Inspired by Waring's feats, the team amassed a total of 128 League goals. Waring's individual scoring record for Villa and the team's tally have yet to be beaten by a Villa side.

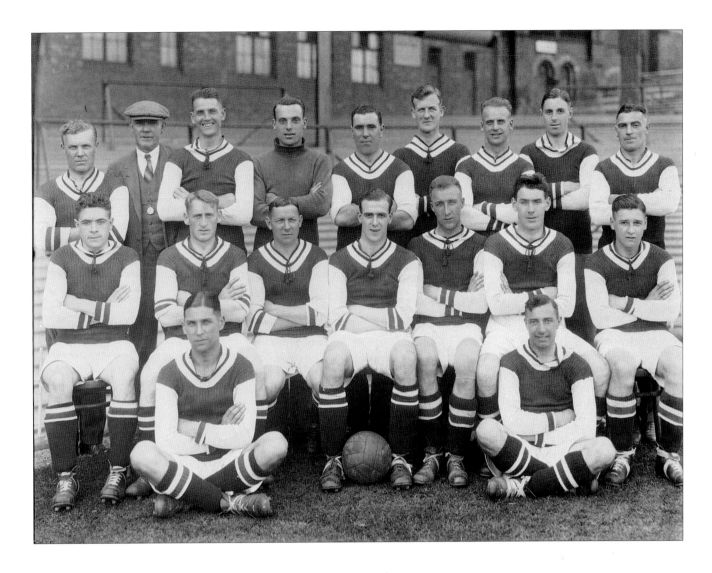

The Aston Villa players who created a club record by accumulating 128 League goals in the 1930–31 season. Back row, from left: E. Bowen, H. Cooch (trainer), A. Talbot, F. Biddlestone, T. Smart, J. Gibson, W. Walker, J. Tate, R. York. Middle row: J. Mandley, T. Mort, A. Dorrell, T. Waring, R. Chester, G. Brown, E. Houghton. Seated on ground: W. Kingdon, J. Beresford.

hard defenders over the coming seasons. Billy Walker remained at his best, while at centre-forward the team now had Tom 'Pongo' Waring. He had scored the first of many goals for Villa on his debut, a 7–2 win in a friendly with Airdrie in 1928.

Villa finished fourth, but well out of contention for the title, in 1929–30. On the opening day of the first full season of the 1930s, Villa travelled to Old Trafford for a match with Manchester United. The team's overall performance was weak. Their passing was awry and the defence conceded its first goal of the season after just two minutes. Two more United goals followed and only one Villa player got on the scoresheet. That man, however, was Pongo Waring.

His first goal was the result of quick anticipation. Outside-right Mandley's shot struck the crossbar and Waring dashed in to put the rebound in the net. Waring's

second was down to balance and deftness in the air, as he headed home a cross from Mandley. His third, a minute later, owed everything to strength, as he brushed off several defenders to charge through the United back line and make the score 3–3. With a minute remaining, and a hat-trick to the good, he was still working away. When United goalkeeper Steward dropped the ball, Waring pounced to turn it over the line and give Villa a 4–3 victory. In that commanding performance Waring had demonstrated the skills which he would continue to display throughout that season. He rarely left the field at the end of 90 minutes without adding at least one goal to his tally.

Waring scored the opening goal in Villa's 2–0 win over Sheffield Wednesday the following Monday and 40,000 were at Villa Park the next Saturday to see a 6–1 win over West Ham United. Villa would go

Jimmy McMullan became Aston Villa's first team manager in 1934. As a player he had been the finest Scottish half-back of the 1920s and had been captain of the 'Wembley Wizards', the Scottish team who had defeated England 5–1 at Wembley in 1928. McMullan failed to transfer his playing magic to his management of Villa during the short period he had in charge at the club. After little more than a year as manager, he resigned from his position at Villa.

on to score 128 goals in the League, still a record for England's top division. Pongo Waring scored 49 of those goals plus one in the FA Cup – a feat which still stands as the club record for goals scored in a season. While Waring and his team-mates scored an impressive number of goals, for overall consistency Villa struggled to match Arsenal. The Highbury side's powerful forward play was backed by a strong defence. Villa's defence was leaky, draining the forwards' efforts by continually conceding crucial goals. Villa ended the season in second position but seven points behind Arsenal.

Two seasons later, Villa again made a strong challenge for the League title. In the autumn of 1932 they were unbeaten in their first 11 games and led the First Division by a point. In the second half of the season, the defence began to creak. Yet in late March, Villa were only three points

Frank Broome (left) was a top-notch goalscorer with Villa. Despite being of light build for a 1930s centre-forward, his alacrity and determination enabled him to score 90 times in 151 League and Cup appearances for the club. On the club's three-game tour of Germany in 1938 Broome scored three of Villa's five goals. He also managed to fit in an appearance for England, who were in Germany that May. Broome helped his national side to a 6-3 win. George Cummings (right), in common with Broome, had his Villa career interrupted by the Second World War. A native of Falkirk, the full-back had been a Villa supporter as a boy and achieved his major footballing ambition when Villa chairman Fred Normansell signed him from Partick Thistle over tea and cakes in a tearoom in Princes Street, Edinburgh, in 1935. Cummings would play 232 games for Villa, becoming captain in 1945 when Alex Massie took the post of team manager.

behind League leaders Arsenal when they faced the London club at Highbury. At one point Villa, playing in white shirts with a claret-and-blue trim, faced just nine Arsenal players, two of the Gunners' forwards having left the field for lengthy treatment to injuries. The Villa defence still struggled to cope with the remaining three Arsenal front men. At half-time Villa were 3-0 down, at full-time it was 5-0 and the championship was on its way to London again.

McMullan appointed manager

Billy Walker left Villa in December 1933 to start a new career as manager of Sheffield Wednesday. Villa plunged to 13th in the First Division at the end of the 1933–34 season. That prompted the board of directors to appoint the club's first team manager, Jimmy McMullan, in the summer of 1934. Prior to this appointment, the team had been selected by committee. A captain of the Scottish international side in the 1920s, McMullan had finished a successful playing career at Manchester

City in 1933. He had been manager of Oldham Athletic for a year before he joined Villa. 'We have some fine players and there is a commendable spirit of keenness and enthusiasm here. I am looking forward to a really good season,' he said in August 1934.

The first major signing during McMullan's time as team manager was Jimmy Allen, who was purchased from Portsmouth for a club record fee of £10,775 in the summer of 1934. Allen introduced the 'third-back' game to Villa. Until then, Villa had employed a traditional 2-3-5 formation, with the centre-half the middle man of the three midfield players. Now, to counter the effect of the new offside rule, many clubs were pulling back their centre-half into defence where he would concentrate more on stopping opponents than on setting up attacks. Successful use of this tactic also required two of the forwards to be brought back into midfield to compensate for the loss of the centre-half in that area.

Villa, traditionally a side geared to going forward, struggled to adjust to the new system and a string of poor results tore team spirit apart. 'I was playing the third-back game at Portsmouth when Villa sought my transfer. Apparently they wanted me for what I was doing. Naturally, being of that opinion, I have carried on,' said Allen in defence of his tactical approach. The situation wasn't helped when Allen missed a lengthy series of games, leaving Villa caught between two styles. They again finished in 13th place in the First Division.

Season of struggle

In the autumn of 1935, Villa made an average start to the League season, taking seven points from seven games. From then, they began to drift downwards and after a 7–0 home defeat by WBA in mid-October they went into freefall. For that game, McMullan had made a total of seven changes; some positional, some personnel. Prior to the match with Leeds United on the last Saturday of October, Jimmy McMullan resigned as Villa's team man-

ager. On his departure, Frank Barson returned to Villa as coach to the players and as training supervisor. Villa were now second-bottom of the First Division and threatened with relegation for the first time in their history. A week at Rhyl brought no cure – it was followed by a 6–2 home defeat by Grimsby Town which put Villa in bottom spot.

The Villa directors dug deep for a solution. Over the next two months, they spent around £35,000 – a massive sum – in an attempt to buy time and a team. George Cummings, a Scottish international full-back, was signed from Partick Thistle in November. The fee of £9,350 was a record paid to a Scottish club. Charles Drinkwater, an outside-left, arrived from Golders Green, an amateur side. Alex Massie, a Scottish international right-half, was signed from Heart of Midlothian for another colossal fee of £6,000. Joe Palethorpe, a centre-forward, arrived from Sheffield Wednesday; Tom Griffiths, a centre-half, came from Middlesbrough;

Fred Rinder and Jimmy Hogan share a chat on the touchline during a Villa training session. Rinder, newly re-elected to the Villa board, had persuaded Hogan to join Villa in 1936 after Hogan had spent two decades on continental Europe, successfully imparting radical ideas to willing listeners in countries where football was growing rapidly. Rinder and Hogan shared an ability to find straightforward solutions to complicated situations.

Tommy Gardner (left), Frank Broome (centre) and Tom Griffiths (right) focusing on a ball tossed to them by Jimmy Hogan during a Villa training session. An increased commitment to ball-work was a mark of Hogan's approach. Hogan, who was a coach first and a manager second, took an active part in training. That set him apart from the other British team managers of the 1930s. Appointing Hogan was a hugely progressive move on Villa's part. Sadly, the experiment could not be concluded. One year after Hogan had led the club back to the First Division, the Second World War broke out and football was sidelined for its duration.

Charlie Phillips, a Welsh international outside-right, cost £9,000 when signed from Wolves. The bad results continued and in mid-December, Arsenal legend Ted Drake scored all seven goals as his team won 7–1 at Villa Park.

The new players had settled by early spring when Villa put together a fair set of results. They were still unable to break clear of the bottom two relegation positions. On 25 April 1936, in their final home game of the season, they lost 4–2 to Blackburn Rovers. That result made Aston Villa the last of the original members of the Football League to suffer the embarrassment of relegation. It was a hurt that was felt particularly sharply by Villa supporters because of their proud history and role in establishing the League. The lack of a youth policy in the preceding years had now taken its toll. The shareholders were angry at Villa's loss of First Division status and at the debts incurred in buying players over the season. Wages, bonuses, benefits and transfers had amounted to £44,590 for the year.

At a highly-charged Aston Villa AGM in July 1936, Mr Arthur Canlett suggested that his fellow shareholders cast their minds back to when Jack Jones had taken over as chairman from Fred Rinder eleven years previously. At that time, said Canlett, a number of young players nurtured by the club were either progressing through the reserve team or holding down a place in the first team. Several of them had gone on to become international players. Since Jones had been chairman, added Canlett, only Eric Houghton had come through the reserves to hold down a place in the first team. 'Where is the blame?' he asked. 'I think that the chief responsibility is on the chairman of the board. It was his duty to lead and advise the younger directors. Did he?' After Canlett had left that question hanging in the air like a noose ready-made for Jones, several other shareholders advocated the return of Fred Rinder as chairman.

Rinder returns

An Emergency General Meeting, held immediately after the AGM, voted Jones off the board and Rinder back on to it as a director after 11 years in the wilderness. Fred Normansell, however, took over as

George Ramsay communes with his dog on the Villa Park pitch in 1928. Ramsay was reputed to have been the last man to kick a ball at the club's Perry Barr ground and the first to do the same on Villa Park. A man who was able to balance the practical necessities of football with a true love of the game, he gave the club 59 years of service from 1876 to his death in 1935. No other individual had a greater or more useful input to the club during its early years.

chairman. Rinder's first major action now that he was back on board was typically dynamic. He travelled to Germany to persuade Jimmy Hogan to become the new Aston Villa team manager. Hogan, a 53-year-old Lancastrian, had been in demand as a coach throughout Europe, passing on his successful ideas in Austria, Hungary, Germany, Switzerland, France and Holland. Frank Barson would work as Hogan's assistant.

Hogan, writing in the Villa News and Record before Villa's opening Second Division fixture, stated: 'The first thing that struck me when I arrived at Villa Park was – despite our relegation of last season – that the average attendance for home games was 40,000. Such loyalty – under adverse circumstances – simply staggered me... I know the class and style of football you require and to which you were always accustomed. Let me say here "right now" you are going to get it so long as I hold the position of manager. I am a teacher and lover of constructive football with every pass, every kick, every movement an object.'

A crowd of 50,000 saw Villa begin their home League programme with a 4–0 win over Southampton. In October, 65,000 – a record crowd for the Second Division – witnessed Coventry City's first visit to Villa Park, a 0–0 draw. Hogan had stressed that it would take time for him to ingrain his ideas in the players' minds and Villa ended the season in ninth position. The following year they were back where they belonged, winning the Second Division title.

The team had the best defensive record in England, conceding just 35 goals – 15 goals fewer than Manchester United, who finished runners-up to Villa in the Second Division. Hogan simultaneously brightened Villa's 1930s FA Cup record. It had proved an inglorious Cup decade for the club. They had gone out in the early rounds in every year except 1934, when they had lost 6–1 to Manchester City in the semi-final. In 1938 Hogan led them to the semi-final where they were beaten 2–1 by Preston North End at Bramall Lane.

Villa bounce back

On 9 May 1938, Villa won their final match of the season, 2–0 against Norwich City in front of 42,000 at Villa Park. A total of 1.1 million spectators had watched Villa's League and Cup games at Villa Park in the 1937–38 season. An incredible 206,000 had been at the three Cup games, with Blackpool, Charlton Athletic and Manchester City. It meant that the average crowd for League games was 42,600, a record for Villa Park. The crowd of 68,029 which had seen Villa draw 1–1 with Coventry City in October 1937 had been the record attendance for a League match at Villa Park. In March 1938, almost 75,500 had been present for a Cup tie with Manchester City, a new attendance record for Villa Park.

Immediately after the Norwich match, Villa left for Southampton where they would sail on the SS Europa to Bremen for a tour of Germany. They had been invited on tour by the German head of the 'physical culture' school in Berlin. A five-day trip to Germany from 12–17 May was available to shareholders for £16 5 shillings (£16.25). In their opening match, against a German select in Berlin, Villa constantly used an offside trap, for which they were booed by the 110,000 crowd from start to finish. Villa won 3–2. They won their next game, in Stuttgart, 2–1 against a team composed chiefly of Austrian players, then travelled to Dusseldorf where they were beaten 1–0 by another select team composed of leading German players.

At the 1938 AGM, Fred Rinder explained his thinking in choosing Hogan as manager: 'It was not so much a manager we wanted. In my judgment the directors ought to manage the club, and if they are not capable of doing so they ought not to be there. What we wanted is what we got – a man who could teach the players how to play football. It had become the system to get a young player and put him in the first team; if he had the "guts" he made good; but if not there was nobody to help him. That was what the game was suffering from. When I tell you that the players presented Mr Hogan with a smoker's cabinet last year I need say no more to indicate their esteem and respect, or to show that older and younger players appreciate what he has done for them…Frank Barson is of wonderful assistance to Mr Hogan, and in charge of the younger players at the Alexander Ground [Birchfield Harriers' home, which Villa used for training] he is doing a great deal of good.' Bringing Jimmy Hogan to Villa was Fred Rinder's last major contribution to the club. The man who had done so much for Villa died on Christmas Day 1938.

During the 1938–39 League season, Villa safely consolidated their regained First Division status, finishing in 12th place. Only the teams in the top five had a better goal difference. That improved record owed much to Villa's greatly strengthened defence. Across the country, other more important defences were being improved simultaneously. Even as Villa had toured Germany in that late spring of 1938, Britain had been preparing for a second major war with that country. Indeed, the Villa team had been asked to give the Nazi salute before their matches in Germany but had refused to do so. In September 1939, the Second World War began. The two national football competitions were suspended for the duration of the conflict. Jimmy Hogan would never have the chance to see how far he could take his new youth policy or his rejuvenated Aston Villa.

The end of the war did not signal the end of troubles for Villa. But amongst the relegations and managerial comings and goings, there was a good deal of breathtaking football not to mention cup success.

5 Postwar Villa: 1945–67

Aston Villa Football Club proved to be one of the first casualties of the Second World War, disappearing from sight almost as soon as Britain had declared war on Germany in September 1939. Villa Park had been commandeered by the military authorities and, without a venue for home fixtures, the Villa directors suspended the team's activities and the players' contracts.

The First Division programme had been abandoned by order of the Government after the first three games of the 1939–40 season, but Midlands clubs continued to play each other in localised competition. Villa were notably absent from the proceedings. It mattered little. Although some Villa players were guesting for other Midlands clubs, others had more important work to do. Jimmy Allen, for example, was engaged in munitions work close to Southampton. By early 1940 Jimmy Hogan was also assisting with the war effort, working with the RAF football team and giving talks on football to members of the British Expeditionary Force in France. Others took part in active service. Terry Cullen, who had joined the club in 1938, spent most of the war years as a prisoner of the Germans in Poland.

The war years

Homeless Villa finally re-emerged in April 1940 for a testimonial match at St Andrews for Birmingham City's long-serving goalkeeper Harry Hibbs. A 15,000 restricted-capacity crowd saw Villa lose 2–1. The Government limited crowd numbers in the early period of the war because of the real fear that such assembled masses could be an enormous sitting target in the event of enemy bombing raids.

Football would continue throughout the war but restrictions on travel meant that it was played on a regional basis. It also became marginalised in most people's minds as they became preoccupied with more important matters.

In 1940, the Villa directors came to an arrangement with Solihull Town to use their ground for home fixtures in the Birmingham and District League. After two seasons ticking over in that competition, Villa competed in the Football League (North). They also took part in the Football League Cup (North), a temporary substitute for the FA Cup. Blackpool defeated Villa in the semi-finals of that tournament in 1943. The two clubs met again in the 1944 final. In the first leg, Villa were 1–0 ahead at Blackpool with six minutes remaining but lost the game 2–1.

For the second leg, on 6 May 1944, the gates at Villa Park were closed half an hour before kick-off. The 55,000 crowd inside was captivated by a spirited contest which Villa won 4–2. Frank Broome scored twice, George Edwards and Bob Iverson once each. For Villa's second goal, the ball appeared to be punched into the Blackpool net by Edwards. Looking back, Edwards admitted: 'Yes, I punched it in. There I was facing an open goal when I was pulled down from behind. As I fell the ball bounced up so I gave it a mighty right-hander. It went in like a rocket and you could have heard a pin drop when the ref gave a goal. Everyone else knew I had handled it!'

That win meant Villa would visit London for the first time since 1939. The winners of cups North and South traditionally took

Peter McParland volleys the winning goal in the 1957 FA Cup final to give Aston Villa their first postwar trophy.

part in a prestigious charity match at Stamford Bridge, the proceeds of which went to King George's Fund for Sailors. The southern cup-winners, Charlton Athletic, were not expected to be able to live with Villa in this match. The game attracted 40,000 spectators who each paid a minimum half-crown (12½ pence) entrance fee. Villa's half-backs Alex Massie, Ernie 'Mush' Callaghan and Ronnie Starling spun an intricate passing web all over the pitch and Eric Houghton opened the scoring early in the second half. Charlton managed to equalise and the match ended 1–1.

With the end of the war in 1945, football gingerly began to take its first steps back to normality. The north-south split in the League remained in place for the 1945–46 season, although Villa had now switched from the northern league to the southern one. Alex Massie took part in the opening games of that season, but a 7–1 victory over Luton Town was his final match as a player. He was promoted to team manager on 22 August 1945. Villa finished the season level on points with Birmingham City at the top of the southern league. Both sides had 61 points from 42 games but the St Andrews club took the title: their goal average was 0.306 better than that of Villa. Villa were the league's top scorers with 106 goals.

A return to League and Cup action

In 1946, the FA Cup competition returned after a seven-year absence and was greeted across the land like a long-lost war refugee. The football-hungry public devoured the fare offered by the tournament. That was reflected in the crowd for the home leg (each tie was played over two legs that year) of Villa's quarter-final with Cup favourites Derby County on 2 March 1946. It drew 76,588 to the ground – the record attendance for Villa Park. Those present saw Villa take the lead three times. With five minutes remaining the home side were winning 3–2. Then a defensive slip allowed Derby's Peter Doherty to make it 3–3. Before the end, Derby scored again for a 4–3 win. In the second leg a 1–1 draw sent Villa out of that year's tournament.

The championship of the First Division of the Football League finally resumed in

August 1946, and that season saw a speedy youngster, Johnny Dixon, make his mark on Villa's right wing. George Cummings, now 34, was still going strong, getting the better of Stoke City's mercurial winger Stanley Matthews in one memorable League game. Early in that season, however, Frank Broome left for Derby County where he would continue to be a regular goalscorer.

On Boxing Day 1946, Eric Houghton joined Notts County after almost 20 years as a Villa man. Houghton had scored 241 goals in all competitions, including 170 goals in the Football League and FA Cup, despite his Villa career having been interrupted by wartime service with the RAF. He would continue to train at Villa Park during his spell at Notts County.

Ernie Callaghan was a key member of the Villa side who won the wartime League Cup in 1944. His final appearance for Villa was in a 3–3 home draw with Grimsby Town in April 1947, aged 39 years, nine months. His best days with Villa were in the 1930s, when he formed a fine full-back partnership with George Cummings.

At the end of the 1946–47 season, Ernie Callaghan made his final appearance for the club. A Villa player since 1930, he was almost 40 when he wore the claret and blue for the last time, making him the oldest player to turn out for Villa. That summer, he took up residence at 'The Cottage' inside the grounds of Villa Park and became the club's on-site maintenance man.

Alex Massie was less content at Villa Park. From early in his time as team manager, the directors had interfered with the running and selection of the team. Massie endured four frustrating years of this before resigning in July 1949. Villa had achieved a respectable placing in the first three seasons of the postwar First Division but had not been in contention for the title. The club had also made little impact on the FA Cup.

After the war, Villa had been top-heavy with older players – 17 pre-war players were still on the club's books for the first League season after the war. There had been little effort on the part of the directors to bring in youth. Johnny Dixon had arrived at the club after writing, from his home town of Hebburn-on-Tyne, to ask for a trial, rather than having been spotted by Villa scouts. The name of Aston Villa still had a great allure for youngsters such as Dixon but this prestige was not being fully utilised by those in charge of the club.

George Martin appointed manager

Minus a manager, Villa tumbled down the First Division in the opening half of the 1949–50 season. By mid-December 1949 they were in 17th position, only two points

better off than bottom club Sheffield Wednesday. The directors then decided it was time to appoint a manager. George Martin was given the job. He had been manager of Newcastle United since the war, leading them out of the Second Division and to fourth position in the top flight in the 1948–49 season. Unlike his three predecessors Martin was, supposedly, to have full control of team selection and team affairs, not simply be team manager.

Martin managed a revival that saw Villa finish 12th in the First Division in the spring of 1950, but over the succeeding three years he would encounter the same problems of directorial interference that Massie had faced. There was still very little strength-in-depth in the reserve team and the club was still failing to nurture young players. The scouting system was virtually non-existent.

Villa finished 1950–51 in 15th position, but the following season took 11 points from their first seven games. In mid-September 1951 Villa, with new signing Danny Blanchflower influential at right-half, were a point behind League leaders Manchester United and had a game in hand. Villa then suffered a spate of injuries in mid-season. With a lack of sufficient cover for the missing players, they finished sixth.

One of George Martin's more unusual moves that season was to establish Con Martin, Villa's Irish international centre-half, as the first-team goalkeeper. 'Last season I noticed that after practice matches he would go into goal and invite the lads to shoot at him,' said the manager. 'He obviously revelled in it and it struck me more and more forcibly that he was a natural. Then when I watched him playing cricket, I noticed that he sighted a ball very quickly. It all helped to build up the idea in my mind that he was a natural goalkeeper.'

Eric Houghton returns to take over the helm

Villa ended the 1952–53 season in eleventh position and Martin remained in place in August 1953, smiling in the centre of the team group as its picture was taken for the new season. Within days he had been dismissed. On the same day as Martin parted company with Villa, Eric Houghton resigned as manager of Notts County after four years

Eric Houghton (left) with Jimmy Hogan (right) on the pitch in front of the Trinity Road stand during the early 1950s. Houghton had been a member of Hogan's promotion-winning side in 1938 and in 1953 Houghton had returned to the club as its manager. Hogan came back to Villa Park as a coach. Under Houghton and his trainer Billy Moore, the players' training sessions (below) again became imaginative.

in that position. He had guided County to promotion from the Third Division (North) but had spent the subsequent three seasons struggling against the threat of relegation from the Second Division. On 3 September 1953, he was appointed manager of Aston Villa. Jimmy Hogan also returned to the club in the same year to take charge of youth policy – an unusual post for a 70-year-old. Hogan inspired moves to promote the club's profile in the community, organising coaching classes for local boys at which first-team players attended.

'George Martin was the old-fashioned type of manager,' remembers Peter McParland, an outside-left who joined Villa from Dundalk in 1952. 'He would watch training but only from the side of the pitch, wearing an overcoat and a Homburg [a hat with a curled brim and a dent in the crown]. He wouldn't get involved in training but he would be watching you to see how you were working. When he got angry at half-time in a match he would sometimes throw his overcoat and his hat around the dressing room. That would backfire on him if it was a muddy day – they'd just get filthy.

'Eric Houghton was similar in his approach but he would sometimes get involved in training, going through a free-kick move or what to do at a throw-in, that sort of thing. His trainer, Billy Moore, was a

Jimmy Dugdale, a centre-half, had been a member of West Bromwich Albion's FA Cup winning side of 1954. Three years later, he was able to draw on that experience as he began his first FA Cup run with Aston Villa.

mutterings from the fans about the inadequacies of the board and manager. Some suggested that Houghton should step down in favour of Hogan. A spurt of good results in April and May 1955 saw Villa finish in sixth place in the First Division. It was an artificially high position – the club had never been in contention for the title and had spent most of the season slumped in the lower half of the table. In December 1954, the talented Danny Blanchflower, disillusioned with the club, had left for Tottenham Hotspur.

Chairman Fred Normansell died in March 1955 at the age of 68. He was replaced by Chris Buckley, who had been centre-half in the Villa team that had won the First Division championship in 1910. He had first been elected to the Villa board at the momentous meeting of 1936.

The following season, 1955–56, Villa were almost relegated, finishing third-bottom of the First Division on the same number of points as demoted Huddersfield Town. Villa missed the abyss of the Second Division by virtue of a slightly superior goal average.

With relegation a real possibility, Houghton had signed Jimmy Dugdale from WBA for a fee of £25,000 in February 1956. The centre-half had strengthened the defence considerably. By January of the 1956–57 season, Villa had the best defensive record in the First Division, having conceded only 30 goals. The team was anchored in mid-table, with little hope of winning the title but also safe from relegation. It looked a decent position from which to launch a run in the FA Cup.

A rare Cup run

In the postwar years, Villa had never gone further in the FA Cup than the sixth round. Their most notable Cup season had been in 1955; only because a fourth round tie with Doncaster Rovers had gone to a fourth replay before Villa lost 3–1 at the Hawthorns. On 5 January 1957, Villa travelled to Luton Town in the third round of the Cup and soon found themselves in the mire. Eric Houghton described the Kenilworth Road surface as the worst he had ever seen. With thick mud clawing at their ankles, Villa quickly used their heads and opted for the aerial route to goal. After 12 minutes,

revelation though. With him, training became much more enjoyable and worthwhile. Before he arrived we would hardly see the ball in training. The thinking was that if we didn't see the ball during the week we'd be hungrier for it on a Saturday. Instead, we just got sent out to lap the pitch. Or we'd have to run up the Holte End carrying weights or bags of sand on our backs. But they stopped giving us sandbags when they found out that some of the boys were tipping the sand out of the bags every time they reached the top; by the end there would be hardly any sand in the bags. Billy had us working in small groups, playing two-a-side and five-a-side and doing things like circuit training. We'd never had that before and it brightened everything up.'

After ending in 13th place in 1954, Villa got off to a sluggish start in the League the following autumn, bringing

Johnny Dixon, now team captain and playing at inside-left, headed Villa into the lead. Luton fought back to go 2–1 ahead. With Villa toiling in the face of the elements, Peter McParland was switched from the left wing to centre-forward with Derek Pace moving in the opposite direction. With just eight minutes of the match remaining, McParland picked his way through the muddy goalmouth to hit the equaliser after Luton keeper Streton had blocked a shot from Pace.

The replay took place the following Monday afternoon; Villa Park did not, as yet, have floodlights. A crowd of 28,356 found the time to get to the game. Two Johnny Dixon goals won the tie for Villa. The odds on Villa to win the Cup were now shortened from 33–1 to 25–1 but they remained distant outsiders. Manchester United, at 6–1, were the clear favourites. A trip to Middlesbrough

One of Villa's most outstanding goalkeepers, Nigel Sims, joined Villa from Wolves in 1956 at the age of 24 and remained with the club until 1964.

in the fourth round saw Dixon, still suffering from stomach trouble which had afflicted him overnight, draw on all his available strength to hit a forceful shot from distance and give Villa a 3–2 win. All three goals had been carefully constructed by Villa's left-half Pat Saward.

A home tie with Bristol City, fourth-bottom of the Third Division, drew 63,000 to Villa Park. Villa pulled through with goals from Jackie Sewell and Derek Pace. 'I remember watching the draw for the last eight on television,' says McParland. 'The one team we didn't want was Burnley. When six names had been drawn there was only us and Burnley left. When their name came out the hat first I nearly choked on a sausage.' In that tie, a headed goal by McParland provided Villa with the equaliser in a 1–1 draw. A fractious game had featured a free-for-all stand-up-fight inside the Burnley penalty area. Burnley's passing game was more sophisticated than that of Villa, but the Villa players had pressed them hard in every area of the pitch, cracking into tackles and rushing the Burnley players into mistakes.

In the Wednesday afternoon replay at Villa Park, watched by 46,531, Villa were wearing red shirts loaned to them at short notice by Birmingham City to avoid a clash with Burnley's all-black strip. The Villa players had expected another tough tie but the win proved an easy one. In the 18th minute, Smith darted past two defenders, Burnley goalkeeper Blacklaw half-stopped the Villa man's shot and Dixon sent the rebound skidding into the Burnley net. Peter McParland zipped through the middle to chip over Blacklaw for a second goal. Villa now faced a semi-final tie against West Bromwich Albion.

In that game, at Molineux, Villa played poorly. Twice they went behind. Twice Peter McParland equalised for a 2–2 draw that gave them a replay the following Thursday at St Andrews. 'There were only six minutes to go when I scored the second equaliser,' says McParland. 'As I was coming in on goal I had time and I thought, "I must keep it down" but I got over the top of the ball and I mishit it – I sidefooted it into the ground but it bounced slowly into the goal. The full-back on the goal-line stretched to get it with his hands but he couldn't quite reach it. So I got away with that one.' In the replay Villa played almost as badly as in the first game, but they were dealt a big advantage when

Albion forward Ronnie Allen had to leave the field after being knocked unconscious in the 17th minute. Allen would return after half an hour, but looking very fragile.

After 38 minutes, Sewell's cross dropped dangerously inside the WBA penalty area. The ever-alert McParland knocked it into Billy Myerscough's path. The centre-forward, who had been in Villa's reserves three weeks previously, angled a header into the Albion net for the only goal of the game. 'We had a bit of luck that day,' says McParland. 'I remember the ball bouncing and rolling along our crossbar and big Nigel Sims eventually jumped up to whack it over the bar. If it had dropped down into the goalmouth there would have been maybe ten people in the back of the net with the ball. In that match Stan Lynn also ran back to make a clearance but the ball came off his heel. Luckily it went the right side of the post for us. When players see things like that they think the luck of the Cup is with them.'

Cup final date with Manchester United

Villa would now return to Wembley for the final after a 33-year absence. Their opponents would be Manchester United. 'We would have preferred to have won against eleven fit men,' said Eric Houghton after the semi-final replay. 'Our fitness played a big part – a tribute to our trainer Billy Moore. There have been cleverer sides at Villa Park but none has been in better condition or played better as a team than the present one. We shall go into the final quietly confident. After all, we drew with Manchester United three weeks ago.' United had won the First Division by an eight-point margin, their third title of the 1950s. Ten days prior to the FA Cup final, they had contested the second leg of an exhilarating European Cup semi-final with Spanish giants Real Madrid at Old Trafford, losing on a 5–3 aggregate. Villa had finished the League season nine places below United.

An ankle injury had kept McParland out of Villa's final League game of the season, but he would be fit to take part in the Cup final. On the Tuesday before the game with United, at a training session at the Bourneville ground in Birmingham, Villa unveiled the new jersey which they would wear in the final; a light blue top with claret pinstripes. 'Someone had said to us that Bourneville had a nice ground that was like Wembley,' says McParland. 'We decided to do two days' training there so we went over there on the Tuesday morning. The place was chock-a-block with people to watch us but the ground was full of bumps. The players weren't too happy with it so although we did our training there that day Billy Moore was worried by the surface and cancelled training on the next day. He didn't want any injuries that week.'

On 3 May, the eve of the game, the Villa party travelled to London where they stayed in Hendon. A few players and manager Eric Houghton spent the evening at the cinema. Many of the 25,000 Villa supporters who had tickets for the final also travelled south that evening.

'After we came out of the film, Eric rang from a phone box for a taxi but was told we would have to wait a while for it to arrive,' says Peter McParland. 'So we were standing around and Eric said, "I'll tell you what I'll do, I'll ring the hotel and have a chat with Billy Moore [the Villa trainer]. I'll tell him I'm Harry Ditton." Harry Ditton was a *News of the World* reporter. So Eric rang Billy and asked him how the preparations had gone. Billy gave him the whole run-down on the day's work, saying, "Yes, we've been up to Wembley and the players tested the boots they're going to wear tomorrow." We were all hanging round the receiver listening. Billy put the phone down believing he'd spoken to Harry Ditton. About five minutes later the taxi came but

even when we got back to the hotel Eric didn't let on about what he had done.'

The following morning, Billy Moore gave a final talk to the players. 'At the end of that talk,' says McParland, 'Billy Moore said, "Right – Stan Lynn, Nigel Sims, Peter Aldis, you three pick Johnny Dixon up and get him on your shoulders after the game with the Cup and we'll all gather round for the photograph." That was how confident Billy was. That was the sort of man he was.

'We had a good side. We had three good defenders in Aldis, the full-back, Nigel Sims, a top goalkeeper, and Jimmy Dugdale, a helluva good player. He should have been England centre-half and Nigel should have been England goalkeeper but they only got "B" games. We had two good wing-halves in Crowther and Pat Saward – they were the best players on the field in the Cup final. Leslie Smith was a Wolves-style winger, a good crosser of the ball. Jackie Sewell and Johnny Dixon, the inside-forwards, were both excellent players. The centre-forward, Billy Myerscough, had had to battle for his place with Derek Pace. So we had this good side and we knew that we could look after ourselves on the day at Wembley. There was a feeling amongst us that we would do well.'

Villa start final the stronger

United were expected to play Villa off the park, but it was Villa who took control from the start. They moved the ball around effectively, while the United players struggled to

Below, left: Villa defenders Jimmy Dugdale, Pat Saward, Peter Aldis and Stan Crowther form a claret and blue barrier to keep Manchester United forward Tommy Taylor from their goal in the 1957 FA Cup final.

Below: After a heavy collision, Peter McParland and Manchester United goalkeeper Ray Wood share severe pain. They had fallen to the Wembley turf together when McParland's shoulder charge resulted in Wood taking the impact of the inrushing Villa forward's body on his jaw. Johnny Dixon, the Villa captain, prepares to give McParland a helping hand.

Above: Jackie
Blanchflower,
United's stand-in
keeper, sees a head-
er from McParland
rush goalwards to
give Villa the lead in
the 1957 final.

Right: Manager Eric
Houghton (extreme
left) and trainer Billy
Moore (third right)
join the Villa players
as they chair Johnny
Dixon, who clutches
the FA Cup after the
1957 final.

pass to one another. After six minutes, Sewell crossed for McParland, whose header was held by the United goalkeeper Ray Wood. McParland then shoulder-charged the goalkeeper, a legal and accepted part of the game in the 1950s. Both men collided and fell prone to the ground. McParland eventually got back on his feet but Wood was carried off on a stretcher, having sustained a fractured cheekbone in the collision.

'When the ball was in flight I was sure I was going to stick it in the back of the net at the far post but I stuck it straight into Woody's hands,' says McParland. 'I followed up for whatever dropped. I kept on going and he took me on for a shoulder charge. He then tried to step away at the last second and unfortunately I hit him on the jaw. I fell to the ground and thought that the match was over for me – the ground was spinning

round and round in my head but I managed to continue.

'That year we had played a midweek game at Burnley that had been postponed because of our Cup run,' adds McParland, 'and when we were coming back we stopped

63

at a pub to have a drink. The match between Real Madrid and Manchester United was on the telly and I remember Gento – who was only a little fellow – flying though the middle. Wood picked the ball up but he then ran into Gento, putting him on the deck. He was that type of goalkeeper.

'I felt sorry for him because I wouldn't have liked to have been playing in a Cup final and been carried off. He did a nice thing at Villa's dinner to celebrate the 40th anniversary of the final. He came up on stage and stood beside me – with an ice bucket on his head for protection.'

With no substitutes allowed, Jackie Blanchflower, Danny's brother and United's centre-half, replaced Wood in goal but Villa rarely tested him. When they did, the Irishman showed some excellent goalkeeping skills. Ten minutes before half-time, Wood returned to the fray but, unfit to continue in goal, took up a position at outside-right.

McParland strikes silence United

After half-time, with the score still 0–0, United came back strongly at Villa, but they were unable to dent a steely Villa defence cleverly organised by Dugdale and reinforced by goalkeeper Nigel Sims, who scooped up anything that came near him.

After coolly coming through continuous United pressure, Villa went careering upfield in the 67th minute. McParland had been subdued since his collision with Wood but as he saw Johnny Dixon move up the right wing he sprang to life. Dixon bent a fast, hard cross into the box at head height, McParland nipped in front of Duncan Edwards and, almost from the penalty spot, steered a fantastically accurate, powerful header into the top right-hand corner of the United net. Villa were in the lead. Again McParland lay flat-out on the turf. This time he was dizzy with delight, not injury. For more than an hour of play, McParland had been constantly booed by United fans. Now his ears were assaulted only by Villa cheers. 'When we came in at half-time,' says McParland, 'Billy Moore had said, "There's only one way to shut that lot up and that's to stick one in the back of the net." It did shut them up.'

Four minutes later, Villa put together a scintillating move. Stan Crowther, Villa's right-half, pierced the defence on the right and crossed for McParland at the back post. His swift, skilfully angled reverse header skimmed off the top of his skull and was effortlessly controlled by Dixon. The speed of the move gave the forward time to spin away from his marker, then turn for a sharp shot that flew down off the crossbar. With the United defenders bewildered by all the movement around them, McParland acted decisively and struck the rebound high into the net. Tommy Taylor scored a consolation goal for United with six minutes remaining, but it was Villa's Cup for a record sixth time. The Villa team was: Sims, Lynn, Aldis, Crowther, Dugdale, Saward, Smith, Sewell, Myerscough, Dixon, McParland.

A double goalscorer in the 1957 final, Peter McParland dons Villa's 1957 FA Cup final strip as he displays the trophy at Villa Park. Before Villa began their 1957 FA Cup ties, McParland had had a feeling that the team could win the cup. His goals did much to turn that premonition into reality.

The team were welcomed back to Birmingham by 75,000 delirious supporters. At New Street, the Villa players boarded an open-topped bus which had to stop several times in Colmore Row as police cleared a path for it through the crowd. At the Council House on Victoria Square, the players displayed the FA Cup from the balcony. They then progressed to Villa Park where thousands more cheered as the Cup was taken on a lap of honour around the pitch. This part of the proceedings was shown on BBC television. 'We are very satisfied with what we have done,' said Houghton, 'but we are ambitious.' The manager clearly felt that there remained much unfulfilled potential at Villa Park.

Houghton, however, struggled to fulfil his hopes for the club. Villa finished in 13th position in the League in 1958. The following season promised even less. By November 1958 Villa had just four wins from their 17 games and were stuck in bottom position in the First Division.

Houghton quits, Mercer arrives

On 19 November 1958, Villa played a friendly match against the Scottish champions Hearts. That game was to mark the official unveiling of the Villa Park floodlights, which had first been used some three months before. After an entertaining 4–2 Villa victory, Eric Houghton walked into the dressing room and told the Villa players that he would be leaving the club.

'I think they should have gone out and bought a couple of good players after the FA Cup win,' says McParland. 'That would have made a good team even better. A couple of good new players might have made us more consistent and helped us push it all the way in the League. Under Eric we would get up to fifth or sixth position in the League but we didn't have that bit extra to push us further up the table. I think ambition was badly needed in the club on the side of the directors and the management. Billy Moore was the most positive-thinking person then at the club. The board tugged at the pursestrings too much instead of going out and signing a few new players.'

At Christmas 1958 Joe Mercer left Sheffield United, where he had been manager for three years, to take the post of Aston Villa manager. As a player, he had been a man of stature in the British game in an illustrious career with Everton, Arsenal and England. Dick Taylor, who had been Mercer's chief coach at Sheffield United, was appointed Villa assistant manager. 'I have no stunts, no gimmicks and, as yet, I have no plans,' Mercer said on taking over. 'I have come with a completely open mind. I don't like guessing and you can only judge football as you see it. But I do know most of the players, and I have played against most of them. I applied for the Villa job because it appealed to me. It was not the prospect of a challenge or a fight because I don't go round looking for fights. I am here because I like the set-up and because I realise the potential is enormous.' Mercer had a five-year contract.

Eric Houghton was a well-liked man but he was too nice a gentleman to be an effective football manager. He did leave a legacy of two very important recent signings. In December 1957 he had spent £22,000 to bring centre-forward Gerry Hitchens to Villa from Cardiff City. And days before his resignation, Houghton had signed Ron Wylie, a tough Scottish inside-left, from Notts County.

Villa adopted a highly demanding defensive system under Joe Mercer. Players were required to provide cover for each other, tackle with great concentration and exert fierce pressure on the man on the ball. As one Villa player confronted his opponent, another would lie in wait in case his teammate was beaten. If that happened, the beaten man was required to double-back immediately to offer similar cover. 'We don't regard it as a defensive game,' said Mercer, 'but we do go back when they are in possession and hold the initiative. Then, when we have the ball, we quickly move up. Defence is not always negative.'

Last day drama: Villa relegated

Mercer's influence showed itself in an enjoyable 1959 Cup run which took his side to a semi-final with Nottingham Forest, now managed by Billy Walker. Villa were unlucky to lose 1–0. In the First Division, under

Mercer's ministrations, Villa made a brief recovery but remained in a critical condition. They went into their final match of the season, against WBA, in third bottom position, ahead of Manchester City only on goal average. With 88 minutes gone, and Villa leading 1–0 through a 65th minute Hitchens goal, Ronnie Allen equalised for WBA. Manchester City won their fixture. Villa were relegated.

'Relegation will not mean any change in our policy,' said Mercer. 'Football teams are not built overnight, but as the result of day in, day out effort and procedure. While we did not want it, we may find it easier to rebuild in the Second Division where the pressure may not be so intense.'

Back at the first attempt

In the close season, John Neal, a left-back, was signed from Swindon Town and Jimmy MacEwan, a 30-year-old outside-right, arrived from Raith Rovers. Bobby Thomson, a combative Scot, was signed from Wolves to partner MacEwan on the right wing. With Hitchens at centre-forward and McParland and Wylie on the left wing, Villa now had a forward line that was a fine blend of touch and toughness. They looked too good for the Second Division and so it proved. Villa were promoted at the first attempt. Hitchens scored 23 goals, McParland 22 and Thomson 20 as Villa took the 1959–60 Second Division title. Villa again reached the semi-finals of the Cup, losing 1–0 to Wolves.

New cup challenge

A stabilising season in 1960–61 saw Mercer's team finish in a respectable ninth position in the First Division. For the third successive year, Villa reached a cup semi-final. This time, however, it was not the FA Cup but the League Cup, a competition solely for League clubs that was being contested for the first time in that 1960–61 season. It was played in midweek, on a two-legged basis, and was a delayed peacetime development of the League Cup competition which had been started during the war years. It also provided clubs with an additional means of revenue. In Scotland, a League Cup had been played in addition to the Scottish

League and Scottish Cup since 1946 and had proved a fair success.

'At the start we didn't want the League Cup,' says McParland, 'but later in the season it replaced the drudgery of training in midweek, when you were already fit anyway. We got a bit of a run going and we were then getting wee bonuses so the players started to become quite happy with the new cup. It was like working overtime – we were only getting a wage of £20 a week then.'

Entry to the tournament was optional and many of the bigger clubs froze at the prospect of additional fixtures and opted out. Villa met only one First Division club, Preston North End, on their way to the semi-final. They also defeated Huddersfield Town, Plymouth Argyle and Wrexham before facing Burnley, a leading First Division side, in the semi. With the tournament yet to capture the imagination of fans across the country, only 20,000 turned up at Villa Park for the second leg of the semi-final with Burnley. That match ended 2–2, leav-

The stresses and strains of football management weighed heavily on Joe Mercer during his years as manager of Aston Villa. He eventually stepped down in the summer of 1964. He went on to enjoy success at Manchester City and in mid-1974 took on the position of caretaker manager of England.

ing the teams level on aggregate over the two legs. They would now face each other in a play-off at Old Trafford during the final week of the season. The cries and shouts of just 7,000 fans bounced around the Manchester United stadium on an evening when Villa took the lead 20 minutes from time; Stan Lynn, Villa's right-back, hammered home a penalty after Thomson had been body-checked inside the penalty area. Burnley equalised inside a minute and another draw looked likely until, with only three minutes of the match remaining, Gerry Hitchens scored with a shot which clipped the inside of the Burnley post on its way into the net.

Villa's reward was a two-legged final with Rotherham United, who had only just escaped relegation from the Second Division. The play-off with Burnley had, however, taken place on 2 May while the final had originally been scheduled for 1 and 4 May. With Villa leaving for a Russian tour on Monday, 8 May, it was not possible to arrange the two legs of the League Cup final for the end of the 1960–61 season. Instead, Villa and Rotherham would face each other at the start of the 1961–62 season, on 22 August and 5 September.

Hitchens departs for Internazionale

Gerry Hitchens had scored 11 of Villa's 26 goals on the way to the League Cup final, but he would not be available for either leg of that tie. While the Villa party had travelled to Russia, he had stayed behind to make his international debut for England against Mexico on 10 May 1961, scoring after just two minutes. 'Gerry Hitchens will not be sold at any price, under any circumstances,' said Chris Buckley as the inevitable transfer speculation followed. Within days Internazionale of Milan had paid £100,000 for Hitchens' transfer.

Hitchens had amassed 96 goals in 159 League, FA Cup and League Cup appearances since joining Villa in December 1957.

A powerful, direct centre-forward in the best English tradition, the boy from Kidderminster had scored 41 goals in 55 games during the 1960–61 season. He appeared to be almost irreplaceable. 'He was a good player Gerry, a flyer,' says Peter McParland. 'We used to call him Champion the Wonder Horse because he was so quick and he had a mane of hair. If he got the ball on the run then that was it, the defenders were gone.'

In Villa's final home game of that 1960–61 season, Johnny Dixon had made his last appearance for the club in a 4–1 win over Sheffield Wednesday. As one great club servant bowed out, a full-back called Charlie Aitken was making his debut. 'I had gone to George Watson's school in Edinburgh,' he says, 'which was a rugby-playing school; it has produced a number of world-class rugby players. When I was about 14 I would play good-quality rugby for the school on a Saturday morning and football for a local youth team in the afternoon. After that I signed for Edinburgh Thistle, one of Hibernian's junior teams, and was training at Easter Road two evenings a week.

'When I was 16 I got asked to come to Villa on trial. I wasn't really bothered because I wanted to get all my exams and go on to university but I thought I'd try it for a year and see how I got on. There were about 50 professionals when I arrived at Aston Villa and athletically they were very very poor; the quality of fitness was horrendous. Most of them were totally unfit. When I was in the third team I was fitter and quicker than anyone else in the club at that time.

'The soccer side was interesting. I was completely out of my depth because I'd come from a completely different kind of world – a middle-class world. Suddenly you had all these people shouting and screaming at you. I was traumatised for the first year I was here. Also I was getting paid twice as much grouse-beating in the Scottish Highlands during the summer as I was making at Aston Villa. I was getting £8 14 shillings (£8.70) a week at the Villa but £4 of that was going on lodgings so I was ready to go back to Scotland. I did learn quite a lot because Joe Mercer and the staff worked hard on the basics at training. So after the first year I stuck it out for another year because I felt I was progressing.'

Early season cup final

Villa's new centre-forward for the 1961–62 season was Derek Dougan, a Northern Ireland international signed from Blackburn Rovers for £15,000 in July 1961. Dougan played in the opening League matches of the 1960–61 season but he was ineligible for the League Cup final, the first leg of which was played at the Millmoor Ground, Rotherham, on 22 August. He was replaced by Ralph

In his four seasons with Aston Villa, Gerry Hitchens produced an abundance of goals. He equalled an Aston Villa record in November 1959, when he scored five goals in the 11–1 win over Charlton Athletic in a Second Division match. After moving to Internazionale of Milan in 1961 at the age of 26, Hitchens spent the remainder of his career in first-class football in Italy, he and his family adapting easily to the language and lifestyle.

Charlie Aitken made his debut for Aston Villa in an end-of-season League match with Sheffield Wednesday in April 1961, a match which also saw Johnny Dixon make his final appearance for the club. Aitken would go on to make 656 appearances for Villa; 559 in the League, 34 in the FA Cup, 61 in the League Cup and two in the UEFA Cup. A natural athlete, his relish for the game made him a perennial favourite with Villa fans during the 1960s and 1970s. He left Villa Park in 1976 to join New York Cosmos, where he played alongside Pele. Charlie Aitken was later made a vice-president of Aston Villa.

minutes later, Harry Burrows' shot was deflected into the Rotherham net to level the tie on aggregate. In the 19th minute of extra-time, MacEwan's cross created a scramble inside the Rotherham penalty area. As bodies flew here and there, McParland kept his eye firmly on the ball and pounced to drive it into the roof of the net. The 31,000 crowd saw Vic Crowe, the Villa captain, presented with the new trophy by Joe Richards, president of the Football League. The Villa team was: Sidebottom, Neal, Lee, Crowe, Dugdale, Deakin, MacEwan, O'Neill, McParland, Thomson, Burrows.

Winning a cup so early in the season should have been a massive boost for Villa, but within hours of victory there was a sense of deflation at the club. After the match, Bobby Thomson had been driving Derek Dougan and the *Wolverhampton Express and Star* reporter Malcolm Williams home when he crashed his Vauxhall into a tree. Tragically, Malcolm Williams was dead on arrival at hospital in Wolverhampton. Thomson emerged relatively unscathed but Dougan was detained in hospital. He would miss the rest of the season, Thomson taking his place at centre-forward.

Villa finished seventh in the First Division in the spring of 1962. Their defensive record was second only to fourth-placed Everton but Villa had scored only 65 goals in comparison to the previous season's 78.

'The tackling was ferocious in the 1960s,' says Charlie Aitken. 'The physical and verbal abuse allowed on the park was just incredible. The verbal abuse that was taken by the referees was just unbelievable. It was a violent, hard game. But once I got in the first team I just loved being out on the pitch playing football – I used to analyse my opponents to work out what they might do in a match.'

Brown, a 17-year-old who had turned professional six months previously. In front of 12,226, Villa conceded two goals shortly after half-time. Stan Lynn had a penalty saved and Peter McParland hit a post, but this was a wooden performance from Villa and Rotherham deserved their victory. The Villa team was: Sims, Lynn, Lee, Crowe, Dugdale, Deakin, MacEwan, Thomson, Brown, Wylie, McParland.

For the return match at Villa Park on Tuesday 5 September, McParland was switched from the left wing to centre-forward. It was the first time he had started a game for Villa in that position. Harry Burrows, who had made his debut for Villa in 1959, came into the team at outside-left. Rain pelted down throughout the evening of the match. Villa were equally relentless as they flooded forward but the Rotherham goal was dammed by the Yorkshire club's defenders, midfielders and forwards.

After a spate of half-chances, Villa had reached the mid-point of the second half without scoring. Then, in the 67th minute, Alan O'Neill, a £10,000 signing from Sunderland in 1960, took Deakin's pass and manoeuvred the ball past three Rotherham men for the opening goal of the night. Two

Mercer resigns

In the following two seasons – 1962–63 and 1963–64 – Villa finished in the lower half of the First Division table. They did reach another League Cup final, losing 3–1 on aggregate to Birmingham City in the spring of 1963. In July 1964, Joe Mercer resigned as manager on grounds of ill-health. Dick Taylor became acting manager.

'Joe was in a bad way – he couldn't handle it,' says Charlie Aitken. 'I felt really sorry for him. We weren't playing well. I had a lot of admiration for him but I think he just didn't adapt his tactics to the changes that were happening in football.

'We played quite well when teams were playing the WM formation, but when the transition came from the WM formation to overlapping full-backs it was never handled properly at this club. With the WM formation the two full-backs picked up the two opposing wingers. You always had a winger to mark. It was so simple. Then all of a sudden you had no winger to mark. Then where did you go? What did you do? At Villa Park nobody ever told us what to do. So you'd be marking nobody, you'd just be a waste of time – spare.

'I did overlap a lot but it was never with knowledge. We weren't coached. We were told we were professionals and that we had to get out and play. The coaching was non-existent. I was playing for the Scotland Under-23s in 1961–62 and I saw quality football there and I thought, "Have I now got to go back to Villa Park after all this?"

I'm not decrying the place but it was wonderful to go and play with people like Alan Gilzean and John White.'

'Joe was very positive when he first came to the club but that gradually faded away,' says Peter McParland. 'He used to get very nervous before games. He was a very nervous man. I used to come in at about twenty to two on a Saturday and Joe would be lying on the treatment table in the middle of the dressing-room. I said to him one day when he was there, tensed up, "If I felt like you now I wouldn't be able to play." He said, "This is the way it gets you when you're the manager." At half-time, when you would maybe need a wee bit of encouragement he would blow his top and he would do the same after the game.'

Under Taylor, Villa became a more attack-minded side but the team lacked balance up front, where only Tony Hateley was a regular goalscorer. Hateley, signed from Notts County when Dougan was transferred to Peterborough United in 1963, scored 20 of Villa's 70 League goals in the 1964–65 season. He was the only Villa man to get into double figures that season. In January, Villa had been bottom of the First Division but a late revival – a Villa speciality – saw them finish 16th. Ron Wylie was voted Midland Footballer of the Year for 1965 but that summer he left for Birmingham City who had just been relegated to the Second Division. That Wylie should wish to leave and that nobody was able to persuade him to stay, indicated the lack of direction and determination at Villa.

Key players depart

In the summer of 1966, after Villa had again finished 16th, Hateley left for Chelsea. Phil Woosnam, the team's driving force in midfield during the mid-1960s, departed for a career in the new football league in the United States. The fee for Hateley had been £100,000, a top-of-the-range price for the time. Yet Taylor, who had been confirmed as manager in 1965, was given only a fraction of that money to work with and had to rely on signing new players at bargain prices.

'There was also always a problem with money here for some reason,' says Charlie Aitken. 'We never seemed to buy good players. This club seemed to drift along. It was a happy little club and there never seemed to be much ambition here. You didn't realise it at the time – this is all in hindsight. Like Joe, Dick never adapted tactically and we were buying players who I thought were pretty poor. We just struggled and struggled. Dick was a nice man, a lovely man, he liked skilful football, but he wasn't tactically up to it.

'To me, we always fell down tactically but even if the tactics had been different I

Tony Hateley's aerial expertise was a constant source of striking power for Villa in the mid-1960s. He moved to Chelsea for £100,000 in 1966. The London club then sold him to Liverpool within a year.

Relegation spectre haunts Villa Park again

Villa entered 1967 in 17th position in the First Division. Mike Rawson, a former European 800-metre champion, was enlisted to give the players sprint training, but the team would spend the rest of the season running backwards down the League. By early March, Villa had reversed into fourth-bottom spot although they were still five points clear of second-bottom Newcastle United. After a 2–0 win at Leeds United and a 3–3 draw at home to Tottenham Hotspur, confidence swept through Villa Park; relegation would surely be avoided. A 2–1 win over Stoke City in late March kept them five points above the two relegation places. A week later, on 1 April, after a series of stunning results for their rivals during the Easter programme, Villa had tumbled into second-bottom spot.

On 6 May, in the final home match of the season, Villa lost 4–2 to Everton, lost their place in the First Division and Dick Taylor lost his job. Whereas in 1959 dropping into the Second Division had appeared a good opportunity to regroup, now there appeared little prospect of any short-term recovery. The team had picked up just two points from their final eight fixtures. Lew Chatterley, a defender, had been top scorer with 13 goals.

'Harry Burrows was a tremendous player,' says Charlie Aitken. 'This was a man with one of the most powerful shots in English football, guaranteed to score you 20 goals a season. He's off to Stoke. Who was going to replace him? Tony Hateley – with 20–30 goals guaranteed a season – was one of the best headers of the ball you'll ever see in your life. I remember one game against Tottenham when we were losing 5–1 just after half-time and Tony Hateley scored four with his head – one of them was from about 18 yards. They sold him. Who was going to replace him? No wonder we got relegated! There was no foresight. Nobody looked two years ahead or anything like that. No players were bought to help us out of relegation.'

Villa were now at the lowest point in their history. The most realistic among the Villa fans expected a long slog before their club was back in the First Division. The only consolation for them was the belief that the club surely couldn't fall any further.

don't think the players were good enough. We were never consistent enough. A tremendous amount of good players came through the club but in any one team we would, at best, have six or seven good players. We would never have 11 players playing consistently well; there were never enough of us in the team to be successful. Dick had a problem because he had Phil Woosnam here who thought a lot about the game. Phil was a coach and wanted to change all sorts of things so there was a bit of conflict there.'

After relegation in 1967 Villa reached their nadir, beginning the 1970s with two seasons in the Third Division. The club's troubles prompted a revolution in the boardroom that took the club in a new direction.

6 Hard times: 1967–74

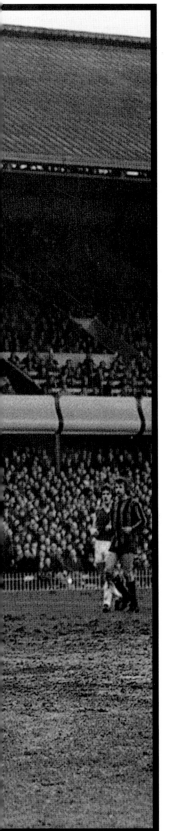

Between the mid-1960s and the mid-1970s, Britain's leading football clubs enjoyed unprecedented success. European trophies were brought to the country by a total of 11 different clubs. For those clubs who missed out on the European triumphs, such as Everton, there was the major consolation of winning a top domestic competition. Almost every major club in Britain laid claim to a sizeable prize. Aston Villa, meanwhile, lived through those years like a down-at-heel aristocrat, forced to struggle for survival in sometimes seedy surroundings.

Tommy Cummings: a short reign

A new manager, Tommy Cummings, took charge of the team in the summer of 1967. As player-manager of Mansfield Town, he had taken them to promotion from the Fourth Division to the Third Division in 1963. Mansfield had come close to winning promotion to the Second Division in the following two years and had comfortably maintained their position in the Third Division.

In the opening nine games of the 1967–68 season, Cummings' Villa took just five points from a possible 18. In September, the new manager returned to his old club to purchase inside-right Tommy Mitchinson. Brian Greenhalgh, a centre-forward, and Brian Godfrey, an inside-left, both arrived from Preston North End, one of Villa's bed-fellows in the Second Division. Villa were rejuvenated in mid-season and put together a good run of results, winning 11 of 15 League games between October 1967 and

February 1968. In their final 17 matches, however, they won just three. Villa finished 16th in the Second Division.

In the summer of 1968, Cummings broke the Villa transfer record when he signed Mike Ferguson, a winger, from Blackburn Rovers for £50,000. In the opening 11 League games of the 1968–69 season, Villa managed just nine goals. On 9 November 1968, an own-goal from Villa centre-half Fred Turnbull presented Preston North End with a 1–0 win at Villa Park and deposited Villa into bottom place in the Second Division. A considerable proportion of the 13,374 crowd shouted for the board to resign; banners dotted around the ground read 'The Board Must Go'. Two days later, Tommy Cummings, who had spent £200,000 on seven players, was dismissed as manager.

This did little to pacify the supporters, who regarded the board as the culprits behind Villa's calamities. The club was now strapped for cash, so much so that in 1964 the board had been forced to sell the beautiful Hercules training ground in Trinity Road. This made Villa one of the few prominent clubs in England without their own training facilities. In the 1967–68 financial year, the club had made a loss of £76,000. Since 1960–61, Villa's average attendance had dropped in tandem with the club's decline as a footballing force, from 33,000 to around 18,000.

Boardroom uncertainty

Norman Smith, aged 66, had become chairman on the retirement of Chris Buckley in 1966. Three of the other worthies on the

A record Third Division crowd of 48,110 look on as Andy Lochhead closes in on the Bournemouth goal at Villa Park in February 1972.

five-man board were in their seventies. A few days before the Preston game, the directors had moved to pacify the supporters. Two new board members had been elected to provide some youthful vigour – Bob Mackay, aged 44, and Roy Ladbrooke, 49. Both had the backing of the Shareholders' Association.

While Villa sought a manager, Arthur Cox, the club's 30-year-old trainer, took over the running of the team. One of his first actions was to tell Barrie Hole, a Welsh international forward, that he was dropped for the following Saturday's match with Portsmouth. Hole responded by walking out of the club. On that same day, 13 November, chairman Smith and vice-chairman Bruce Normansell stated that they would resign if Villa dropped into the Third Division.

The Villa directors had looked at the possibility of a share issue, but had apparently baulked at the prospect of their shareholdings and their control of the club being diluted by incomers who would gain a considerable stake in the club. The number of shares in Aston Villa had remained static since 1896: 2,000 shares with a face value of £5 each.

On 21 November, amidst continued agitation from supporters, the edifice began to crumble. At a board meeting, one of the directors, George Robinson, 71, resigned. Sir Theodore Pritchett, the Villa president, read out a statement after the meeting: 'Sympathetic consideration was given to a proposed substantial increase in the capital of the company and the conditions upon which further shares might be issued. It was appreciated that this would necessitate changes in the board but members had willingly indicated to make available, by their resignations, such seats as the new financial arrangements might require.' In other words, the directors would quit if the price for their shares was right.

That evening, at Digbeth Civic Hall, 1,000 Villa supporters gathered for a protest meeting. Brian Evans, who chaired proceedings, said: 'I now ask for someone from the many shareholders, perhaps from the industrialists of the Midlands, to step forward and seize this golden opportunity.'

In the following days, Ron Harrison, a wealthy industrialist and the chairman of Walsall FC, hinted that he might be prepared to make a move on Villa. Harry Kartz, owner of a string of racehorses, had previously made efforts to get on the board and was interested once more following the

Dissatisfied Aston Villa supporters attend a protest meeting in Digbeth Civic Hall on 21 November 1968 to express their ideas on the future direction of the club.

Doug Ellis (left), Villa's new chairman, and Pat Matthews (right), the London financier who helped construct a reorganisation plan for the club, on 16 December 1968, the day a new board was appointed to take Villa in a new direction.

new developments. There was also a suggestion that the Atlanta Chiefs, a United States soccer club, whose management personnel had strong Villa connections, were interested in buying Aston Villa. The Shareholders' Association, too, were keen on forming a new board with Mackay and Ladbrooke, but the small shareholders looked unlikely to be able to raise the funds necessary to buy out the existing directors' holdings. A business consortium, led by alderman Sir Frank Price, mayor of Birmingham in 1964–65, also stated an interest.

On 7 December 1968, with behind-the-scenes financial negotiations dragging on, just 12,747 attended the 0–0 draw with Charlton Athletic at Villa Park. The following Monday, a deputation of four Villa supporters, led by Brian Evans, met the board. Afterwards, frustrated by the answers they had received, they proposed a boycott of Villa Park until the four longest-serving directors resigned.

Change at the top

The board then made a decisive move. They accepted a proposal from Mr Pat Matthews to create a reorganisation plan for the club's executive. Matthews, a wealthy London financier, was managing director of First National Finance Corporation and chairman of Birmingham Industrial Trust. His plans included a buy-out of the Villa directors' shares at £60 for each £5 share by B.I.T. and the appointment of a new board. Once those two steps had been carried out, a share issue would take place to recapitalise the club. B.I.T. would, in addition, give Aston Villa a loan of £50,000 to bolster the club's finances.

Matthews also intended to install Tommy Docherty as the new manager. Docherty, a Scottish international right-half with 25 caps, had enjoyed a successful playing career with Celtic, Preston North End, Arsenal and Chelsea. On 5 December, he had walked out on QPR after just a month as manager there. He had won his managerial spurs at Chelsea between 1962 and 1967, achieving promotion to the First Division and taking them to two FA Cup semi-finals and a final in three successive seasons, 1965–67, before resigning after an internal dispute in October 1967. He had discussed taking over as manager at Villa after Dick Taylor's departure in 1967, but he instead joined Rotherham United, then QPR. In February 1968 his Rotherham side had knocked Villa out of the FA Cup at Villa Park.

Doug Ellis arrives

For the chairmanship, Matthews had in mind Doug Ellis, a Cheshire man who had been successful in business in Birmingham. Ellis had been a director of Birmingham City for three years and was the chairman of a group of companies which included the Ellis Travel Agency.

On Monday 16 December, a new board of directors took over at Aston Villa, comprising Doug Ellis as chairman, Harry Kartz, Bob Mackay and Harry Parkes. The last-named was a former Villa full-back of the 1940s and 1950s who had prospered after his playing career as the proprietor of a sports goods business in Birmingham.

Ellis had put a substantial sum into Villa. 'I don't have to work,' he told John Slim of *The Birmingham Post* shortly after taking the position, 'but I do work because I love work and I still do 12 to 14 hours a day. And obviously now I have taken Aston Villa on I expect to give Aston Villa at least four or five hours a day which means there will be that much less time for other business. Football is not the same as a normal business by any means. It is run on commercial lines, to some extent, but the average businessman would tear his hair out with the problems of football over and above the normal everyday commercial demands. I love it!'

The Doc issues his cautious prescription

Two days after the boardroom rearrangement, Tommy Docherty was appointed Aston Villa manager. 'Every week we have got to play cautious football,' he said. 'While we shall be looking for goals, we must be careful not to give any away. In fact, we must play like a club in Europe where away goals count double.' For his first game as manager, a Villa Park crowd of 19,923 saw Villa defeat Norwich City 2–1 and move off the bottom of the Second Division.

Docherty moved wing-half Dick Edwards to centre-half and Villa became meaner at the back. The team won their first five matches under 'The Doc' and finished the season in 18th position. One of Docherty's

Aston Villa's ninth team manager, Tommy Docherty (second from left), welcomes three new signings to the club in the summer of 1969: Bruce Rioch (left), Ian 'Chico' Hamilton (second from right) and Neil Rioch (extreme right).

first moves had been to sign Brian Tiler, a left-half, for a fee of £35,000 from Rotherham United. He also introduced the Villa players to the new experience of a 20-minute warm-up in the gymnasium before a match. His major asset, however, was his strong motivational power.

'That was the turning point: Doug, Pat Matthews and Tommy coming to the club,' says Charlie Aitken. 'Tommy was the catalyst that made the whole thing work at Villa Park. It was a complete change. He brought personality – you felt you had to do well because the TV cameras were here and so on. Tommy's enthusiasm and charisma and the aura about him rubbed off on the players. The work-rate from all the players at the club increased tremendously – everybody wanted to do well for Tommy initially. He changed things tactically that first season. We did adapt more to what was going on. We were successful, we had some fine players, and we escaped relegation.'

In the second half of that 1968–69 season, shares in Aston Villa could be purchased after Villa's home matches from the Lions Club, a social club that had been built on the Trinity Road side of the ground in 1966. In total, the share issue would raise approximately £210,000. In the summer of 1969, Docherty invested some of that money in the purchase of forwards Neil and Bruce Rioch from Luton Town for a combined fee of £100,000. Ian 'Chico' Hamilton, another forward, came from Southend United at a price of £40,000. Pat McMahon, a midfielder, arrived on a free transfer from Celtic. Assembled at a total cost of around £400,000, Villa were now the most expensive side in the Second Division.

Too much claret

For the 1969–70 season, Villa took the field minus their traditional blue sleeves – their shirts were now all-claret with a blue collar. In the eyes of most observers this was an unnecessary and crass break with tradition. The matter was remedied in February 1970 when, after many complaints from the Villa supporters, the blue sleeves were restored to the shirts. There would be no such straightforward solution to the problems of the team, however. Villa made an even worse start to the 1969–70 season than they did to

the 1968–69 campaign, losing five of their opening six games. They failed to win until their 10th League game, 3–2 against Hull City. A 5–3 home defeat by Portsmouth in January 1970 had the Holte End chanting: 'Walsall, Walsall, here we come!' as Villa again clung to the foot of the Second Division. Two days later, Docherty was dismissed. The cohesion and confidence he had engendered so quickly, had evaporated equally swiftly. Morale had plummeted.

'That second season Tommy tried all sorts of things, like man-to-man marking,' says Charlie Aitken. 'We were still working hard and we were fit but the enthusiasm had gone. The Second Division is different. You've got to match teams physically. You can't just go out and knock the ball about. You might be superior players but you've got to wear the other team out and impose your will on them. It might take 89 minutes but you've got to do that. We never seemed to do that. I thought we were trying to play too much football. We'd lose the most stupid games. Tommy tried everything but nothing seemed to work.

'We'd also been out in Atlanta in a competition for six weeks in the summer of 1969. So we started the season knackered. We'd been travelling all over America for six weeks. We'd hardly got back home before we were back in training and playing. After just a week's training we were playing the Italian Under-23 side. We should have had a good rest and then started training.'

Crowe flies straight to a new division

Vic Crowe, a Villa centre-half and captain between 1952 and 1966, took over as manager on 19 January 1970. Crowe had been brought on to Docherty's staff to coach the second team at the start of the 1969–70 season. He had spent the previous three years at Atlanta Chiefs. The new manager brought in Ron Wylie as first-team trainer and coach. 'It was a complete change,' says Charlie Aitken. 'Vic was quiet, kind of dour and totally the opposite of Tommy. Vic brought in Ron Wylie and I thought they worked very well together.'

One of Crowe's first acts was to sign Andy Lochhead, a centre-forward from Leicester City. Villa had been without a prolific

Vic Crowe (second from left), who took over from Tommy Docherty as Villa manager in January 1970, leads out the Villa team for the 1971 League Cup final with Tottenham Hotspur at Wembley.

goalscorer since the departure of Tony Hateley in 1966. The new management team were unable to repeat the trick of the previous season. Villa finished next to bottom and sank into the Third Division.

'We got relegated but we nearly escaped,' says Aitken, 'We really did improve under Vic and Ron. At Leicester Pat McMahon scored a tremendous goal that hit the back stanchion and came out – it left a big mark on it. At Leicester there was very little depth on the stanchion and the goal was never given. We went berserk. There was no score then and Leicester went on to win 1–0. If we had won that game we would have escaped relegation. We got relegated but Vic and Ron were good. They introduced a more personal, quieter approach and had us working hard at tactics. Vic and Ron were the first people who really did coach us. They would talk to us collectively then individually.'

Despite their relegation in 1969–70, Villa had been the best-supported club in the division; their average attendance over the season was almost 28,000. Yet it was fitting that Villa should begin their Third Division career away from the splendour of Villa Park. Their first fixture, in August 1970, was a truer reflection of Villa's newly reduced circumstances: a visit to homely Saltergate for a match with Chesterfield Town. Pat McMahon sent the ball zipping into the Chesterfield net in the second minute. Two thunderous long-range shots from Bruce Rioch gave Villa a 3–2 win and their first victory outside Birmingham since April 1969.

On the final day of August 1970, however, at Mansfield Town, Bruce Rioch was injured. He subsequently underwent cartilage operations to both knees, a process which required a lengthy recovery time in the 1970s. Rioch, playing in a position just behind the forward line, had developed into a highly influential individual. He would now be absent for the bulk of the season. The team would miss his hard tackling, precision passing and shooting power.

League Cup challenge

Despite the drop in divisions, Villa were again watched by an average of almost 28,000 at home, with their biggest League attendance 37,642 for the derby match with Walsall. Villa's biggest crowd of the season, however, was the 62,500 who assembled at Villa Park on 23 December for the second leg of the League Cup semi-final with a Manchester United side that featured George Best, Denis Law and Bobby Charlton. On that momentous evening, however, United's legends were cast in the shadows as Villa overwhelmed their illustrious opponents. The first leg had ended 1–1, and a Brian Kidd goal at Villa Park had put United ahead on aggregate. Villa responded strongly and two headers, from Lochhead and McMahon, put them in the final.

The League Cup had grown in importance since the early 1960s. It now attracted the full complement of League clubs and since 1967 the final had been played at Wembley. Thirty thousand Villa fans were in the crowd of 100,000 at the national stadium as Villa took on Tottenham Hotspur in the final. Villa were the better side throughout. Andy Lochhead had a shot cleared off the line by Spurs' Steve Perryman. A 30-yard drive from Chico Hamilton nicked the top of the Spurs crossbar. With 12 minutes remaining, Spurs' centre-forward Martin Chivers opened the scoring and three minutes later, with Villa still reeling, he made it 2–0 to Tottenham, prising the cup out of Villa's grasp. The Villa team was: Dunn, Bradley, Aitken, Godfrey, Turnbull, Tiler, McMahon, Rioch, Lochhead, Hamilton, Anderson.

As they had approached the League Cup final, Villa had been two points clear at the top of the Third Division and had looked assured of promotion. A 3–1 defeat at Bury a week before the final saw them fall back to second and, following the final, the team continued to falter in the League. Villa collected just 15 points from a possible 36 in their final series of matches.

Villa finished fourth in the Third Division, seven points short of the top two promotion places. Despite this, Villa announced record profits for 1970–71 thanks to consistently high crowds at Villa Park and the League Cup run.

In the summer, Ray Graydon was signed from Bristol Rovers in exchange for a combination of £55,000 and Brian Godfrey. Graydon, a goalscoring winger, added a direct approach to the Villa attack. Centre-forward Andy Lochhead also regained the support of a fit-again Bruce Rioch. By mid-October 1971 Villa were top of the Third Division. Four months later, a decisive clash with promotion rivals Bournemouth at Villa Park, which had been anticipated for weeks, drew a crowd of 48,110, the record attendance for a Third Division match. Goals from Geoff Vowden, a forward signed from Birmingham City a year earlier for £14,000, and Lochhead gave Villa a 2–1 win. 'Every game in the Third Division was like a cup final,' says Aitken. 'Teams would go at us like maniacs. We knew we were better than them. We trained hard and we had a good group of players.'

An even bigger crowd – 54,437 – turned up for the visit of Pele and Santos, his Brazilian club, for a friendly in February 1972. At the time, Britain was undergoing a national energy crisis, necessitating drastic conservation of the country's resources. In order to use the floodlights for the Santos match, therefore, Villa had to hire their own electricity generator at a cost of £5,000. At the start of the second half the lights began dimming. It was then discovered that a mem-

Fred Turnbull climbs to clear the ball during a Spurs attack at Wembley in 1971. Villa, then in the Third Division, were the better side on the afternoon but would unluckily lose the final 2–0.

ber of the staff had switched on the electricity for the players' baths, diverting some of the power needed for the lights. Pele displayed sublime skills but a Pat McMahon header and a Ray Graydon penalty gave Villa a 2–1 win. Before the end of the season, Villa strengthened the side again. Chris Nicholl, a centre-half who wore contact-lenses, was signed from Luton Town for a fee of £90,000. Ian Ross, also a central defender, arrived from Liverpool for £70,000.

On leaving Villa Park, Tommy Docherty had predicted that the youth set-up he had started would show results in two to three years' time. In 1972, Aston Villa won the FA Youth Cup through a two-legged victory over Liverpool. Outstanding members of that side included John Gidman, a full-back, and Brian Little, a striker. Coached by Frank Upton, the youth team also won the Dusseldorf International Youth Tournament that year. Little made his full debut in the match against Torquay United which clinched the Third Division title. In front of 38,000 at Villa Park, Little scored once and set up two of the other goals in a 5–1 win. Villa's final total of 70 points was a Third Division record.

'The Second Division holds no fears for us,' said a confident Bruce Rioch as Villa celebrated. 'Everyone is looking forward to the challenge because we know that we are a much better side than two years ago. The Third Division was an experience none of us wanted but I am sure that it has helped harden a few players' approach to the game. I feel myself that I am a much better player than when I came to Villa and I am sure the same applies to some of the younger players.'

Boardroom changes

Prior to the new season, Villa lost 1–0 to Manchester City in the Charity Shield before 33,000 at Villa Park. There was little charity in the boardroom. Over the previous two years, Harry Parkes and Doug Ellis had had numerous disagreements and in August 1972 the split between the two became public. There was also some resentment among the other directors that Ellis was being given excessive publicity. 'I have opposed the chairman many times on the grounds that he never allows sufficient credit to go to Vic Crowe and Ron Wylie,' said Parkes.

Ellis sought the removal of Parkes from the board but his four fellow directors opposed him. At a meeting on 7 August they voted Ellis out of his position as chairman, replacing him with vice-chairman Jim Hartley, the most recent addition to the board. At a meeting with Villa supporters on 8 August, Hartley said: 'I will tell you some of the quarrels – without the details. We differed over the terms of the manager's contract and some of us thought that he was not given a big enough rise when promoted as manager. There were other differences which were all resolved within the board-room and the matter of the publicity Mr Ellis got, and Mr Parkes' criticism of it, should also have been resolved there.'

The supporters were firmly behind Doug Ellis. They were pleased with the progress made on the field of play and off it, with developments such as the new purpose-built 20-acre training ground at Bodymoor Heath on a plot of land which Ellis had purchased from a farmer. Constructed in 1971, it had four training pitches, on-site catering facilities and a lecture theatre for the manager to give talks to the players.

Signed by Vic Crowe from Bristol Rovers in 1971, Ray Graydon, a goalscoring winger, helped inject impetus into Villa as they sought a speedy exit from lower division football during the early 1970s.

A memorable match with Santos of Brazil in February 1972 brought some much-needed glamour to Villa Park in an era when the club was playing Third Division football.

Since 1968, 42,517 ordinary shares, each carrying one vote, had come into the hands of 7,000 supporters. Crucially, Pat Matthews, the financial mind behind the 1968 take-over, also supported Ellis. Over the succeeding weeks, Ellis waited patiently to fight back at an EGM on 25 September. At that meeting, he was reinstated as chairman by the shareholders. They also voted for Ellis' nominees, one of whom was Eric Houghton, to replace the other four directors on the board.

Promotion push

In the 1972–73 season, Brian Little established himself alongside Andy Lochhead in the forward line. Villa had started at a gallop, topping the Second Division table in the early part of the season, but this position could not be maintained. In mid-season Bruce Rioch lost form and found himself being booed by the Villa fans. On 6 January, a section of fans in a 38,000 crowd at Villa Park chanted 'Crowe Must Go' as Villa lost 3–0 to Burnley, now the Second Division leaders. Villa ended the season in third position, 11 points behind second-placed QPR, and thus missed out on promotion.

Crowe adjusted the team only very slightly in the summer of 1973, bringing in journeyman defender Trevor Hockey from Norwich City and centre-forward Sammy

Morgan from Port Vale. Morgan was to team up with Little, who was always more suited to an inside-forward role. It had appeared that such minor changes might be enough to nudge Villa into one of the top two promotion spots. It was not to be. Consecutive defeats away to Swindon Town, Sunderland and Luton Town in the run-up to Christmas saw Villa fixed firmly in a mid-table position. The only bright spot for Villa supporters in this period was seeing full-back Charlie Aitken break the club record for League appearances. Aitken beat Billy Walker's tally on 22 December when he wore the Villa shirt for the 479th time, in a 1–1 draw with Notts County.

By February 1974, Villa, who had been second in November, had slipped to fifth-bottom of the Second Division. In the final week of that month, Bruce Rioch moved to Derby County for a fee of £200,000. One of the reasons he gave for his departure was that he believed there wouldn't be First Division football at Villa Park 'for a couple of years at the earliest'. He was an ever-present for Derby as they won the championship the next season.

On the first Saturday of March 1974, 100 years to the month of Villa's first-ever game, they faced one of their oldest rivals, WBA, at Villa Park. On the terraces, young supporters of both sides 'rushed' each other, an increasingly common sight at football during the hooligan-infested 1970s. On the park, WBA hit Villa with three goals inside ten first-half minutes for a 3–1 win. Villa gave it everything but minus Rioch they were outmanoeuvred in midfield. Only 12,007 turned up at Villa Park the following midweek for the match with Carlisle United. Villa finished 14th in the Second Division. In May 1974, Crowe was offered the job of manager of Wales but refused it because of his commitments with Villa. That week, he and his assistant Ron Wylie were dismissed by the board.

Much had happened in the previous six years but little appeared to have changed. As in 1968 the team were stuck in the lower half of the Second Division, looking uninspired. Star players saw a more promising future elsewhere. Crowds were down to an unacceptable low and the team was without a manager. The Shareholders' Association was again stirring into life after a dormant period. The board's next move would have to be a good one.

In the 1980s Villa at last regained their status as Britain's premier team. Following promotion in 1975, Ron Saunders and Tony Barton guided Villa on an upward path to the top prize in club football: the European Cup.

7 Back in the Big Time: 1974–82

Ron Saunders slipped quietly into position as the new manager of Aston Villa on Tuesday 4 June 1974. With the country captivated by the World Cup in West Germany, he was allowed to get down to work unobtrusively. It was a low-key entrance entirely suited to a man who preferred action to words. Initially, Villa had appeared set to make a more high-profile appointment. Sir Alf Ramsey, recently dismissed as England manager, and Brian Clough, the loquacious manager of Brighton and Hove Albion, were among those who had been considered for the vacancy. Saunders was less of a name but he would engineer an era at Aston Villa that was more exhilarating than any of his rivals could have managed.

Saunders' managerial career had taken him to Yeovil Town, Oxford United, Norwich City and Manchester City. He had won the Southern League title with Yeovil, won promotion to the First Division with Norwich in 1972 and had taken both Norwich and Manchester City to the League Cup final. He had left Norwich in the autumn of 1973 after a disagreement with the board. At Manchester City, Saunders had been brought in to instil some discipline into the club, but after a players' revolt against his tough methods he was dismissed in April 1974.

Saunders sets his sights

The first signing of the Saunders era came from Maine Road: Frank Carrodus, an outside-left who would become known as 'the roadrunner' to his Villa Park team-mates. Otherwise, Saunders used a positional change or two to freshen up the squad that he had inherited from Vic Crowe. The new manager declared that his initial ambition was to get Villa back into the First Division within three years.

A crowd of 8,740 was at York City for the first step on a potentially long and winding road. Ray Graydon's header equalised an early York goal and although Brian Little hit the underside of the bar, Villa had to settle for a 1–1 draw. Two more 1–1 draws – at Hull City and at home to Norwich City – suggested that Villa fans would be forced to play patience throughout Saunders' first season. Then the early return match with Hull at Villa Park yielded a 6–0 win. Saunders' policy of fielding a settled side started to look a wise one. The next home game brought a 3–1 win over Orient. In the League Cup, a difficult tie at home to Everton ended in a 1–1 draw. In the replay at Goodison Park, goals from Morgan, Carrodus and Graydon gave Villa a deserved 3–0 win. The 25,000 crowd applauded Villa off the park.

Saunders had already succeeded in turning Villa into a highly industrious side, prepared to run and work to his specifications. In September 1974 he had signed Welsh international midfielder Leighton Phillips from Cardiff City for £100,000. Carrodus and Phillips in midfield were key elements in Saunders' team: they dictated the pace of the game and both players combined a high workrate with a ration of skilful play. Little time or energy was wasted in forcing the ball forward. Graydon, a direct wide player, fitted into the system well. By mid-October 1974, Graydon was the top goalscorer in England with 12 goals in cup and League. The previous season, he and Little had been Villa's joint top scorers with

Ian Ross, the Aston Villa captain, is hoisted high with the League Cup after Villa's victory over Norwich City in the 1975 final.

eight goals each. That October, Villa were third in the Second Division, six points behind leaders Manchester United.

'Ron Saunders was tremendous for the first year,' says Charlie Aitken. 'He had tremendous organisation and repetition. He would go over everything we had to do on the park hundreds and hundreds of times – even every corner-kick and every throw-in. We went through all the attacking and defensive moves repeatedly and repeatedly and repeatedly. It was just like automation under Ron. Everybody knew their job. He was talking to us, he was friendly with us. The reserves played in the same way as the first team. Everything slotted into place. We had a good team. We were very, very difficult to beat and Ron had everything organised to a tee.'

At Old Trafford in mid-November Villa were much the better side. A Chico Hamilton header gave Villa an early lead and Phillips struck a United post. A dubious penalty turned the match in United's favour and a disheartened Villa went down 2–1 in front of 55,000. A slump in form followed and by the end of 1974 Villa had lost their footing at the top of the table. After a sloppy 3–1 defeat at Cardiff City on the final Saturday of the year, Villa were in seventh position in the Second Division.

Saunders' remedy was to hammer the players with extra fitness training of a pre-season nature. For Villa's next match, an FA Cup tie at Boundary Park, Oldham, he brought hungry, young players into the team in the shape of Bobby McDonald, a 19-year-old midfielder, and Frank Pimblett, a 17-year-old forward. Villa won 3–0. After this match, Doug Ellis said: 'Last week, for the first time in my chairmanship, I went into our dressing-room and said things to the players which I never believed I would say. I was bitterly disappointed and told them so in no uncertain fashion. But I hope all that can be forgotten now, particularly after the way they won today.'

Following the victory over Everton in the League Cup, Villa had progressed in that competition by defeating Crewe Alexandra, Hartlepool United and Colchester United. Those wins took them to a two-legged semi-final with Chester City in January 1975. Goals from Bobby McDonald and Ray Graydon helped Villa to a 2–2 draw at Chester's Sealand Road ground.

In the second leg, at Villa Park, 47,632 saw Villa meet their Fourth Division opponents. Villa were jittery from the start, but Keith Leonard – a centre-forward who had responded positively to Saunders' exacting methods – scored twice to give Villa a 2–0 lead. Defensive errors on Villa's part let Chester get back on level terms at 2–2, but with ten minutes to go McDonald jumped to head Graydon's cross down to Little. The forward turned sharply to score and send Villa into a third League Cup final. 'Brian Little was a world-class player,' says Charlie Aitken. 'He was brilliant at running across the back four. He'd watch your foot come back then go with perfect timing.'

Ron Saunders, Villa manager, is congratulated by fans in the front section of the Trinity Road stand after the team had won promotion to the First Division in 1975.

A month later, on 22 February, Manchester United, now managed by Tommy Docherty, arrived at Villa Park. Villa consummately outplayed United from start to finish. Goals from Graydon and Aitken gave Villa a 2–0 win, modest reward for the amount of work they had put into their football that afternoon. Between winning at Oldham in January and the League Cup final on 1 March, Villa had won eight matches, drawn two and lost just one, a fifth round FA Cup tie at Ipswich Town.

A third League Cup final

Prior to the League Cup final, Saunders said: 'I prefer to let performances and results speak for themselves. We all know about Villa's vast potential – it's been talked about for years – but now we are on the verge of doing something about it. This club is near to an explosion.' Villa's opponents in the final were to be Norwich City, who, like Villa, were chasing promotion from the Second Division. It would be the first Wembley final not to feature a First Division side.

From the start, Norwich retreated into defence, fearful of Villa's strength in midfield. With Carrodus and McDonald

Villa players and officials prepare to take flight for Belgium and the club's first step into European competition. The match with Royal Antwerp would be one of the most eventful in the club's modern history.

dominant and Little looking sharp, Villa roved forward incessantly. The ball rarely strayed from the vicinity of the Norwich goal, but as the match trundled to an end the score remained 0–0. Strangely, the best chance of the match had fallen to Norwich on a rare breakaway, Ian Ross heading Ted McDougall's scoring effort off the line.

With ten minutes remaining, Nicholl headed on target. Norwich's goalkeeper Kevin Keelan was beaten but Mel Machin, his right-back, dived to palm the ball off the line. Ray Graydon took the resultant penalty but Keelan, who had once been on Villa's books, dived to his right and knocked the ball off the inside of his post. The ball rushed back into Graydon's path. The winger stayed steady, controlled the ball with his instep, drew back his right leg and, as Keelan scurried to his left, directed a strong shot into the Norwich net. It won Villa the League Cup and their first place in European competition – winning the League Cup provided entry to the UEFA Cup. Saunders commented after the match: 'After getting to Wembley I stepped up training and became more critical, both with individuals and the team. The players have responded marvellously.' The Villa team for the final was: Cumbes, Robson, Aitken, Ross, Nicholl, McDonald, Graydon, Little, Leonard, Hamilton, Carrodus.

Return to the top flight

From there, Villa's push for promotion gathered even more momentum. On 23 April, a 4–0 win at Sheffield Wednesday guaranteed them one of the three promotion places. They finished the season in second place in the Second Division, runners-up to Manchester United and ahead of Norwich City. Saunders would initially remain loyal to the players who had taken Villa out of the wilderness and back into the First Division. He continued to remain supportive of his team after their first game back in the top division resulted in a 2–1 home defeat by Leeds United. 'We learned a lot today,' he said afterwards. 'I know we will be all right in the First Division.'

With the Villa players still adjusting to survival at a higher level of English football, they were thrust into the even more hazardous zone of European competition, in

the shape of the UEFA Cup. The draw had paired Villa with Royal Antwerp of Belgium. It was a tie that looked neither particularly hard nor easy – no Belgian club had won a European trophy but their national league was impressively strong in the mid-1970s.

Villa visited the Bosuilstadion for the first leg on 17 September 1975. 'We arrived in Belgium and it was freezing cold,' says Charlie Aitken. 'They made us walk about a quarter of a mile to the ground from our coach. They put no heating on in the dressing-room. We were numb with the cold. We thought we'd be in luxury but it was horrendous – I'd been better treated in juvenile football in Scotland. There was a gas geyser on the wall. Ron went to light it and the thing blew up. There was a great explosion – Ron nearly got blown away. So there was this tremendous psychological battle before the game.'

Carrodus, Little and Leonard were all missing through injury as Villa took the turf for their first competitive match in Europe. There were around 1,500 Villa fans in the 21,000 crowd. From the early stages, Villa put Antwerp under heavy pressure. For the opening half hour, the home side had to concentrate all their energies on preventing Villa from scoring. The Belgian team were given the chance of a brief breather when awarded a free-kick 30 yards from the Villa goal. Jos Heylighen took the kick and his shot swept past Jim Cumbes, the Villa goalkeeper, and under the crossbar for the opening goal of the tie.

Karl Kodat, Antwerp's Austrian centre-forward, encouraged by Heylighen's success, tried a strike from distance himself. His shot spun off a Villa defender and the ball darted past Cumbes to make it 2–0. Kodat then tried the same trick again. This time his long shot beat Cumbes without the aid of a deflection. With half-time approaching, Kodat took possession a long way from goal and decided to see if he could get lucky a third time. His shot raced across the turf to be stopped only by the back of the Villa net. It left Villa 4–0 down at half-time and looking

From his debut in 1975, Andy Gray (second left) endeared himself to the Villa fans with his all-action approach.

distinctly bereft of riches in the world's diamond capital. Ray Graydon was the only scorer in the second half. Saunders insisted that the 4–1 first leg scoreline could be turned around at Villa Park, but before a 31,513 crowd Antwerp won 1–0. Villa were out of the competition on a 5–1 aggregate.

'I don't think we were mentally, physically and tactically aware of what was required for playing in Europe,' says Charlie Aitken. 'You can't play your normal game in Europe. I think Ron learned a tremendous amount from that game. We didn't change our tactics for that game but we should have played totally differently. I hated that game in Antwerp. It was one of my lowest ebbs ever in football. We just went to pieces, which was unbelievable because we'd never, ever done that before. I don't think we concentrated on our jobs properly. We were in a bit of a daze and that was the only time in all my years at Villa Park I felt that. It's all about tactics in Europe, it's like a chess game. You've got to use your brain.'

The power and drive of Dennis Mortimer was essential to Villa's successes from the mid-1970s to the mid-1980s. The midfielder's positive approach to the game and his strength of character made him a natural choice when Ron Saunders was looking to select a team captain.

Saunders makes key signings

Cumbes had looked at fault for three of the Antwerp goals. He was immediately replaced by Jake Findlay, a 20-year-old, for Villa's next game, a 3–0 defeat at Liverpool in the League. The following week, Saunders paid Blackpool £90,000 for goalkeeper John Burridge. Cumbes' career at Villa was as good as over. The manager also had problems up front. Leonard's knee had been damaged when Jimmy Rimmer, the Arsenal goalkeeper, had fallen on it at Villa Park four days before the visit to Belgium. The forward needed a cartilage operation. With Villa struggling to score goals, Saunders acted quickly, signing striker Andy Gray from Dundee United for £110,000.

Gray scored on his home debut, a 2–1 League Cup defeat by Manchester United on 8 October. He also scored on his home League debut, a 1–1 draw with Tottenham

Hotspur three days later. After a shaky spell in mid-season, Villa finished 16th in the League. In the FA Cup, Villa again made a negligible impact, going out in a third round replay with Southampton. In the 15 seasons since they had reached the semi-finals in 1960, Villa's FA Cup record had been consistently poor.

The burden of goalscorer-in-chief would be on Gray's shoulders for the 1976–77 season. It was a load that the confident Glasgow lad appeared to carry lightly. Before the season began he was joined at the club by his fellow countryman Gordon Smith, a left-back who cost £80,000 from St Johnstone. He teamed up with John Gidman, a pacy overlapping right-back. Saunders also moved Phillips into central defence alongside Nicholl. The midfield was now driven by Dennis Mortimer, a £175,000 signing from Coventry City in December 1975.

'I was aware of Villa's potential but when I joined the club I didn't know any of the players,' remembers Mortimer. 'When you've played in the First Division, as it was then, all your career, you don't tend to spend a great deal of time looking at Second or Third Division sides, which Villa had been. Anyway, Ron impressed on me that it was a good club and that we were going to go places. I thought that Villa was a club where I had a better chance of gaining honours than I could have if I'd stayed at Coventry City. At that time, £175,000 was a big fee and it was a bit nerve-racking to think that someone thought you were good enough to justify spending such a sum on you. It was near Christmas so the press asked me to do something rather silly. They wrote a headline, "Villa's Christmas present to the fans", and they made me stand in a box, wrapped up in some wrapping paper. The idea was that I was Villa's Christmas present from Ron Saunders.'

The 1976–77 season had barely started when, on 1 September, Doug Ellis resigned as chairman. 'The time is right to let someone else take over at the helm,' he said. Sir William Dugdale, a Villa director since 1973, became chairman. Ellis remained on the board. That evening, two smartly taken Brian Little goals and one from Graydon gave Villa a 3–0 win over Manchester City in the second round of the League Cup. Little had suffered an injury-hampered season in 1975–76. Now recovered from cartilage trouble, he was

looking an exciting player; lithe and lively in and around the 18-yard box. His thoughtful, slightly languid approach to the game worked perfectly alongside that of the more direct, quickfire Gray.

Three Gray goals in a 5–2 win over Ipswich Town, three days after the Manchester City match, took Villa to the top of the First Division. They stayed there for just a week before a 2–1 defeat at QPR saw them drop down to fourth position. Gray's was the first hat-trick scored in the First Division by a Villa player since a Tony Hateley triple in 1966. 'I did all right last season but on several occasions I was disappointed with my performances,' said Gray. 'But it's been different this season and I have been quite pleased with my game. Teaming

up with Brian Little has helped tremendously. I think we complement each other and it has been an exciting experience playing alongside him. He has scored some fantastic goals, goals which I don't think I would have got.'

Cowans makes debut at 17

In late September, Villa defeated Norwich City 2–1 at Villa Park in the third round of the League Cup, a match notable for the

Villa full-back John Robson guides the ball away from the feet of Everton forward Duncan McKenzie during the 1977 League Cup final at Wembley.

Gordon Cowans made his debut for Villa as a 17-year-old during the 1976–77 season. Equally adept with either foot, the midfielder developed into one of the most talented players ever to grace the Aston Villa shirt.

debut of Gordon Cowans, a 17-year-old mid-fielder. A light, slight player, Cowans had the sleight of foot to place any pass, long or short, on a team-mate's toe. The day after Cowans' debut, Saunders bought himself another excellent midfielder when he paid Arsenal £125,000 for Alex Cropley, a Scottish international.

'We had a knock on the door when I was a ten-year-old in Mansfield,' remembers Cowans. 'A Villa scout came to the door and invited us to Villa Park to have a look around. They took the whole school team through to watch a game, have a look at the ground and have lunch, which was lovely. When I was 13, Villa offered me schoolboy terms but at that time a few clubs were interested in me so my dad thought I should leave my options open until I was a bit older. Then Villa offered my dad the job of running the youth hostel if I'd sign. For my dad it was an opportunity to get out of the pits – he'd been working on the coalface for 25 years. So we ended up moving down to Birmingham from Mansfield.'

Following his youthful first-team bow, Cowans was returned to the Villa reserves to complete his footballing apprenticeship. Cropley and Mortimer immediately came to a profitable understanding in midfield. When Villa went to Anfield to play League champions Liverpool on the final Saturday in October 1976 they were still very much in contention for the title. With 10,000 fans in

support, Villa, as in the previous season, lost 3–0. However, Ron Saunders stated that the performance was '20 times better' than that of 1975. Had Villa's passing been just a mite more precise the points would already have been theirs before Liverpool scored three times in the final 15 minutes.

Mighty Reds humbled at Villa Park

When Liverpool, the League leaders, came to Villa Park for the return fixture on 15 December, Villa were six points behind them but with a game in hand. Since the Anfield match John Deehan, a 19-year-old, had replaced the injured Graydon alongside Gray, 21, and Little, 23, in a three-pronged strikeforce that sparkled with the effervescence of youth.

In the ninth minute, Andy Gray met the ball with a header on the run and whipped it high over Liverpool's England goalkeeper Ray Clemence and into the net. Two minutes later Deehan poked the ball under Clemence's body to make it 2–0. Deehan was quickly alive to a mistake in the Liverpool defence to score Villa's third. Little met a Gidman cross in style for 4–0 on the half-hour. Shortly before half-time, with the score 4–1 to Villa, Gray sprang to meet Mortimer's corner and score his 19th League goal of the season. Gray's second goal give Villa a 5–1 lead. That was also the final score. Villa had comfortably defeated a team that would go on to win the European Cup that season. 'We must not go over the moon about this victory. We gave a highly professional performance not just in the first half but throughout,' said Saunders. 'The First Division title? There is still a long way to go but obviously I am hoping we shall be able to continue our challenge.'

'It was quite an amazing scoreline,' recalls Dennis Mortimer, 'because that kind of thing just never happened to Liverpool. That was one of the big highlights of that season. That just summed up how good a side we were. We had a very well-balanced side, with lots of hard-working players but with lots of ability as well. All through my time at Villa I don't think the media gave us a billing as a skilful side and yet we had some very, very skilful players. You don't win things by not having a skilful side. There's got to be ability in a side to win things.'

The new North Stand at Villa Park, flanked by floodlights that spelled out the letters 'A V'. A monument to modernity 1970s-style, the stand replaced terracing that had been open to the elements. The new stand was built in anticipation of the fans of the future looking for greater comfort when watching a match.

A late Deehan goal allowed Villa to squeeze a 2–1 win at home to Newcastle United the following Saturday and move two points behind new leaders Ipswich Town. Two days after Christmas, however, Villa – missing Gidman, Nicholl, and Cropley through injury and with teenagers filling the gaps in the side – went down 3–2 at Middlesbrough. Saunders stated that he needed to be able to buy two or three players to give him strength in depth. The seven players he had bought until then had become the backbone of the team. 'It is not fair to always pitch so many teenagers into games like this, particularly as we are hoping to continue our championship challenge,' he said. 'There is such a gap between the experienced men and the promising teenagers on the staff. I believe the point was admirably made this afternoon.'

'A few of us young players thought he was a bit hard on us,' says Gordon Cowans of his early days under Ron Saunders. 'He forever seemed to be getting on at us and knocking us down but really, when you look back on it, it was just to keep our feet on the ground. He brought us up in the right way, making sure nobody got big-headed or started thinking they were better than they were. At the same time he knew when to compliment you and

put his arm around you and have a word with you. His ways were probably a lot more beneficial to us than if we'd had a manager who was a lot easier on us and was letting us get away with things we shouldn't have been doing. He built three sides in the time he was at Villa and I've got nothing but admiration for him.'

Gray had scored his 21st goal of the season against Middlesbrough. He was the top goalscorer in England but his all-action style of play, his bravery and lack of regard of danger in pursuit of goals attracted injury. Throughout the second half of the season he would struggle for full fitness in the face of niggling injuries. On New Year's Day 1977, a 2–0 defeat away to Manchester United left Villa nine points behind Liverpool at the top of the First Division, a sizeable gap at a time when two points were awarded for a win.

A new North Stand

The progressive team on the field would soon be playing in front of a suitably modern backdrop. In the final week of 1976, Sir William Dugdale had announced that the north end of Villa Park would undergo reconstruction at a projected cost of

£1million. The terracing there would be replaced by a two-tiered edifice. A stand on the upper tier would seat 4,000 people while the lower tier would have standing accommodation for a further 6,000 fans. Sandwiched in between, a middle section would hold 38 six-seater executive boxes. Work on the new North Stand would begin in January 1977. It would be open to spectators for the start of the 1977–78 season. The Holte End was now the only part of Villa Park that still consisted of vast swathes of terracing. The Witton Lane side of the ground had been fitted with seats for the World Cup in 1966. The lower tier of the Trinity Road side of the ground had been converted to seating in 1971. At the same time, executive boxes had been built behind the seats on that tier.

'We have done our sums conservatively,' said Dugdale, 'and we consider that we can go ahead without impeding the normal servicing of players in the side. The manager is a very selective purchaser and the board is aware that because of injuries he is anxious to strengthen the squad. He has never been refused money before when he has come to us and I do not expect he will be turned down in the future. But he has not yet asked for further money.'

Villa hone in on Wembley

Villa's chances of the title were fading slowly, but they remained one of the chief contenders for the League Cup. After defeating Norwich, wins over Wrexham and Millwall had taken Villa to a two-legged semi-final with QPR. In the first leg, at Loftus Road, the Villa defence, which had at times in the season been both shaken and stirred, formed a tight protective seal around Burridge's goal. Villa captured a 0–0 draw. Midway through the second half of the second leg, the tie remained scoreless. Then Deehan finished off a fast, four-man move to put Villa ahead. The 48,500 present remained happy until ten minutes from time when QPR's Gerry Francis headed the equaliser. Seven minutes into extra-time, a raft of heads rose to a Gidman free-kick as it dipped into the QPR goalmouth. Deehan rose above the competition to head Villa into the lead for a second time but six minutes from the end of a superb match Peter Eastoe equalised for QPR. There had been some fearsome tackling at Villa Park and the play-off, scheduled for Highbury the following midweek, threatened to be a wild one. In the opening minute Cropley was clattered by

Brian Little resists a challenge from Everton's Roger Kenyon as he prepares to cross the ball during the first replay of the 1977 League Cup final, at Hillsborough. In the 1976–77 season Little scored 26 goals in 56 appearances for Villa. His goals helped the team become the highest scorers in the First Division that season.

QPR's Frank McLintock as part of some left-over business from the Villa Park match. From then on, it was a clean-cut affair. Three strikes from Brian Little sent Villa sailing into a final with Everton.

The following Aston Villa team lined up in front of 100,000 for the League Cup final at Wembley on 12 March 1977: Burridge, Gidman, Robson, Phillips, Nicholl, Mortimer, Deehan, Little, Gray, Cropley, Carrodus. It was a forgettable final, dissolving dully into a 0–0 draw. At the end of the match, Andy Gray refused to join in a lap of honour with his team-mates because he felt he hadn't played well enough to merit the Villa fans' applause. The following evening, the Professional Footballers' Association, at their annual dinner in London, awarded Gray the unique double of Player of the Year and Young Player of the Year.

The replay of the League Cup final was watched by a crowd of 55,000 at Hillsborough, Sheffield, on 16 March. Villa made just one change to the previous Saturday's team, Cowans coming in for the injured Cropley. It was a more spirited affair than the Wembley game, although the quality of the football was poor. An own goal from Everton's Roger Kenyon, ten minutes from time, appeared to have settled matters in Villa's favour. In the dying seconds, however, Bob Latchford equalised for Everton to set up a second replay.

Cup final part three

A month had elapsed before Villa and Everton met for a third instalment of the League Cup final at Old Trafford on Wednesday 13 April. By then, Villa were seventh in the League and ten points behind Norwich City and Liverpool at the top of the table. Carrodus and Gray were both injured. Graydon, who had himself been fighting injury all season, came in for Gray with Deehan moving inside to centre-forward. Cowans replaced Carrodus. This time there would be a winner on the night. The Football League had decided that if the score was level at the end of 120 minutes, penalty kicks would decide the final. Shortly before half-time, Everton centre-back Ken McNaught headed the ball to Latchford to put Everton ahead. Villa were the better side throughout but their constructive, well-crafted moves

had failed to bring an equaliser.

Nicholl had given away the foul that led to Everton's goal. Ten minutes from time he made amends. Taking possession on Villa's right wing, he eluded an Everton challenge to move inside. From 30 yards he sent a left-footed shot goalwards. The ball went swirling through the air, then dipped just in front of the Everton posts, escaping goalkeeper David Lawson's fingertips by a fraction of an inch and burying itself in the corner of the net. Two minutes later, Little pounced on a defensive mistake, veered wide to his right and, almost from the goalline, teased the ball between goalkeeper, defender and post to put Villa ahead. Within a minute, Villa faced another test of character when Mick Lyons equalised for Everton.

Villa had deserved to win over the three games, but with two minutes of extra-time remaining, two tired teams looked set to face the test of penalties. Then Gordon Smith, on as a substitute for Gidman, crossed goalwards from the right wing. The ball took a deflection off a weary Everton leg and passed in front of Everton left-back Terry Darracott who decided to let it run on. That was a mistake. Little, hovering behind him, danced into the six-yard box and flicked the ball beyond Dawson to make it 3–2 to Villa. The League Cup was on its way to Villa Park for a record third time. The winning Villa team was: Burridge, Gidman (Smith), Robson, Phillips, Nicholl, Mortimer, Graydon, Little, Deehan, Cropley, Cowans.

Afterwards, Saunders praised Dennis Mortimer for a 'simply superb' performance. The manager added: 'We would have settled for winning the League Cup at the start of the season. This is a young side and we do not have enough senior or experienced players so I think it is a tremendous effort to have won at least one trophy. This is just the start. I still believe we are two or three years away from becoming a top side.' Villa finished fourth in the League, a position which would have won them a UEFA Cup place even if they hadn't triumphed in the League Cup. 'I'm certain that if we had not had those two replays we could have gone on to win the League that season,' says Mortimer. 'And that would have been something totally out of the blue for everybody.'

Sir William Dugdale stated that, while victory in the League Cup had been hugely enjoyable, Villa's ultimate aim was winning

Ron Saunders with the League Cup at Wembley in March 1975 after the 1–0 win over Norwich City in the final. The manager led a recon-structed Villa team to another victory in the same competition, two years later. Only four players who had played in the 1975 final were in the team that won the League Cup in 1977.

the League title and becoming a team that possessed the consistency of Liverpool. The profits from the League Cup run would be used to allow Saunders to strengthen his team in the summer of 1977. He spent £350,000 on three players: Jimmy Rimmer, a goalkeeper, from Arsenal; Ken McNaught, a centre-back, from Everton; and John Gregory, a man with the ability to play in either defence or midfield, from Northampton Town.

Villa return to European competition

The following September Villa made a sec-ond venture into European competition, meeting Fenerbahce of Turkey in the first round of the UEFA Cup. Before the first leg, at Villa Park, Saunders said he wanted a 2–0 lead for the second leg in Turkey. Villa were halfway there early in the first half when Gray met Cropley's pass to make it 1–0. Ten minutes from half-time, Mortimer's corner was headed into goal by Deehan. Villa hit the bar three times in the second half. In addition, Little and Deehan each hit the net to give Villa a close to invulnerable 4–0 lead to take to Istanbul. So it proved, Villa saun-tering to a 2–0 victory in the Inonu Stadium.

Before Villa's second round tie, it was revealed that Ron Saunders had been offered £100,000 to become national coach in Saudi Arabia for 18 months. Saunders, on a salary of £36,000 a year at Villa, thought over the opportunity for several days in mid-October 1977. He opted to stay at Villa Park, saying: 'There are some things that money just can't buy.'

A week after Saunders made his decision to stay, Villa faced Gornik Zabrze of Poland at Villa Park in the UEFA Cup. Ten minutes into the first half, Mortimer's corner parted the air above the six-yard box and Ken McNaught leapt to head his first goal for Aston Villa. Ten minutes into the second half, McNaught leapt to meet another cor-ner from Mortimer for his second goal for Aston Villa. It gave his side a useful 2–0 win. Whether playing at home or away, Villa had shown themselves expert at slicing the oppo-sition open on the break. Cropley and Mortimer were the two fulcrums on which Villa's moves turned as they quickly revolved passes on to Deehan, Gray and Little.

In Zabrze, Gornik pressurised Villa from the start and after 40 minutes the Poles opened the scoring through Janusz Marcinkowski. The Villa back four had done well to beat back the Polish forwards until then, but the second half stretched long in

front of them. Shortly after the break, Andy Gray relieved the pressure, heading an equaliser from Carrodus' cross. Villa had a precious away goal and Gornik now needed three goals to take the tie. Their deflated players were unable to get even one more. The 1–1 draw put Villa into the third round.

Spanish test for Saunders

The steadily improving quality of Villa's UEFA Cup opposition continued when they were drawn against Athletic Bilbao. The Spanish side had been UEFA Cup finalists the previous season, losing a two-legged final to Juventus on away goals. An experienced European club, Bilbao had lost only twice at home in 29 European ties. Their goalkeeper, José Iribar, was familiar with Villa Park, having played excellently there for the Spanish national team in the 1966 World Cup. The Bilbao team had also beaten Villa in a pre-season friendly in their San Mames stadium a few months earlier.

The UEFA Cup was a different matter and, with the first leg of the tie at Villa Park, 33,000 fans anticipated seeing their side build up another good first leg lead that November night. A corner-kick again provided the key to unlock a mean continental defence. After half an hour, Iribar palmed Cropley's kick into his own net. Ten minutes from time, Gidman's free-kick dropped in Deehan's direction and he sent a header speeding past Iribar to give Villa a 2–0 victory. Again the Villa midfield had been exceptional in propelling the ball forward on a night of heavy rain that had made the pitch heavy and the surface slow.

A week before the second leg with Bilbao, a 4–2 defeat at top-of-the-table Nottingham Forest ended Villa's defence of the League Cup. A 2–0 defeat at Ipswich Town the following Saturday came as no great surprise – Villa's League form was unpredictable throughout the 1977–78 season. They were set firmly in mid-table, equidistant from the division's pace-setters Nottingham Forest and the bottom club Newcastle United.

Johan Cruyff (left) of Barcelona challenges Frank Carrodus during the second leg of Villa's UEFA Cup tie with the Spanish side in 1978. A total of 140,000 spectators watched the two legs of a captivating tie.

In Bilbao, the timing of Villa's opening goal could not have been bettered. Two minutes before half-time, Gidman sent a smoothly-struck cross to the far post where Mortimer dipped his head at the ball to score his first goal of the season. It was a fitting finish to a first half that had been filled with elegant, stylish football from Villa. In the second half Bilbao drove themselves hard but were constantly rebuffed by Villa's craggy defence of Gidman, Smith, Phillips and McNaught. A Bilbao equaliser four minutes from time was almost irrelevant – the 1–1 draw was enough to put Villa into the quarter-finals in March.

Cropley would be missing for that tie – in December he had suffered a double leg fracture in a match with WBA. Gray was also missing through injury despite desperate efforts to get him fit.

Barca and Cruyff visit Villa

A 50,000 crowd was at Villa Park on the opening day of March 1978. Watching Villa compete in a European quarter-final was an exciting prospect, as was that of seeing Barcelona, one of the continent's elite football clubs. Adding delicious extra flavour to the occasion was the chance to see Europe's most distinguished footballer, the Dutchman Johan Cruyff, the leading light of the Barcelona team. Cruyff, then 30, had announced that he would be retiring from football at the end of the season. This was expected to be his last game in Britain.

Midway through the first half, Cruyff picked up a stray Villa pass close to the halfway line. With his long, loping stride, he moved gracefully to the fringes of the Villa penalty area. From there, he cleanly clipped a shot that swooped past Rimmer and into the Villa net to put Barcelona 1–0 ahead. Eleven minutes of the match were remaining when Barcelona forward Zuviria sent a header high into the Villa net. With Barcelona 2–0 ahead, Cruyff, who had been carrying a leg injury, departed for the dressing room.

Just as Cruyff had inspired his Barcelona team-mates, so his absence appeared to pep up Villa. With five minutes remaining, McNaught flew into the air to greet Smith's cross with a powerful, downward header to bring Villa within a goal of the Spanish team.

Three minutes later, substitute defender Allan Evans headed the ball on to Deehan who stretched to nudge it over the Barcelona line. A 2–2 draw gave Villa hope for the second leg.

'I honestly believe we can win,' said Saunders on arrival in Barcelona. With 90,000 home fans glowering down on them from the Nou Camp's towering stands, the following 11 took the field for Villa: Rimmer, Gidman, Smith, Phillips, McNaught, Mortimer, Gregory, Little, Deehan, Cowans, Carrodus. Midway through the first half, Gidman was dismissed after kicking Barcelona's Jesus de la Cruz in retaliation for a sly foul. Villa survived to half-time with the score at 0–0. Then, ten minutes into the second half, Smith's free-kick was only half-cleared by the Barcelona defence. Little instantaneously whisked the ball into the Barcelona net. No sooner had Villa's hopes been raised than they were dashed: goals from Zuviria and Asensi put Barcelona 2–1 up. Near the end, McNaught struck the bar but Villa were unable to get the equaliser. Barcelona went into the semi-finals on a 4–3 aggregate. 'I'm proud of how my ten players conducted themselves on the night,' said Saunders. 'They were all magnificent and we can look to the future with confidence. We deserved to get a draw at least.'

'We played out of our skins in Barcelona,' recalls Dennis Mortimer. 'We were looking as if we were going to win that game. I remember Brian Little had one of those chances where you think, "If that goes in, we're going to win this game." Unfortunately, he missed and it was the type of chance with which Brian would normally score. We put up a great performance that night and if John Gidman hadn't been sent off we'd have been through to the semi-final of the UEFA Cup.'

Gordon Cowans also has good memories of that UEFA Cup run. 'It was nice for us as players to get the chance to play against a different style of football and pit our wits and our own game against continentals. Playing against Barcelona and Johan Cruyff is an outstanding memory. I was excited at the prospect of being on the same pitch as him. At the time he was the best player in the world and, as a lad, he had always been one of my heroes. Cruyff showed touches of his class at Villa Park but over in Barcelona he was fantastic, in world-class form.'

Injuries halt progress

Villa finished the 1977–78 season eighth in the First Division. For the 1978–79 season the club had a record number of season-ticket holders – 12,000 – attracted by the positive play of the team. Before the season began, Sir William Dugdale resigned as chairman after a boardroom row. Dugdale had been in favour of giving Saunders a long-term contract but other directors had hesitated before doing so. Harry Kartz took over from Dugdale. On the field of play, the season began more smoothly. A typical display of razor-sharp reflexes from Andy Gray gave Villa a 1–0 win over Wolves in front of 44,000 at Villa Park on 19 August 1978.

It would, however, turn out to be a season disrupted severely by injuries. The saddest news came in September 1978 when John Robson, a full-back cum midfielder, was forced to quit football after being diagnosed as having multiple sclerosis. Gidman struggled with an ankle injury early in the season; Gray was still bothered by the previous season's thigh strain for the first half of the campaign and in the second half he needed three cartilage operations; Cowans broke a bone in his foot; Smith underwent a cartilage operation; Carrodus had two cartilage operations and suffered an ankle ligament injury; Little was out for three months with a stomach injury; Cropley was still recovering from his broken leg.

Vital players were missing in almost every game and when they were in the side they were often feeling their way back to fitness after a recovery period. Tommy Craig, a clever midfielder signed for £250,000 from Newcastle United in January 1978, had been hampered by injury since joining the club. When he was fit to play, from September 1978, he struggled for form. The only positive aspect of the situation was the introduction of young players, such as full-back Gary Williams and forward Gary Shaw, who gained experience as replacements for the wounded.

The situation was aggravated by Saunders' falling out with Gidman and Smith. After a 2–0 home defeat against Luton Town in the League Cup, Saunders gave Gidman a verbal battering, accusing him of not starting to play until Luton had scored. Gidman put in a transfer request

A modest, self-effacing professional, Des Bremner was held in high regard by his Villa team-mates. He was already a fine player when he arrived at Villa in 1979 but his willingness to learn enabled his game to develop throughout his career. An overhead kick from Bremner started the scoring in a 3–0 win against Southampton in October 1979. That win sparked Villa's season into life and, from then, the club enjoyed years of unbroken success.

although, after a few weeks, he withdrew it. Gordon Smith also issued a transfer request after a disagreement with Saunders at Bodymoor Heath, stating that he 'could no longer work with the manager'.

Allan Evans, a £30,000 signing from Dunfermline Athletic in 1977, now formed Villa's central defence alongside Ken McNaught. With Leighton Phillips having lost his place to Evans, Dennis Mortimer took over as Villa captain. Saunders waited and watched to see how his players recovered from injury. His only major signing that 1978–79 season was Kenny Swain, a £100,000 purchase from Chelsea. Swain took Carrodus' place on the left wing. Amidst the injury chaos, Villa did well to finish eighth in the First Division.

The summer of 1979 saw further fallout at Villa. John Gregory, dissatisfied that he had not been offered improved terms after some excellent performances at both centre-half and in midfield, asked for a transfer. He left for Brighton with mutual recriminations between him and Saunders. Brian Little also submitted a transfer request that summer, saying that he was looking for a new challenge. A £615,000 move to Birmingham City was on the verge of going through, when a routine medical examination by the

Villa's 'heavy team', the solid Scottish central defenders Allan Evans and Ken McNaught, add their weight to a Villa attack in an encounter with Ipswich Town at Portman Road. During the 1980–81 season, Ipswich were favoured by the national media but the Villa players were content as long as their own supporters and people in the Birmingham area were satisfied with the team's performances.

St Andrews club resulted in the discovery of a back problem and the deal was called off. Little would stay at Villa Park. In August 1979, Gidman walked out on Villa after a meeting with Ron Saunders and the Villa board over his contractual terms. The defender would return but would remain unhappy at the club. At the same meeting, it was decided that Aston Villa would accept offers for Andy Gray, who had also chafed against Saunders' abrasive ways. John Deehan was another player on the move, sold to WBA in September 1979.

A new team takes shape

Saunders now began to construct a new team; the third he had assembled in his time at Villa Park. In June 1979, Saunders had paid £200,000 to Burnley for winger Tony Morley. Before the season began, Terry Donovan, a striker, was signed from Grimsby Town for £80,000. Swain made a diagonal change in position, Saunders switching him from the left wing to right-back to cover for the discontented Gidman.

With Andy Gray playing in the reserves, Villa suffered an awful start to the season. In September, they failed to score in six of their

seven matches and tumbled to second-bottom of the First Division. That month, Gray was sold to Wolverhampton Wanderers for a British record fee of £1,469,000. Saunders moved swiftly to spend some of the money from that transfer. Mike Pejic, a left-back, arrived from Everton for £200,000 but on suffering a pelvic injury in October he was replaced by Colin Gibson, a youngster who had been brought through the Villa youth system. Des Bremner, a midfielder, arrived from Hibernian for £300,000. David Geddis, a striker, was signed from Ipswich Town, also for £300,000. In October, John Gidman was transferred to Everton for £500,000. Gordon Smith also left Villa Park, sold to Tottenham Hotspur for £150,000.

As the new players quickly settled in, the team began to make swift progress up the table. While they did so, another struggle for power broke out in the boardroom. At an Emergency General Meeting in November 1979, Doug Ellis brought a resolution to remove father and son Ron and Donald Bendall, together with chairman Harry Kartz, from the board. The majority of small shareholders voted for Ellis' resolution, but he was overpowered by the Bendalls and their sizeable block shareholding. In December, following that setback, Ellis resigned as a director, selling the majority of his shares to Ron Bendall. 'In Mr Bendall and myself,' he said, 'there were two immovable objects. So I bowed my head for the sake of the club to try and bring back harmony… I remain a small shareholder and I shall continue to follow Aston Villa… The money I have received from the shares is on ice in case the club needs it at any time.' Eric Houghton also resigned from the board that December. The Bendalls now had total control of the running of the club.

Striking vacancy

By Christmas, the team had climbed to fifth in the First Division. It was a remarkable achievement in light of the number of players who had arrived and departed just a few weeks earlier. Additionally, Villa had a persistent problem with the centre-forward position. Geddis, who had previously been in Ipswich's reserves, had struggled to get goals in the First Division. Since signing in September he had failed to score until a 2–1 Villa win at Tottenham in mid-December. To add to his ongoing bad luck, an ankle injury sustained at White Hart Lane would keep him out of the side until February 1980. Donovan replaced Geddis but he too had limited success. Saunders would also try Evans, who had been a centre-forward at Dunfermline, as the leader of the Villa attack. Morley, who had struggled against inconsistency and injury throughout the season, was also tried in a central attacking role but by the end of the season Villa still had a vacancy for a proven goalscorer.

Since 1960, Villa's best FA Cup run had been in 1977, when, three days after their first League Cup replay with Everton, they had met Manchester United in a quarter-final at Villa Park. Brian Little had scored with a coruscating 30-yard shot but Villa had unluckily lost 2–1 in front of more than 57,000 supporters. They reached that stage of the competition again in 1980, when they were drawn away to West Ham United. Badly weakened in defence by injuries, Villa were drawing 0–0 when an extremely dubious penalty awarded two minutes from time gave the Londoners a lucky 1–0 win.

'Ken McNaught went up for a cross right on the edge of the box,' says Dennis Mortimer. 'Ken's hand was right by his head.

Gary Shaw was 17 years old when he made his Villa debut in 1978. His light-footed touches made him the perfect partner for Peter Withe who arrived at Villa in 1980. A finisher of the highest class, Shaw's career at the top level was sadly cut short by a series of crippling knee injuries.

He went up for the ball and it hit his hand. The ball was going nowhere; no one was going to gain anything from Ken handling the ball. We were devastated when we got into the dressing room after that game.' Another cup, the 1980 Youth Cup, did come to Villa Park through a 3–2 aggregate win in the final against Manchester City. Paul Birch, Noel Blake, Mark Walters and Brian McClair were among the members of the winning Villa side.

Saunders signs striker

The senior side had finished seventh in the First Division in the spring of 1980 and days after the last ball of the League season had been kicked Saunders signed Peter Withe, a striker, from Newcastle United for a club record fee of £500,000. Villa would be the tenth club for the 28-year-old, an experienced Liverpudlian who had been a First Division title-winner with Nottingham Forest in 1978. Saunders made no further major signings over the coming year. 'What we'd always lacked was a true out-and-out centre-forward,' states Dennis Mortimer, 'a man we could rely on to be in the box and someone who could hold the ball up for midfield players either to get beyond him or support him. We were just lacking someone who could do that job for us. Also, a young player came on the scene then, Gary Shaw, an 18-year-old striker. Brian Little was struggling by then and was about to retire. Ron was never afraid to put a young player in the team. He'd done it with Gordon Cowans at 18 and he wasn't going to be afraid to do it with Gary.'

In Villa's opening game of the 1980–81 season, away to Leeds United, they went a goal down from a penalty after two minutes. Two minutes later, Leeds winger Arthur Graham struck a Villa post. Late in the first half, with Villa having come through Leeds' early pummelling, Cowans floated a pass to Morley. In a blur of movement, the winger controlled the ball, moved it on and shot for the equaliser. Villa's magnificent fitness left Leeds standing – a notable result of Saunders having had all of his new men with him throughout pre-season training. In the second half Gary Shaw attacked a Mortimer cross to give Villa a deserved 2–1 win. 'I am not going to make any forecasts about the championship after just one game and a good victory,' said the Villa manager. 'But if after 12 games we are in the top six, I feel that we will be there or thereabouts at the end of the season.'

On 18 October 1980 Villa took the field for that 12th game of the season, a home fixture against Tottenham Hotspur. Morley, now a regular at outside-left, chivvied Spurs defenders into mistakes all afternoon. Two such moments, either side of half-time, saw him pinch the ball from flailing feet before dinking it into the net. 'Tony being the flair player he was, I think it took him longer to come to terms with Ron Saunders and the way he wanted him to play than most other players,' is Gordon Cowans' viewpoint. 'He didn't expect his wingers just to be waiting out on the wings for the ball to come to them. They were expected to get back and defend as well and do their fair share of work. That didn't come naturally to Tony. He had fantastic ability. He was great going forward, had two great feet and was a fine crosser of the ball. He came up with his fair share of goals as well, and they were usually spectacular. And Ron seemed to get the best out of him. Tony was probably our match-winner; on his day he could turn things round and create things for us.'

A late goal from Withe neatly rounded off the match against Spurs. The 3–0 win in front of Villa's biggest crowd of the season up to that point – 30,940 – took Villa into second place behind Ipswich Town on goal difference. 'We have got off to a good start,' said Saunders. 'But it is far too early to start making rash forecasts. My assessment must be that so far the team have played very well. Now we must wait and see how we are placed after the next 12 matches.'

Twelve games further on, Villa met Stoke City on Boxing Day 1980. A hard-fought match ended in a 1–0 Villa win, courtesy of a Peter Withe strike. 'Every time someone on our side had the ball,' says Gordon Cowans, 'Peter was always available to be hit. He'd pull off to make angles or he'd pull away from the shoulders of people. All you can ask of your team-mates is for them to be helping you when you've got the ball and to be giving you options. Like Des Bremner, Peter was another player who was underrated. He had a lot more ability than people gave him credit for. He had good control, could hold the ball up and knock balls down for people. He scored a lot of goals with his head as well.'

Three-way title fight

Villa were now jostling for leadership of the First Division with Liverpool and Ipswich Town, each team taking turns to head the table. After the Stoke game, Villa were second to Liverpool on goal difference. The following day, Villa shared a 2–2 draw with European champions Nottingham Forest.

Villa started 1981 with a 1–0 FA Cup defeat at Ipswich Town. They had also gone out of the League Cup in the third round. Their early defeats in the cup competitions freed them to fix their eyes solely on the League. Villa continued the new year with seven successive League victories. The first of those games had been against Liverpool, League champions in 1979-80, at Villa Park. The danger of Kenny Dalglish, Liverpool's most potent forward, was snuffed out by centre-back Ken McNaught. Withe opened the scoring for Villa. Then Mortimer pushed the ball forward on a determined run. He carried it audaciously through the centre of the Liverpool defence before planting it past Clemence to cap a spectacular 2–0 win. It took Villa to the top, a point clear of Ipswich.

After seeing-off Liverpool, Villa and Ipswich were soon left alone to tussle for the title.

'I think the favourites to win the title, going into the new year, were Ipswich,' says Dennis Mortimer. 'They were playing good football. They had the two Dutchmen – Arnold Muhren and Franz Thijssen – in the side. Eric Gates and Paul Mariner were performing well. They had Russell Osman and Kevin Beattie at the back. So they had a good side and more stars than we were being credited with. They had names who were playing international football. We didn't have too many of those in our side. We were a side who had a lot of unsung heroes who worked hard for one other, with a lot of ability. You could probably say that we were only getting recognition for our ability and the way we were playing from the local press but that didn't perturb us in any way.'

Villa remained leaders when their biggest home crowd of the season – 47,988 – turned up for a midweek derby against WBA in early April. Villa Park's capacity was by then restricted to 48,000 for safety reasons. With two minutes remaining, and the score 0–0, Rimmer's kick-out dropped deep inside the WBA half. Albion's Brendan Batson tried a passback that fell short of his goalkeeper Tony Godden. Withe sprinted on to the ball to lob it into the net and put Villa three points ahead of Ipswich Town.

Throughout the 1980–81 season, the Villa starting 11 rarely altered. Villa played a fast passing style, so it was vital that teammates knew each others' games inside out. For the WBA match, however, Gary Shaw, a 20-year-old who had stood on the Villa Park terraces as a boy, was left out of the side. After making an explosive impact early in the season he had been struggling to score goals. He required rest but would return for the next match, at home to Ipswich Town. 'Gary Shaw was the ideal partner for Peter Withe,' says Cowans. 'His touches and awareness around the box were absolutely fantastic. He would just float around Peter Withe picking up knockdowns. He was a natural goalscorer.'

Leaders meet at Villa Park

The Ipswich manager Bobby Robson admitted before the top two met at Villa Park that a Villa win would end his club's title bid. Gary Williams was in central defence in place of Evans, who had been excelling there throughout the season. Another massive crowd – 47,495 – saw Villa stutter and get off to a disastrous start. Two defensive mistakes led to the goals which saw Ipswich establish a 2–0 lead. Shaw, with an outstanding left-footed drive, guided the ball past Ipswich goalkeeper Cooper near the end but Ipswich held on to win. They were now one point behind Villa with a game in hand. 'We threw it away,' said Saunders. 'We gave Ipswich a goal start with a misunderstanding at the back and it was like walking into a right-hander. But then we created enough chances to win by a street – and missed them. It's our own fault but it makes it interesting, doesn't it?'

That defeat affected the support more than the players. The Villa Park crowd was down to 35,000 the following Saturday, but a Villa side inspired from within constructed a smooth victory over Nottingham Forest. With Ipswich losing to Arsenal, Villa were back in control of their championship chances. A nervy performance at Stoke City on Easter Monday resulted in a 1–1 draw but with Ipswich again losing, Villa were now four points ahead of their closest challengers.

A 71-year wait comes to an end

In Villa's final home game, against Middlesbrough, a sleek, streamlined display of passing and movement encapsulated the qualities that had taken Villa to the top. Goals from Shaw, Withe and Evans saw Villa roll to a 3–0 win. At the end, Villa players trotted round the pitch, some wearing scarves and bobble hats thrown to them by fans. Villa's four point lead meant that a win or a draw in their final match of the season – away at Arsenal – would take the title to Villa Park even if Ipswich were to win their final two matches. However, Ipswich had a better goal difference than Villa so a point had to be secured at Highbury for Villa to make sure of the championship. Seventeen thousand Villa fans were in North London that afternoon, but to their dismay they saw their team lose a goal in each half. Villa stumbled through the afternoon and rarely looked like scoring. It remained 2–0 to Arsenal at the end, but the sour taste of defeat was removed by the sweet news that Middlesbrough had beaten Ipswich 2–1. It was Villa's title, the first since 1910 and won with 60 points – a Villa record. 'If we were not equipped we would not have won the championship,' said Saunders. 'We have always tried to seek perfection and I think the major thing about our displays has been our consistency.'

'The whole season was amazing,' says Dennis Mortimer. 'We had a good pre-season and I knew, within myself, that we had a side capable of winning the title – if we could keep free from injury. In our first game of the season we played Leeds off the park. I thought, on that day, "We're going to go all the way this year." I just knew we had a great side.

'Going into the Arsenal game we were very relaxed and confident. I think we were probably too relaxed. We lost two poor goals from our point of view and I don't think we rose to the occasion. Then all of a sudden we saw the crowd starting to cheer and jump up and down. As soon as the final whistle went, the crowd came over the wall. So we made a quick dart and got off the pitch and everyone was telling us we'd won the title. We wanted to go back out on to the pitch. We were waiting in the dressing-room for the police to give us the word but the crowd had remained on the pitch.

'Winning the title was, literally, a dream come true. I'd gone to the same school as Phil Thompson, the captain of Liverpool, and whenever I'd seen him lift the trophy, I'd always said to myself, "I want to do what you're doing, I want to lift that trophy one day." We'd worked really hard that season. When you think that we'd only used 14 players it was a quite phenomenal achievement. I thought we were so consistent in our play over the season. It's great being in a side where you know that when you go out on the field of play every player is going to be working hard for you, where you know each other's play so well and you read one another so easily.

'Winning the championship is about how many points you have at the end of the season. It's got nothing to do with whether people think romantically that somebody else should have won the title. The best team in the League was the team that won the championship. That wasn't Ipswich; it was us.'

An open-topped bus, carrying Villa players, officials and the League championship trophy, travelled from St Martin's Square to Colmore Row and the Council House the following day. One hundred thousand fans, who had waited anything up to 71 years to

Dennis Mortimer clutches the League championship trophy in celebration of Villa's stirring efforts in the 1980–81 season. Colin Gibson (left) and Kenny Swain (centre) savour the moment along with the Villa captain.

enjoy that moment of glory, packed the streets and squares of the city centre to acclaim the team. Seven players had been ever-present in the side: Rimmer, Swain, McNaught, Mortimer, Cowans, Morley and Bremner. 'I think our strength was the way we worked and chased,' says Gordon Cowans. 'There were no big-time players at the club, players who thought they were better than anyone else. Ron made sure it stayed that way and the players he brought to the club complemented those who were already there. He signed players who fitted into his system, players who had the right attitude.'

Villa had been watched by an average 33,650 at Villa Park over the 1980–81 season. This was a very healthy figure, given that Britain was in the midst of the most severe economic recession since the Second World War. Saunders had established a settled team during the championship season and in addition to the seven ever-presents, three players – Shaw, Withe and Evans – were close to permanent fixtures in their positions. Striker Shaw was also voted Young Player of the Year by the PFA. The left-back position had been shared by Williams and Gibson throughout the season.

Withe was top scorer with 20 goals, Shaw had scored 18 and Morley 10. In 1979–80 Morley had struggled both with a persistent injury and in coming to terms with the workrate required at Villa Park. In 1980–81 his form had been a revelation.

Morley and Withe now came into contention for the English national side as the 1982 World Cup approached. Overall, however, the majority of this Villa team were overlooked in terms of international recognition. Villa players who deserved a chance at international level, such as Bremner, McNaught and Mortimer, missed out on the honour. This was a blessing in disguise for Villa. The majority of their men did not suffer the distractions of international football, where midweek fixtures often produce tiredness and injuries. For the 1981–82 season, Villa's regular 11 were again left alone to concentrate on their club duties.

Championship defence

The team would again virtually pick itself as Villa set about defending their title. However, Shaw suffered a damaged instep

and ankle and missed the first fixtures of the 1981–82 season. In Villa's opening match, at home to newly-promoted Notts County they sagged to a 1–0 defeat in front of 30,000. Ken McNaught suffered a knee injury and left the pitch after just 10 minutes of the match. In common with Shaw he would now be missing for the early part of the League programme. Geddis had replaced Shaw for that match, but he in turn would be replaced by Terry Donovan for the next match, at Roker Park, Sunderland. Donovan scored but Villa lost 2–1. A 3–2 win at White Hart Lane gave Villa their first win of the season, with Donovan scoring twice. It was the first time Villa had taken three points for a win – the new system had come into operation for that 1981–82 season.

European Cup debut

A 1–1 home draw with Manchester United meant that Villa were in the lower half of the First Division as Valur Reykjavik came to Villa Park on 16 September 1981. The match with the champions of Iceland was Villa's first European Cup tie. The tournament, inaugurated in 1955, was played on a knockout basis over two legs with the champions of every European nation, large, middle-sized and small, being thrown together in the draw for the opening round. A crowd of 20,481 saw Villa cut through the gap-happy defence of the Icelandic amateurs to notch a 5–0 first-leg win. Morley opened the scoring and Withe and Donovan each scored twice. The return leg in Iceland saw Shaw given his first start of the season. McNaught, meanwhile, entered hospital for a knee operation. Brendan Ormsby, another homegrown talent, took McNaught's place in central defence for the match in the Laugardalsvollur stadium. The pockmarked pitch appeared a severe danger to Shaw's recently healed instep and ankle, while an icy wind whipped the players throughout the match. Shaw ignored the conditions to score both goals in a 2–0 win.

Villa now got down to more demanding European business. In the second round they were drawn away to Dynamo Berlin. Dynamo were champions of East Germany. Villa flew into the eastern sector of Berlin on 19 October. Saunders' team was prepared for a tie in which their opponents were likely

In August 1981 Villa made their fourth appearance in the Charity Shield. Their opponents would be Keith Burkinshaw's Cup-winning Spurs. Peter Withe (centre) is congratulated by Ken McNaught (left) and Allan Evans (right) after scoring one of his two goals in the 2-2 draw. After losing their three previous Charity Shields, the draw meant Villa were at least able to share the Shield that season.

to be their equals in terms of concentration, teamwork and fitness. Villa could, however, take a certain amount of confidence from their victory over the East German national side in a pre-season friendly at Villa Park two months previously. 'If we get into the last eight we will have come a long way in the last seven years – from Second Division nonentities to the championship, a couple of League Cups and into the final phase of a competition acknowledged to be the best in the world,' said Saunders.

With four minutes gone, Bremner chipped a cross on to Shaw's head. The striker pushed his header into Morley's path and from the edge of the penalty area he volleyed Villa's opener. Villa felt the fury of the roused Germans, backed by a full house of 20,000 fans in their compact Sportspark stadium. Shortly after half-time the Villa defence was breached, Hans Jurgen Riediger heading the equaliser. A narrow 2–1 defeat – a decent result – looked likely when Dynamo were awarded a penalty close to the end of the match. Ullrich stepped up to shoot but Rimmer saved to keep Villa level.

With five minutes remaining, Morley, midway inside his own half, took possession of the ball and accelerated forwards with players of both sides scampering to keep up with him. He did not release it until he had reached the Dynamo penalty area. From there he pushed the ball under goalkeeper Rudweilet's outstretched left arm and into the Dynamo net. For style, individual determination and importance, this was the most outstanding solo goal in Villa's history. It was also deeply important for Morley at that point in his Villa career – he had started the season again struggling for consistency and confidence. 'Once I start getting goals,' he said afterwards, 'I have the confidence to keep trying with shots from any range with either foot.'

Prior to the second leg the feeling in Birmingham was that Villa were through to the quarter-finals. This was reflected in the crowd of only 28,175 which turned up on 4 November for the return with Dynamo Berlin. Those present saw Villa exert exceptional pressure on the Berlin goal all evening. In return, the Dynamo players defended with considerable nerve, rarely allowing themselves to be flustered by Villa's attacks. After a quarter of an hour, Dynamo's Terletzki sent a low shot skimming past Rimmer. It left the tie balanced beautifully for the remaining 75 minutes, but with no further scoring Villa went through on the away goals rule, the two they had scored in Berlin counting double. Now the Villa supporters could relax for four months as they awaited the prospect of the European Cup quarter-finals.

Saunders quits

In the boardroom, Harry Kartz had moved aside as chairman in October 1980, and Ron Bendall, 72 years old and a resident of the Isle of Man, had taken over. He envisaged a day when his son Donald would also become Aston Villa chairman. On 2 February 1982, Bendall told Ron Saunders that his three-year rollover contract would now be modified to become a straightforward three-year contract. The rollover agreement had meant that Saunders would have had a three-year payoff at any time if the board decided to terminate his contract. Under the modified contract he would now be entitled only to whatever was left on his three-year agreement if the board decided to dismiss him.

'I have always said that I wanted to spend the rest of my life with Villa,' said Saunders. 'But the present situation means that the odds of this happening are stacked against me. I am worse off now than I was three years ago when I was originally given a six-year contract, which became a permanent three-year agreement, on their suggestion... The players need to know that their manager is on a long-term contract because that helps to engender confidence throughout the club.' On 9 February Saunders terminated his contract as manager of Aston Villa. 'If they want me to be their paid manager then I will have to be the manager,' he said. 'But I will not be the office boy.' Ron Bendall expressed surprise at Saunders' resignation and stated: 'The directors, contrary to some reports, have never attempted to select the team and differences arose when the manager wanted to be responsible for the complete control of the club, to which the board could not agree.'

The day after his resignation, Saunders said his farewells to his players at Bodymoor Heath. Tony Barton, who had been assistant to Saunders since 1976, took over as Villa's acting manager.

'I enjoyed working with Ron,' says Dennis Mortimer. 'I found him to be a very honest person, a decent manager who did well for his players. We were a very, very fit team, full of natural athletes but our training wasn't geared to fitness, it was geared to playing football. There wasn't hard running every day. It was basically down to playing football.

'The players took his resignation the way all players take things like that. They get on with it. Players realise that managers are there as a front man. They're there to pick the team, buy players and sell players but, to me, when you've got a good side the side takes care of itself. If you've got enough quality and experience in a side then a manager, to me, is there just to keep things ticking over. The side was playing so well that it didn't need any stimulus.

'The night before he resigned he phoned me up at home and said there was a big fight going on between himself and the Bendalls. He said there would be no way he would be resigning from the job. Lo and behold, the next morning the phone starts ringing and people are asking me what I think about Ron resigning. One day, he might spill the beans as to why he resigned but I've never asked

Tony Morley's special skills were carefully shaped and honed by Ron Saunders to fit Aston Villa's requirements. His speed and predatory eye for goal were essential factors in Villa enjoying an extended run in the European Cup during the 1981–82 season. Morley played a decisive role in every tie.

him about it. He had his reasons for doing so but it was a big surprise, especially with the quarter-final with Dynamo Kiev approaching. He must have had good reasons to resign, particularly with us in the quarter-finals of the European Cup.'

Eastern bloc cup tie

Although Barton inherited a team that had reached the latter stages of the European Cup, Villa were struggling in the First Division, having now slipped to 15th position. Saunders, a week after leaving Villa Park, took the post of Birmingham City manager. On taking over at St Andrews he said that he had no wish to become a club director but added: 'I think that a manager should be allowed to manage. If that means having a finger in every pie I do not believe that should be a bad thing.' At Birmingham he was given a three-year rollover contract. By chance, his first match as City manager was against Villa at St Andrews. Villa were well worth their 1–0 win, a victory which signalled the beginning of a revival in the League.

The following week Villa jetted out to Simferopol on the Black Sea for their European Cup quarter-final first leg. There they would face Dynamo Kiev, the champions of the Soviet Union. Villa had been given only a week's notice that the game had been switched from Kiev, where freezing temperatures had made the pitch at Dynamo's Republic Stadium unplayable. In Simferopol, Villa found that their Soviet hosts had billeted them in barracks-style accommodation at the Moscow Hotel. Their rooms were cold and basic but the Villa party had wisely brought their own food – bulk supplies of steak, eggs and potatoes.

'If you hadn't been to a communist country before then a trip there opened your eyes to the way people in those countries lived,' says Cowans. 'I remember in Simferopol we brought our own food. Well, on the first night we got there it wasn't unpacked so we had soup and bread rolls. I broke my roll open and there was a dead cockroach in the middle of the roll. Obviously I couldn't eat then. The people were extremely poor and it was a dour, miserable place. We always took loads of stuff with us; pennants, badges, that sort of thing. We gave them away, something the locals always enjoyed.'

The good form which Villa had displayed in their recent League games continued in the Locomotiv Stadium. Dynamo forward Oleg Blokhin hit a Villa post in the first half but Shaw responded by doing the same thing at the same end in the second half. Otherwise, Villa carried out a sound exercise in negating Dynamo's attacking threat and flew back home to Birmingham with a creditable 0–0 scoreline under their wing. Villa's performance had been especially commendable as Bremner had filled in at centre-back in place of the injured Evans. 'Blokhin was running riot in the first half in Simferopol,' says Gordon Cowans. 'We were fighting for our lives but we still created a couple of chances ourselves. We didn't go out and play for a draw in games like that, but we would be cautious and not throw too many people forward or give silly goals away and make it easy for them. It was never our style just to sit back and soak things up. With the players we had we needed to try and get forward.'

Kiev KO'd

After five minutes of the second leg, Shaw and Cowans combined in an act of great significance to Aston Villa's future. Shaw's perceptive pass to Cowans was returned to the forward with interest, setting him up perfectly to shoot past Chanov, the Dynamo goalkeeper, and put Villa into the lead. Shortly before /half-time, Cowans sent a corner kick drifting high over the Dynamo Kiev penalty area. Ken McNaught, Villa's specialist in European affairs, got his full weight behind a header to make it 2–0. The 38,579 crowd expected Kiev to kick back into life in the second half. It didn't happen. The only blow the Ukrainian side managed was one by Demyanenko seconds from the final whistle which left Mortimer with a worrying injury to his arm. The victory over Kiev was the seventh match in an unbeaten run under Barton but he remained only 'acting manager'.

'Going into the European Cup,' remembers midfielder Gordon Cowans, 'we never thought we would go all the way and win it. We hoped we could go a long way and do ourselves justice in the tournament. Once we got past Dynamo Kiev we began thinking we could go all the way. Deep down I think

Aston Villa supporters show the colours during Villa's 1981–82 European Cup campaign. The club's followers, throughout the 1980s and 1990s, have done much to give Villa a positive image during their foreign travels.

we knew that we were a good side. Our strength was in doing the best for each other. And you don't go all the way to the European Cup final without being a good side.'

Along with Bremner and Cowans, Mortimer had been the inspiration behind a fine Villa win. Bremner was often seen as the worker in that trio. He did get through a mountain of work in every game, but he also provided frequent touches of subtlety and grace. Mortimer was expert in shuttling the ball through the midfield, while Cowans' refined skills took spectators' breaths away almost as a matter of routine.

'Dennis was a good captain,' says Cowans. 'He was vocal and would say his piece but he probably led more by example. He was also a very good player, an inspirational player. I think he and I in the middle of midfield complemented each other because we were different sorts of players. I liked to sit a little bit more and get on the ball and try and pass it, while Dennis would make surging runs through the middle and get on the ends of things, knockdowns from Peter Withe and things like that. Des Bremner, on the right-hand side, was absolutely fabulous. He was very underrated. We, the guys at the club, felt that Des was probably the most important member of the side because he got through so much work for us working from in to out as a right-sided midfield player, fly-ing up the wing, getting crosses in and getting on the end of crosses.'

Back in Belgium

The semi-final draw took Villa to Belgium, scene of their first European adventure seven years previously. This time, they would face that nation's premier club, Anderlecht. The Belgian champions had overcome considerable opposition to reach the semis, beating Widzew Lodz, Juventus and Red Star Belgrade on the way. The club also had a long and successful history in European competition: in the late 1970s they had twice won the European Cup Winners' Cup.

The first leg against Anderlecht was to be played at Villa Park on 7 April 1982. A week before the match, Barton was confirmed as the Villa manager. 'I think we are good enough to win the European Cup,' he said, 'even though in some eyes we may seem inexperienced in European competitions. More important, the players believe they can win it too.'

Major ties in European competition during the 1970s and 1980s often saw the away side set out simply to frustrate the opposition. At that time the laws of football did much to help teams who adopted such tactics and time-wasting was commonplace.

The kicked passback to the goalkeeper was fully legal and defenders could knock the ball back to him as often as they wished. When they did so, there was no limit on how long the keeper could hold on to the ball. He could also drop the ball, roll it along the ground and pick it up again without penalty. For an attacking player to remain onside he had to have two men between him and goal. The rule whereby a player is onside if level with the last defender (and has the keeper in front of him) had not yet been passed. This all meant that a team could comfortably and successfully turn their skills towards mass frustration of the opposition – not to mention paying spectators – without much of a risk, even if this was not their normal game.

Anderlecht were expert at this type of football – it was close to the style they adopted every week in the Belgian League. They were also accomplished at Villa's own speciality of shuttling the ball swiftly from defence into attack as the 38,539 Villa crowd soon discovered that April evening.

'I never came up against a side who played the offside the way they did,' says Cowans. 'A blanket of players just stepped up all the time; they caught us offside so many times. They did it so well they limited us to very few chances. Their side was packed with internationals. One of their midfielders, Lozano, was one of the best players I've ever played against. He was absolutely brilliant on the ball. When he got the ball he was causing havoc. Coeck, a left-footer, was another very good player, as was Vercauteren.'

Ten minutes before half-time, Shaw and Cowans twisted and turned to release the catch on an explosive Villa attacking move. The ball was worked forward to Morley who stole into a rare square of space to snatch a shot that nicked the inside of an Anderlecht post before making its way into the net. The goal jabbed Anderlecht into a series of stinging counter-attacks. With half-time on the horizon, Frankie Vercauteren sent a quick, powerful shot speeding towards the upper reaches of Rimmer's goal. The goalkeeper cut a gymnastic shape as he dived through the air to repel the scoring effort, turning it round the post.

The interval brought a natural break in the Anderlecht-induced storm and in the second half conditions settled to Villa's advantage. Neither side was able to add to the score, leaving the second leg finely poised. 'It was absolutely imperative that we did not concede a goal,' said Barton afterwards. 'And now we will be looking to score a goal over there to ensure that we go through without any trouble.'

The Villa team had been: Rimmer, Swain, Williams, Evans, McNaught, Mortimer, Bremner, Shaw, Withe, Cowans, Morley. 'The hero of the night against Anderlecht was Jimmy Rimmer,' is Dennis Mortimer's opinion. 'Jimmy made two or three super saves which prevented Anderlecht getting that away goal. We knew it would be a tough game away so we needed to be sure that we kept a clean sheet.'

Crowd trouble in Brussels

The same players strode out in front of 40,000 at the Stade Emile Versé in the tidy surroundings of the Parc Astrid, Brussels, for the second leg. The picturesque setting was, however, tarnished that evening as the game began to a backdrop of fighting on the terracing behind the Villa goal. Sadly, the away supporters appeared to be the instigators of the fighting. Some Villa fans had over-indulged in alcohol on the long cross-channel day-trip from Birmingham. Other individuals, looking for a fight, had attached themselves to the club for the evening. One person, a 17-year-old British soldier, ran onto the pitch midway through the first half to escape a beating from the Belgian police. However, instead of simply escaping the trouble, he decided to lay down inside the penalty area. Others departed the terraces for the fringes of the pitch. The referee stopped the match for seven minutes, during which Villa players appealed to the people behind the goal to cease the conflict. They had only limited success in penetrating the senses of the alcohol-dazed individuals responsible for the trouble.

The two sets of supporters were only separated when riot police moved into the crowd in numbers, beating offenders with their batons. They then formed a line to prevent the opposing fans from making further attacks on each other.

'The fans ruined it for us,' said Barton afterwards. Amidst the mayhem, Villa had managed to obtain a 0–0 draw that took them into the final. The team had started

The Aston Villa team and substitutes on the pitch at the Feyenoord Stadium before the 1982 European Cup final. From left to right, back row: Peter Withe, Andy Blair, Nigel Spink, Pat Heard, Gary Shaw, Ken McNaught, Allan Evans, Dennis Mortimer, Jimmy Rimmer. Front row: David Geddis, Colin Gibson, Gordon Cowans, Gary Williams, Tony Morley, Des Bremner, Kenny Swain.

the match cautiously and had been on the point of playing more expansively, when the trouble had grown increasingly serious. The hooliganism had unsettled the players, but they managed to maintain their concentration and stop Anderlecht scoring. 'We were magnificent last night,' said Barton, 'especially in the first half. I was proud that we did it for Aston Villa, Birmingham and the whole of Britain. We can now go on and win the cup.'

'After the Anderlecht game,' says Cowans, 'realising that you had got to the European Cup final was nearly as good as winning it. Getting through that second leg in Brussels was the most difficult task we faced on the way to the final. We were hanging on a bit by the end of that game.'

Villa await UEFA verdict

Villa now awaited a meeting of UEFA's Control and Disciplinary Committee on 29 April, eight days after the second leg of their European Cup semi-final. Possible punishments mooted were a ban on Villa competing in the European Cup final or on Villa fans attending that match, which was scheduled for Rotterdam, Holland, on 26 May. On 30 April, after a meeting that had started the previous afternoon and had

stretched through to midnight, UEFA handed down Villa's punishment for the behaviour of the miscreants who had soiled the club's name in Brussels. Villa were fined £14,500 and were ordered to play their next home match in European competition behind closed doors. It was a punishment that was far less severe than it might have been. Unsurprisingly, Ron Bendall and his fellow directors decided not to risk appealing against UEFA's ruling.

Although the appalling scenes in the Parc Astrid could not be excused, Anderlecht had sold tickets openly in the environs of the stadium on the day of the match. This was a flagrant breach of UEFA rules and may have helped move the UEFA committee to be more lenient towards Villa. For the final against West German champions Bayern Munich, Villa were allocated 14,000 tickets and these could only be obtained through the Travellers' Club. There would be a strict alcohol ban on transport to and from Rotterdam. At the Feyenoord Stadium, supporters of Villa and Bayern Munich would be segregated, each group occupying one end of the stadium. In

Holland, no more than two tickets would be sold to any one individual to prevent touts obtaining and selling tickets to fans. Villa officials had made several visits to the continent and had done a considerable amount of excellent work in helping to draw up these plans.

Bayern beckon in final

In the seven League fixtures between the match in Brussels and the European Cup final, Villa's form was mediocre. Three defeats, two draws and just one win preceded Villa's final match of the season, at home to Swansea City. There were 18,294 at Villa Park to see Barton's team warm-up for the final with a quality display. Confident and certain in their control of the play, Villa eased to a 3–0 win that saw them finish the domestic season in 11th place in the First Division. Bayern general manager Uli Hoeness had watched the match and had afterwards identified Villa's teamwork and swiftness on the break as their major strengths. He viewed Evans, Morley and Withe as their three most impressive players.

Two days before the final, the Villa squad alighted in Rotterdam, ready for the most prestigious, exhilarating and enjoyable occasion in the club's history. On the day before their departure, Gary Shaw, who had been the only regular to miss the Swansea game, was passed fit to play against Bayern. That was a major boost for Villa. The European Cup final looked likely to be a suitable setting for Shaw's subtle touches.

'Teams can get tense on these occasions,' said Barton before the match. 'But we hope to win, playing as normally as we possibly can. That will mean playing it tight at the back and getting as many players forward as possible when the opportunity presents itself. We have learned very quickly in Europe this season. The last two rounds, against Dynamo Kiev and Anderlecht, were a tremendous test of discipline and patience and that will be an important factor tomorrow.'

In their semi-final Bayern had scored seven times against CSKA Sofia although, encouragingly for Villa, they had also conceded three goals. This would be the Germans' first final since the mid-1970s when they had won the European Cup three times in succession. Their centre-forward Karl-Heinz Rummenigge had been voted European Footballer of the Year in 1980 and 1981, the sixth successive occasion that the award had gone to a German-based player. Bayern were strong favourites to triumph in Rotterdam and, to help them along, had the incentive of a £10,000 bonus per man if they were to take the trophy to Bavaria for the fourth time. Villa were on £2,750 per man if they could bring the European Cup to the Midlands.

Villa make speedy start

Villa were unchanged from the semi-final. Wearing an all-white strip, a relaxed-looking Villa team posed for photographs on the pitch in front of a 46,000 crowd inside the Feyenoord Stadium. The Villa line-up was Rimmer, Swain, Williams, Evans, McNaught, Mortimer, Bremner, Shaw, Withe, Cowans, Morley.

It was a side that had first played together in a local derby with West Bromwich Albion on 8 November 1980, in a 0–0 draw. During the 1981–82 season, that side had been picked for the first time by Tony Barton, in his third game in charge after Ron Saunders' departure. Saunders' selections had approximated this team but it was Barton who firmly inserted Gary Williams as the team's regular left-back. Between that match, in mid-February 1982, and the final this team had played together eight times.

In the early stages of the final, Villa, whenever possible, took the game to Bayern. After two minutes a header from Allan Evans floated from left to right across the face of the Bayern goal and only narrowly wide. Another header, by Withe from Cowans' free-kick, drifted past a post. Bayern were slowly feeling their way into the game in the opening ten minutes while Villa were speeding forward whenever the opportunity presented itself. Des Bremner and Gary Shaw, with his creative, almost artistic touches, looked particularly bright.

After nine minutes, the line-up had to be changed when Villa made one of the most unusual substitutions seen in a European Cup final. Jimmy Rimmer, without having made contact with an opponent, walked off the field. He was replaced by Nigel Spink. Rimmer had cricked his neck in training the

previous day but the injury had been kept a secret inside the club. After testing the injury in a match situation, the experienced goal-keeper realised that he was not fit enough to continue. Rimmer had touched the ball just twice; once at a goal-kick, the other time to handle a passback from Kenny Swain.

Spink, 23 years old, was making only his second full appearance for Villa and his first of the 1980s. His debut had been on Boxing Day 1979 in a 2–1 defeat at Nottingham Forest. 'Jimmy always had knocks and strains but he always came through and strapped himself up and played,' says Nigel Spink about the substitution that made him a European Cup hero.

'In my naïvety I thought, "Don't even think about it. He's going to play." So myself and the other substitutes made sure that we spent three-quarters of an hour warming up to make the most of the night because we were sure we would spend the rest of the night on the bench. After I came on for Jimmy the night went very quickly but funnily enough that is the one match where I can clearly remember every single thing that went on during the game.'

By midway through the first half Villa were well on top. Peter Withe cleverly made space for himself on the edge of the Bayern box and turned quickly, but he sent his shot wide of goal. Evans was defending energetically, constantly ranging back and forth across the edge of the Villa penalty area, denying the Germans in general, and Rummenigge in particular, the space to create constructive attacks. One interception by the centre-back, midway inside the Villa half, saw him streak 60 yards downfield with the Germans struggling in his wake. His final pass to Shaw was just inches off target. Had it been slightly more accurate, Shaw would have been clean through on goal. Instead, the ball was nicked off his toe by Bayern defender Weiner.

Bayern begin to boss the game

It took Bayern half an hour to carve out their first chance. Durnberger cut inside Swain and swiped a low, 15-yard shot at Spink's goal. The goalkeeper responded in style,

Jimmy Rimmer (left) is forced to concede defeat to the injury that had worried him in the hours before the European Cup final. He leaves the pitch after nine minutes to be replaced by Nigel Spink, a 23-year-old who had been on the Villa Park staff for four years but had, as yet, played only one match for the first team. Spink had not expected to play any part in the match and, accordingly, had no time to suffer from pre-match worries. He produced a nerveless performance against Bayern.

Peter Withe turns the ball past Bayern Munich goalkeeper Muller for the goal that brought European football's top club prize to Villa Park. The ball had bobbled in the dry, dusty penalty area before it reached Withe and it pitched off the inside of the post before carrying on to the back of the net. It was only after the match that Withe discovered that the ball had made contact with the woodwork en route to goal.

snatching the ball cleanly then despatching it, without fuss, to Morley. A minute later, Bayern captain Paul Breitner teed the ball up perfectly for Rummenigge in front of goal. The forward swayed into space, thundered on to the ball and struck an iron-hard shot towards goal. Spink stood up to beat the ball down for his second excellent save of the evening. Inside another minute, Breitner lofted the ball from the goal-line to the edge of the penalty area where Rummenigge leapt into the air with his back to goal. The resultant overhead kick bounced narrowly past Spink's post with the goalkeeper beaten.

As the second half started, Bayern maintained their momentum. On the hour, a run from deep by Augenthaler saw the sweeper push into a good shooting position inside the Villa box, but he screwed his shot wide. A minute later, Durnberger cut into space inside the penalty area. His low, awkward shot was aimed inside the Villa post but Spink swooped to hold the ball.

A stunningly swift move from Bayern saw the Germans transport the ball from one end of the pitch to the other. It ended with Augenthaler rising above McNaught for a header that evaded Spink. As the ball sped toward the net, Swain did well to twist his body and head it off the line. Bayern were exuding quality and Villa looked in danger of being overrun.

Withe hits winner

Morley responded to the German pressure with a 20-yard shot that soared high over the Bayern crossbar. It showed Villa's fighting spirit remained intact. With 67 minutes gone they did even better. Mortimer, on the halfway line, sidefooted a pass to Shaw, who turned inside Wolfgang Dremmler, leaving the German sprawled on the turf. The Villa man quickly nudged the ball into the path of Morley, leaving two German defenders out of position and behind the play. Dremmler had been brought into the Bayern team specifically to mark Morley, so the winger now made the most of his few moments of freedom. He turned inside, then outside, Weiner, leaving the Bayern centre-back in a whirl of confusion. Morley then hit a low,

111

Goalscorer Withe is grounded as celebrations take place for his European Cup final goal. Villa had survived sustained Bayern pressure and would now draw on all their resources to protect their lead. The despondency shown by the Bayern players after the goal was matched by the Germans' weary performance in the remaining minutes of the match.

left-footed cross that zipped inside Weiner and Augenthaler to the feet of Withe, on the edge of the six-yard box and directly in front of goal. As the ball approached the centre-forward, it bobbled in the grass-free goalmouth. Withe still managed to make decisive contact with the ball and it nudged off the inside of the post before hitting the back of the Bayern net. To cap the moment of glory, the goal had been scored in front of the vast bank of Villa supporters. Their celebrations and those of the players were unrestrained. The collective release from the pressure exerted by the Germans in the previous ten minutes made the outpouring of joy particularly exuberant.

The goal smoothed Villa's defensive worries while their attacking movements grew in confidence. A 20-yard spinning shot from Cowans forced the goalkeeper, Muller, into a save low down in front of his line. Bayern had only a couple of half-chances as the game slipped from their grip. Dieter Hoeness, their centre-forward, had the ball in the net but he was ruled to have been offside. At the other end, Withe was denied a penalty when he was sent tumbling after a clash with Dremmler.

'We were very relaxed about the whole thing in the days before the match,' remembers Gordon Cowans, 'especially when you consider the calibre of our opponents. But on the night, we were really geared up for the game. I was a bit nervous before the match but as soon as you kick off you concentrate on what you're doing and nerves just go out the window. Playing in the game I always felt we were okay. I felt as though they caused us a few problems but not too many. It looks a bit more nerve-racking when you watch it on video! But it was a tremendous achievement to win the European Cup, especially when you consider that only five British clubs have managed to do so. We won it and no one can take that away from us.'

Villa celebrate top prize

At the final whistle, the Villa players raced to acclaim their fans. Those fans then saw Dennis Mortimer lift the European Cup. 'All the lads had disappeared to the other side of the ground to wave to the fans and all I wanted to do was get up the steps to pick up the trophy,' says the captain. 'The noise was incredible. I remember one of the officials coming down and saying, "Can you get your team together?" And I said, "How can I? They're all at the other side of the ground. You'll just have to wait until they come back." After five or ten minutes they returned and it was up the steps to get the trophy. I always think that the greatest thing about being the captain of a side is that you get your hands on a trophy first. You just cannot describe the feeling of lifting such a trophy. It's the

Tony Barton, the Aston Villa manager (fourth from right), rises from the Villa bench as the last tense seconds tick away at the end of the European Cup final. Barton's careful stewardship of his players through the final three rounds of the competition maintained the spirit that had brought Villa to the edge of excellence in the European Cup.

Peter Withe, wearing a Bayern shirt exchanged with an opponent, crowns himself as one of Villa's twelve kings of Europe as he lifts the European Cup on to his head in the aftermath of the 1982 final.

ultimate prize, the ultimate achievement.'

Of the team that won the trophy, Gary Shaw was the only native of Birmingham. Gary Williams, from Wolverhampton, was a fellow Midlander. Nigel Spink was an Essex boy. Five members of the team – Mortimer, Swain, Withe, Morley and Rimmer – were from the Liverpool area. Cowans hailed from the North-East. In light of the influence of Scots in the club's origins it was appropriate that there were three Scots in the side on the greatest night in the club's history – McNaught, Evans and Bremner. The average age of the team that won the trophy was 26. 'Afterwards, during the celebrations back in Amsterdam and in Birmingham, I was dumbstruck,' says Spink. 'The whole thing didn't sink in until weeks later. Nothing I did in my career matched that, not even playing for England.'

Dennis Mortimer adds: 'The one thing I'm pleased about is that we'll always be part of the club, the history of the club, because we were so successful as a team. I'd have hated to have played for the number of years I did and not have won anything. To have won the two big ones was immense.'

On Friday 28 May, an open-topped bus carried the Villa party and the European Cup from Villa Park to Victoria Square where they were greeted ecstatically by thousands of claret-and-blue-clad celebrating supporters. It was an awesome sight – the most elusive, fought-over, magnificent trophy in club football standing tall on the balcony of the Council House. The symbol of success that every club in Europe wished to possess had come to rest in Birmingham. Aston Villa had become only the 12th club in the European Cup's 27-year history to win the trophy. The club's name had always been famous throughout the world for its feats in the early days of the game. Now Aston Villa had joined the game's modern elite.

The euphoria of European success didn't last long at Villa Park. A succession of managers tried to halt the club's sudden decline but relegation could not be avoided. Graham Taylor took Villa back to the top.

8 Glamour and grit: 1982–90

Cosmopolitan cup competitions would dominate Aston Villa's footballing affairs during their first season as European champions. It would be the most colourful year in the club's history, during which the players would become experienced international travellers. The club were chasing no fewer than five cups, together with the First Division championship. Two of those competitions were new to Aston Villa: the European Super Cup and the World Club Cup. Villa were also set to defend the European Cup, while fitting in matches in the FA and League cups.

After losing their opening League match to Sunderland, Villa went down 5–0 at Everton. The defence's unsettled performance in that game was reflected in problems off the park. Kenny Swain and Allan Evans were seeking transfers. Ken McNaught, who, with puzzling timing, had announced before the European Cup final that it would be his last game for Villa, was now prepared to stay but was negotiating a new contract with the club. A 1–0 defeat at Southampton saw Europe's premier team stuck in bottom place in the First Division of the Football League after three games.

Villa play European tie behind closed doors

Two back-to-back 4–1 wins in the League secured some stability before Villa began their defence of the European Cup with a home tie against Turkish champions Besiktas. There were two changes to the team that had taken the field in Rotterdam four months earlier. Pat Heard replaced Swain who had played the first two games of

the season but, unhappy with his situation at the club, had then been dropped. Swain had played his last game for Villa and would move on to Nottingham Forest in January 1983. This meant that the European Cup-winning side's last game together had been the final itself. For the Besiktas match, Andy Blair, signed from Coventry City in 1981, was in midfield to compensate for Bremner moving to centre-back in place of Evans, who had missed the previous four matches through an injury he had sustained in the match at Everton.

The game with Besiktas would provide the most highly visible evidence of UEFA's disciplinary action for the events in Brussels the previous April. There were no Villa fans inside the ground although 200 gathered in Aston Park, opposite the Trinity Road stand, to sing and chant while listening to the game on the radio. With no need to accommodate spectators, the match was played in the afternoon. The only witnesses to the action were club officials, a cluster of photographers and pressmen and the occasional policeman and his dog. Withe, Williams and Mortimer scored the goals that put Villa 3–0 up after half an hour. Besiktas pulled a goal back before the end.

'It felt like a bit of a practice match with no one there so we were maybe not as fired up as we should have been. In the return we faced one of the most hostile atmospheres I've ever experienced,' states Gordon Cowans. 'We stayed in the Hilton Hotel, which was around a mile away from the ground, and from there you could look down on the ground. Five hours before kick-off, the stadium was packed. It was full of men – no women – and the noise was incredible. On the field, you had to shout to

Gordon Cowans scores Villa's second goal in the highly-charged 3–0 Super Cup victory over Barcelona at Villa Park in January 1983.

115

make yourself heard even if you were only inches away from someone else. You couldn't get a bigger contrast between that and the first match.'

Dynamo left powerless in Bucharest

At the Inonu Stadium, Istanbul, Villa kept Besiktas under control, comfortably gaining a 0–0 draw that put the defending champions into a second round tie with Dynamo Bucharest of Romania. One good omen for this game was that Dynamo's conquerors in their two previous European runs of the 1980s had gone on to win the respective competitions. There were 80,000 Romanian fans in the August 23 Stadium on that October night, a suitably sizeable audience for one of Villa's most accomplished European performances.

The team smoothly whirred on to the counter attack throughout the match, demoralising their opponents with their efficiency and creating chance after chance. The opening goal saw Morley masterfully manipulating the ball down the wing before crossing for Withe. The centre-forward directed a header towards Shaw, who guided the ball from boot to goal. In the second half, Morley was again the creator for Villa's second goal. The winger quickly shifted the ball forward and crossed for Shaw to head the ball past goalkeeper Moraru to make it 2–0 and give Villa an impressive advantage to take forward into the second leg.

Barton believed that his team's efforts in Bucharest represented Villa's best European performance during his time as manager. He said: 'We have never received the praise we deserved for winning the European Cup and neither did we when we won the First Division title. But we are a good team and if we can defeat Dynamo to reach the quarter-finals I am sure it will make our opponents respect us even more.'

Before the return match against Dynamo at Villa Park, Evans signed a six-year contract with Villa. McNaught had also resolved his differences with the club. Three goals from Shaw and one from his substitute Mark Walters saw Villa coast to a 4–2 win to complete their dismissal of Dynamo from that season's European Cup. Villa were now through to the quarter-finals.

Allegations and investigations

Prior to the European Cup final the previous spring, a story had surfaced that thousands of pounds had gone missing in connection with work carried out on offices built inside the new North Stand. An internal report by a design consultancy commissioned by the club concluded that £700,000 could not be accounted for from a total bill of £1,300,000. There was some evidence that duplication of charges had occurred on costs of work that had been completed on behalf of the club.

Another report, by the club's auditors Deloitte, Haskins and Sells, called into question the position of Mr Terry Rutter being both the employers' representative and the site engineer for the work. The report stated: 'Under the Institution of Civil Engineers' conditions of contract, the engineer is responsible for issuing instructions, for controlling quality and progress and for measuring and pricing the works. We consider that, as a result of Mr Rutter having to perform this role, together with his other duties for and on behalf of the club in an increasingly complex contract, detailed control of the progress, quality and cost of the works would have been difficult to maintain.'

On Monday 27 September 1982, while the Villa team and officials were on their way to Istanbul for the second leg of their tie with Besiktas, Villa Park received a visit from the police. Detective Superintendent Harry West, head of the West Midlands police commercial branch, and Detective Chief Inspector Graham Trevis met vice-chairman Donald Bendall and directors Harry Kartz and Trevor Gill at the ground.

Kartz and Gill had taken the initiative of calling in the police. The police then began investigations into the club's finances. Three years later, at Birmingham Crown Court, Terry Rutter and Harry Marsden, who had been the architect for the North Stand, faced fraud-related charges and were each sentenced to 12 months in prison. Both sentences were suspended.

More immediately, in 1982, the club was labouring under a financial burden that had been exacerbated by these affairs. At an AGM in October it was revealed that Aston Villa now had debts of £1,600,000. On 30

Trip to Orient for World Club Cup

One of the new chairman's first duties was to join the Villa party for a trip to Japan. Villa were to play the South American champions Penarol of Uruguay there on 12 December for the World Club Cup of 1982. Barton was in a positive mood on arrival in Tokyo. The Villa manager declared: 'We are here to win. We will treat the game just as seriously as we did when we won the European Cup against Bayern Munich in May.' There were 62,000 in the National Stadium, Tokyo, to see the following Villa team take on Penarol: Rimmer, Jones, Williams, Evans, McNaught, Mortimer, Bremner, Shaw, Withe, Cowans, Morley. Mark Jones, a right-back who'd come through the Villa youth system, was the only change from the team that had taken the field for the European Cup final.

Before the match, Barton expressed dissatisfaction with the replacement of the expected Adidas Tango ball with one he described as being so light that it flew around like a beach ball. After three minutes, Cowans curled a free-kick which struck the Penarol crossbar. Villa had the game in their grip during the opening stages, but midway through the first half McNaught gave away a free-kick midway inside Villa's half. Jair, a Brazilian, took the kick for Penarol and the ball swayed through the air before dipping towards the target. Rimmer stretched to get a hand to it but could only touch the ball on to his post before watching it drop into the net. From then, Penarol turned the screw and a second half goal from Siba made the final score 2–0 to the Uruguayans.

'The World Championship game was played on the world's worst football pitch,' says Dennis Mortimer. 'There wasn't a blade of grass on the pitch. It was a good venue and the build-up was very, very good but the pitch itself was just a joke. I think it's a lot better now. Overall, we were very disappointed with that game because I do believe we could have won it. They weren't such a great team, Penarol. On the day we didn't play our best football. We would have been the first British club to win the World Championship and that would have been nice for the club.'

Nigel Spink took over from Jimmy Rimmer as Villa's regular goalkeeper midway through the 1982–83 season. Spink would remain the number one choice in goal until the early 1990s, eventually giving the club 20 unbroken years of excellent service.

November 1982, Ron and Donald Bendall resigned from the board. Initially, Harry Parkes claimed that he was about to buy Bendall's shares and become the new chairman of the club. Then Doug Ellis stepped in to buy Ron Bendall's 42% shareholding and returned to the club as Villa chairman. In the years since Ellis' departure in 1979, players had been paid hefty wages and bonuses. This had helped engender success on the park. However, with unemployment soaring in the early 1980s, attendances across the country had been hit hard. Villa, despite the team's triumphs at home and abroad, proved no exception to this trend. That, together with the costly building work, had seen the club's debts escalate.

Bad tempered clash with Catalans

While Villa had been in Japan, the draw for the European Cup quarter-finals had been made in Switzerland. Villa had been drawn at home to Juventus who, with Liverpool, were one of the two teams Barton had wished to avoid. Before that tie, scheduled for March 1983, Villa would face yet another of world football's biggest names. On 19 January, they met Barcelona in the Spaniards' spectacular Nou Camp stadium for the first leg of the European Super Cup.

The Super Cup was a two-legged play-off between the European Cup holders and the European Cup Winners' Cup holders. It had been inaugurated in 1972 after European clubs had become disillusioned with the World Club Cup which, in the late 1960s and early 1970s, had become scarred by violence on the pitch. When, in 1980, that competition changed from a two-legged affair to a one-off game in Japan it took on a more healthy hue.

The Super Cup had, however, survived and 45,000 Spanish fans were in attendance at the Nou Camp as this Villa team stepped out on to the park: Spink, Jones, Williams, Evans, McNaught, Mortimer, Bremner, Shaw, Withe, Cowans, Morley. Villa held their own in the first half but Barcelona's German midfielder Bernd Schuster began to exert an increasing influence on the game. Shortly after half-time, a shot from Barcelona's Marcos flew past Spink's right hand and into the Villa net. From then, Barcelona dominated but Villa held out to the end without conceding another goal.

'They are likely to be more physical over here,' said Gary Shaw before the return leg at Villa Park. 'The kicks and elbows to stop you playing, that kind of thing. But it will be good practice for the European Cup match with Juventus. We are meeting the two most physical sides in Europe, something we haven't encountered in previous continental matches.' The Villa team for the second leg was: Spink, Williams, Gibson, Evans, McNaught, Blair, Bremner, Shaw, Withe, Cowans, Morley. A 31,500 crowd saw Barcelona's Alberto sent off in the first half for deliberate handball but Barcelona handled Villa's attacks competently until ten minutes from time, when Shaw sent a shot spinning past the Barcelona keeper and into the net.

In the 99th minute Walters, a substitute for Morley, was tripped in the penalty area. Cowans had his spot kick saved by Urruti, the Barcelona goalkeeper, but the midfielder followed up to squirt the ball over the line. When the ball rebounded from the back of the net, Cowans, in celebration, smacked it into the net a second time. Urruti snapped and, with a vicious flying kick, swiped the Villa man's legs from underneath him. It looked a sure sending-off offence but the referee failed to take the appropriate action. McNaught, with a diving header, sealed the win. On a night of gruesome tackling, Barcelona's Marcos was dismissed before the end, as was Allan Evans, for a second bookable offence. It meant that Evans would now be automatically suspended for the first leg of the European tie with Juventus. 'People are continually knocking British football and saying what is wrong with it,' said Barton.

'But I thought all my players showed remarkable restraint and control even though they faced the most severe provocation. I was proud of them. When we looked at the event before the game it seemed worth competing for because it was another European tournament, another medal to be won. Now my feelings are bittersweet.' Nigel Spink remembers the match with affection, though he has not forgotten some the gamesmanship and indiscipline of the Catalans: 'The home leg against Barcelona was a night that probably equalled the European Cup for excitement. The Spaniards tried every trick in the book.'

Villa face the Old Lady of Turin

Five weeks later, a Juventus team bristling with style flew to the West Midlands for the first leg of their European Cup quarter-final with Villa. Six of the Juventus players who started the match at Villa Park had been members of the Italy side that had won the World Cup in Spain eight months earlier.

Also in the side was Michel Platini, the most outstanding individual talent at the 1982 World Cup, and the Polish forward Zbigniew Boniek who had also been impressive at that tournament. The Italian champions didn't dither in planting their imprint firmly on the game. Inside the first minute, a tidy move took the ball from midfield down the Villa wing. Cabrini crossed and Paolo Rossi sent a confident, clean header dashing into the Villa net. No Villa player had yet touched the ball. McNaught appeared to have equalised in the 13th minute but his effort was ruled out by the West German referee, who had spotted an offence by another Villa man. Half-time came with Villa still behind but shortly after the restart Cowans stealthily found a gap in the Juventus defence and steered a precise header past Zoff.

The score remained 1–1 as the game reached its latter stages. Then Platini directed a pass through the Villa defence, Boniek took it in his stride and shot to put Villa 2–1 behind. 'We have a good record in away ties,' said Barton afterwards, 'and I am still convinced that we can defeat Juventus. We were given a lesson tonight. We were asleep when we conceded the first goal and we were punished by their winner because we were attempting to force a winner ourselves. Juventus played tremendously. They defended in depth and Rossi and Bettega caused us many problems on the counter attack. Juventus are the best team we have played in Europe.'

The Villa players and manager were defiant in defeat, and as they flew out to Turin for the second leg they maintained that they could turn the tie in their favour. Those beliefs took a blow after 15 minutes on a rainy night at the Stadio Communale. Platini's shot from distance slipped across the turf then through Spink's hands and legs for the opener. Ten minutes later, Rossi crossed for Tardelli to score with a superb header which sent 70,000 fans wild with delight. A third Juventus goal arrived when Boniek put the ball into Platini's path for the

Frenchman to guide the ball into the net. Withe scored for Villa late in the match but it was no consolation for a Villa side who had suffered the rare experience of being outclassed. It was no disgrace – Juventus were one of the outstanding European sides of the time, reaching the final in 1983, then winning the Cup Winners' Cup in 1984 and the European Cup in 1985.

UEFA Cup consolation

The domestic cup competitions had also ended in disappointment for Villa. A lacklustre performance at Highbury four days before the match in Turin had seen Villa lose 2–0 to Arsenal in an FA Cup quarter-final. Notts County had been their conquerors in the third round of the League Cup. Despite having played 15 cup ties in 1982–83, Villa had finished in a commendable sixth place in the First Division. That placing meant they would be in European competition again in 1983–84 as one of the English representatives in the UEFA Cup. During the summer, Ken McNaught departed for WBA and Jimmy Rimmer for Swansea City. Mervyn Day, a goalkeeper, was signed from Leyton Orient. Steve McMahon, a midfielder, was bought from Everton for £375,000 and Paul Rideout arrived from Swindon Town for £175,000. Gordon Cowans, however, would miss the season after suffering a broken leg in a pre-season tournament in Spain. Alan Curbishley was signed from Birmingham City for £100,000 as cover for Cowans.

Following a 5–1 aggregate victory over Vitoria Guimaraes of Portugal, Villa faced Spartak Moscow in the second round of the UEFA Cup. Villa obtained an impressive 2–2 draw in Moscow, but they were outplayed in the return at Villa Park by a Spartak side whose movement of the ball was mesmerising. Despite Spartak's superiority, Villa remained on level terms at 1–1 as the game entered its final seconds and the near-30,000 crowd expected the home side to enter the third round of the tournament on the away goals rule. Then Spartak's Fyodor Cherenkov moved swiftly inside from the wing and hit a shot that slapped off Mortimer's thigh and arced into the net. Villa were out of the UEFA Cup. Barton's team enjoyed a better run in the League

Cup, where they reached the two-legged semi-final but lost 2–1 on aggregate to Everton. Eleventh position was achieved in the League, not high enough to attain a European place.

Since taking over as chairman in 1982, Doug Ellis had implemented measures to reduce the club's overdraft. However, by 1984 it remained high, at around £1,500,000. During the 1983–84 season, Tony Barton had refused requests from Doug Ellis to cut the playing staff from 29 to 24 and to make cutbacks to the youth team. The manager insisted that he would make such reductions, but only as and when he saw fit, and over an extended period of time. In the summer of 1984 he maintained that he still wished to take his time in making the necessary cuts over the course of the new season. Consequently he was sacked on 18 June. 'Tony didn't have Ron's discipline or strength of character,' says Cowans, 'but he was a lovely fellow, an absolute gentleman. The one thing he did was let people go out and express themselves a little bit more. Tony would encourage you to try things

whereas Ron would just tell you to play it simple and not get carried away.'

Barton and his assistant Roy McLaren left the club exactly ten years after the Ron Saunders era – in which both had played an integral part – had begun. Ellis said: 'I want only the best for Villa and our supporters and that must mean that we have to make progress. The status quo is no good for us.' The chairman attempted to persuade Ron Atkinson, manager of Manchester United, to join Villa but after a series of discussions he decided to stay at Old Trafford.

In July 1984, Ellis appointed Graham Turner, a 36-year-old, as the new manager of Aston Villa. Turner had been manager of Shrewsbury Town for the previous six years, winning the Third Division title in his first year as manager then consolidating Shrewsbury's position in the Second Division for the next five years. Turner, who signed a five-year contract with Villa, would have full control of the playing and coaching side at the club, but he would be forced to work within a restricted budget at debt-laden Villa Park.

Graham Turner became the youngest manager in Villa's history when, at the age of 36, he took charge of the team in the summer of 1984. His arrival brought an end to the Villa careers of several players who had helped bring the League championship and European Cup to Villa Park. Turner's jettisoning of those players, who still had a considerable amount to contribute to the team, appeared premature.

Frenchman Didier Six became the first continental player to attain a place in the Villa first eleven when he signed in 1984. He was an established international but found it difficult to reproduce his sophisticated skills in English league football.

New boss signs Six

The new manager's first signing was an intriguing one: Didier Six, a French international forward and a team-mate of Platini at the 1982 World Cup. Six was Villa's first foreign first-team player. He was signed on a free transfer from Mulhouse who had been relegated to the French Second Division and were looking to cut their wage bill. Six started his Villa career in style, crossing for Peter Withe to open the scoring in a 3–0 win over Manchester United in October 1984. However, a series of poor results, including some truly shocking ones, meant that Villa went into 1985 in sixth-bottom position in the First Division.

Turner was unable to buy players until he had sold others, so his first year at the club was spent carefully assessing the playing staff. The only significant new addition to the first team that season, other than Six, was Tony Dorigo, a player who had joined the club as a youth. An 18-year-old Australian, the left-back was particularly impressive in his skilful overlapping. 'I would hope that we will be able to strengthen the staff soon,' said Turner at the end of 1984. 'Money has been tight and I've been determined only to sign players who will be an improvement on what we have got. All the while that has been going on we have been slowly sorting the staff out.'

There was enough quality in the Villa side to ensure that their First Division place was secure long before the end of the season. They finished tenth in the First Division. Again the team had failed to secure a European place. That, however, became academic a few weeks later. The tragic deaths of 39 Italian fans at the 1985 European Cup final between Liverpool and Juventus led to English clubs receiving an indefinite ban from European competition.

Turner forced to rebuild

Six was dissatisfied with the contract offered to him by Villa at the end of the 1984–85 season. He had also found it difficult to adjust to the English game, where his clever, intricate skills often looked out of place. Six returned to Mulhouse on a free transfer in the summer of 1985. Within days of Six' last appearance for Villa in April 1985 another

Experienced midfielder Gordon Cowans was fit to return to the Villa team for the 1984–85 season and there was further good news for the supporters when Holte End favourite Gary Shaw, who had been linked with a move to Manchester United, signed a new two-year contract with the club. However, in September Shaw underwent his fourth operation in a year, an injury to his right knee requiring extensive surgery and a five-night stay in hospital. Villa were without his skills throughout the season. He would, in total, have six knee operations; four on one knee, two on the other.

winger, a 17-year-old called Tony Daley, made an eye-catching debut in a 5–2 home win over QPR. Daley signed a three-year contract with Villa in the summer of 1985.

Paul Rideout had been Villa's top scorer in the 1984–85 season with 15 goals in League and cup but in the summer of 1985 he and Gordon Cowans were transferred to Bari, an Italian Serie A club, for a combined fee of £850,000. Two goals from Rideout in that match with QPR had prompted Bari to add his purchase to their original target of Cowans. Steve McMahon, a key midfielder along with Cowans, left for Liverpool for a £375,000 fee.

With so much talent leaving the club, Turner's replacements would have to be good ones. With some of the incoming cash, Turner purchased Steve Hodge, an industrious midfielder, from Nottingham Forest for £400,000 and Andy Gray, from Everton, for a fee of £150,000. Now 29, the striker had been outstanding for Everton in the 1984–85 season as they won the First Division and the European Cup Winners' Cup. He would replace Peter Withe who moved to Sheffield United on a free transfer. 'We've got a very young squad at Villa,' said Gray, 'just as the side at Everton was very young. They grew up very quickly and the lads at Villa Park will have to do the same. Hopefully, the little bit of experience I can bring them will help.' Other than Evans, 27, and Spink, 26, all of the other members of Villa's first-team pool were in their early twenties. The team that Saunders and Barton had built was now no more. Nigel Spink remained between the posts for Villa, but he had his doubts about the wholesale team rebuilding which had taken place under Turner. 'I felt a little a bit that the team that had won the European Cup was broken up a little bit too early. Graham Turner had his own ideas about the team but I felt some of those players he let go still had more to offer the club,' says the goalkeeper.

Dark days for football

The backlash from Heysel, combined with the general decline in attendances, saw English football at an all-time loveless low. Villa suffered with everyone else. Their first home match of the 1985–86 season was with Liverpool. Normally one of the fixtures of the season, it attracted a crowd of only 20,197. For Villa's next two home games,

Opposite: Billy McNeill acknowledged that taking over a struggling Aston Villa side in 1986 was a gamble. His tenure at Villa Park proved the most difficult and challenging period of a long and distinguished career in football.

Tony Daley displays his exquisite balance and control of the ball. His fascinating wing play brightened many an afternoon for Villa fans in the late 1980s and early 1990s. Daley's success was all the more celebrated by the Villa faithful as he was a local boy, from Aston. His pace, unpredictability and clever goals would earn him seven England caps.

Right: Graham Taylor's thorough organisational skills revitalised Villa during the late 1980s although he, like McNeill, found himself with a battle on his hands to stay clear of relegation.

United, the lowest 8,456 for the meeting with Southampton.

Old Bhoy is Villa's new man

Turner made two other major signings during the season: Simon Stainrod, a forward, from Sheffield Wednesday for £250,000 and Paul Elliott, a centre-back, from Luton Town for £400,000. Stainrod finished the season as the club's top scorer with 10 goals in the League and 11 in the League Cup. His League Cup goals took Villa to the semi-finals, where they lost on aggregate to Oxford United. In the First Division, however, Villa finished the season in 16th position, just three points above the relegation places. Some of Turner's signings had taken a considerable time to settle at Villa. The loss of McMahon and Cowans had left the midfield badly depleted.

Turner spent £1,000,000 to strengthen the spine of his team for the 1986–87 season, signing Martin Keown, a central defender, from Arsenal, Neale Cooper, a central midfielder, from Aberdeen, and Garry Thompson, a striker, from Sheffield Wednesday. Villa suffered five defeats in their opening six matches of the season, leaving the club bottom of the First Division. On the day after the fifth of those setbacks, a 6–0 defeat at Nottingham Forest, Graham Turner was dismissed. 'I always had a good relationship with the chairman,' said the departing Turner. 'He sacked me and then we talked about my successor. If I had a choice it would be Billy McNeill. I feel he is the right man for the job.'

McNeill it was – on 22 September 1986 he was appointed Aston Villa manager. McNeill was best-known to British football fans as the captain of the Celtic side that had won the European Cup in 1967. He had managed Clyde and Aberdeen before returning to Celtic Park where, as Celtic manager from 1978 to 1983, he had won three Scottish League titles, one Scottish Cup and one League Cup. McNeill then moved to Manchester City where he won promotion to the First Division in 1984–85, his second season at the club. As he left Maine Road for Villa Park in September 1986, Manchester City were 15th in the First Division. 'It's a totally new experience for me to come into a club when the season has started, without

with QPR and Luton Town, crowds of little over 10,000 turned up on each occasion. The club would average 15,237 over the League season, the highest attendance being 27,626 for the match with Manchester

the benefit of the summer preparations,' said McNeill. 'During the close season you can get to know the players so much better as well as your way about the place. But my first impressions have been encouraging. There isn't an awful lot wrong with the appetite and attitude of the players in training. Their confidence has simply taken an awful hammering because of the results.'

McNeill's greatest strength as a manager was his motivational skill. By late November the fresh impetus he brought to the club saw them move up to 16th position in the First Division. On 29 November, however, a brief switch to a sweeper system was cut short with a 4–0 home defeat to Arsenal. Keown, the sweeper, had started the scoring with an own goal. It was the end of Villa's brief resurgence. McNeill tried other positional changes and means of freshening up the team but things did not improve. Villa were not only poor defensively, they were also struggling to score goals. Thompson worked hard without scoring success, while Shaw and Gray had injury-disrupted seasons. Allan Evans finished the season as Villa's top scorer with eight goals in all competitions.

England international midfielder Steve Hodge, who had issued a transfer request within days of Turner's dismissal, moved on to Tottenham Hotspur for £400,000 in December 1986. McNeill, who, like Turner, was unable to buy before selling, now had some money to spend on new players. His first signing for the club was Warren Aspinall, a 19-year-old centre-forward who had made just eight substitute appearances in the First Division and cost £200,000 from Everton. However, by the time Aspinall made his debut in late February 1987, Villa were back in the bottom two and heading for the Second Division.

They finished the season bottom of the First Division. McNeill was sacked on 8 May, the day before the team played their final match of the season, at Old Trafford. His eight months in charge was the shortest tenure of all Villa's managers. 'I knew this was a daunting task when I took over,' said McNeill, 'but I don't think anyone appreciated the size of it. When a big club like Villa starts to slide, it's difficult to stop. I always knew there would not be a quick and simple solution.'

Alan McInally rushes to the Villa fans after scoring against Millwall in a 2–2 draw on the opening day of the 1988–89 season. Andy Gray and Gordon Cowans attempt to catch up with the scorer. Known as 'Rambo' because of his hard-running, committed style of play, McInally scored a total of 22 goals to finish as Villa's leading scorer that season. He moved to Bayern Munich in the summer of 1989 for a £1,100,000 fee.

Taylor fits the bill

Taylor's team takes shape

Derek Mountfield joined Villa in 1988 and spent his first season with the club alternating between full-back and centre-back. For the 1989–90 season he became established at the centre of defence alongside Kent Nielsen and Paul McGrath. That three-man partnership afforded Villa high security in defence. It also provided Mountfield with a springboard to make forward runs, which brought him eight goals over the season.

Ron Atkinson again appeared poised to take over, but a fortnight after McNeill's dismissal Graham Taylor became Aston Villa's third manager within nine months. Taylor had been forced to end his playing career with Lincoln City at the age of 28 because of injury. He had then taken over as manager and had led Lincoln into the Third Division in 1976. Taylor moved on to Watford in 1977 and took the Hertfordshire club from the Fourth to the First Division in five years. He then led the Hornets to a runners-up position in 1982–83 and the FA Cup final in 1984. Taylor's assistant would be Steve Harrison, who came with him from Watford. 'I'm not saying we will get back at the first time of asking,' said the new manager. 'The Second Division will be very tough but I want us to establish ourselves as the team to beat. We must have desire and passion. If we achieve that, the supporters will take us the rest of the way. So often, managers take a job and ask supporters to be patient. How on earth can I do that when Villa were European champions only five years ago?'

One of Taylor's initial tasks was to rebuild the Villa defence. This was a compulsory matter as full-backs Tony Dorigo and Gary Williams were leaving the club; Dorigo for Chelsea, Williams for Leeds United. Paul Elliott had moved to Pisa of the Italian League for £400,000. New centre-backs Steve Sims, from Watford, David Hunt, from Notts County, and Mark Lillis, from Derby County, were purchased for a total sum of £180,000. Kevin Gage, a right-back, cost £110,000 from Wimbledon; Bernard Gallacher, a left-back, stepped up from the reserves. Stainrod and Gray had both left the club by the beginning of the 1987–88 season. A new striker arrived in the shape of Alan McInally, who cost £225,000 from Celtic.

Taylor maintained a settled side throughout the season, especially in defence and in midfield. Villa again became a difficult side to beat. Two lengthy unbeaten runs in the League, each consisting of 12 games, saw Villa steadily accumulate points towards promotion. Taylor, who had described the state

of the club as 'a shambles' shortly after his arrival, instilled discipline in the players. For home games, the first-team was expected to report to the ground at 10.00am so that they could focus their minds on the game ahead. A morning jogging and stretching session would find Taylor giving the players the benefit of his views on the match which was to come. Taylor's ordered approach was appreciated by the Villa players. 'Graham Taylor reorganised the club. The club was on a slippery slope, not just at first-team level,' remembers Taylor's goalkeeper Nigel Spink. 'Footballers appreciate being organised and having everything done for them so that they can get on with their football and not have anything to distract them from it. Graham, who was one of the best club managers that I've played under, introduced those conditions to the club. I think they are benefiting now from the stability he gave the club.'

On the final day of the season a 0–0 draw at Swindon Town appeared likely to leave Villa in third position in the division. That would have put them into the recently introduced First/Second Division play-offs where they would have been one of four teams competing for a single First Division place. Then news came through that Middlesbrough

had lost their final match, which meant that Villa were promoted as runners-up to John Docherty's Millwall.

Among Taylor's mid-season signings in the Second Division had been David Platt, an attacking midfielder, from Crewe Alexandra for £200,000; Andy Gray, a midfielder, from Crystal Palace for £150,000; and Stuart Gray, a forward, from Barnsley for £175,000. For the First Division, Taylor would rely largely on the same corps of players who had brought the club promotion, but there would be some important additions to his team. Chris Price, a right-back signed from Blackburn Rovers, replaced Gage, who moved into central defence. Derek Mountfield, a centre-back, joined Villa from Everton. Gordon Cowans returned to the club from Bari.

'Graham Taylor was probably the most thorough manager I've ever played under,' says Cowans. 'He would know everything about the opposition, not only as individuals but their strengths as a team, the way they played, what they would do at set-pieces. He left nothing to chance. He got the best out of players by playing to their strengths. With the players we had at Villa Park at the time, that meant a passing game, not a long-ball game.'

Below left: Kent Nielsen a dependable Danish international, was signed by Graham Taylor for £500,000 in July 1989. Over the following two seasons he rarely missed a game, a tackle or a header.

Below: A Villa attack during a pre-season match with Hibernian in August 1989 sees Derek Mountfield (left) and Paul McGrath (centre) join their forwards to put pressure on the Hibs defence. McGrath had become the best-paid player in Villa's history that summer when he agreed terms that would see him earn £2,000 per week.

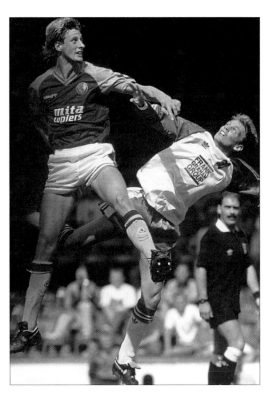

Ian Ormondroyd uses his six feet four inches to best effect as he challenges for the ball in the air with Hibernian's Gordon Hunter. A centre-forward with Bradford City, Ormondroyd was switched to the left wing by Graham Taylor, one of several changes the manager made to enliven his team early in the 1989–90 season.

were particularly expert at making effective runs at defences from deep and this helped bring the duo a combined total of 27 goals, 14 in the League, by the end of December. Between then and the club's final match of the season, at home to Coventry City, they managed only a further five League goals between them. Goals were not forthcoming from other members of the team. It meant that Villa drifted downwards in the League.

Going into their final fixture, only a victory over Coventry would guarantee Villa's First Division status. The match ended 1–1 on a fractious afternoon when 57 arrests were made inside Villa Park. Villa now had to watch and wait for other results. Ten days after Villa's final match, relegation rivals West Ham United lost 5–1 at Liverpool and Villa lived to fight another season in the First Division. They would do so without Alan McInally, who was transferred to Bayern Munich for £1,100,000. Ian Olney, a 19-year-old, took over at centre-forward.

Goal drought

Villa had a good first half of the season in 1988–89 with Platt and McInally forming an exciting partnership in attack. Both players

Back in the title hunt

The final days of the following season would prove equally tense but this time it would be through the fine tension of a championship chase. In mid-February 1990, a 1–0 win over Sheffield Wednesday at Villa Park left Villa second in the First Division, one point behind Liverpool with two games in hand. Champions Arsenal, in third place, were seven points behind Villa. In the summer of 1989 Taylor had strengthened the defence. The experienced Paul McGrath, a 29-year-old Irish international centre-back, was signed from Manchester United, and Kent Nielsen, a 27-year-old Danish international, arrived from Brondby. Martin Keown had moved to Everton for £750,000.

'We are not the sort of side who do stupid and careless things when we are defending and we do have the players who can break,' said Taylor. 'Nielsen is the nearest thing to what you might call an old-fashioned centre-half. We all recognise McGrath's ability as a defender – he's capable of so many different tasks – and these two players allow Mountfield to occasionally go forward and contribute to the play up front. It's a very solid foundation and something that means a lot to the team.'

127

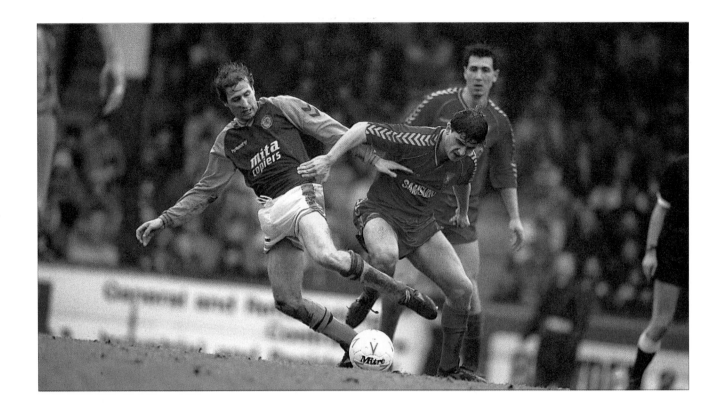

Tactical changes

A poor start to the 1989–90 season had made Taylor radically rethink the formation of his team. He remodelled it, using the skills of his players to best effect. 'Sometimes managers and coaches must be prepared to observe and discover what players like doing and what they are good at doing,' said Taylor. The new system was founded on the skills of the three tall, dominating centre-backs – McGrath, Nielsen and Mountfield. Mountfield told the author, in an interview for *Inside Football* magazine, in the spring of 1990: 'Paul McGrath was a bargain at £450,000. He is the best centre-half with dodgy knees in the business! Kent Nielsen took a while to settle into the hurly-burly of English football but both he and Paul McGrath have over 30 caps – they're quality players. The manager put the three of us together and the system clicked. All three of us are fairly orthodox centre-backs. I sometimes drop back behind the other two but I won't play in that position for the full 90 minutes.'

The most fascinating aspect of Villa's tactics during that 1989–90 season was that they were playing a WM formation, albeit an updated version for the 1990s. The three half-backs – Nielsen, McGrath and Mountfield – formed solid support for five attackers. The two wide players in the front line, Ian Ormondroyd and

Tony Daley, were markedly different. Daley was close in style to a traditional winger, blessed with beautiful balance that allowed him to right himself instantaneously as he coasted clear of tackles before accelerating with the effortless grace of a thoroughbred. His speed could carry him deep into danger areas at will. Mountfield said: 'Tony has to be one of the fastest wingers in the First Division. The manager has been coaching him closely, trying to get him to slow down a bit just before he crosses the ball.' Ormondroyd, six feet four inches tall, was playing wide on the left, adding his skills to the attack by making well-timed, late runs into the box.

In the centre of the attack, Platt was using his acceleration, exceptional control and heading power to break into the penalty area from the midfield to optimum effect. Ian Olney, a 20-year-old, willingly made numerous runs in the centre-forward position, but he struggled to score in his first season of top-class football. Cowans, meanwhile, was as steadily influential as ever. With the speed of Platt and Daley, the height of Ormondroyd and the runs from deep by Mountfield for him to look for, Cowans had a variety of targets to hit with his accurate passes. He rarely failed to select the best option.

'Tony Daley has been mature enough to listen and learn from the manager and his

Gordon Cowans works the ball away from Wimbledon midfielder Vaughan Ryan but in this home League match, in February 1990, Villa would lose 3–0. The defeat knocked Villa off the top of the League and was the first of several setbacks that would leave their championship hopes in tatters.

David Platt breaks forward to start a Villa attack. Platt's piercing runs into opposing penalty areas frequently ended with the ball being despatched into the back of the net. He was Villa's leading goalscorer in the 1989–90 season although the team became over-reliant on Platt to put the ball in the net. Had he been paired with an equally prolific goalscoring partner, Villa might have sustained their title challenge to the end of the season.

crossing has improved,' said Mountfield. 'He, Ormondroyd and Ian Olney have all shown great maturity in adapting to the way the manager wants them to play. They've all been great in the way they've taken on responsibility and worked at their game.'

Title hopes fade

A 2–0 victory at Tottenham Hotspur in late February put Villa on top of the First Division. However, consecutive defeats by Wimbledon and Coventry City eroded the advantage Villa had held over Liverpool in terms of games in hand. They were still top when they went to Crystal Palace in late March but a flat performance led to a 1–0 defeat. Villa were knocked off the top spot and a series of indifferent results in the remaining weeks of the season presented the title to Liverpool.

Villa finished nine points behind the Anfield side in second place in the First Division. There was still cause for optimism, and many pundits believed that this team could go one better in its second season together. The players and supporters also had European competition to look forward to once again. English clubs were readmitted to UEFA's competitions for the 1990–91 season and Villa's second place in the League guaranteed them entry to the UEFA Cup.

A few weeks after Villa's final League fixture, David Platt – wearing England colours in Bologna, Italy – swung his right boot to volley a ball delivered to him by Paul Gascoigne. The resultant goal saw England knock Belgium out of the World Cup and helped engender an unexpected revival of interest in English football that would go a long way towards ensuring that the game would undergo radical changes during the 1990s. That summer, other England business would have a more immediate effect on Aston Villa. Bobby Robson completed his time as England manager and his place was taken by Graham Taylor. Villa were now looking for a new manager and the 1990 World Cup would also have a strong bearing on that particular aspect of Villa's future.

The 1990s proved to be one of the most exciting decades in Villa's history, with Wembley victories and regular European football. As the millennium approached, Villa's future looked safe in the hands of John Gregory.

9 New Football, New Villa: the 1990s

Aston Villa began the 1990s with a radical gambit. In the summer of 1990 they became the first club in England's top division to entrust an individual from outside the British Isles with the management of their playing affairs. The appointee in question was Doctor Jozef Venglos, a Czechoslovakian who had a university doctorate in philosophy and physical education and who could speak four languages. His achievements as a coach in international football made him equally qualified as a footballing thinker.

Venglos' most recent triumph had been to guide the Czechoslovakian national team to the quarter-finals of the 1990 World Cup, where they had lost unluckily by 1–0 to the eventual world champions West Germany. A distinguished midfielder with Slovan Bratislava, Venglos, 53, had moved into management with the same club, twice winning the Czechoslovakian League title and once winning the cup. In 1976 he had been assistant to Vaclav Jezek when Czechoslovakia had won the European Championship.

Venglos had spent two periods in charge of the Czechoslokian national side: 1978–82 and 1987–90. During each of his spells in charge, he had succeeded in winning his country a place in the World Cup finals, in 1982 and in 1990. In 1980 he had taken the Czechs to third place in the European Championship. He had also worked as a coach in Australia, Malaysia, Indonesia and in Portugal, with Sporting Lisbon.

The appointment of Venglos was a daringly imaginative move on the part of the Villa board and chairman Doug Ellis, a move that had the potential to widen the horizons of English football. With the lifting of the European ban in 1990, Villa and Manchester United, England's only two representatives in European competition, would have to adjust to the more sophisticated demands of continental fixtures.

Football back in fashion

Football, in that summer of 1990, was enjoying renewed popularity after the English national team's incident-packed journey to the semi-finals of the 1990 World Cup. People old and young, male and female, had been gripped by the action. When the English squad returned to Luton Airport, a crowd of 100,000 welcomed them home. It was important for the clubs to draw on this positive mood and make sure it lasted by attracting the new potential audience to the delights of League football. This was unlikely to happen if the new fans were presented with the sight of two teams wrestling for the ball rather than manipulating it in the skilful fashion that they had seen during the World Cup. Villa's appointment of Venglos appeared to be a major step in the right direction. The strength of his Czechoslovakian teams had been the intelligent shuttling of the ball at speed and with high precision on ground level.

Villa also had an added attraction in comparison to most other English clubs. They possessed three players who had enjoyed leading roles in the World Cup: David Platt of England and Paul McGrath and Tony Cascarino of the Republic of Ireland. Cascarino, a tall, powerfully built striker, had been signed by Graham Taylor from Millwall for a club record fee of £1,500,000 in the spring of 1990. Taylor had hoped

Dalian Atkinson prods the ball into the Manchester United net for Villa's opening goal in the 1994 League Cup final.

131

Cascarino would supply a stream of goals to help take Villa to the 1989–90 title. The forward had played in Villa's final ten fixtures but struggled to find the goalscoring form that had brought him 42 goals in two and a half seasons with Millwall. At the end of the campaign, Cascarino had managed just two goals, one in each of Villa's last two games of the season.

Early homecoming for Venglos

Venglos' first European excursion as manager of Aston Villa would be considerably less exotic for him than for the other members of the Villa party. The draw for the first round of the UEFA Cup paired Villa with Banik Ostrava, one of the tournament's entrants from Venglos' homeland. Before that, however, Venglos would be introduced to the less familiar demands of League football.

'British players are changing,' he said a week before the season began. 'Those such as Platt and Daley are more flexible, skilful players, with aesthetic feelings. Our boys have confidence that they're able to compete with the best in England. Through our training sessions we can try to adapt, bring something that is a little different to them. When I worked for Slovan Bratislava and Sporting Lisbon they had to be in Europe, and it's the same here. I was in charge for 76 games as manager of Czechoslovakia, including two World Cups, so I know about pressure.'

Cascarino scored in Villa's opening League game, a 1–1 draw at home to Southampton that was watched by a near-30,000 crowd. 'If I could have found the net more regularly Villa might have run Liverpool much closer for the title last season,' admitted the Irish international. 'I should have scored more goals. Then it might have been a different story.' It would, however, be another difficult season for Cascarino. He would score just nine League goals for Villa; Platt would again be the main source of goals for the club.

As Villa visited Czechoslovakia for the second leg of their UEFA Cup tussle with Banik Ostrava they were 11th in the First Division. They were, however, nicely poised in the UEFA Cup tie, having constructed a 3–1 lead at Villa Park.

Doctor Jozef Venglos, who took control of the team in 1990, introduced new ideas on players' positional play, diets and approach to the game.

UEFA Cup date with Internazionale

Shortly before half-time in Czechoslovakia, Radin Necas, a Banik forward, stepped up to take a free-kick. The ball flew from his foot and went skipping past Spink to take the home side within a goal of Villa on aggregate. Early in the second half, Mountfield screwed the ball into the Banik net from close range to make it 1–1. When Ivo Stas, Banik's centre-back, headed a Cowans free-kick past his own goalkeeper the tie was finished, in Villa's favour. The second round offered Villa a more sumptuous stage for their talents – the San Siro, Milan. Villa were drawn to play the first leg there, against

Internazionale, who share the 80,000-capacity stadium with AC Milan. However, with AC Milan drawn at home to Club Bruges in the European Cup on the same night, the first leg of the Inter-Villa tie was switched to Villa Park.

The Inter side contained five of the Italian internationals who had reached that year's World Cup semi-finals, together with three of the dominant members of the German team that had won the trophy: Jurgen Klinsmann, Lothar Matthaus and Andreas Brehme. With Platt and Cascarino fielded by Villa, the spirit of Italia 90 lived on that October night at Villa Park and, despite the match being live on television, a crowd of almost 37,000 was present. McGrath, unfortunately, was injured. Andy Comyn, who had made only five previous appearances for Villa, took his place alongside Nielsen and Mountfield in central defence.

Villa accelerated into attack from the start and went close to scoring several times. After a quarter of an hour, Paul Birch crossed for Cascarino. He played the ball to Nielsen who lashed a shot past Walter Zenga, the Inter goalkeeper, to put Villa 1–0 ahead. Midway through the second half, a Cowans pass fluttered through the air before dropping neatly for Platt to send the ball past Zenga. The score remained unchanged after that. The 2–0 win had been achieved against an Inter side who had attacked with verve throughout the evening. All the Italians'

efforts had been repelled successfully by Villa. They had used the pace of Daley and Platt to hit back on the break in Villa's traditional European fashion. It was as if they had never been away.

Home European ties, even against England's finest, do not always guarantee massive crowds for Internazionale. The Italian side had, however, switched their first round tie against Rapid Vienna to Verona because of the appalling condition of the pitch in the San Siro. As compensation to their fans, they had offered those who travelled to Verona free tickets for the match with Villa. This, together with the finely balanced nature of the tie, produced a 75,000 crowd for the second leg.

The crowd created a screeching cacophony of noise inside the stadium. Inter quickly branded their mark on the game, Klinsmann putting them 1–0 ahead shortly after the start. On the hour, Nicola Berti brought Inter level on aggregate. With a quarter of an hour remaining, Alessandro Bianchi put the ball in the Villa net for the third time although when Fausto Pizzi had crossed to him the ball had appeared to be out of play. Villa, however, had been thoroughly outmanoeuvred. 'The third goal might have been dodgy,' said David Platt, 'but even if it had been disallowed they would still have got another. We know we didn't play well. If we had, we would still be in the competition.'

Kent Nielsen (fourth left) elegantly swings a leg to connect with the ball and send Villa into the lead in their 1990 UEFA Cup meeting with Internazionale of Milan at Villa Park.

Domestic decline

One of Venglos' more notable innovations that season was the introduction of mineral and vitamin supplements to the players' diets. He also cut out the half-time cup of tea. He believed that if tea was taken while a player's adrenaline levels were high it acted as a depressant on the muscles.

Villa were in ninth place in the First Division as they turned their thoughts back to domestic competition following the UEFA Cup adventure. In the wake of the Inter defeat, Villa took seven League points from a possible 24. The team struggled throughout the remainder of the season, finishing 19th, fourth-bottom, just four points above the bottom three relegated clubs.

The closing games in the First Division programme had seen Villa concede five goals twice in successive matches. On the Monday after a 5–2 defeat at Leeds United, David Platt was in Bari, Italy, for a look around the facilities at that town's football club. At a press conference, the Italian club announced that they were on the verge of signing him.

Platt heads back to Italy

Platt, with 22 goals (including eight penalties), had been Villa's top scorer over the 1990–91 season. He would move to Bari that summer for a stunning fee of £5,500,000. This was £4,000,000 more than Villa's previous record sale: Andy Gray to Wolves in 1979. Some brightness had been shone on the situation two days after Platt's visit to Italy. Villa finally secured their First Division place with a 2–1 home win over Norwich City. Dwight Yorke, a talented 19-year-old forward who had left the St Clairs club in Trinidad and Tobago to join Villa, scored the winning goal, his second for the club.

Venglos went on Villa's two-week end-of-season tour of Malaysia but on his return to Villa Park it was announced that his two-year contract had been terminated. Known affectionately as 'Gentleman Jo', he had endeared himself to the people at Villa Park. 'I came to Villa because I had a reputation for achievement,' he had said shortly before the end of his time at the club. 'To have been at the epicentre of English football has been an honour and a privilege. I'm happy that I came and wiser for the experience. I believe that I could get a job anywhere in football. I have been widely described as an honest, gentlemanly person. This is very nice but I would much prefer to make an impression as a successful coach here.'

Gordon Cowans remembers that season well. 'The appointment of Jo Venglos was a total shock to us all. Nobody, honestly, knew him. He was really up against it, being the first foreign manager, coming in with his ideas on how to play the game and with strict ideas on the way players should live – for example he didn't particularly like people going out drinking. I liked his ideas and the way he wanted to play the game but trying to put that over to us British players, with the mentality we've got, was very difficult. I think that's the reason it didn't work. I think we were very set in our ways. Yet now you see so many foreign managers coming in, changing things and doing well.

'Maybe if he had had another year he might have done better but in the first year we struggled. You can't really knock Jo Venglos for what he did because I thought he had some very good ideas and I agreed with the way he wanted to play the game. So in the end you've got to look at the players and think, "Did they let him down?" And I think in the end we probably did by not really giving him the chance to instil those ideas into us and play the game the way he wanted us to.

'He thought we weren't very fluent at all as a side and that people couldn't adapt to different situations. If we ended up in a different position to our own he wanted us to sit there and fill in. If a left-sided midfield player ended up on the right wing, for example, he wanted them to just adapt to that and fill in there. We always wanted to get back to our starting position. That is something you are brought up to do as kids: get back to your starting position, get your shape. He was also trying to coax us into playing a short passing game rather than a long passing game. I think he really needed more time to work with us and get his ideas over to us. He was a lovely fellow, a really, really nice fellow. It was hard on him that it worked out the way it did.'

Nigel Spink comments: 'When Graham left there was a little bit of instability again. Jo Venglos knew his stuff but foreign footballers are a lot more disciplined. They will go home and eat pasta and drink water whereas British players tend to be go-out-on-a-Saturday-night merchants. I did that all my career and I don't regret it. I don't think it affected my game at all although things are changing nowadays with the demands of the Premier League and young players are approaching the game differently. There was a lot more technical stuff with Jozef. The actual set-up of play was a lot more technical. But when players start getting doubts in their minds and start talking among themselves in the dressing-room there are problems. Doug Ellis realised that and pulled the plug. Fair play to Jozef. He came over and had a go at introducing his methods.'

Ron Atkinson: a return to British methods

Doug Ellis, stung into conservatism by the failure of what he described as 'an experiment' now announced that he was looking for an 'experienced British manager'. It was a description that fitted perfectly Ron Atkinson, whom Ellis approached in late May 1991 with a lucrative contract. Atkinson, the manager of Sheffield Wednesday, appeared on the verge of accepting Villa's offer as he attended Hillsborough for a meeting with his chairman.

After a three-hour discussion, however, Atkinson announced that he was remaining with the Yorkshire club, stating that he had decided to stay with Wednesday because they were 'the best club I have ever worked for. I must be barmy to think of leaving.' Within days, Atkinson had changed his mind and had joined Villa as manager, provoking fury among Wednesday fans. As the reason for his decision, he said he wished to cease making a daily 200-mile round-trip to Sheffield. Atkinson lived in the elegant Birmingham suburb of Barnt Green. Villa had also made him an improved offer of £750,000 over his four-year contract.

Atkinson had been on Villa's books as a teenager but had failed to make the breakthrough into the first-team. His 20-year managerial career had begun at Kettering Town, whom he had twice taken to the Southern League championship. During his four years at Cambridge United the club had won the Fourth Division title. At WBA, between 1978 and 1981, he had put together a fine side, one which had challenged for the League championship. His

Ron Atkinson's vigorous, enthusiastic approach to the manager's job revitalised Villa in the early 1990s. Soon Villa were challenging again for the English game's top trophies.

achievements attracted Manchester United, with whom he won two FA Cups.

However, after failing to bring the First Division title to Old Trafford he was dismissed in October 1986. Thereafter, Atkinson had brief stints at WBA and Atletico Madrid before he had joined Wednesday in 1989. During the 1990–91 season Wednesday had won the League Cup, their first post-war trophy. They had also finished third in the Second Division to win promotion after being relegated in Atkinson's first season at the club. 'I haven't come here to mess around,' said Atkinson on his arrival at Villa Park. 'Villa are potentially as big a club as you can get and my intention is to build a successful team.'

Ron rings the changes

Atkinson brought in Andy Gray as his assistant, replacing Peter Withe, who had performed that function for Jozef Venglos. Gray had been working as a football commentator with Sky TV, the new satellite channel. The new manager, who came with a reputation as a big spender, immediately broke the club's transfer record with the purchase of Dalian Atkinson, a former Wednesday striker who had been with Real Sociedad of Spain, for £1,600,000.

Steve Staunton, an Irish international left-back, cost £1,100,000 from Liverpool. Bournemouth were paid £300,000 for Shaun Teale, a centre-back. Kevin Richardson, an experienced central midfielder who had been at Real Sociedad with Dalian Atkinson, cost £450,000. Paul Mortimer, a left-sided midfielder, cost £500,000 from Charlton Athletic. Striker Cyrille Regis arrived from Coventry City to play alongside Dalian Atkinson.

On 17 August, as Villa lined up for their first League match of the season, there were six changes to the team that Venglos had put out for the final fixture of the previous season. The team formation had also changed. While Venglos had retained Graham Taylor's players and his 3-5-2 system, Atkinson reverted to 4-4-2. During the season, Ron Atkinson would again break the club transfer record in signing Earl Barrett, a right-sided defender, from Oldham Athletic for £1,700,000. He would also purchase Garry Parker, to play alongside Richardson in central midfield, from Nottingham Forest for £650,000.

Atkinson's extensive spending silenced the previously loudening grumbles that Villa was a parsimonious club unwilling to pay the price necessary to compete at the highest level. Galvanised by the new manager and signings, Villa finished seventh in the First Division in the 1991–92 season.

Richardson, who had been a championship winner with Arsenal in 1989, proved a cool captain. From his position in front of the two centre-backs, his forward momentum and incisive passing constantly nudged Villa forward. Yorke established himself in the side, chiefly playing in a wide-left position. He finished the season as top scorer with 17 goals in 35 League and cup appearances. His instantaneous control, quickness and accuracy allowed him to score from all angles and distances and he was equally adept with foot and head at landing the ball in the net. His distinguishing characteristic was his decisiveness, his instinctive ability to know exactly what was required in any given situation and his ability to act on it without hesitation. 'Dwight Yorke is a hugely talented player,' says Nigel Spink. 'I've seen him in the dressing-room standing in a bin keeping the ball up 100 times with his head when it was impossible for him to move his feet. The other players would bet him he couldn't do it but he would always succeed.'

Tony Daley was another who found the new manager's emphasis on attack to be to his liking and he turned in some of this best performances in a Villa shirt over that 1991–92 season. Veteran striker Cyrille Regis scored some spectacular goals. The form of Regis almost made up for the absence of Dalian Atkinson, who had missed much of the season through injury. Dalian's injury problems led to a strained relationship between him and manager Ron Atkinson.

A new league is formed

Away from the League, an engaging FA Cup run had ended with a 1–0 defeat from Liverpool at Anfield in the quarter-finals. Villa's average crowd over the season was just under 25,000, a slight drop on 1990–91, but a near-32,000 crowd was at Villa Park on the final day of the 1991–92 season. The sup-

Steve Staunton, a left-back, was one of several Republic of Ireland internationals who graced the Villa shirt in the 1990s. Ray Houghton, Andy Townsend and Paul McGrath also filled the Irish jersey in the World Cups of 1990 and 1994.

porters saw smartly taken headers from Yorke and Regis give Villa a 2–0 win over Coventry City.

The scene on that sun-bathed day at Villa Park would surely have gladdened the heart of William McGregor. After 104 years, his idea of league football retained enormous appeal for the public. That summer of 1992, however, a series of meetings among the chairmen of England's leading clubs resulted in a collective decision to quit the Football League that had been established by McGregor and their predecessors. They were not about to abandon league competi-

tion altogether. Instead, a new league, the FA Premier League, was to be established. Instead of league competition among the leading 22 clubs being administered by the Football League it would be run by a branch of the Football Association.

Chairmen of the First Division clubs had been discussing a breakaway move since the 1980s. They wished to harness television money for themselves instead of having to share it among the 92 Football League clubs. The impetus behind the final severance from the smaller clubs in 1992 came because of the irresistible sums of money on offer from Sky television for an exclusive deal.

Sky, owned by the Australian Rupert Murdoch, had begun transmitting programmes to Britain in 1989. By 1992, obtaining the rights to top-class English football was seen by Sky's executives as the perfect vehicle to drive up sales of satellite decoders, dishes and subscriptions. In return for exclusive rights to broadcast two live Premier League matches per week – one on a Sunday afternoon, the other on a Monday evening – SKY would pay the top 22 English clubs £304,000,000 over the following five seasons.

At the end of each season, clubs in the Premier League would receive a payment, the size of which depended upon their position in the League – the champions would be given £848,000, the club in 22nd place £38,000. Every time a club appeared in a live match, it would be paid a further £78,000. Such regular, large amounts of television money had never previously been known in the British game.

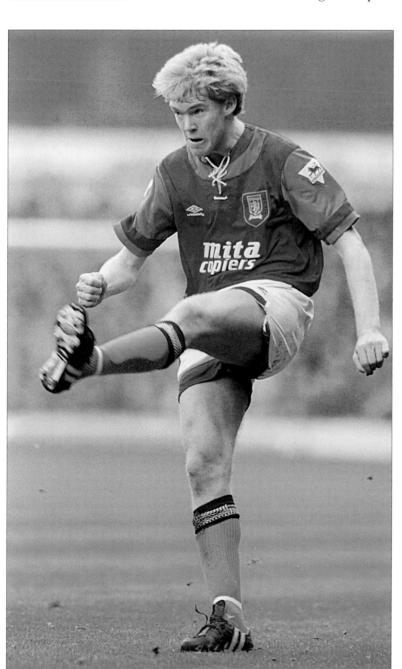

Football's brave new world

To the supporter, initially, little would appear to have changed. Clubs would still be promoted and relegated but instead of dropping into the Second Division they would now go into the First Division of the Football League. Other minor changes would be apparent. Referees, who had traditionally worn all-black, would now wear a green shirt. At the end of the 1994–95 season, four clubs would be relegated with two replacing them, reducing the number of clubs in the Premier League to 20.

Four weekends a season would be free of Premier League fixtures to allow the English national squad extended time together before a midweek match. Instead of two substitutes, teams would now be able to name three replacements, although one would have to be a goalkeeper and only two of the substitutes could be used. Other changes included the half-time interval being extended to a uniform 15 minutes throughout the Premier League. Players would wear a new Premier League badge on the sleeves of their shirts.

FIFA had also been busy that summer, introducing new rules, of which the most far-reaching was the elimination of the kicked backpass, one of the most loved tactics of timewasting teams. It would do much to keep matches flowing, which was helpful for the televised spectacle.

For those watching on television, coverage of football would be more exhaustive than ever before. Filming was now aided by a minimum of 15 new, lightweight cameras at every ground. On the television screen, a clock in the top corner of the picture would let viewers know exactly how much time had expired in the match. Unlike the BBC and Britain's other landbound independent television stations, Sky could devote as much time as it wished to its football programmes. Their Super Sunday programme, for example, would be centred around one live football match but with extensive build-up and post-match analysis the programme would last five hours.

Football followers who were without satellite television would also benefit from the deal. The FA Premier League looked after those supporters' interests by signing a deal with the BBC to broadcast highlights of matches. This led to the welcome revival of Match of the Day, the BBC's Saturday night programme. One immediate result for Villa of Sky's deal was that assistant manager Andy Gray quit his position with the club to return to Sky Sports as its chief football analyst and co-commentator. Jim Barron became Atkinson's new assistant.

The century-old established routine of a match every Saturday during the season was now at an end. For those who had grown up with this, there was some sentimental sadness at its passing, although it was possible to become too maudlin. As a Perthshire man, William McGregor had known all about husbanding resources and his plan for the Football League had been driven by the idea of maximising revenue and improving competition through guaranteed, consistent income. The new league was an adjustment to the conditions and circumstances surrounding football as it approached the 21st century.

Traditional values at Villa Park

There was a concession to sentiment on Villa's part in their selection of a new strip for the 1992–93 season. They were now wearing an old-fashioned shirt with tie-up lacing at the neck. This new jersey was modelled on the one worn by the Villa players of the 1890s. An increasing number of fans

The original steps leading from the dressing-rooms to the pitch remain in place at Villa Park, more than a century after the ground was built. Greats such as Johan Cruyff, Pele, Bobby Moore, George Best, Kenny Dalglish, Franz Beckenbauer, and various Villa maestros, have all made their way down these long looked-after stairs.

were now attending matches wearing replica team shirts. The Villa jerseys retailed at £31.99 for an adult-sized jersey and £24.99 for a child's.

It was widely anticipated that the increased income from the Premier League would result in managers having greater sums to spend on players, including high-profile names from abroad. Ron Atkinson stayed local in mid-1992, returning to his home town, Liverpool, to purchase Ray Houghton, a midfielder, for £850,000. 'I just had a gut feeling about Villa and the title,' said Houghton, 30, an experienced Irish international. 'Money didn't come into it.'

Dalian Atkinson was restored to fitness for the 1992–93 season but with Regis now 34 years old, the manager was looking for a

The Doug Ellis stand rises into view as the players make their way down the tunnel and on to the pitch.

central striking partner for his namesake. The matter was emphasised when Villa's League fixtures began with three 1–1 draws, two defeats and just one victory. After those six matches, Villa were 15th in the new FA Premier League.

Within days, Ron Atkinson had made his third signing from Anfield, breaking the Villa transfer record for a third time with the £2,300,000 purchase of Dean Saunders, a Welsh international striker. Saunders was an immediate success, scoring six goals in his first five matches for Villa. By the first Saturday in November, when they played host to Manchester United, Villa were third in the Premier League, two points behind leaders Arsenal. A crowd of 39,063, Villa Park's biggest of the season, saw the match go to form. Villa were barely troubled by mid-table United all afternoon and a 10th minute goal from Dalian Atkinson gave them a 1–0 win and three points. The score would have been more heavily in Villa's favour had Peter Schmeichel not been out-standing in United's goal.

The team Ron Atkinson had built was beautifully balanced. Both full-backs, Staunton and Barrett, were adept at pushing forward in support of the attackers. At cen-tre-back, the aggressive, highly charged Teale worked well alongside the refined McGrath. Houghton toiled busily on the right-hand side of midfield, harrying opponents into mistakes and running hard at defences. Parker, inside of him, was more deliberate in his actions, selecting and spooning choice passes rather than running with the ball. Richardson pressed when necessary but was equally happy to play an incisive pass when the opportunity arose. With none of the midfielders frequent scorers, the team relied heavily on the front two of Atkinson and Saunders to convert their service into net results.

Villa challenge for new prize

Atkinson had scored 11 League goals and Saunders eight by the turn of the year. However, as 1993 began, Atkinson was again struggling against injury. For the home match with Middlesbrough in mid-January, Saunders was paired with Yorke. The after-noon produced a scintillating 5–1 win and, for the first time, Villa were top of the Premier League. It had been a wonderfully relaxed performance, the players moving the ball with ease, obviously deriving great pleasure from their work. The goals had come from all parts of the team: central defenders McGrath and Teale, Parker and the front two of Yorke and Saunders. 'It's your ambition to sit in the stand and just enjoy it,' said Ron Atkinson afterwards, 'and I could do that today which, if it is not the first time I've ever done it, I can't remember the other occasion.'

In the succeeding weeks, Villa dropped down to second then third, then went back up to second and first again. By March, only three clubs remained in contention for the title: Villa, Norwich City and Manchester United. Four days before their return with Manchester United at Old Trafford, Villa again lost their grip on the leadership when they drew 0–0 at home to Tottenham Hotspur. A crowd of 37,000-plus had turned up that evening. It was a healthy attendance as, in the early 1990s, Britain was going through a severe recession. The club did help ease the strain on the supporters' pockets by frequently offering discounted entry prices, most notably to the Holte End. The average attendance at Villa Park over the season would be close to 30,000.

Mark Bosnich, who had previously been on Manchester United's books, had, in February 1993, taken over from Nigel Spink as Villa's regular goalkeeper. Bosnich, a 21-year-old Australian, had played for United three times but had been unable to obtain a work permit. He had returned to Australia in 1991 where he had played for Sydney Croatia. Having married a British citizen and bought out his contract with the Australian club, he had joined Villa in February 1992.

As they went into the match with United, Villa were second to the Old Trafford side on goal difference; United's goal difference was +24, Villa's +17. Both teams had ten of their 42 fixtures to complete. The match was played on a Sunday afternoon as one of Sky's cherry-picked games. Sky needed all the camera angles their extensive new coverage could provide as the action flashed incessantly from goal to goal. Ten minutes after half-time, Staunton's shot curved from left to right and finished its journey inside a United post. Two minutes later, Bosnich,

who had been in unbeatable form until then, was finally defeated when Hughes' lunging header flew past him. The match ended 1–1.

The chairman's new stand

The club's enthralling present was complemented by its ambitions for the future. On the final day of March 1993, preliminary work began on the foundations of a new stand on the Witton Lane side of the ground. The new, two-tiered edifice, to be named after chairman Doug Ellis, would be open in the 1993–94 season. It would hold 10,000 people and was the first major stage in the club complying with the Taylor Report. Compiled by Lord Justice Taylor, who had headed the inquiry into the Hillsborough Disaster, the report required every Premier League ground to be all-seater, primarily for safety reasons. His requirements had to be fulfilled throughout the land by the beginning of the 1994–95 season. Income from

Mark Bosnich was Villa's regular goalkeeper for the majority of the club's matches in the 1990s. Agile and adept at shot-stopping, the Australian international was also a great improviser, displaying numerous unconventional and entertaining ways of keeping the ball from the net.

Below: The ornate mosaic on the Trinity Road stand's exterior remained proudly in place in the 1990s. The Corner Flag, the club restaurant that has superb views on to the pitch, nestles neatly in the old stand's shadow.

Sky television and government grants would help Villa pay for the work.

At Nottingham Forest in early April, Villa produced a champion performance. Staunton swept a corner-kick on to McGrath's head for the only goal of the game. The win put Villa one point ahead of Manchester United and two clear of Norwich. All three teams had six games left to play. When Villa drew 0–0 at home to Coventry City the following Saturday, United took over from them at the top. Villa

once in the previous 12 games. Atkinson, who had recently returned to the team, had not scored since early December 1992. For a team that relied so heavily on its twin strikers this was a mind-numbing problem. At Ewood Park, Atkinson hit a post in the opening minutes. Then Blackburn scored three times before the half-time break. It remained 3–0 at the end. Gordon Cowans, who had been allowed to join Blackburn for £250,000 in 1991, had been the most creative player on the pitch. 'We have now got

The Trinity Road stand (right) and the Doug Ellis stand (above right) provided comfortable seated accommodation for the 1990s, helping to make Villa Park a welcoming, accessible place for all varieties of supporters.

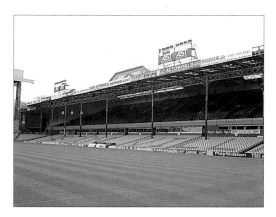

then defeated Arsenal and Manchester City to remain just a point behind United with three games to play. Norwich were by now out of contention.

Villa goal drought

As Villa travelled to Blackburn for their final fixture in April, Saunders had scored just

to pull ourselves back into shape,' said Ron Atkinson. 'The ironic thing was that every time we had a chance they went up the field and scored.'

With two matches to go, Villa were four points behind United. However, a hapless performance at Villa Park, Villa's worst of the season, resulted in a 1–0 defeat at the hands of Oldham Athletic. The title race was over. 'We haven't scored enough goals in the run-in,' said Atkinson, 'and this was typical. We must have hit the woodwork about 155 times this season. It's been nip and tuck at the top all season and it looks as if they might win it by a street in the end, which wouldn't be a fair reflection on the way it has gone.' Villa lost their final fixture, at QPR, while United won both their remaining games. Villa finished in second position, ten points behind United.

'Ron was one of the best motivators,' says Nigel Spink. 'He could get players to perform for him even when they were injured. He did know his stuff. He was very knowledgeable about football. You could never beat him with a quiz question on football. The team Ron Atkinson put together was a bit more flamboyant than the team Graham [Taylor] put together. When we came second in the League in 1990 we were very organised. Ron Atkinson's teams were a bit more adventurous.'

Saunders and Dalian Atkinson had scored 30 goals between them. Among that tally, each had scored one particularly outstanding goal, both of which would live long in the memory. Saunders, in a match against Ipswich Town in February 1993 had got under the ball 35 yards from goal, lofting it high into the air before watching it dip over the goalkeeper's head, to fly just below the crossbar and into the net. Atkinson, in the rain at Wimbledon in October 1992, had taken the ball on an evasive, diagonal run from the halfway line before stopping a couple of feet outside the penalty area and scooping the ball over the goalkeeper's head and into the back of the net. That effort was named Goal of the Season by the BBC's Match of the Day panel.

Atkinson shops again

In preparation for the 1993–94 season, Atkinson acted to shore up the weaknesses in his team. He paid £1,200,000 for Guy Whittingham, a forward who had scored 44 goals for Football League side Portsmouth the previous season. Andy Townsend was signed from Chelsea for £2,100,000 to play on the left-hand side of midfield. That position had been filled by several players during 1992–93 but the team required a settled specialist. Tony Daley was again available after missing much of the previous season with a knee injury and Gordon Cowans returned to Villa Park from Blackburn Rovers.

Another European adventure began in Czechoslovakia, at Slovan Bratislava's Brick Field stadium. An inventive performance from Cowans helped Villa to a 0–0 result that saw them return home confident of reaching the second round. In the second leg, watched by 25,000, two early goals, from Atkinson and Townsend, led the way to a 2–1 victory. By then – late September – Villa were third top in the League, which was now sponsored and renamed the FA Carling

Andy Townsend added a fiery, competitive edge to the Villa midfield when he joined the club in 1993. His surging runs from deep powered many Villa victories in the mid-1990s.

Premiership. The team's form had at times been indifferent, with McGrath and Teale occasionally looking unsteady, but a series of one-nil wins had pushed them up the table.

Deportivo defeat at Villa Park

Deportivo La Coruña, from northern Spain, were Villa's next opponents in the UEFA Cup. Another away draw, 1–1 this time, saw the Villa players again return from Europe in high spirits. The result was more than Villa could have hoped for after conceding a third minute penalty. The spot kick was taken by Deportivo's Brazilian World Cup striker Bebeto. Bosnich dived the right way and saved the South American's penalty. The Villa Park leg of the tie, however, saw Villa go out of the tournament after a 1–0 defeat. 'They should be ashamed of themselves,' Ron Atkinson said after that match. 'There were a lot of experienced players involved who didn't do their stuff, that's for sure. We were a very, very poor advert for English football and I wish I knew the answer to why that was.'

The manager had changed Villa's playing system to a 4-3-3 formation early that season, which accommodated new signing

Two young Villa fans do their bit to add to the colourful spectacle at Wembley in the 1994 League Cup final.

Whittingham alongside Dalian Atkinson and Saunders in the forward line. After a 2–0 home defeat in the League to Southampton in late November, when the team was booed off the pitch, Atkinson reverted to 4-4-2. Whittingham would figure in only four more fixtures that season – his goal tally for the season would be three. Prior to the Southampton match, Villa had been second to Manchester United in the Premiership, although there was an 11-point chasm separating the two sides.

A 2–1 defeat at Liverpool knocked Villa down to fifth in the League, 15 points behind United and with the title already out of their sights. An unsteady run of results in December meant that when Villa lost 1–0 at Blackburn on New Year's Day 1994 they had fallen to tenth in the Premiership. That was where they finished the League season.

League Cup keeps Euro hopes alive

Throughout the second half of the campaign the club had maintained hopes of qualifying for the UEFA Cup through an elevated League position. As those hopes became clouded, Villa's chances of reaching Europe through the alternative route of the League Cup became more clear. Home and

away victories over Birmingham City had kicked off a bracing run that had produced away victories over Sunderland, the holders Arsenal and Tottenham Hotspur.

At the semi-final stage, the competition reverted to a two-legged format. Villa had been drawn against Tranmere Rovers and the first leg of the tie was at Prenton Park. A last-minute goal from Dalian Atkinson saved face in a 3–1 defeat at the hands of the First Division side. In the return match, Villa surged forward from the start to go 2–0 ahead and level on aggregate after only 24 minutes. A John Aldridge penalty after 26 minutes put Tranmere a goal ahead over the two legs but, with only two minutes remaining, Dalian Atkinson again made a late intervention to give Villa a 3–1 win over the 90 minutes and a 4–4 aggregate scoreline.

Extra-time brought no further scoring, so the tie would be settled on penalties. When John Aldridge hit home Tranmere's fifth kick, the score on penalties was 4–4. The penalty competition now became a sudden death shoot-out. Kevin Richardson sent his kick high into the North Stand and Villa were facing elimination. Tranmere's Liam O'Brien would take their penalty. In the 90th minute of the match, O'Brien's shot had struck the angle of post and crossbar and now he would give Villa another reprieve – his penalty kick, low to Bosnich's

right, was stopped by the goalkeeper. Tony Daley slid the next kick into the corner of the net then Bosnich made his third penalty save of the afternoon, from Rovers' Ian Nolan. Villa were at Wembley for the first time in the 1990s.

United at Wembley once more

For the final, with Manchester United, Villa supporters could choose to go to London on any of several weekend trips organised by the Aston Villa Official Travel Club. A return ticket on a 'Champagne Special Train' cost £94. On board, supporters would be served a full English breakfast after leaving Witton Station at 11.00am on the Sunday morning of the final and a three-course meal on the 8.45pm return from London.

'United are a better team now than when they won the title last season,' said Ron Atkinson before the final. 'We will have to play better than at any time this season if we are going to win.' Villa would be facing the champions-elect, who had lost just two League games up to that point. United also had the chance of winning the treble of England's major trophies. Villa had lost three consecutive League matches before the final but were cheered by the knowledge that Peter Schmeichel, United's giant Danish international goalkeeper, would be suspended.

Villa adopted an unusual 4-5-1 formation, with Saunders alone up front and five Villa men restricting United's midfield freedom. This meant that United's deep-lying attackers – Eric Cantona and wingers Andrei Kanchelskis and Ryan Giggs – had to work hard to win themselves space. Villa would be running at United's central defenders Gary Pallister and Steve Bruce from midfield rather than taking them on, man-to-man, up front.

Early in the match, United twice went dangerously close to scoring, through Hughes and Keane. Villa's first on-target effort was a Steve Staunton corner that streaked out from his boot then in towards the United goal where Les Sealey stretched backwards to palm the ball over the bar. Villa now began to flex their muscles, their constant movement in midfield drawing United's defenders out of position. Villa's growing confidence was evident after 25 minutes, when Townsend knocked the ball forward to Saunders. He directed a first-time pass over the United defence for Atkinson who controlled it on his left instep to guide the ball away from Bruce. The Villa forward then quickly edged the ball under Sealey, using his right shin. It was a wonderful goal and it sent half the 77,231 crowd into raptures.

Villa's tactics worked well – chances arrived so rarely for United that they had to snatch at them. With only 15 minutes remaining, and the score still 1–0 to Villa,

Above: Dean Saunders makes certain of Villa's first trophy of the 1990s as he sends his 90th-minute penalty, straight and true, into the heart of Sealey's goal for the final flourish of the 1994 League Cup final.

Above, left: Villa's second goal in the 1994 League Cup final sees Dean Saunders redirect Kevin Richardson's free-kick past Les Sealey, the Manchester United goalkeeper. When Richardson took the kick, the Villa attackers had turned as one, confusing their opponents and creating a glimpse of goal for Saunders.

Bottom: Villa captain Kevin Richardson celebrates after the 1994 League Cup victory, a triumph he regarded as the greatest of his career.

Below: The new Holte End stand, built in 1994, brought Villa Park's capacity for the late 1990s to almost 40,000.

Tony Daley was flipped into the air on the left wing by Paul Parker, the United right-back. From the free-kick, Richardson sent the ball into the United penalty area where Saunders connected to dink it into the net from the edge of the six-yard box.

When Mark Hughes scored for United in the 83rd minute, Villa began living on their nerves. Four minutes later, Hughes sent a 20-yard shot towards the bottom right-hand corner of Bosnich's goal. The Australian responded with an exceptional save, instantaneously extending his left arm to divert the ball round the post.

With the seconds melting away, Villa broke free and Daley pelted a pacy shot against the post. The ball fell at Atkinson's feet and he toe-ended goalward. Kanchelskis handled the ball before it could cross the line. The United winger was immediately dismissed and, from behind the goal, watched as Saunders prepared to exact justice with his penalty. Saunders said afterwards that he knew Sealey would dive to one side so he decided to hit the ball straight down the middle of the goal. The ball slapped against the back of the net and Villa had won 3–1. The victorious Villa side was: Bosnich, Barrett, Staunton (Cox), Teale, McGrath, Richardson, Atkinson, Townsend, Saunders, Fenton, Daley. 'Andy Townsend was phenomenal,' said Atkinson afterwards. 'He was the big difference.'

It had been a thoroughly splendid occasion, on and off the park. A thunderous, fiery game had rushed incessantly from one goal to the other throughout the 90 minutes. The excitement charged the crowd and both teams' supporters were fittingly vociferous.

Richardson, the Villa captain, had won the League championship with Everton and Arsenal. 'This has to be better because everybody had written us off,' he said after the League Cup final. 'People said we had to win something this season to justify the money the manager has spent. But I don't think we were under as much pressure as United. They only had to turn up to win, didn't they?' Atkinson had spent £17,000,000 on players with £11,000,000 coming into Villa Park through sales.

The League Cup was displayed at Villa Park on the following Wednesday night before a match with Everton. Despite steady rain, a crowd of 36,000 turned up to acknowledge the players who had contributed to such a magnificent spectacle the previous weekend. There was further good cheer for Villa that week when the club was given planning permission to build a new two-tier stand at the Holte End of the ground. Preliminary work began on the new construction that April, with both tiers scheduled for completion in December 1994.

Holte End redevelopment

The building work meant that for the first half of the 1994–95 season Villa would have to operate with a restricted capacity of around 30,000, which included several rows of seats in the lower tier of the stand still

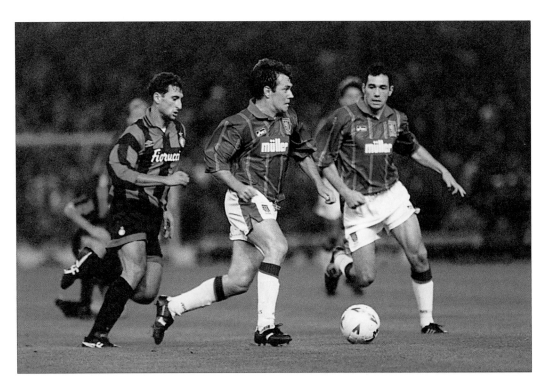

Ray Houghton, Villa's industrious Scottish-Irish midfielder, busies himself with a darting run deep into the Internazionale defence during the 1994 UEFA Cup tie at Villa Park.

being built at the new Holte End. Early in the 1994–95 season, these seats would be open to the public during matches, while building work would continue around them through the week. Once the new Holte End stand was complete, however, the ground's capacity would seat close to 40,000. The new stand, which would have 13,500 seats, would cost £6,000,000.

Following the 1994 League Cup final, McGrath missed seven successive games through neck and shoulder injuries. Ugo Ehiogu, a 22-year-old centre-back whom Atkinson had purchased from WBA for £40,000 in 1991, was given an extended run in the team. He would remain in the starting line-up as the 1994–95 season kicked off. With a UEFA Cup place already theirs through the League Cup win, Villa played out time in the weeks between the League Cup final and the end of the season. Yet their biggest home crowd of 1994 turned up on 7 May for their final fixture, a match with Liverpool.

Nineteen thousand of the 45,347 were there to stand on the Holte End for one last time. At one time in its history the massive terrace had taken the weight of nearly 30,000 bodies. Every individual passing through the Holte End turnstiles that afternoon received a certificate testifying to their presence. A number of post-war Villa stars were on the pitch before the match to acknowledge the swaying masses for the last time. Two goals from Dwight Yorke gave Villa a 2–1 win. Both goals, appropriately, were scored in front of the Holte End.

Three major signings helped cheer the Villa fans over the summer but none of them involved players moving in or out of the club. Mark Bosnich signed a five-year contract; Steve Staunton a four-year deal. Paul McGrath, now 34, signed on for another year. These were vital signings. Following the ruling of the European Commission in the Jean-Marc Bosman case, players who were out of contract would soon be free to move to a club in a different EC country with no transfer due to their previous club.

One player who was leaving Villa in 1994 was Tony Daley. He had asked for a transfer in the autumn of 1993 and had been on the verge of a £2,000,000 move to Udinese, an Italian club, when the deal collapsed. In the early summer of 1994 he moved to Wolverhampton Wanderers for £1,250,000, leaving the Villa supporters with many fond memories.

Incoming individuals that summer of 1994 were Nii Lamptey, a 19-year-old Ghanaian forward signed from Anderlecht, and John Fashanu, a 32-year-old striker from Wimbledon. Phil King, a left-back, joined Villa from Sheffield Wednesday.

Phil King's penalty pelts against the back of Gianluca Pagliuca's net to give Villa a win on penalties in the 1994 tie with Internazionale. The 1990s saw Villa develop into consistent competitors in Europe. The club won a place in the UEFA Cup almost every season during that decade.

Fashanu cost £1,200,000 while Lamptey's initial price was £300,000 with additional sums payable depending on the number of first-team appearances he made. King cost £250,000. These were modest signings for a club of Villa's size – the club was having to divert funds to the redevelopment of Villa Park, the total cost of which would be in the region of £14,000,000. 'If the manager wants someone else,' said Doug Ellis at the Villa AGM, 'we will always do our best to provide the funds to support his choice.'

Penalties decide Inter clash

There would be no gentle easing into that year's UEFA Cup competition for Villa. They were drawn with the holders, Internazionale. The first leg in Milan saw a Dennis Bergkamp penalty give the Italian side a 1–0 victory. Nigel Spink, in goal for the injured Bosnich, got the tips of his fingers to the ball but it drifted into the net. In the return, wave upon wave of Villa attacks crashed down on the Inter defence but by the end of 120 minutes Villa had only one goal – from Houghton – to show for their efforts. With the teams level on aggregate and with neither having scored away goals the tie would be decided on penalties.

Parker, Staunton and Townsend scored Villa's first three penalties. Bia, Bergkamp and Seno accomplished the same task for Inter. When Fontolan missed Inter's fourth penalty Whittingham did the same for Villa. Ruben Sosa then made it three missed penalties in a row, striking the underside of the bar with his kick. Phil King stepped up to sweep the last penalty of the night into the net to put Villa into the second round.

Villa fully deserved their win – it had been an imaginative, committed performance and they had been unlucky not to have scored six or seven goals inside the 90 minutes. 'I can't remember enjoying a result so much before,' said Ron Atkinson afterwards. 'You have to bear in mind the competition we faced. We have seen some very, very talented players on the field today who we pressurised into very basic mistakes.'

Villa take on Turks

Ron Atkinson had welcomed the early meeting with Internazionale, saying that he hoped that Villa's next tie would be in Madrid so that players and supporters could experience another glamorous occasion. Instead, the second round draw took them to Turkey and a meeting with Trabzonspor. Again Villa lost the away leg 1–0, Orhan hammering a header past Spink for the Turks' goal.

With 13 minutes remaining in the return at Villa Park, Trabzonspor goalkeeper Victor saved a Steve Staunton penalty. From the rebound, Dalian Atkinson put Villa ahead. With the Turks down to ten men, extra-time looked a possibility. It also appeared likely to go in Villa's favour even though they had made and missed a score of chances already. Two minutes into injury time, however, Orhan turned and hit a shot that flew high over Bosnich's shoulder and into the net.

Villa now needed two more home goals to overcome the Turkish side's one away goal, which would count double in the event of an aggregate draw. In the seven minutes of injury time that was played, Ugo Ehiogu did get another goal for Villa but it was not enough. Villa were out of Europe. 'I just couldn't believe it when they scored. It seemed like their only attack of the second half,' said Ron Atkinson after the match. 'It was a freak result and it was very cruel.'

By the time the euphoria of the UEFA Cup run had died away, in early November, Villa were fourth bottom of the Premiership. It was a worrying situation, especially in the 1994–95 season: four clubs were to be relegated to the First Division. Villa lost their next League game, at home to Manchester United. Then, at Wimbledon, they were 3–1 ahead but, after having had Andy Townsend sent off, lost 4–3. On 10 November, Ron Atkinson was dismissed from his position as Aston Villa manager.

'Of course I understand the depth of the problem in taking just one Premiership point from 27,' said Atkinson. 'Something drastic had to be done. I just don't think my head had to roll to help Villa's revival. All my life I had an obsession, a great private desire to manage Villa and take them to the top. All I hope is that whoever gets the job after me does not have the kind of luck that has deserted the players in the last couple of months.'

Nigel Spink recalls: 'There was a bit of a problem over confidence. We had a bad run. These things happen. Nowadays, in the Premier League, if you go seven or eight games in a row without winning you drop like a stone. There are a lot of teams who are on a similar level – and it's a very high level – and any of them can beat any of the others at any time. So if a manager has a bad run

nowadays it can cost him his job whereas before it would maybe be judged over a season. Now a bad run of injuries can cost a manager his job. That's football.'

Several names were linked with the Villa job but Brian Little, who was manager at Leicester City, soon became the focus of attention. His chairman, Martin George, refused Doug Ellis permission to speak to Little. He stated that Little would not be allowed to leave the club – Little was contracted to stay at Filbert Street until 1997.

Villa old boys return

But on 22 November 1994, Brian Little resigned as Leicester City manager. 'I have had no approach personally from Aston Villa.' he said, 'and, at this moment, I have no idea what my plans will be. It's time for me to do something different with my life, although I intend to stay in football. Where that will be I have not the slightest knowledge. I'm leaving because I have always said that the day the enjoyment stops and job satisfaction goes is the day I leave.' On the following day, John Gregory also resigned from Leicester City, where he had been first-team coach. Another former Villa player, Allan Evans, had been Little's assistant. On Little's departure, Evans took temporary charge of the Leicester first team.

Three days after his resignation from Leicester, Brian Little was back at Villa Park, where his appointment as the new Aston Villa manager was announced at a press conference. John Gregory would be Villa's new first-team coach. On the same day as those two appointments were announced, Allan Evans resigned from Leicester. He would, in mid-January, become assistant manager at Villa.

Little's final competitive appearance as an Aston Villa player had been in April 1980. He had retired the following year, at the age of 27, after persistent knee injuries had rendered him unfit to continue playing. After working in Villa's commercial department for four years he had been appointed youth team coach. He had moved to Wolverhampton Wanderers in January 1986 to be assistant manager to Sammy Chapman and was promoted to manager in August 1986. Seven weeks later he was dismissed to make way for Graham Turner who had

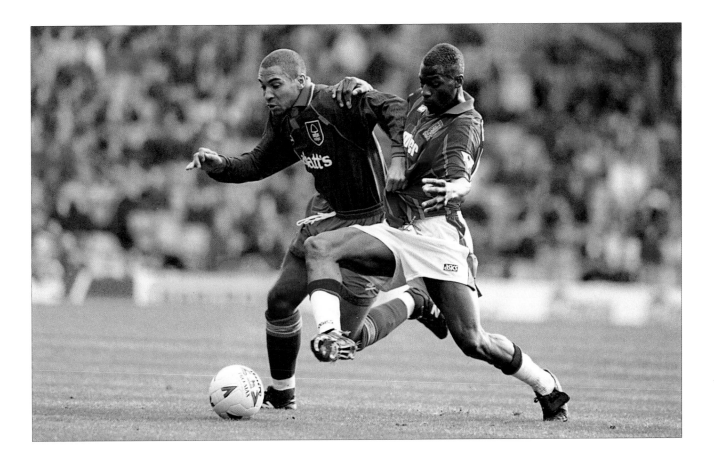

Ugo Ehiogu (right), Villa's dependable centre-back, tackles Stan Collymore, then of Nottingham Forest, in a League match at Villa Park in October 1994.

recently departed from the manager's post at Villa.

After two years' coaching at Middlesbrough, where Bruce Rioch was manager, Little moved to Darlington as manager in February 1989. The club was relegated to the GM Vauxhall Conference three months later but in the following two seasons Little led them to the Conference title and the Fourth Division title. He moved to Leicester in 1991, winning the Foxes promotion to the Premiership in 1994. On his departure, however, Leicester were bottom of the Premiership.

'It's a great feeling for me,' said Little, on taking charge at Villa on his 41st birthday. 'I've not been one to shout about my ambitions and when you are a player you never really think about it but once I got into coaching it was always at the back of my mind. I hadn't expected the chance to arrive when it did but nothing surprises you in football. Opportunities come along and you have to go with those.'

Little's first game in charge, at home to Sheffield Wednesday, ended in a 1–1 draw. 'I have to make some decisions and I have to make them fast to win us some football

games,' said the new manager after casting an eye over his new players in a competitive situation. 'I wouldn't call them hard decisions – I'm paid to make decisions. Whatever I have to do I will do and hopefully what I do will be right. The club is in the wrong position and my motto in football has always been "whatever it takes". I will do that.'

A week later, Little returned to Leicester as Aston Villa manager and was subjected to a collective verbal assault by the crowd from start to finish of the 1–1 draw. The previous Wednesday, 30 November, Villa had lost their grip on the League Cup, having been knocked out of the tournament courtesy of a 4–1 defeat at Crystal Palace. Earlier that day, across London, Leicester City had gone to the High Court to attempt to gain an injunction preventing Little continuing as Villa manager. Leicester had claimed that Little had given them an assurance that he would not take the Villa manager's job after his resignation from the manager's post at Filbert Street. Mrs Justice Smith refused to grant the injunction.

Despite a colourful, champagne-drinking image, Ron Atkinson had been relatively cautious during his managerial tenure at

Villa Park. He tended to play safe with his signings, investing heavily in experienced players of proven ability who had given good service to other clubs. By the time they reached Villa they would have only a certain amount left to give. It was a short-term approach that did little for the club's long-term future.

Brian Little, grey-haired, polite and softly spoken had a more sober public image but he was more adventurous in his signings than Atkinson. Little would buy young players who were hungry and who, if they fitted in, could give the club years of service. He quickly adopted a new 3-5-2 formation, consisting of three central defenders, two wing-backs flanking three central midfielders and two forwards. After the Sheffield Wednesday match, Little had commented that he wished to have more pace on the flanks, with crosses quickly whipped in for the forwards. He wanted to see less of the tactic of lobbing the ball over the heads of the opposing defence.

The Villa careers of Kevin Richardson, Ray Houghton and Garry Parker were soon over. Gary Charles and Alan Wright were brought in to play as specialist wing-backs. Both cost £900,000; Wright from Blackburn Rovers and Charles from Derby County. Ian Taylor, a hard-running midfielder who had stood on the Holte End as a youth, was

brought in from Sheffield Wednesday at a cost of £1,300,000. Dwight Yorke, who had never been certain of his place in the team under Atkinson, became a more regular starter. The West Indian would take on the pivotal role of withdrawn striker in Little's new formation. Townsend moved from his role on the left of a midfield quartet to become one of a central trio. Tommy Johnson, a pacy forward, cost £2,000,000 from Derby County.

Last day escape

Villa's form fluctuated over the second half of the 1994–95 season and by the time of their final fixture the situation was critical. If Villa failed to beat Norwich City at Carrow Road, while Crystal Palace won at Newcastle, Little's team would be relegated. A simple header from Steve Staunton in the eighth minute gave Villa an early lead and their travelling support enjoyed further relief when they heard that Palace were losing 3–0 at Newcastle. Norwich equalised and Palace pulled two goals back to ensure a few last drops of tension would be squeezed out of a nerve-racking season. The scoring ended there. Villa had survived, finishing in fifth-bottom place in the Premiership. Brian Little would have the chance to start afresh

Dwight Yorke, one of the most exciting players on Villa's books during the 1990s, shows the concentration and control that made him such a potent performer for the club.

in the top division for the 1995–96 season.

Over the summer Little would gather together more players whom he saw as suitable to fit into his 3-5-2 system. Several high-profile internationals were linked with Villa: midfielder Paul Gascoigne of Lazio and strikers Stan Collymore of Nottingham Forest, Dennis Bergkamp of Internazionale and Les Ferdinand of QPR. Ferdinand was the only one for whom Villa made a firm offer but he decided to move to Newcastle United. In the event, Villa's eventual signings were young players eager to make a name for themselves in the game. Little made three key signings, one for each part of the team.

Gareth Southgate, the captain of Crystal Palace, joined Villa for £2,500,000. The 24-year-old had been playing a holding role in the Palace midfield but Little saw him as ideal for a role in Villa's three-man central defence. Paul McGrath's ongoing excellence ensured that he would be alongside Southgate for the new season. The Irish international had been given another 12-month contract.

'Paul McGrath's ability to go out week after week without training through the days between matches was exceptional,' says Nigel Spink. 'I couldn't do it, mentally. I wouldn't be able to play without training through the week. It took great character not to have worked with the ball all week and to then be able to prepare yourself to play a game of football on the Saturday. He read the game brilliantly. His positioning, passing and heading ability was immense. He was international class.'

For his midfield, Little returned to Leicester City to purchase Mark Draper, a 25-year-old, for £3,250,000. That was a move that Little-watchers might have predicted but his final signing that summer was a total surprise. Little and Doug Ellis made an unpublicised flight to Belgrade to sign Savo Milosevic, a 21-year-old striker from the city's Partizan club for a club record fee of £3,500,000. Milosevic had scored 71 goals for Partizan in the previous three seasons and had five caps for Yugoslavia. It brought Little's spending in six months at Villa to £15,000,000. Around £8,000,000 had been brought in by selling players, including Dean Saunders, who had moved on to Galatasaray of Turkey.

Villa defeated Partizan Belgrade 2–0 in a Villa Park friendly before the 1995–96 season began. Bosnich said of Milosevic afterwards: 'There's three important points to remember before people start forming any hard and fast opinions about him. First and foremost, he's in a new country and can't speak any English. He's only 21 and English football is far different to the former Yugoslav league. It's a new, young side the manager is putting together. We all need to

Savo Milosevic managed 34 goals in three full seasons at Villa Park. It was an unsatisfactory tally for a striker who had been, in 1995, the club's record signing. The Yugoslav struggled to come to terms with football and life in England. In the summer of 1998, he was sold to Real Zaragoza for £3,500,000, the price Villa had paid for him three years previously.

pull together for everyone's benefit, not least Savo's. We all believe we're on the verge of something tremendously exciting.'

Nigel Spink comments: 'Brian Little was very organised. Training was very organised. He introduced the three centre-backs – a system he had used at Leicester – and the players he wanted to play that way, bringing in Gareth Southgate to play alongside Paul McGrath and Ugo Ehiogu. They were a very solid threesome. With Gary Charles and Alan Wright as the wing-backs Brian very quickly had quite a balanced team.

'He was very impressive with his organisation and professionalism – at a big club like Villa everything has to be very well organised. He got a staff in that people liked working with. Brian was very quiet – not a bawler or shouter in the way big Ron would sometimes be. Brian did it in his own quiet way. John Gregory was also very impressive. He's got an arrogant streak which is something that a manager needs. John was a good motivator. He, Allan Evans and Brian all took turns to take team talks.'

Opening day clash with United

The opening match of the 1995–96 season pitched Villa against Manchester United,

League champions in 1993 and 1994 and runners-up in the FA Cup and the League in the 1994–95 season. Bosnich was the Villa goalkeeper with Ehiogu, McGrath and Southgate the three defenders in front of him. Charles and Wright were the wing-backs with Townsend and Taylor on either side of central midfielder Draper. In attack, Milosevic was paired with Yorke.

Little's alchemy met with the full approval of the Villa fans as their team flowed sweetly to a 3–1 win over United. The opener arrived when Taylor tweaked Charles' cross into the net. The second was the result of some crafty control inside the penalty area by Milosevic which was rounded off nicely by a suave, disguised shot from Draper. Yorke got the third with a penalty after a forceful run from Milosevic was terminated with Schmeichel felling the 6ft 1in, 13st 7lb Yugoslav striker.

Little had described the final months of 1994–95 as the toughest in all his years in the game. 'Now I am aiming to put out a team full of passion, commitment and flair – a team that will not lie down. That team will be led by a manager who has no desire to fail.' By late September, Villa were second in the League but a month later they had

Brian Little introduced a calm, controlled approach to management when he took over in 1994 but he quickly built a team that was a highly explosive attacking force.

slipped to sixth. Milosevic was struggling to adapt to the English game. Villa would remain respectably placed throughout the season without challenging for the title.

New Villa put on Wembley show

Milosevic's stated ambition for the season had been to score 25 goals but he had managed just 11 in the League by March. He had scored only one other goal that season, in an FA Cup tie with non-League Gravesend and Northfleet. In the League Cup he had failed to score even once. He did, however, have one more opportunity to break his duck in that competition – Villa were in the final against Leeds United on 24 March 1996.

The Wembley setting would be graced by one of the finest goals seen at that venue. With 20 minutes gone, Milosevic took possession just inside the Leeds half of the field. He moved carefully forward until he was 25 yards from goal. As Ian Taylor made a run to the right, creating a brief distraction for the Leeds defence, Milosevic took a couple of steps to his left, bent over the ball and sent a hefty left-footed shot high into the Leeds net for an unforgettable opener.

Ten minutes after half-time, Alan Wright's crisp cross to the back post was half-cleared by Leeds left-back Lucas Radebe. Ian Taylor, from close to the penalty spot, sent a first-timed shot flashing past Leeds goalkeeper John Lukic to make it 2–0 to Villa. In the final minute, Draper intercepted the ball in midfield and sent a smart pass to Milosevic. The Yugoslav cannily rolled his foot over the ball, keeping the Leeds defenders guessing as to his intentions. When the moment was right, he slipped a pass to Yorke whose shot licked the underside of the crossbar before nestling in the Leeds net. The 3–0 win, watched by 77,056, was attained by: Bosnich, Charles, Wright, Southgate, McGrath, Ehiogu, Taylor, Draper, Milosevic, Townsend, Yorke.

Villa's fifth League Cup win made them joint-record winners along with Liverpool. 'It was the best goal of my life and the best day of my life,' said Milosevic. 'This was a wonderful occasion for the whole team but one I shall remember forever. I have been a bit disappointed with my scoring. I've missed too many chances. I think this goal made up for a lot.'

Little continues to build

Villa finished the 1995–96 season fourth in the Premiership. In the summer Little signed Sasa Curcic, an attacking midfielder

Ian Taylor volleys Villa's second goal in the 1996 League Cup final win over Leeds United. Dwight Yorke follows the trajectory of the ball as it speeds unerringly towards goal.

from Bolton Wanderers. Belgrade-born Curcic had left Partizan Belgrade at the same time as Milosevic and had shown impressive form for Bolton despite their relegation from the Premiership that year.

Villa's other notable new signings that summer were Fernando Nelson, a Portuguese international signed from Sporting Lisbon, and Julian Joachim, a forward from Leicester City. Nelson would fill the right wing-back role during the 1996–97 season in the absence of Gary Charles, who would miss the season through an ankle injury. Foreign players were now becoming increasingly common in the British game, which had become even more popular as a result of the exciting 1996 European Championships, held in England. The hosts had reached the semi-finals, again creating enormous interest in the game throughout the country.

Another factor in the game's revival was improved facilities for supporters. With Britain's leading clubs now having smart, refurbished all-seater stadiums to comply with the Taylor Report, matches could be watched in considerable comfort. Villa Park had been one of the eight venues for matches during the finals, playing host to group games involving Scotland, Holland and Switzerland and a quarter-final between the Czech Republic and Portugal. Birmingham city centre had been besieged by thousands of well-behaved, colourful supporters from those five countries. Euro' 96 further improved the status of a game that, a decade before, had dragged a tarnished reputation behind it everywhere it went.

With work on the stadiums now complete and Sky's money kicking in, English clubs could afford to lavish enormous sums on some of the world's finest players, making the game even more attractive. Villa's average attendance in the 1995–96 season had been 32,609. For 1996–97 it would be 36,027. Those fans saw Villa sustain their form of the previous season – by the beginning of 1997 Villa were seven points behind leaders Liverpool with a game in hand. That month, Brian Little signed a five-year contract to remain at Villa Park as manager.

Matters were not proceeding entirely smoothly on the field of play. Curcic was stating publicly that he regretted his move to Villa Park and that he wanted to leave the club. Milosevic was again struggling to score

goals and the goalscoring burden was falling heavily on Dwight Yorke. Little, in the autumn of 1996, had offered £4,500,000 for Liverpool striker Stan Collymore. Joachim had cost £1,500,000 but a lack of match fitness after injury saw him spend most of his first year at Villa in the reserves.

The UEFA Cup effort had spluttered out almost as soon as it had begun, with Villa going out on the away goals rule to Helsingborgs of Sweden. By the end of January, Villa were out of both domestic cup competitions. They would finish sixth in the League, 14 points behind the champions Manchester United but with the compensation of a UEFA Cup place for the 1997–98 season.

Villa go public

Off the field, the club was achieving ongoing success. By the 1990s, careful budgeting had ensured that Villa was in good financial health. The club could be relied upon to produce a multi-million pound annual profit. At the beginning of February 1997, the board announced that the club would become a public limited company that year. Aston Villa was valued at between £120,000,000 and £140,000,000. A figure of £15,000,000-£20,000,000 was expected to be raised by the share issue.

Financial backing was provided for Brian Little before the 1997–98 season began. The club transfer record was doubled at a stroke when Stan Collymore was signed from

The League Cup is presented to Aston Villa for the fifth time in the club's history after the win over Leeds United in the spring of 1996. Captain Andy Townsend shows it to the proud Villa supporters.

Liverpool for £7,000,000. Simon Grayson arrived from Leicester City to stiffen the midfield. Andy Townsend left for Middlesbrough. Little would perm any two from his three midfielders – Grayson, Draper and Taylor – to support Dwight Yorke, who began the season playing behind strikers Collymore and Milosevic. With McGrath having departed for Derby County in October 1996, Ehiogu, Southgate and Staunton were the three centre-backs.

High expectations

A poor start to the 1997–98 season saw Villa slumped in the lower half of the Premiership table. The team finally appeared to have completed a turn for the better on the first Saturday in December, when they played host to Coventry City. Stan Collymore, who had scored just once all season, looked prepared to please. After 21 minutes his willingness to get in the hunt for goals was rewarded. His 20-yard shot took a deflection off a Coventry defender and veered into the net for Villa's opening goal.

Collymore's goal was received with delight by the Villa faithful but on the half hour he received an even more enthusiastic cheer when he moved on to the ball in midfield and, on a 40-yard run, swayed past three defenders before being blocked as he accelerated towards goal. The Villa fans badly wanted him to do well and they were off their seats to applaud and encourage him after that promising glimpse of his fleet footed potential.

An equally significant move was made by the Villa management five minutes after that incident. Dwight Yorke, who had aggravated a long-term calf problem, was replaced by Lee Hendrie, a 20-year-old who had made seven previous appearances in a Villa shirt but who had yet to appear during the 1997–98 season. The young, home-grown midfielder initially appeared to be struggling to keep up with the pace of the game. By the middle of the second half, he had righted himself and was showing some eye-catching touches.

With 18 minutes remaining, Alan Wright intercepted a Coventry clearance and pushed the ball on to Hendrie. He swayed past three players and pitched a neat shot past Coventry goalkeeper Steve Ogrizovic and into the net. Julian Joachim added a third goal on an afternoon when Coventry's frustration in the face of Villa's finesse saw two of their players sent off.

Mark Bosnich and Mark Draper clutch the cup after the 3–0 win over Leeds United at Wembley in 1996. Draper, a stylish play-maker in midfield, showed the potential to become an international after joining Villa from Leicester City in 1995.

Europe: a welcome distraction

Hendrie's performance against Coventry saw him retain his place for the match with Steaua Bucharest three days later. The gloomy domestic season had been lightened only by the side's performances in the UEFA Cup. Demanding opposition, in the shape of Bordeaux and Athletic Bilbao had already been eliminated from the tournament on exciting nights at Villa Park. Another spectacular display against Steaua, watched by 35,302, gave Villa a 2–0 win and took the club into the quarter-finals.

In domestic competition, Villa's season was riddled with frustrating inconsistency. Progress in one or two matches would then be counterbalanced by equivalent setbacks. By Christmas, Villa were just three points above third-from-bottom Tottenham Hotspur, who would be Villa's visitors for the live Sky TV match on Boxing Day.

A stirring 4–1 win over Spurs was particularly encouraging because of two Stan Collymore goals – one a stunning 20-yard free-kick that glided into the top corner of the Spurs net. A 1–1 draw at Leeds two days later saw 1997 end on an encouraging note.

The early matches of the new year were less pleasurable. Villa were two minutes away from going out of the FA Cup at Portsmouth before Simon Grayson's 88th minute equaliser gave them a 2–2 draw. A Savo Milosevic strike earned Villa a 1–0 win in the replay but after his 21st minute goal it was another disappointing evening for the Villa fans, only 23,000 of whom turned up for this third round match.

A late equaliser from substitute Julian Joachim against his former club Leicester City, brightened up a dull 1–1 draw in the first League game of the year. However, the following week Villa found their season's nadir. Their visit to Blackburn Rovers, then third in the Premiership, resulted in a 5–0 defeat, Villa's biggest beating of the 1997–98 season.

Close to the end of the match, Villa fans howled abuse at Savo Milosevic after he failed to control the ball in front of the Blackburn goal. Fans ran down the terrace to scream at Milosevic and Blackburn stewards had to intervene. Milosevic, in response, spat in the direction of the fans. The following midweek, after outraged protests by Villa followers in the Birmingham press and directly to the club, Milosevic was placed on the transfer list.

Ian Taylor stays steady to drive the ball past Athletic Bilbao goalkeeper Imanol Etxeberria in the 2–1 UEFA Cup victory over the Spanish side in November 1997. The win put Villa into the third round of the European competition but their good form in that tournament was not matched in the League. Taylor's goal was only Villa's second in six games and at the time of this match they were in 15th position in the Premiership.

Savo Milosevic puts a firm, accurate shot past Zoltan Mitli, the Steaua Bucharest goalkeeper, for the opening goal in Villa's 2–0 win over the Romanian side at Villa Park in December 1997. The victory put Villa into their first quarter-final in European competition for 15 years.

With the supporters temporarily placated, Villa faced up to a home fourth round tie with West Bromwich Albion in the FA Cup. It brought out the best in the Villa fans, their vociferous encouragement as the game kicked off creating a rumbustious atmosphere that was capped by a tremendous volley by Simon Grayson high into the Albion net in the fifth minute. That goal tipped Villa towards a 4–0 victory but in the following round they bent placidly to a 1–0 defeat at home to Coventry City.

Little takes his leave

On 21 February, following another listless, insipid Villa performance, in a 2–1 defeat at Wimbledon, Brian Little trudged towards the dressing rooms a couple of yards behind Joe Kinnear. Little had to look on enviously as the Wimbledon manager repeatedly mimed putting three points in his pocket for the benefit of the cheering Wimbledon fans. It left Villa sixth-bottom of the Premiership and in serious danger of relegation. Three days later, Little resigned as Villa manager. 'There were certain things going on behind the scenes which were affecting my own managerial position,' he said. 'My decision to resign was not taken lightly and it most definitely was not on the spur of the moment. It was done with the well-being of Aston Villa uppermost in my mind.'

The following day, John Gregory was appointed Aston Villa manager. He had left the coaching staff at Villa Park 16 months previously to become manager at Wycombe Wanderers. 'I'm fully aware that people were expecting a bigger name or a more experienced manager,' he said, 'but what are the credentials for being a big name? Are you an experienced manager or a big name if you've had the sack five times?

'I've been brought here to keep us up. I believe that the club were left at three o'clock on Tuesday afternoon without a football manager and with a decision to make about it. Had it been the summer months when they had two or three months to make a decision I'm sure I wouldn't have been the man for the job. I was available, I was handy, I know the place inside out, I know the staff. I know everyone connected with Aston Villa Football Club – and I'm quite cheap.' Gregory's first game, on the final Saturday in February, resulted in a gritty 2–1 victory over Liverpool, with Stan Collymore scoring a goal in each half against his former Anfield team-mates.

Stan Collymore (right) celebrates his goal against Atletico Madrid in March 1998 with Ian Taylor (left) and Dwight Yorke (centre). Collymore scored eight goals in 36 games during the 1997/98 season. It was a disappointing return for the club's £7,000,000 record signing, who only occasionally showed the pace and control that had made him such a highly valued player.

Villa thriller against Atletico

In the first leg of the UEFA Cup quarter-final, on 3 March, Villa voyaged to the Estadio Vicente Calderon, Spain, to confront Atletico Madrid. Prior to the tie, Steve Harrison was appointed assistant to John Gregory. A decade earlier, Harrison had been Graham Taylor's assistant at Villa. After a nervous start, when Villa's immediate future in the competition looked bleak, they burst back into contention in the tie. Shortly before half-time, however, the leggy Taylor swiped José Luis Caminero into the air and the referee pointed to the spot. Bosnich plunged to his right and got an arm to Christian Vieri's penalty but the momentum of the centre-forward's strike carried the ball into the net. Bosnich's excellence in a tough first-half gave Villa the platform to seek an equaliser in the second 45 minutes. The clearest opportunity fell to Julian Joachim but the substitute failed to make clean contact with the ball and the chance was gone. Villa lost 1–0.

The improvement in Villa's play during the second half in Madrid gave cause for optimism for the long sold-out second leg at Villa Park on 17 March. Villa started briskly but failed to put the Madrid goal under sustained pressure. After 28 minutes, Atletico forward Kiko's clever through-ball rolled off Ehiogu's back. When the ball ran free, Aguilera got to it before Bosnich and squeezed it into the path of Caminero. The forward directed a low, precise shot past three Villa defenders and into the corner of the net.

Mark Draper had a powerful shot beaten down at the second attempt by Atletico's impressive goalkeeper José Molina and early in the second half Dwight Yorke headed against the bar. It looked then as though Villa were not going to get the required breakthrough. With 20 minutes remaining, however, Ian Taylor scored from a similar position to Caminero.

Three minutes later, Stan Collymore effortlessly created space for himself 20 yards from goal. He sent a coruscating shot ripping into the roof of the Atletico net before the Spanish defenders could think.

Lee Hendrie eludes Simon Rodger of Crystal Palace to carve out a cross in a 1998 FA Premiership match at Villa Park. Hendrie's surging runs from midfield, his sleek passing and his clear-sightedness in front of goal made the Birmingham-born youngster one of the most promising players to have come through the Villa youth system during the 1990s.

With the players now sparking off the fiery atmosphere inside the ground, a fine game roared into flame. Atletico exercised their marvellous ball control and speed to create several swift breaks towards the Villa goal and should have scored from at least one.

Villa, meanwhile, continued to pick away at the Atletico defence. In the dying minutes, Lee Hendrie, who had been heavily involved in the build-up to both Villa goals, curved a shot round a defender. Molina saw it at the last split-second and pushed it off his goal-line and away from danger. It ended 2–1 to Villa, but the away goals rule ensured their elimination. Both sets of players were applauded off the pitch by a crowd still enthralled by the high-grade football they had witnessed. The Villa fans took great encouragement for the future from the way Gregory's team had played in the second half.

A late dash for Europe

In ten League games between Gregory taking charge in late February and the end of the season, Villa won eight and lost two. In

their final game, against Premiership champions Arsenal at Villa Park, a Dwight Yorke penalty – cheekily chipped over England keeper David Seaman – gave Villa a 1–0 win and seventh place in the Premiership. Three days later, Chelsea won the European Cup Winners' Cup. The London side had qualified for the UEFA Cup by virtue of their League postion, but would defend the Cup Winners' Cup in the 1998–99 season, freeing a UEFA Cup place for Villa. It was undreamed-of bounty for the Villa supporters, who had suffered a tortured opening six months of the season.

'I've been up there at the training ground since John took over,' says Nigel Spink, 'and there's a marked difference. The atmosphere is very light-hearted. Steve Harrison is a marvellous coach, especially with defenders. He's a great joker as well but if people aren't working for him the way they should he'll soon let you know. Sometimes it's not good for the manager to be out every day at training. John has got Steve Harrison to take over from him. It's important for a manager to come in and take training and command respect.

'There are very few players who have come to Villa and not enjoyed playing there,' adds Spink. 'It's a fantastic club. The training facilities are superb. They make you want to train hard and play football. It's still a family club. There are people at Villa who have been there for years and years. Having to leave the club brought a lump in the throat. It's then you realise just what you are leaving behind. I could have moved three or four times in my career and made three or four times the money that I did make but I wanted to stay at Villa just to play for the club.'

Prior to the match with Arsenal on 10 May, Gareth Barry, a central midfielder, had been presented with his award of Youth Team Player of the Year by Steve Staunton. That afternoon, Barry, making his first full appearance of the season, had been impressive in his composure and calm distribution of the ball. Before the match, the youth team paraded around the ground, taking deserved applause for having won the Midland Youth Cup.

The capacity crowd of 39,372 for the Arsenal game provided Villa with an average attendance of 36,136 over the 1997–98 season. It was the highest average crowd since 1975–76 and reflected the increasing numbers being drawn to the ground to watch the resurgent Villa of the 1990s.

In the final minute of the match, a Dwight Yorke shot clattered off the foot of an Arsenal post. As the referee put his whistle to his lips to signal the end of the League season, Lee Hendrie was getting his weight behind the rebound for a drive that thoroughly tested David Seaman in the Arsenal goal. Villa were ending the season on the attack, with their fans on their feet and with every indication that the club's immediate future would be as captivating as its past. Little more could be desired of a club with a history as illustrious as Aston Villa.

John Gregory took over as manager of Aston Villa in February 1998. Since Gregory's resignation as first-team coach 16 months earlier, Villa had steadily gone into decline. Gregory got the team winning again and put together an exceptional run of results between February and May 1998.

Facts and Figures

This section gives the results of every competitive game played by Aston Villa from the formation of the English Football League in 1888 to the present day. The War years are not included. From Season 1980–81, it includes all the players, goalscorers and playing substitutes. An asterisk (*) indicates an own goal.

SEASON 1888–1889 FOOTBALL LEAGUE (DIVISION 1)

8 Sep	Wolverhampton Wanderers	A	D	1–1
15 Sep	Stoke City	H	W	5–1
22 Sep	Everton	H	W	2–1
29 Sep	Notts County	H	W	9–1
6 Oct	Everton	A	L	0–2
13 Oct	Blackburn Rovers	H	W	6–1
20 Oct	Bolton Wanderers	A	W	3–2
27 Oct	Accrington Stanley	H	W	4–3
3 Nov	Stoke City	A	D	1–1
10 Nov	Preston North End	A	D	1–1
17 Nov	Blackburn Rovers	A	L	1–5
24 Nov	Wolverhampton Wanderers	H	W	2–1
8 Dec	Notts County	A	W	4–2
15 Dec	Accrington Stanley	A	D	1–1
22 Dec	Burnley	H	W	4–2
29 Dec	Derby County	H	W	4–2
5 Jan	Burnley	A	L	0–4
12 Jan	Bolton Wanderers	H	W	6–2
19 Jan	West Bromwich Albion	H	W	2–0
26 Jan	West Bromwich Albion	A	D	3–3
9 Feb	Preston North End	H	L	0–2
9 Mar	Derby County	A	L	2–5

FA Cup

2 Feb	Witton	H	W	3–2
16 Feb	Derby County	H	W	5–3
2 Mar	Blackburn Rovers	A	L	1–8

SEASON 1889–1890 FOOTBALL LEAGUE (DIVISION 1)

7 Sep	Burnley	H	D	2–2
14 Sep	Notts County	H	D	1–1
21 Sep	Preston North End	H	W	5–3
28 Sep	West Bromwich Albion	A	L	0–3
5 Oct	Burnley	A	W	6–2
12 Oct	Derby County	H	W	7–1
19 Oct	Blackburn Rovers	A	L	0–7
26 Oct	West Bromwich Albion	H	W	1–0
2 Nov	Wolverhampton Wanderers	H	W	2–1
9 Nov	Notts County	A	D	1–1
16 Nov	Bolton Wanderers	A	L	0–2
23 Nov	Everton	H	L	1–2
30 Nov	Accrington Stanley	A	L	2–4
7 Dec	Stoke City	H	W	6–1
14 Dec	Blackburn Rovers	H	abandoned	
21 Dec	Wolverhampton Wanderers	A	D	1–1
25 Dec	Preston North End	A	L	2–3
26 Dec	Accrington Stanley	H	L	1–2
28 Dec	Derby County	A	L	0–5
4 Jan	Everton	A	L	0–7
25 Jan	Bolton Wanderers	H	L	1–2
17 Mar	Stoke City	A	D	1–1
31 Mar	Blackburn Rovers	H	W	3–0

FA Cup

18 Jan	South Shore (Blackpool)	A	W	4–2
1 Feb	Notts County	A	L	1–4

SEASON 1890–1891 FOOTBALL LEAGUE (DIVISION 1)

6 Sep	Wolverhampton Wanderers	A	L	1–2
13 Sep	Notts County	H	W	3–2
20 Sep	Burnley	A	L	1–2
27 Sep	West Bromwich Albion	H	L	0–4
4 Oct	Bolton Wanderers	A	L	0–4
11 Oct	Everton	H	D	2–2
18 Oct	Derby County	A	L	4–5
25 Oct	Derby County	H	W	4–0
1 Nov	West Bromwich Albion	A	W	3–0
8 Nov	Burnley	H	D	4–4
15 Nov	Accrington Stanley	H	W	3–1
22 Nov	Bolton Wanderers	H	W	5–0
29 Nov	Notts County	A	L	1–7
6 Dec	Blackburn Rovers	A	L	1–5
13 Dec	Blackburn Rovers	H	D	2–2
26 Dec	Sunderland	H	D	0–0
1 Jan	Everton	A	L	0–5
10 Jan	Sunderland	A	L	1–5
24 Jan	Preston North End	A	L	1–4
9 Mar	Preston North End	H	L	0–1
14 Mar	Wolverhampton Wanderers	H	W	6–2
21 Mar	Accrington Stanley	A	W	3–1

FA Cup

17 Jan	London Casuals	H	W	13–1
31 Jan	Stoke City	A	L	0–3

SEASON 1891–1892 FOOTBALL LEAGUE (DIVISION 1)

5 Sep	Blackburn Rovers	H	W	5–1
12 Sep	West Bromwich Albion	H	W	5–1
19 Sep	Preston North End	A	W	1–0
28 Sep	Sunderland	H	W	5–3
3 Oct	Derby County	A	L	2–4
10 Oct	Bolton Wanderers	H	L	1–2
17 Oct	Burnley	A	L	1–4
24 Oct	Stoke City	A	W	3–2
31 Oct	Darwen	A	W	5–1
7 Nov	Notts County	H	W	5–1
14 Nov	West Bromwich Albion	A	W	3–0
21 Nov	Stoke City	H	W	2–1
28 Nov	Everton	A	L	1–5
5 Dec	Burnley	H	W	6–1
19 Dec	Wolverhampton Wanderers	A	L	0–2
26 Dec	Darwen	H	W	7–0
28 Dec	Everton	H	L	3–4
2 Jan	Notts County	A	L	2–5
4 Jan	Accrington Stanley	A	L	2–3
12 Mar	Accrington Stanley	H	W	12–2
26 Mar	Sunderland	A	L	1–2
2 Apr	Bolton Wanderers	A	W	2–1
16 Apr	Preston North End	H	W	3–1
18 Apr	Wolverhampton Wanderers	H	L	3–6

FA Cup

16 Jan	Heanor Town	H	W	4–1
30 Jan	Darwen	H	W	2–0
13 Feb	Wolverhampton Wanderers	A	W	3–1
27 Feb	Sunderland	N	W	4–1
19 Mar	West Bromwich Albion (F)	N	L	0–3

SEASON 1892–1893 FOOTBALL LEAGUE (DIVISION 1)

5 Sep	Burnley	A	W	2–0
10 Sep	Everton	H	W	4–1
12 Sep	Stoke City	A	W	1–0
17 Sep	Sunderland	H	L	1–6
19 Sep	West Bromwich Albion	A	L	2–3
24 Sep	Bolton Wanderers	A	L	0–5
1 Oct	Everton	A	L	0–1
8 Oct	Wolverhampton Wanderers	A	L	1–2
10 Oct	Stoke City	H	W	3–2
15 Oct	Nottingham Forest	H	W	1–0
22 Oct	Preston North End	A	L	1–4
29 Oct	Derby County	H	W	6–1
5 Nov	West Bromwich Albion	H	W	5–2
12 Nov	Nottingham Forest	A	W	5–4
19 Nov	Newton Heath	A	L	0–2
26 Nov	Preston North End	H	W	3–1
3 Dec	Sheffield Wednesday	A	L	3–5
10 Dec	Blackburn Rovers	H	W	4–1
17 Dec	Derby County	A	L	1–2
24 Dec	Bolton Wanderers	H	D	1–1
31 Dec	Notts County	A	W	4–1
7 Jan	Sheffield Wednesday	H	W	5–1
14 Jan	Sunderland	A	L	0–6
11 Feb	Blackburn Rovers	A	D	2–2
6 Mar	Newton Heath	H	W	2–0
18 Mar	Notts County	H	W	3–1
25 Mar	Accrington Stanley	H	W	6–4
3 Apr	Wolverhampton Wanderers	H	W	5–0
4 Apr	Burnley	H	L	1–3
15 Apr	Accrington Stanley	A	D	1–1

FA Cup

21 Jan	Darwen	A	L	4–5

SEASON 1893–1894 FOOTBALL LEAGUE (DIVISION 1)

2 Sep	West Bromwich Albion	H	W	3–2
9 Sep	Sunderland	A	D	1–1
11 Sep	Stoke City	H	W	5–1
16 Sep	Everton	A	L	2–4
23 Sep	Everton	H	W	3–1
30 Jan	Derby County	H	D	1–1
2 Oct	Sheffield United	A	L	0–3
7 Oct	Nottingham Forest	A	W	2–1
14 Oct	Darwen	A	D	1–1
16 Oct	Stoke City	A	D	3–3
21 Oct	West Bromwich Albion	A	W	6–3
28 Oct	Burnley	H	W	4–0
30 Oct	Sheffield United	H	W	4–0
4 Nov	Blackburn Rovers	A	L	0–2
11 Nov	Sunderland	H	W	2–1
18 Nov	Bolton Wanderers	A	W	1–0
25 Nov	Preston North End	H	W	2–0
2 Dec	Derby County	A	W	3–0
9 Dec	Sheffield Wednesday	H	W	3–0
16 Dec	Newton Heath	A	W	3–1
23 Dec	Wolverhampton Wanderers	A	L	0–3
26 Dec	Darwen	H	W	9–0
6 Jan	Sheffield Wednesday	A	D	2–2
18 Jan	Preston North End	A	W	5–2
3 Feb	Newton Heath	H	W	5–1
3 Mar	Bolton Wanderers	H	L	2–3
24 Mar	Blackburn Rovers	H	W	2–1
26 Mar	Wolverhampton Wanderers	H	D	1–1
7 Apr	Burnley	A	W	6–3
14 Apr	Nottingham Forest	H	W	3–1

FA Cup

27 Jan	Wolverhampton Wanderers	H	W	4–2
10 Feb	Sunderland	A	D	2–2
21 Feb	Sunderland (R)	H	W	3–1
24 Feb	Sheffield Wednesday	A	L	2–3

SEASON 1894–1895 FOOTBALL LEAGUE (DIVISION 1)

1 Sep	Small Heath	H	W	2–1
8 Sep	Liverpool	A	W	2–1
15 Sep	Sunderland	H	L	1–2
22 Sep	Derby County	A	W	2–0
29 Sep	Stoke City	A	L	1–4
6 Oct	Nottingham Forest	A	L	1–2
13 Oct	West Bromwich Albion	H	W	3–1
20 Oct	Small Heath	A	D	2–2
22 Oct	Sheffield United	A	L	0–1
27 Oct	Liverpool	H	W	5–0
3 Nov	Sheffield Wednesday	A	L	1–2
10 Nov	Preston North End	H	W	4–1
12 Nov	Sheffield United	H	W	5–0
17 Nov	West Bromwich Albion	A	L	2–3
24 Nov	Nottingham Forest	H	W	4–1
1 Dec	Blackburn Rovers	A	W	3–1
3 Dec	Sheffield Wednesday	H	W	3–1
8 Dec	Blackburn Rovers	H	W	3–0
22 Dec	Wolverhampton Wanderers	A	W	4–0
26 Dec	Stoke City	H	W	6–0
2 Jan	Sunderland	A	D	4–4
5 Jan	Derby County	H	W	4–0
12 Jan	Preston North End	A	W	1–0
17 Jan	Everton	A	L	2–4
26 Jan	Bolton Wanderers	H	W	2–1
23 Feb	Burnley	A	D	3–3
23 Mar	Bolton Wanderers	A	L	2–3
6 Apr	Burnley	H	W	5–0
15 Apr	Wolverhampton Wanderers	H	D	2–2
24 Apr	Everton	H	D	2–2

FA Cup

2 Feb	Derby County	H	W	2–1
16 Feb	Newcastle United	H	W	7–1
2 Mar	Nottingham Forest	H	W	6–1
16 Mar	Sunderland	N	W	2–1
20 Apr	West Bromwich Albion (F)	N	W	1–0

SEASON 1895–1896 FOOTBALL LEAGUE (DIVISION 1)

2 Sep	West Bromwich Albion	H	W	1–0
7 Sep	Small Heath	H	W	7–3
14 Sep	Sheffield United	A	L	1–2
21 Sep	Derby County	H	W	4–1
28 Sep	Blackburn Rovers	A	D	1–1
30 Sep	Everton	H	W	4–3
5 Oct	Sunderland	H	W	2–1
12 Oct	West Bromwich Albion	A	D	1–1
19 Oct	Blackburn Rovers	H	W	3–1
26 Oct	Small Heath	A	W	4–1
2 Nov	Burnley	H	W	5–1
9 Nov	Sunderland	A	L	1–2
16 Nov	Sheffield United	H	D	2–2
23 Nov	Burnley	A	W	4–3
7 Dec	Preston North End	A	L	3–4
14 Dec	Bolton Wanderers	H	W	2–0
21 Dec	Everton	A	L	0–2
26 Dec	Wolverhampton Wanderers	A	W	2–1
28 Dec	Bury	H	W	2–0
4 Jan	Stoke City	A	W	2–1
11 Jan	Preston North End	H	W	1–0
18 Jan	Sheffield Wednesday	A	W	3–1
25 Jan	Nottingham Forest	H	W	3–1
8 Feb	Derby County	A	D	2–2
22 Feb	Stoke City	H	W	5–2
7 Mar	Bolton Wanderers	A	D	2–2
14 Mar	Sheffield Wednesday	H	W	2–1
21 Mar	Bury	A	L	3–5
3 Apr	Nottingham Forest	A	W	2–0
6 Apr	Wolverhampton Wanderers	H	W	4–1

FA Cup

1 Feb	Derby County	A	L	2–4

SEASON 1896–1897 FOOTBALL LEAGUE (DIVISION 1)

2 Sep	Stoke City	H	W	2–1
5 Sep	West Bromwich Albion	A	L	1–3
12 Sep	Sheffield United	H	D	2–2
19 Sep	Everton	A	W	3–2
26 Sep	Everton	H	L	1–2
3 Oct	Sheffield United	A	D	0–0

---

10 Oct	West Bromwich Albion	H	W	2–0
17 Oct	Derby County	A	W	3–1
24 Oct	Derby County	H	W	2–1
31 Oct	Stoke City	A	W	2–0
7 Nov	Bury	H	D	1–1
14 Nov	Sheffield Wednesday	A	W	3–1
21 Nov	Sheffield Wednesday	H	W	4–0
28 Nov	Blackburn Rovers	A	W	5–1
19 Dec	Nottingham Forest	H	W	3–2
25 Dec	Liverpool	A	D	3–3
26 Dec	Wolverhampton Wanderers	A	W	2–1
2 Jan	Burnley	H	L	0–3
9 Jan	Sunderland	A	L	2–4
16 Jan	Sunderland	H	W	2–1
6 Feb	Bury	A	W	2–0
8 Feb	Burnley	A	W	4–3
22 Feb	Preston North End	H	W	3–1
6 Mar	Nottingham Forest	A	W	4–2
13 Mar	Liverpool	H	D	0–0
22 Mar	Bolton Wanderers	H	W	6–2
27 Mar	Bolton Wanderers	A	W	2–1
17 Apr	Blackburn Rovers	H	W	3–0
19 Apr	Wolverhampton Wanderers	H	W	5–0
26 Apr	Preston	A	W	1–0

FA Cup

30 Jan	Newcastle United	H	W	5–0
13 Feb	Nottingham Forest	H	W	2–1
27 Feb	Preston North End	A	D	1–1
3 Mar	Preston North End	H	D	0–0
10 Mar	Preston North End	N	W	3–2
20 Mar	Liverpool	N	W	3–0
10 Apr	Everton (F)	N	W	3–2

SEASON 1897–1898 FOOTBALL LEAGUE (DIVISION 1)

1 Sep	Sheffield Wednesday	H	W	5–2
4 Sep	West Bromwich Albion	H	W	4–3
11 Sep	Notts County	A	W	3–2
18 Sep	Bury	H	W	3–1
25 Sep	Blackburn Rovers	A	L	3–4
27 Sep	Sheffield Wednesday	A	L	0–3
2 Oct	Bolton Wanderers	H	W	3–2
9 Oct	West Bromwich Albion	A	D	1–1
16 Oct	Notts County	A	W	4–2
23 Oct	Sunderland	A	D	0–0
30 Oct	Liverpool	H	W	3–1
6 Nov	Preston North End	A	L	1–3
13 Nov	Everton	H	W	3–0
20 Nov	Bolton Wanderers	A	L	0–2
27 Nov	Sunderland	H	W	4–3
11 Dec	Blackburn Rovers	H	W	5–1
18 Dec	Stoke City	A	D	0–0
25 Dec	Everton	A	L	1–2
27 Dec	Wolverhampton Wand	A	D	1–1
8 Jan	Sheffield United	A	L	0–1
15 Jan	Sheffield United	H	L	1–2
22 Jan	Derby County	A	L	1–3
5 Feb	Preston North End	H	W	4–0
5 Mar	Derby County	H	W	4–1
12 Mar	Bury	A	W	2–1
26 Mar	Nottingham Forest	A	L	1–3
2 Apr	Stoke City	H	D	1–1
11 Apr	Wolverhampton Wanderers	H	L	1–2
16 Apr	Liverpool	A	L	0–4
30 Apr	Nottingham Forest	H	W	2–0

FA Cup

29 Jan	Derby County	A	L	0–1

SEASON 1898–1899 FOOTBALL LEAGUE (DIVISION 1)

3 Sep	Stoke City	H	W	3–1
10 Sep	Bury	A	L	1–2
17 Sep	Burnley	A	W	4–2
24 Sep	Sheffield United	H	D	1–1
1 Oct	Newcastle United	A	D	1–1
8 Oct	Preston North End	H	W	4–2
15 Oct	Liverpool	A	W	3–0
22 Oct	Nottingham Forest	H	W	3–0
29 Oct	Bolton Wanderers	H	W	2–1
5 Nov	Derby County	H	W	7–1
12 Nov	West Bromwich Albion	A	W	1–0
19 Nov	Blackburn Rovers	H	W	3–1
26 Nov	Sheffield Wednesday	A	L	1–4

---

3 Dec	Sunderland	H	W	2–0
10 Dec	Wolverhampton Wanderers	H	D	1–1
17 Dec	Everton	H	W	3–0
24 Dec	Notts County	A	L	0–1
26 Dec	Newcastle United	H	W	1–0
31 Dec	Stoke	A	L	0–3
2 Jan	Bolton Wanderers	A		abandoned
7 Jan	Bury	H	W	3–2
14 Jan	Burnley	H	W	4–0
21 Jan	Sheffield United	A	W	3–1
4 Feb	Preston North End	A	L	0–2
18 Feb	Nottingham Forest	A	L	0–1
4 Mar	Derby County	A	D	1–1
18 Mar	Blackburn Rovers	A	D	0–0
25 Mar	Sheffield Wednesday	H	W	3–1
1 Apr	Sunderland	A	L	2–4
3 Apr	Wolverhampton Wanderers	A	L	0–4
15 Apr	Everton	A	D	1–1
17 Apr	Bolton Wanderers	A	D	0–0
22 Apr	Notts County	H	W	6–1
24 Apr	West Bromwich Albion	H	W	7–1
29 Apr	Liverpool	H	W	5–0

FA Cup

28 Jan	Nottingham Forest	A	L	1–2

SEASON 1899–1900 FOOTBALL LEAGUE (DIVISION 1)

2 Sep	Sunderland	A	W	1–0
4 Sep	Glossop	H	W	9–0
9 Sep	West Bromwich Albion	H	L	0–2
16 Sep	Everton	A	W	2–1
23 Sep	Blackburn Rovers	H	W	3–1
30 Sep	Derby County	A	L	0–2
7 Oct	Bury	H	W	2–1
14 Oct	Notts County	A	W	4–1
21 Oct	Manchester City	H	W	2–1
28 Oct	Sheffield United	A	L	1–2
4 Nov	Newcastle United	H	W	2–1
11 Nov	Wolverhampton Wanderers	H	D	0–0
13 Nov	Stoke City	A	W	2–0
18 Nov	Liverpool	A	D	3–3
25 Nov	Burnley	H	W	2–0
2 Dec	Preston North End	A	W	5–0
9 Dec	Nottingham Forest	H	D	2–2
16 Dec	Glossop	A	L	0–1
23 Dec	Stoke City	H	W	4–1
30 Dec	Sunderland	H	W	4–2
1 Jan	Bury	A	L	0–2
6 Jan	West Bromwich Albion	A	W	2–0
13 Jan	Everton	H	D	1–1
20 Jan	Blackburn Rovers	A	W	4–0
3 Feb	Derby County	H	W	3–2
17 Feb	Notts County	H	W	6–2
3 Mar	Sheffield United	H	D	1–1
10 Mar	Newcastle United	A	L	2–3
19 Mar	Manchester City	A	W	2–0
24 Mar	Liverpool	H	W	1–0
31 Mar	Burnley	A	W	2–1
7 Apr	Preston North End	H	W	3–1
14 Apr	Nottingham Forest	A	D	1–1
16 Apr	Wolverhampton Wanderers	A	W	1–0

FA Cup

27 Jan	Manchester City	A	D	1–1
31 Jan	Manchester City (replay)	H	W	3–0
10 Feb	Bristol City	H	W	5–1
24 Feb	Millwall	A	D	1–1
28 Feb	Millwall (replay)	H	D	0–0
5 Mar	Millwall (replay)	N	L	1–2

SEASON 1900–1901 FOOTBALL LEAGUE (DIVISION 1)

1 Sep	Stoke City	H	W	2–0
3 Sep	Preston North End	H	W	4–0
8 Sep	West Bromwich Albion	A	W	1–0
10 Sep	Bury	H	W	1–0
15 Sep	Everton	H	L	1–2
22 Sep	Sunderland	A	D	0–0
29 Sep	Derby County	H	W	2–1
6 Oct	Bolton Wanderers	A	L	0–1
13 Oct	Notts County	H	L	1–2
20 Oct	Preston North End	A	W	2–0
27 Oct	Wolverhampton Wanderers	H	D	0–0
29 Oct	Blackburn Rovers	H	D	3–3

3 Nov	Sheffield Wednesday	A	L	2-3
10 Nov	Liverpool	A	L	1-5
17 Nov	Newcastle United	H	D	2-2
24 Nov	Sheffield United	A	D	2-2
1 Dec	Manchester City	H	W	7-1
8 Dec	Bury	A	L	1-3
15 Dec	Nottingham Forest	H	W	2-1
22 Dec	Blackburn Rovers	A	D	2-2
26 Dec	Bolton Wanderers	H	W	3-0
29 Dec	Stoke City	A	D	0-0
5 Jan	West Bromwich Albion	H	L	0-1
12 Jan	Everton	A	L	1-2
19 Jan	Sunderland	H	D	2-2
16 Feb	Notts County	A	L	0-2
9 Mar	Sheffield Wednesday	H	W	2-1
16 Mar	Liverpool	H	L	0-2
30 Mar	Sheffield United	H	D	0-0
8 Apr	Wolverhampton Wanderers	A	D	0-0
17 Apr	Newcastle United	A	L	0-3
20 Apr	Nottingham Forest	A	L	1-3
22 Apr	Derby County	A	L	0-3
27 Apr	Manchester City	A	L	0-4

FA Cup

9 Feb	Millwall	H	W	5-0
23 Feb	Nottingham Forest	H	D	0-0
27 Feb	Nottingham Forest (R)	A	W	3-1
23 Mar	Small Heath	A	D	0-0
27 Mar	Small Heath (R)	H	W	1-0
6 Apr	Sheffield United	N	D	2-2
11 Apr	Sheffield United (R)	N	L	0-3

SEASON 1901-1902 FOOTBALL LEAGUE (DIVISION 1)

7 Sep	Bury	A	D	0-0
9 Sep	Notts County	H	W	2-0
14 Sep	Blackburn Rovers	H	D	1-1
16 Sep	Sheffield United	H	L	1-2
21 Sep	Stoke City	A	L	0-1
28 Sep	Everton	H	D	1-1
5 Oct	Sunderland	A	L	0-1
12 Oct	Small Heath	A	W	2-0
19 Oct	Derby County	A	L	0-1
26 Oct	Sheffield Wednesday	H	W	4-1
2 Nov	Notts County	A	W	3-0
9 Nov	Bolton Wanderers	H	W	1-0
23 Nov	Wolverhampton Wanderers	H	W	2-1
30 Nov	Liverpool	A	L	0-1
7 Dec	Newcastle United	H	D	0-0
14 Dec	Grimsby Town	H	W	4-1
25 Dec	Everton	A	W	3-2
26 Dec	Small Heath	H	W	1-0
28 Dec	Nottingham Forest	H	W	3-0
1 Jan	Sheffield United	A	L	0-6
4 Jan	Bury	H	W	2-0
11 Jan	Blackburn Rovers	A	L	0-4
18 Jan	Stoke City	H	D	0-0
1 Feb	Sunderland	H	L	0-1
15 Feb	Derby County	H	W	3-2
17 Feb	Manchester City	A	L	0-1
22 Feb	Sheffield Wednesday	A	L	0-1
8 Mar	Bolton Wanderers	A	D	2-2
22 Mar	Wolverhampton Wanderers	A	W	2-0
29 Mar	Liverpool	H	L	0-1
31 Mar	Manchester City	H	D	2-2
1 Apr	Nottingham Forest	A	D	1-1
5 Apr	Newcastle United	A	L	1-2
12 Apr	Grimsby Town	A	L	1-4

FA Cup

25 Jan	Stoke City	A	D	2-2
29 Jan	Stoke City (R)	H	L	1-2

SEASON 1902-1903 FOOTBALL LEAGUE (DIVISION 1)

6 Sep	Derby County	H	D	0-0
13 Sep	Nottingham Forest	A	L	0-2
20 Sep	Bury	H	D	2-2
27 Sep	Blackburn Rovers	A	W	2-0
4 Oct	Sunderland	H	L	0-1
11 Oct	Stoke City	A	L	0-1
18 Oct	Everton	H	W	2-1
1 Nov	West Bromwich Albion	H	L	0-3
8 Nov	Notts County	A	L	1-2
15 Nov	Bolton Wanderers	H	W	4-2

22 Nov	Middlesbrough	A	W	2-1
29 Nov	Newcastle United	H	W	7-0
6 Dec	Wolverhampton Wanderers	A	L	1-2
13 Dec	Liverpool	H	L	1-2
20 Dec	Sheffield United	A	W	4-2
26 Dec	Sheffield Wednesday	H	W	1-0
27 Dec	Grimsby Town	H	D	2-2
1 Jan	Sheffield Wednesday	A	L	0-4
3 Jan	Derby County	A	L	0-2
10 Jan	Nottingham Forest	H	W	3-1
17 Jan	Bury	A	W	1-0
24 Jan	Blackburn Rovers	H	W	5-0
31 Jan	Sunderland	A	L	0-1
14 Feb	Everton	A	W	1-0
28 Feb	West Bromwich Albion	H	W	2-1
14 Mar	Bolton Wanderers	A	W	1-0
28 Mar	Newcastle United	A	L	0-2
30 Mar	Notts County	H	abandoned	
4 Apr	Wolverhampton Wanderers	H	W	3-1
11 Apr	Liverpool	A	L	1-2
13 Apr	Stoke City	H	W	2-0
15 Apr	Notts County	H	W	2-1
18 Apr	Sheffield United	H	W	4-2
25 Apr	Grimsby Town	A	W	2-0
27 Apr	Middlesbrough	H	W	5-0

FA Cup

7 Feb	Sunderland	H	W	4-1
21 Feb	Barnsley	H	W	4-1
7 Mar	Tottenham Hotspur	A	W	3-2
21 Mar	Bury	N	L	0-3

SEASON 1903-1904 FOOTBALL LEAGUE (DIVISION 1)

2 Sep	Newcastle United	A	D	1-1
5 Sep	Sunderland	A	L	1-6
12 Sep	West Bromwich Albion	H	W	3-1
19 Sep	Small Heath	A	D	2-2
26 Sep	Everton	H	W	3-1
3 Oct	Stoke City	A	L	0-2
10 Oct	Derby County	H	W	3-0
17 Oct	Manchester City	A	L	0-1
24 Oct	Notts County	H	W	4-0
31 Oct	Sheffield United	A	W	2-1
7 Nov	Newcastle United	H	W	3-1
14 Nov	Wolverhampton Wanderers	H	W	2-0
21 Nov	Middlesbrough	A	L	1-2
28 Nov	Liverpool	H	W	2-1
5 Dec	Bury	A	D	2-2
12 Dec	Blackburn Rovers	H	L	2-3
19 Dec	Nottingham Forest	A	W	7-3
26 Dec	Sheffield Wednesday	H	W	2-1
28 Dec	Derby County	A	D	2-2
2 Jan	Sunderland	H	W	2-0
9 Jan	West Bromwich Albion	A	W	3-1
16 Jan	Small Heath	H	D	1-1
23 Jan	Everton	A	L	0-1
30 Jan	Stoke City	H	W	3-1
13 Feb	Manchester City	H	L	0-1
27 Feb	Sheffield United	H	W	6-1
12 Mar	Wolverhampton Wanderers	A	L	2-3
19 Mar	Middlesbrough	H	W	2-1
26 Mar	Liverpool	A	D	1-1
1 Apr	Notts County	A	D	0-0
2 Apr	Bury	H	L	0-2
9 Apr	Blackburn Rovers	A	W	3-0
16 Apr	Nottingham Forest	H	W	3-1
23 Apr	Sheffield Wednesday	A	L	2-4

FA Cup

6 Feb	Stoke City	A	W	3-2
20 Feb	Tottenham Hotspur	A	abandoned	
25 Feb	Tottenham Hotspur (R)	H	L	0-1

SEASON 1904-1905 FOOTBALL LEAGUE (DIVISION 1)

1 Sep	Preston North End	H	L	1-2
3 Sep	Stoke City	H	W	3-0
10 Sep	Blackburn Rovers	A	L	0-4
12 Sep	Everton	H	W	1-0
17 Sep	Nottingham Forest	H	W	2-0
24 Sep	Sheffield Wednesday	A	L	2-3
1 Oct	Sunderland	H	D	2-2
8 Oct	Woolwich Arsenal	A	L	0-1
15 Oct	Derby County	H	L	0-2

22 Oct	Everton	A	L	2-3
29 Oct	Small Heath	H	W	2-1
9 Nov	Manchester City	A	L	1-2
12 Nov	Notts County	H	W	4-2
19 Nov	Sheffield United	A	W	3-0
26 Nov	Newcastle United	H	L	0-1
3 Dec	Preston North End	A	W	3-2
10 Dec	Middlesbrough	H	D	0-0
17 Dec	Wolverhampton Wanderers	A	D	1-1
24 Dec	Bury	H	W	2-0
26 Dec	Woolwich Arsenal	H	W	3-1
31 Dec	Stoke City	A	W	4-1
7 Jan	Blackburn Rovers	H	W	3-0
14 Jan	Nottingham Forest	A	D	1-1
21 Jan	Sheffield Wednesday	H	L	0-2
28 Jan	Sunderland	A	W	3-2
11 Feb	Derby County	A	W	2-0
25 Feb	Small Heath	A	W	3-0
11 Mar	Notts County	A	W	2-1
18 Mar	Sheffield United	H	W	3-0
5 Apr	Newcastle United	A	L	0-2
8 Apr	Middlesbrough	A	L	1-3
22 Apr	Bury	A	W	3-2
27 Apr	Wolverhampton Wanderers	H	W	3-0
29 Apr	Manchester City	H	W	3-2

FA Cup

4 Feb	Leicester Fosse	H	W	5-1
18 Feb	Bury	H	W	3-2
4 Mar	Fulham	W	W	5-0
25 Mar	Everton	N	D	1-1
29 Mar	Everton (R)	N	W	2-1
15 Apr	Newcastle United (F)	N	W	2-0

SEASON 1905-1906 FOOTBALL LEAGUE (DIVISION 1)

2 Sep	Blackburn Rovers	A	D	1-1
9 Sep	Sunderland	H	W	2-1
11 Sep	Liverpool	H	W	5-0
16 Sep	Birmingham City	A	L	0-2
23 Sep	Everton	H	W	4-0
30 Sep	Derby County	A	L	0-1
7 Oct	Sheffield Wednesday	H	W	3-0
14 Oct	Nottingham Forest	A	D	2-2
21 Oct	Manchester City	H	W	2-1
28 Oct	Bury	A	W	1-0
4 Nov	Middlesbrough	H	W	4-1
11 Nov	Preston North End	A	L	0-2
13 Nov	Stoke City	A	W	1-0
18 Nov	Newcastle United	H	L	0-3
25 Nov	Wolverhampton Wanderers	H	W	6-0
2 Dec	Liverpool	A	L	0-3
9 Dec	Sheffield United	H	W	4-1
16 Dec	Notts County	A	L	1-2
23 Dec	Stoke City	H	W	3-0
26 Dec	Bolton Wanderers	H	D	1-1
27 Dec	Woolwich Arsenal	H	W	2-1
30 Dec	Blackburn Rovers	H	L	0-1
2 Jan	Bolton Wanderers	A	L	1-4
6 Jan	Sunderland	A	abandoned	
20 Jan	Birmingham City	H	L	1-3
27 Jan	Everton	A	L	2-4
10 Feb	Sheffield Wednesday	A	D	2-2
17 Feb	Nottingham Forest	H	W	3-1
28 Feb	Sunderland	A	L	0-2
3 Mar	Bury	H	D	3-3
10 Mar	Middlesbrough	A	W	2-1
14 Mar	Manchester City	A	W	4-1
17 Mar	Preston North End	H	L	0-1
24 Mar	Newcastle United	A	L	1-3
31 Mar	Wolverhampton Wanderers	A	L	1-4
13 Apr	Woolwich Arsenal	A	L	1-2
14 Apr	Sheffield United	A	D	1-1
16 Apr	Derby County	H	W	6-0
21 Apr	Notts County	H	W	2-1

FA Cup

13 Jan	King's Lynn	H	W	11-0
3 Feb	Plymouth Argyle	H	D	0-0
7 Feb	Plymouth Argyle (R)	A	W	5-1
24 Feb	Manchester United	A	L	1-5

SEASON 1906–1907 FOOTBALL LEAGUE (DIVISION 1)

Date	Opponent			
1 Sep	Blackburn Rovers	H	W	4–2
3 Sep	Stoke City	A	W	2–0
8 Sep	Sunderland	A	L	1–2
10 Sep	Stoke City	H	W	1–0
15 Sep	Birmingham City	H	W	4–1
22 Sep	Everton	A	W	2–1
29 Sep	Woolwich Arsenal	H	D	2–2
6 Oct	Sheffield Wednesday	A	L	1–2
13 Oct	Bury	H	W	3–1
20 Oct	Manchester City	A	L	2–4
27 Oct	Middlesbrough	H	L	2–3
3 Nov	Preston North End	A	L	0–2
10 Nov	Newcastle United	H	D	0–0
17 Nov	Derby County	A	W	1–0
24 Nov	Liverpool	A	L	2–5
1 Dec	Bristol City	H	W	3–2
8 Dec	Notts County	A	D	1–1
15 Dec	Sheffield United	H	W	5–1
22 Dec	Bolton Wanderers	A	W	2–1
24 Dec	Preston North End	H	W	3–0
26 Dec	Manchester United	H	W	2–0
29 Dec	Blackburn Rovers	A	L	1–2
1 Jan	Manchester United	A	L	0–1
5 Jan	Sunderland	H	D	2–2
19 Jan	Birmingham City	A	L	2–3
26 Jan	Everton	H	W	2–1
9 Feb	Sheffield Wednesday	H	W	8–1
16 Feb	Bury	A	W	3–0
23 Feb	Manchester City	H	W	4–1
2 Mar	Middlesbrough	A	L	0–1
16 Mar	Newcastle United	A	L	2–3
23 Mar	Derby County	H	W	2–0
30 Mar	Liverpool	H	W	4–0
1 Apr	Woolwich Arsenal	A	L	1–3
6 Apr	Bristol City	A	W	4–2
13 Apr	Notts County	H	D	0–0
20 Apr	Sheffield United	A	D	0–0
27 Apr	Bolton Wanderers	H	L	0–2

FA Cup

Date	Opponent			
12 Jan	Burnley	A	W	3–1
2 Feb	Bolton Wanderers	A	L	0–2

SEASON 1907–1908 FOOTBALL LEAGUE (DIVISION 1)

Date	Opponent			
2 Sep	Manchester United	H	L	1–4
7 Sep	Blackburn Rovers	A	L	0–2
9 Sep	Sunderland	H	W	1–0
14 Sep	Bolton Wanderers	H	W	2–0
21 Sep	Birmingham City	A	W	3–2
28 Sep	Everton	H	L	0–2
5 Oct	Sunderland	A	L	0–3
12 Oct	Woolwich Arsenal	H	L	0–1
19 Oct	Sheffield Wednesday	A	W	3–2
25 Oct	Bristol City	H	D	4–4
2 Nov	Notts County	A	W	3–0
9 Nov	Manchester City	H	D	2–2
16 Nov	Preston North End	A	L	0–3
23 Nov	Bury	H	D	2–2
30 Nov	Newcastle United	H	D	3–3
7 Dec	Liverpool	A	L	0–5
14 Dec	Middlesbrough	H	W	6–0
21 Dec	Sheffield United	A	D	1–1
25 Dec	Nottingham Forest	H	L	4–0
26 Dec	Nottingham Forest	A	D	2–2
28 Dec	Chelsea	H	D	0–0
4 Jan	Blackburn Rovers	H	D	1–1
18 Jan	Birmingham City	H	L	2–3
25 Jan	Everton	A	L	0–1
8 Feb	Woolwich Arsenal	A	W	1–0
15 Feb	Sheffield Wednesday	H	W	5–0
2 Mar	Notts County	H	W	5–1
7 Mar	Manchester City	A	L	2–3
11 Mar	Bristol City	A	D	2–2
14 Mar	Preston North End	H	W	3–0
21 Mar	Bury	A	L	1–2
4 Apr	Liverpool	H	W	5–1
8 Apr	Newcastle United	A	W	5–2
11 Apr	Middlesbrough	A	W	1–0
17 Apr	Bolton Wanderers	A	L	1–3
18 Apr	Sheffield United	H	W	1–0
20 Apr	Manchester United	A	W	2–1
25 Apr	Chelsea	A	W	3–1

FA Cup

Date	Opponent			
11 Jan	Stockport County	H	W	3–0
1 Feb	Hull City	H	W	3–0
22 Feb	Manchester United	H	L	0–2

SEASON 1908–1909 FOOTBALL LEAGUE (DIVISION 1)

Date	Opponent			
1 Sep	Liverpool	A	L	2–3
5 Sep	Sheffield Wednesday	H	D	1–1
12 Sep	Nottingham Forest	A	W	2–1
19 Sep	Sunderland	H	W	2–0
26 Sep	Chelsea	A	W	2–0
3 Oct	Blackburn Rovers	H	D	1–1
10 Oct	Bradford City	A	D	1–1
17 Oct	Manchester United	H	W	3–1
24 Oct	Everton	A	L	1–3
31 Oct	Leicester Fosse	H	D	1–1
7 Nov	Woolwich Arsenal	A	L	1–0
14 Nov	Notts County	H	D	1–1
21 Nov	Newcastle United	A	W	2–0
28 Nov	Bristol City	H	D	1–1
5 Dec	Preston North End	A	L	2–3
12 Dec	Middlesbrough	H	L	0–3
19 Dec	Manchester City	A	L	0–2
25 Dec	Liverpool	H	D	1–1
26 Dec	Bury	H	W	3–0
1 Jan	Bury	A	W	2–1
2 Jan	Sheffield Wednesday	A	L	2–4
9 Jan	Nottingham Forest	H	L	1–2
23 Jan	Sunderland	A	L	3–4
30 Jan	Chelsea	H	D	0–0
6 Feb	Sheffield United	A	L	1–3
13 Feb	Bradford City	H	L	1–3
15 Feb	Blackburn Rovers	A	L	1–3
27 Feb	Everton	H	W	3–1
13 Mar	Woolwich Arsenal	H	W	2–1
20 Mar	Notts County	A	D	1–1
27 Mar	Leicester Fosse	A	L	2–4
31 Mar	Manchester United	A	W	2–0
3 Apr	Bristol City	A	D	0–0
9 Apr	Sheffield United	H	W	3–0
10 Apr	Preston North End	H	L	2–4
17 Apr	Middlesbrough	A	L	0–1
24 Apr	Manchester City	H	W	2–1
26 Apr	Newcastle United	H	W	3–0

FA Cup

Date	Opponent			
16 Jan	Nottingham Forest	A	L	0–2

SEASON 1909–1910 FOOTBALL LEAGUE (DIVISION 1)

Date	Opponent			
1 Sep	Woolwich Arsenal	H	W	5–1
4 Sep	Bolton Wanderers	A	W	2–1
6 Sep	Woolwich Arsenal	A		abandoned
11 Sep	Chelsea	H	W	4–1
18 Apr	Blackburn Rovers	A	L	2–3
25 Sep	Nottingham Forest	H	D	0–0
2 Oct	Sunderland	A	D	1–1
9 Oct	Everton	H	W	3–1
16 Oct	Manchester United	A	L	0–2
23 Oct	Bradford City	H	W	3–1
30 Oct	Sheffield Wednesday	A	L	2–3
6 Nov	Bristol City	H	W	1–0
13 Nov	Bury	A	W	2–0
20 Nov	Tottenham Hotspur	H	W	3–2
27 Nov	Preston North End	A	L	0–1
4 Dec	Notts County	H	D	1–1
11 Dec	Newcastle United	A	L	0–1
18 Dec	Liverpool	H	W	3–1
25 Dec	Sheffield United	A	W	1–0
27 Dec	Sheffield United	H	W	2–1
1 Jan	Nottingham Forest	A	W	4–1
8 Jan	Bolton Wanderers	H	W	3–1
22 Jan	Chelsea	A	D	0–0
29 Jan	Blackburn Rovers	H	W	4–3
12 Feb	Sunderland	H	W	3–2
26 Feb	Manchester United	H	W	7–1
5 Mar	Bradford City	A	W	2–1
12 Mar	Sheffield Wednesday	H	W	5–0
14 Mar	Everton	A	D	0–0
19 Mar	Bristol City	A	D	0–0
25 Mar	Middlesbrough	H	W	4–2
26 Mar	Bury	H	W	4–1
28 Mar	Middlesbrough	A	L	2–3
2 Apr	Tottenham Hotspur	A	D	1–1
9 Apr	Preston North End	H	W	3–0
11 Apr	Woolwich Arsenal	A	L	0–1
16 Apr	Notts County	A	W	3–2
27 Apr	Newcastle United	H	W	4–0
30 Apr	Liverpool	A	L	0–2

FA Cup

Date	Opponent			
15 Jan	Oldham Athletic	A	W	2–1
5 Feb	Derby County	H	W	6–1
19 Feb	Manchester City	H	L	1–2

SEASON 1910–1911 FOOTBALL LEAGUE (DIVISION 1)

Date	Opponent			
3 Sep	Oldham Athletic	H	D	1–1
10 Sep	Sunderland	A	L	2–3
17 Sep	Woolwich Arsenal	H	W	3–0
24 Sep	Bradford City	A	W	2–1
1 Oct	Blackburn Rovers	H	D	2–2
8 Oct	Nottingham Forest	A	L	1–3
15 Oct	Manchester City	H	W	2–1
22 Oct	Everton	A	W	1–0
29 Oct	Sheffield Wednesday	H	W	2–1
5 Nov	Bristol City	A	W	2–1
12 Nov	Newcastle United	H	W	3–2
19 Nov	Tottenham Hotspur	A	W	2–1
25 Nov	Middlesbrough	H	W	5–0
3 Dec	Preston North End	A	W	1–0
10 Dec	Notts County	H	W	3–1
17 Dec	Manchester United	A	L	0–2
24 Dec	Liverpool	H	D	1–1
26 Dec	Bury	H	W	4–1
28 Dec	Sheffield United	A	L	1–2
31 Dec	Oldham Athletic	A	D	1–1
2 Jan	Bury	A	L	0–1
7 Jan	Sunderland	H	W	2–1
21 Jan	Woolwich Arsenal	A		abandoned
28 Jan	Bradford City	H	W	4–1
11 Feb	Nottingham Forest	H	W	3–1
18 Feb	Manchester City	A	D	1–1
25 Feb	Tottenham Hotspur	H	W	4–0
4 Mar	Sheffield Wednesday	A	L	0–1
11 Mar	Bristol City	H	W	2–0
15 Mar	Woolwich Arsenal	A	D	1–1
18 Mar	Newcastle United	A	L	0–1
27 Mar	Everton	H	W	2–1
1 Apr	Middlesbrough	A	W	1–0
8 Apr	Preston North End	H	L	0–2
14 Apr	Sheffield United	H	W	3–0
15 Apr	Notts County	A	W	2–1
22 Apr	Manchester United	H	W	4–2
24 Apr	Blackburn Rovers	A	D	0–0
29 Apr	Liverpool	A	L	1–3

FA Cup

Date	Opponent			
14 Jan	Portsmouth	A	W	4–1
4 Feb	Manchester United	A	L	1–2

FA Charity Shield

Date	Opponent			
5 Sep	Brighton & Hove Albion	A	L	0–1

SEASON 1911–1912 FOOTBALL LEAGUE (DIVISION 1)

Date	Opponent			
2 Sep	Bradford City	A	L	1–2
4 Sep	West Bromwich Albion	H	L	0–3
9 Sep	Woolwich Arsenal	H	W	4–1
16 Sep	Manchester City	A	W	6–2
23 Sep	Everton	H	W	3–0
30 Sep	West Bromwich Albion	A	D	2–2
7 Oct	Sunderland	H	L	1–3
14 Oct	Blackburn Rovers	A	L	1–3
21 Oct	Sheffield Wednesday	H	L	2–3
23 Oct	Sheffield United	A	W	1–0
28 Oct	Bury	A	D	1–1
4 Nov	Middlesbrough	H	W	2–1
18 Nov	Tottenham Hotspur	H	D	2–2
25 Nov	Manchester United	A	L	1–3
2 Dec	Liverpool	H	W	5–0
9 Dec	Preston North End	H	W	1–0
16 Dec	Newcastle United	A	L	2–6
23 Dec	Sheffield United	H	W	1–0
26 Dec	Oldham Athletic	H	W	6–1
30 Dec	Bradford City	H	D	0–0
1 Jan	Bolton Wanderers	A	L	0–3
6 Jan	Woolwich Arsenal	A	D	2–2

20 Jan	Manchester City	H	W	3–1
27 Jan	Everton	A	D	1–1
10 Feb	Sunderland	A	D	2–2
17 Feb	Blackburn Rovers	H	L	0–3
24 Feb	Sheffield Wednesday	A	L	0–3
2 Mar	Bury	H	W	5–2
9 Mar	Middlesbrough	A	W	2–1
13 Mar	Notts County	A	L	0–2
16 Mar	Notts County	H	W	5–1
23 Mar	Tottenham Hotspur	A	L	1–2
30 Mar	Manchester United	H	W	6–0
5 Apr	Bolton Wanderers	H	L	0–1
6 Apr	Liverpool	A	W	2–1
8 Apr	Oldham Athletic	A	W	2–1
13 Apr	Preston North End	A	L	1–4
20 Apr	Newcastle United	H	W	2–0

FA Cup

13 Jan	Walsall	H	W	6–0
3 Feb	Reading	H	D	1–1
7 Feb	Reading (R)	A	L	0–1

SEASON 1912–1913 FOOTBALL LEAGUE (DIVISION 1)

2 Sep	Chelsea	H	W	1–0
7 Sep	Bradford City	H	W	3–1
9 Sep	Oldham Athletic	A	D	2–2
14 Sep	Manchester City	A	L	0–1
16 Sep	Woolwich Arsenal	A	W	3–0
21 Sep	West Bromwich Albion	H	L	2–4
28 Sep	Everton	A	W	1–0
5 Oct	Sheffield Wednesday	H	W	10–0
12 Oct	Blackburn Rovers	A	D	2–2
19 Oct	Derby County	H	W	5–1
26 Oct	Tottenham Hotspur	A	D	3–3
2 Nov	Middlesbrough	H	W	5–1
9 Nov	Notts County	A	D	1–1
16 Nov	Manchester United	H	W	4–2
23 Nov	Sunderland	A	L	1–3
30 Nov	Liverpool	A	L	0–2
7 Dec	Bolton Wanderers	H	D	1–1
14 Dec	Sheffield United	A	L	2–3
21 Dec	Newcastle United	H	W	3–1
26 Dec	Oldham Athletic	H	W	7–1
28 Dec	Bradford City	A	D	1–1
4 Jan	Manchester City	H	W	2–0
18 Jan	West Bromwich Albion	A	D	2–2
25 Jan	Everton	H	D	1–1
8 Feb	Sheffield Wednesday	A	D	1–1
15 Feb	Blackburn Rovers	H	D	1–1
1 Mar	Tottenham Hotspur	H	W	1–0
12 Mar	Derby County	A	W	1–0
15 Mar	Notts County	H	W	1–0
21 Mar	Chelsea	A	W	2–1
22 Mar	Manchester United	A	L	0–4
24 Mar	Woolwich Arsenal	H	W	4–1
5 Apr	Liverpool	H	L	1–3
9 Apr	Middlesbrough	A	D	1–1
12 Apr	Bolton Wanderers	A	W	3–2
23 Apr	Sunderland	H	D	1–1
26 Apr	Newcastle United	A	W	3–2
28 Apr	Sheffield United	H	W	4–2

FA Cup

11 Jan	Derby County	A		abandoned
15 Jan	Derby County	A	W	3–1
1 Feb	West Ham United	H	W	5–0
22 Feb	Crystal Palace	H	W	5–0
8 Mar	Bradford Park Avenue	A	W	5–0
29 Mar	Oldham Athletic	N	W	1–0
19 Apr	Sunderland (F)	N	W	1–0

SEASON 1913–1914 FOOTBALL LEAGUE (DIVISION 1)

1 Sep	Manchester City	H	D	1–1
6 Sep	Bradford City	A	D	0–0
13 Sep	Blackburn Rovers	H	L	1–3
20 Sep	Sunderland	A	L	0–2
27 Sep	Everton	H	W	3–1
4 Oct	West Bromwich Albion	A	L	0–1
11 Oct	Sheffield Wednesday	H	W	2–0
18 Oct	Bolton Wanderers	A	L	0–3
25 Oct	Chelsea	H	L	1–2
1 Nov	Oldham Athletic	A	W	1–0
8 Nov	Manchester United	H	W	3–1

15 Nov	Burnley	A	L	0–4
22 Nov	Preston North End	H	W	3–0
29 Nov	Newcastle United	A	D	2–2
6 Dec	Liverpool	H	W	2–1
13 Dec	Tottenham Hotspur	H	D	3–3
20 Dec	Middlesbrough	A	L	2–5
25 Dec	Derby County	A	W	2–0
26 Dec	Sheffield United	H	W	3–0
27 Dec	Bradford City	H	L	0–1
1 Jan	Sheffield United	A	L	0–3
3 Jan	Blackburn Rovers	A	D	0–0
17 Jan	Sunderland	H	W	5–0
24 Jan	Everton	A	W	4–1
7 Feb	West Bromwich Albion	H	W	2–0
14 Feb	Sheffield Wednesday	A	W	3–2
25 Feb	Bolton Wanderers	H	W	1–0
28 Feb	Chelsea	A	W	3–0
14 Mar	Manchester United	A	W	6–0
18 Mar	Oldham Athletic	H	D	0–0
21 Mar	Burnley	H	W	1–0
1 Apr	Preston North End	A	L	2–3
4 Apr	Newcastle United	H	L	1–3
10 Apr	Manchester City	A	L	1–3
11 Apr	Liverpool	A	W	1–0
13 Apr	Derby County	H	W	3–2
18 Apr	Tottenham Hotspur	A	W	2–0
25 Apr	Middlesbrough	H	L	1–3

FA Cup

10 Jan	Stoke City	H	W	4–0
31 Jan	Exeter City	A	W	2–1
21 Feb	West Bromwich Albion	H	W	2–1
7 Mar	Sheffield Wednesday	A	W	1–0
28 Mar	Liverpool	N	L	0–2

SEASON 1914–1915 FOOTBALL LEAGUE (DIVISION 1)

2 Sep	Notts County	H	W	2–1
5 Sep	Sunderland	H	L	1–3
12 Sep	Sheffield Wednesday	A	L	2–5
19 Sep	West Bromwich Albion	H	W	2–1
26 Sep	Everton	A	D	0–0
3 Oct	Chelsea	H	W	2–1
10 Oct	Bradford City	A	L	0–3
17 Oct	Burnley	H	D	3–3
24 Oct	Tottenham Hotspur	A	W	2–0
31 Oct	Newcastle United	H	W	2–1
7 Nov	Middlesbrough	A	D	1–1
14 Nov	Sheffield United	H	W	1–0
25 Nov	Manchester City	A	L	0–1
28 Nov	Liverpool	A	W	6–3
5 Dec	Bradford (Park Avenue)	H	L	1–2
12 Dec	Oldham Athletic	A	D	3–3
19 Dec	Manchester United	H	D	3–3
25 Dec	Blackburn Rovers	A	W	2–1
26 Dec	Bolton Wanderers	H	L	1–7
1 Jan	Bolton Wanderers	A	D	2–2
2 Jan	Sunderland	A	L	0–4
16 Jan	Sheffield Wednesday	H	D	0–0
23 Jan	West Bromwich Albion	A	L	0–2
6 Feb	Chelsea	A	L	1–3
10 Feb	Everton	H	L	1–5
13 Feb	Bradford City	H	D	0–0
22 Feb	Burnley	A	L	1–2
27 Feb	Tottenham Hotspur	H	W	3–1
13 Mar	Middlesbrough	H	W	5–0
20 Mar	Sheffield United	A	L	0–3
2 Apr	Blackburn Rovers	H	W	2–1
3 Apr	Liverpool	H	W	6–2
5 Apr	Notts County	A	D	1–1
10 Apr	Bradford (Park Avenue)	A	D	2–2
17 Apr	Oldham Athletic	H	D	0–0
21 Apr	Manchester City	H	W	4–1
26 Apr	Manchester United	A	L	0–1
28 Apr	Newcastle United	A	L	0–3

FA Cup

9 Jan	Exeter City	H	W	2–0
30 Jan	Manchester City	A	L	0–1

SEASON 1919–1920 FOOTBALL LEAGUE (DIVISION 1)

30 Aug	Sunderland	A	L	1–2
1 Sep	Derby County	H	D	2–2
6 Sep	Sunderland	H	L	0–3
8 Sep	Derby County	A	L	0–1
13 Sep	Liverpool	A	L	1–2
20 Sep	Liverpool	H	L	0–1
27 Sep	Bradford (Park Avenue)	A	L	1–6
4 Oct	Bradford (Park Avenue)	H	W	1–0
11 Oct	Preston North End	A	L	0–3
18 Oct	Preston North End	H	L	2–4
25 Oct	Middlesbrough	A	W	4–1
1 Nov	Middlesbrough	H	W	5–3
10 Nov	West Bromwich Albion	A	W	2–1
15 Nov	West Bromwich Albion	H	L	2–4
22 Nov	Sheffield United	A	W	2–1
29 Nov	Sheffield United	H	W	4–0
6 Dec	Manchester United	H	W	2–0
13 Dec	Manchester United	A	W	2–1
20 Dec	Oldham Athletic	H	W	3–0
23 Dec	Chelsea	H	W	5–2
27 Dec	Oldham Athletic	A	W	3–0
1 Jan	Newcastle United	A	L	0–2
3 Jan	Burnley	H	D	2–2
17 Jan	Burnley	A	D	0–0
24 Jan	Arsenal	A	W	1–0
7 Feb	Everton	A	D	1–1
11 Feb	Arsenal	H	W	2–1
14 Feb	Everton	H	D	2–2
28 Feb	Bradford City	H	W	3–1
13 Mar	Bolton Wanderers	A	L	1–2
17 Mar	Bradford City	A	L	1–3
20 Mar	Blackburn Rovers	H	L	1–2
2 Apr	Chelsea	A	L	1–2
3 Apr	Notts County	H	W	3–1
5 Apr	Newcastle United	H	W	4–0
7 Apr	Bolton Wanderers	H	L	3–6
10 Apr	Notts County	A	L	1–2
15 Apr	Blackburn Rovers	A	L	1–5
17 Apr	Sheffield Wednesday	H	W	3–1
26 Apr	Manchester City	H	L	0–1
29 Apr	Sheffield Wednesday	A	W	1–0
1 May	Manchester City	A	D	2–2

FA Cup

10 Jan	Queens Park Rangers	H	W	2–1
31 Jan	Manchester United	A	W	2–1
21 Feb	Sunderland	H	W	1–0
6 Mar	Tottenham Hotspur	A	W	1–0
27 Mar	Chelsea	N	W	3–1
24 Apr	Huddersfield Town (F)	N	W	1–0

SEASON 1920 – 1921 FOOTBALL LEAGUE (DIVISION 1)

28 Aug	Arsenal	H	W	5–0
30 Aug	Manchester City	A	L	1–3
4 Sep	Arsenal	A	W	1–0
6 Sep	Manchester City	H	W	3–1
11 Sep	Tottenham Hotspur	H	W	4–2
15 Sep	Bolton Wanderers	A	L	0–5
18 Sep	Tottenham Hotspur	A	W	2–1
25 Sep	Oldham Athletic	H	W	3–0
2 Oct	Oldham Athletic	A	D	1–1
9 Oct	Preston North End	H	W	1–0
16 Oct	Preston North End	A	L	1–6
23 Oct	Sheffield United	H	W	4–0
30 Oct	Sheffield United	A	D	0–0
6 Nov	West Bromwich Albion	H	D	0–0
13 Nov	West Bromwich Albion	A	L	1–2
20 Nov	Bradford (Park Avenue)	H	W	4–1
27 Nov	Bradford (Park Avenue)	A	L	0–4
4 Dec	Newcastle United	A	L	1–2
11 Dec	Newcastle United	H	D	0–0
18 Dec	Liverpool	A	L	1–4
25 Dec	Manchester United	H	L	3–4
27 Dec	Manchester United	A	W	3–1
1 Jan	Liverpool	H	L	0–2
15 Jan	Everton	H	L	1–3
22 Jan	Everton	A	D	1–1
5 Feb	Burnley	A	L	1–7
9 Feb	Burnley	H	D	0–0
12 Feb	Sunderland	H	L	1–5
23 Feb	Sunderland	A	W	1–0
26 Feb	Bradford City	H	L	1–2
7 Mar	Bradford City	A	L	0–3

165

12 Mar	Huddersfield Town	H	D	0–0
19 Mar	Huddersfield Town	A	L	0–1
26 Mar	Middlesbrough	A	W	4–1
28 Mar	Chelsea	H	W	3–0
29 Mar	Chelsea	A	L	1–5
2 Apr	Middlesbrough	H	L	0–1
9 Apr	Blackburn Rovers	A	W	1–0
16 Apr	Blackburn Rovers	H	W	3–0
23 Apr	Derby County	A	W	3–2
30 Apr	Derby County	H	W	1–0
7 May	Bolton Wanderers	H	W	2–0

FA Cup

8 Jan	Bristol City	H	W	2–0
29 Jan	Notts County	A	D	0–0
2 Feb	Notts County (R)	H	W	1–0
19 Feb	Huddersfield Town	H	W	2–0
5 Mar	Tottenham Hotspur	A	L	0–1

SEASON 1921–1922 FOOTBALL LEAGUE (DIVISION 1)

27 Aug	Manchester City	A	L	1–2
29 Aug	Cardiff City	H	W	2–1
3 Sep	Manchester City	H	W	4–0
5 Sep	Cardiff City	A	W	4–0
10 Sep	Preston North End	A	L	0–1
12 Sep	Blackburn Rovers	H	D	1–1
17 Sep	Preston North End	H	W	2–0
24 Sep	Tottenham Hotspur	A	L	1–3
1 Oct	Tottenham Hotspur	H	W	2–1
8 Oct	West Bromwich Albion	A	W	1–0
15 Oct	West Bromwich Albion	H	L	0–1
22 Oct	Middlesbrough	A	L	0–5
29 Oct	Middlesbrough	H	W	6–2
5 Nov	Bradford City	A	L	2–3
12 Nov	Bradford City	H	W	7–1
19 Nov	Manchester United	H	W	3–1
26 Nov	Manchester United	A	L	0–1
3 Dec	Liverpool	H	D	1–1
10 Dec	Liverpool	A	L	0–2
17 Dec	Newcastle United	A	W	2–1
24 Dec	Newcastle United	H	W	1–0
26 Dec	Sheffield United	A	W	3–2
27 Dec	Sheffield United	H	W	5–3
31 Dec	Burnley	A	L	1–2
14 Jan	Burnley	H	W	2–0
21 Jan	Everton	A	L	2–3
4 Feb	Sunderland	A	W	4–1
8 Feb	Everton	H	W	2–1
11 Feb	Sunderland	H	W	2–0
25 Feb	Huddersfield Town	H	W	2–0
11 Mar	Birmingham City	H	D	1–1
15 Mar	Birmingham City	A	L	0–1
18 Mar	Arsenal	H	W	2–0
25 Mar	Arsenal	A	L	0–2
1 Apr	Blackburn Rovers	A	W	2–1
5 Apr	Huddersfield Town	A	L	0–1
14 Apr	Chelsea	A	L	0–1
15 Apr	Bolton Wanderers	H	W	2–1
17 Apr	Chelsea	H	L	1–4
22 Apr	Bolton Wanderers	A	L	0–1
29 Apr	Oldham Athletic	H	W	2–0
6 May	Oldham Athletic	A	L	1–3

FA Cup

7 Jan	Derby County	H	W	6–1
28 Jan	Luton Town	H	W	1–0
18 Feb	Stoke City	A	D	0–0
22 Feb	Stoke City (R)	H	W	4–0
4 Mar	Notts County	A	D	2–2
8 Mar	Notts County (R)	H	L	3–4

SEASON 1922–1923 FOOTBALL LEAGUE (DIVISION 1)

26 Aug	Blackburn Rovers	H	W	2–0
28 Aug	Cardiff City	A	L	0–3
2 Sep	Blackburn Rovers	A	L	2–4
4 Sep	Cardiff City	H	L	1–3
9 Sep	West Bromwich Albion	H	W	2–0
16 Sep	West Bromwich Albion	A	L	0–3
28 Sep	Middlesbrough	H	D	2–2
30 Sep	Middlesbrough	A	D	2–2
7 Oct	Tottenham Hotspur	H	W	2–0
14 Oct	Tottenham Hotspur	A	W	2–1
21 Oct	Bolton Wanderers	H	W	2–0
28 Oct	Bolton Wanderers	A	L	0–3

4 Nov	Oldham Athletic	A	W	2–0
11 Nov	Oldham Athletic	H	W	3–0
18 Nov	Liverpool	A	L	0–3
25 Nov	Liverpool	H	L	0–1
2 Dec	Sheffield United	A	D	1–1
9 Dec	Sheffield United	H	L	0–1
16 Dec	Newcastle United	H	D	1–1
23 Dec	Newcastle United	A	D	0–0
25 Dec	Burnley	A	D	1–1
26 Dec	Burnley	H	W	1–0
30 Dec	Preston North End	H	W	1–0
6 Jan	Preston North End	A	L	2–3
20 Jan	Nottingham Forest	A	L	1–3
27 Jan	Nottingham Forest	H	W	4–0
3 Feb	Manchester City	H	W	2–0
10 Feb	Manchester City	A	D	1–1
17 Feb	Stoke City	H	W	6–0
24 Feb	Stoke City	A	D	1–1
3 Mar	Huddersfield Town	H	W	2–1
10 Mar	Huddersfield Town	A	W	5–3
17 Mar	Birmingham City	A	L	0–1
24 Mar	Birmingham City	H	W	3–0
30 Mar	Chelsea	H	W	1–0
31 Mar	Arsenal	A	L	0–2
2 Apr	Chelsea	A	D	1–1
7 Apr	Arsenal	H	D	1–1
14 Apr	Everton	A	L	1–2
21 Apr	Everton	H	W	3–0
28 Apr	Sunderland	A	L	0–2
5 May	Sunderland	H	W	1–0

FA Cup

13 Jan	Blackburn Rovers	H	L	0–1

SEASON 1923–1924 FOOTBALL LEAGUE (DIVISION 1)

25 Aug	Birmingham City	A	L	0–3
29 Aug	Manchester City	H	W	2–0
1 Sep	Birmingham City	H	D	0–0
5 Sep	Manchester City	A	W	2–1
8 Sep	Chelsea	A	D	0–0
12 Sep	Everton	H	D	1–1
15 Sep	Chelsea	H	D	0–0
19 Sep	Everton	A	L	0–2
22 Sep	Preston North End	A	D	2–2
29 Sep	Preston North End	H	W	5–1
6 Oct	Burnley	A	W	2–1
13 Oct	Burnley	H	D	1–1
20 Oct	West Bromwich Albion	A	L	0–1
27 Oct	West Bromwich Albion	H	W	4–0
3 Nov	Notts County	H	D	0–0
10 Nov	Notts County	A	W	1–0
17 Nov	Liverpool	H	D	0–0
24 Nov	Liverpool	A	W	1–0
1 Dec	Middlesbrough	H	D	0–0
8 Dec	Middlesbrough	A	W	2–0
15 Dec	Sheffield United	A	L	1–2
22 Dec	Sheffield United	H	D	2–2
25 Dec	West Ham United	H	D	1–1
26 Dec	West Ham United	A	L	0–1
29 Dec	Cardiff City	H	W	2–1
1 Jan	Newcastle United	A	L	1–4
5 Jan	Cardiff City	A	W	2–0
19 Jan	Bolton Wanderers	A	L	0–1
26 Jan	Bolton Wanderers	H	W	1–0
9 Feb	Sunderland	H	L	0–1
13 Feb	Sunderland	A	L	0–2
16 Feb	Arsenal	A	W	1–0
1 Mar	Blackburn Rovers	A	L	1–3
12 Mar	Arsenal	H	W	2–1
15 Mar	Tottenham Hotspur	H	D	0–0
22 Mar	Tottenham Hotspur	A	W	3–2
2 Apr	Blackburn Rovers	H	W	1–0
5 Apr	Huddersfield Town	A	L	0–1
12 Apr	Nottingham Forest	A	D	0–0
19 Apr	Nottingham Forest	H	W	2–0
21 Apr	Newcastle United	H	W	6–1
30 Apr	Huddersfield Town	H	W	3–1

FA Cup

12 Jan	Ashington	A	W	5–1
2 Feb	Swansea Town	A	W	2–0
23 Feb	Leeds United	H	W	3–0
8 Mar	West Bromwich Albion	A	W	2–0
29 Mar	Burnley	N	W	3–0
26 Apr	Newcastle United (F)	N	L	0–2

SEASON 1924–1925 FOOTBALL LEAGUE (DIVISION 1)

30 Aug	Liverpool	A	W	4–2
1 Sep	Bury	H	D	3–3
6 Sep	Newcastle United	H	D	0–0
8 Sep	Bury	A	L	3–4
13 Sep	Sheffield United	A	D	2–2
20 Sep	West Ham United	H	D	1–1
27 Sep	Blackburn Rovers	A	D	1–1
2 Oct	Nottingham Forest	A	W	2–0
4 Oct	Huddersfield Town	H	D	1–1
11 Oct	Birmingham City	A	L	0–1
18 Oct	Arsenal	A	D	1–1
25 Oct	West Bromwich Albion	A	W	1–0
1 Nov	Tottenham Hotspur	A	W	3–1
8 Nov	Bolton Wanderers	H	D	2–2
15 Nov	Notts County	A	D	0–0
22 Nov	Everton	H	W	3–1
29 Nov	Sunderland	A	D	1–1
6 Dec	Cardiff City	H	L	1–2
13 Dec	Preston North End	A	L	2–3
20 Dec	Burnley	H	W	3–0
25 Dec	Leeds United	A	L	0–6
26 Dec	Leeds United	H	W	2–1
3 Jan	Newcastle United	A	L	1–4
17 Jan	Sheffield United	H	D	1–1
21 Jan	Liverpool	H	L	1–4
24 Jan	West Ham United	A	L	0–2
7 Feb	Huddersfield Town	A	L	1–4
14 Feb	Birmingham City	H	W	1–0
28 Feb	West Bromwich Albion	H	L	1–4
7 Mar	Tottenham Hotspur	H	L	0–1
14 Mar	Bolton Wanderers	A	L	0–4
21 Mar	Notts County	H	D	0–0
28 Mar	Everton	A	L	0–2
1 Apr	Arsenal	H	W	4–0
4 Apr	Sunderland	H	L	1–4
10 Apr	Manchester City	H	W	2–1
11 Apr	Cardiff City	A	L	1–2
13 Apr	Manchester City	A	L	0–1
18 Apr	Preston North End	H	W	1–0
25 Apr	Burnley	A	D	1–1
29 Apr	Blackburn Rovers	H	W	4–3
2 May	Nottingham Forest	H	W	2–0

FA Cup

10 Jan	Port Vale	H	W	7–2
31 Jan	Swansea Town	A	W	3–1
21 Feb	West Bromwich Albion	A	D	1–1
25 Feb	West Bromwich Albion (R)	H	L	1–2

SEASON 1925–1926 FOOTBALL LEAGUE (DIVISION 1)

29 Aug	Burnley	H	W	10–0
2 Sep	Manchester United	A	L	0–3
5 Sep	Leeds United	A	D	2–2
7 Sep	Manchester United	H	D	2–2
12 Sep	Newcastle United	H	D	2–2
19 Sep	Bolton Wanderers	A	W	3–1
26 Sep	Notts County	H	W	2–1
3 Oct	West Bromwich Albion	A	D	1–1
5 Oct	Sunderland	H	W	4–2
10 Oct	Leicester City	A	W	2–1
17 Oct	Birmingham City	H	D	3–3
24 Oct	Bury	A	W	3–2
31 Oct	Cardiff City	H	L	0–2
7 Nov	Sheffield United	A	L	1–4
14 Nov	Huddersfield Town	H	W	3–0
21 Nov	Everton	A	D	1–1
28 Nov	Manchester City	H	W	3–1
5 Dec	Tottenham Hotspur	A	D	2–2
12 Dec	Blackburn Rovers	H	L	1–2
19 Dec	Sunderland	A	L	2–3
25 Dec	West Ham United	A	L	2–5
26 Dec	West Ham United	H	W	2–0
1 Jan	Liverpool	A	L	1–3
2 Jan	Burnley	A	W	3–2
16 Jan	Leeds United	H		abandoned
23 Jan	Newcastle United	A	D	2–2
3 Feb	Leeds United	H	W	3–1
6 Feb	Notts County	A	L	0–1
13 Feb	West Bromwich Albion	H	W	2–1
27 Feb	Birmingham City	A	L	1–2
6 Mar	Bury	H	D	1–1
10 Mar	Leicester City	H	D	2–2
13 Mar	Cardiff City	A	L	0–2
20 Mar	Sheffield United	H	D	2–2

27 Mar	Huddersfield Town	A	L	1–5
2 Apr	Arsenal	H	W	3–0
3 Apr	Everton	H	W	3–1
5 Apr	Arsenal	A	L	0–2
6 Apr	Liverpool	H	W	3–0
10 Apr	Manchester City	A	L	2–4
17 Apr	Tottenham Hotspur	H	W	3–0
24 Apr	Blackburn Rovers	A	L	1–3
26 Apr	Bolton Wanderers	H	D	2–2

FA Cup

9 Jan	Hull City	A	W	3–0
30 Jan	West Bromwich Albion	A	W	2–1
20 Feb	Arsenal	H	D	1–1
24 Feb	Arsenal (R)	A	L	0–2

SEASON 1926–1927 FOOTBALL LEAGUE (DIVISION 1)

28 Aug	Newcastle United	A	L	0–1
30 Aug	Liverpool	H	D	1–1
4 Sep	Burnley	H	D	1–1
8 Sep	Liverpool	A	L	1–2
11 Sep	Cardiff City	A	W	3–2
15 Sep	Leeds United	A	L	1–3
18 Sep	Bury	H	L	1–2
25 Sep	Bolton Wanderers	H	L	3–4
2 Oct	Manchester United	A	L	1–2
9 Oct	Derby County	H	W	3–1
16 Oct	Sunderland	A	D	1–1
23 Oct	West Bromwich Albion	H	W	2–0
30 Oct	Birmingham City	A	W	2–1
6 Nov	Tottenham Hotspur	H	L	2–3
13 Nov	West Ham United	A	L	1–5
20 Nov	Sheffield Wednesday	H	D	2–2
27 Nov	Leicester City	A	L	1–5
4 Dec	Everton	H	W	5–3
11 Dec	Blackburn Rovers	A	W	2–0
18 Dec	Huddersfield Town	H	W	3–0
25 Dec	Sheffield United	H	W	4–0
27 Dec	Sheffield United	A	L	1–3
28 Dec	Leeds United	H	W	5–1
15 Jan	Newcastle United	H	L	1–2
22 Jan	Burnley	A	L	3–6
29 Jan	Blackburn Rovers	H	W	4–3
31 Jan	Cardiff City	H	D	0–0
5 Feb	Bury	A	W	1–0
12 Feb	Bolton Wanderers	A	W	2–0
19 Feb	Manchester United	H	W	2–0
26 Feb	Derby County	A	W	3–2
5 Mar	Sunderland	H	W	3–1
12 Mar	West Bromwich Albion	A	L	2–6
19 Mar	Birmingham City	H	W	4–2
26 Mar	Tottenham Hotspur	A	W	1–0
2 Apr	West Ham United	H	L	1–5
9 Apr	Sheffield Wednesday	A	L	1–3
15 Apr	Arsenal	A	L	1–2
16 Apr	Leicester City	H	W	2–0
18 Apr	Arsenal	H	L	2–3
23 Apr	Everton	A	D	2–2
7 May	Huddersfield Town	A	D	0–0

FA Cup

8 Jan	Cardiff City	A	L	1–2

SEASON 1927–1928 FOOTBALL LEAGUE (DIVISION 1)

27 Aug	Leicester City	H	L	0–3
31 Aug	Portsmouth	A	L	1–3
3 Sep	Liverpool	A	D	0–0
5 Sep	Portsmouth	H	W	7–2
10 Sep	Arsenal	H	D	2–2
17 Sep	Burnley	A	L	2–4
24 Sep	Bury	H	W	1–0
1 Oct	Sheffield United	A	W	3–0
8 Oct	Middlesbrough	H	W	5–1
15 Oct	Sunderland	H	W	4–2
22 Oct	Huddersfield Town	A	D	1–1
29 Oct	Newcastle United	H	W	3–0
5 Nov	Birmingham City	A	D	1–1
12 Nov	Tottenham Hotspur	H	L	1–2
19 Nov	Manchester United	A	L	1–5
26 Nov	Blackburn Rovers	H	W	2–0
3 Dec	Cardiff City	A	L	1–2
10 Dec	Everton	H	L	2–3
17 Dec	Bolton Wanderers	A	L	1–3

24 Dec	Sheffield Wednesday	H	W	5–4
26 Dec	Derby County	A	L	0–5
27 Dec	Derby County	H	L	0–1
31 Dec	Leicester City	A	L	0–3
7 Jan	Liverpool	H	L	3–4
21 Jan	Arsenal	A	W	3–0
4 Feb	Bury	A	D	0–0
8 Feb	Burnley	H	W	3–1
11 Feb	Sheffield United	H	W	1–0
25 Feb	Sunderland	A	W	3–2
10 Mar	Newcastle United	A	L	5–7
17 Mar	Birmingham City	H	D	1–1
21 Mar	Middlesbrough	A	D	0–0
24 Mar	Tottenham Hotspur	A	L	1–2
31 Mar	Manchester United	H	W	3–1
6 Apr	West Ham United	A	D	0–0
7 Apr	Blackburn Rovers	A	W	1–0
9 Apr	West Ham United	H	W	1–0
14 Apr	Cardiff City	H	W	3–1
21 Apr	Everton	A	L	2–3
28 Apr	Bolton Wanderers	H	D	2–2
2 May	Huddersfield Town	H	W	3–0
5 May	Sheffield Wednesday	A	L	0–2

FA Cup

14 Jan	Burnley	A	W	2–0
28 Jan	Crewe Alexandra	H	W	3–0
18 Feb	Arsenal	A	L	1–4

SEASON 1928–1929 FOOTBALL LEAGUE (DIVISION 1)

25 Aug	Leeds United	A	L	1–4
27 Aug	Manchester United	H	D	0–0
1 Sep	Liverpool	H	W	3–1
8 Sep	West Ham United	A	L	1–4
15 Sep	Newcastle United	H	D	1–1
22 Sep	Burnley	A	L	1–4
29 Sep	Cardiff City	H	W	1–0
6 Oct	Sheffield United	A	W	3–1
13 Oct	Bury	H	W	7–1
20 Oct	Bolton Wanderers	H	L	3–5
27 Oct	Birmingham City	A	W	4–2
3 Nov	Derby County	H	L	2–3
10 Nov	Sunderland	A	W	3–1
17 Nov	Blackburn Rovers	H	W	2–1
24 Nov	Arsenal	A	W	5–2
1 Dec	Everton	H	W	2–0
8 Dec	Huddersfield Town	A	L	0–3
19 Dec	Manchester City	H	W	5–1
22 Dec	Sheffield Wednesday	A	L	1–4
25 Dec	Portsmouth	A	L	2–3
26 Dec	Portsmouth	H	W	3–2
29 Dec	Leeds United	H	W	1–0
1 Jan	Manchester United	A	D	2–2
5 Jan	Liverpool	A	L	0–4
19 Jan	West Ham United	H	W	5–2
2 Feb	Burnley	H	W	4–2
9 Feb	Cardiff City	A	W	2–0
20 Feb	Sheffield United	H	W	3–2
23 Feb	Bury	A	D	2–2
9 Mar	Birmingham City	H	L	1–2
13 Mar	Newcastle United	A	L	1–2
16 Mar	Derby County	A	L	0–1
25 Mar	Sunderland	H	W	3–1
30 Mar	Blackburn Rovers	A	W	5–2
1 Apr	Leicester City	A	L	1–4
2 Apr	Leicester City	H	W	4–2
6 Apr	Arsenal	H	W	4–2
13 Apr	Everton	A	W	1–0
17 Apr	Bolton Wanderers	A	L	1–3
20 Apr	Huddersfield Town	H	W	4–1
27 Apr	Manchester City	A	L	0–3
4 May	Sheffield Wednesday	H	W	4–1

FA Cup

12 Jan	Cardiff City	H	W	6–1
26 Jan	Clapton Orient	H	D	0–0
30 Jan	Clapton Orient (R)	A	W	8–0
16 Feb	Reading	A	W	3–1
2 Mar	Arsenal	H	W	1–0
23 Mar	Portsmouth	N	L	0–1

SEASON 1929–1930 FOOTBALL LEAGUE (DIVISION 1)

31 Aug	Birmingham City	H	W	2–1
4 Sep	Derby County	A	L	0–4
7 Sep	Leeds United	A	L	1–4
9 Sep	Derby County	H	D	2–2
14 Sep	Sheffield Wednesday	H	L	1–3
21 Sep	Burnley	A	W	4–1
25 Sep	Arsenal	H	W	5–2
28 Sep	Sunderland	H	W	2–1
5 Oct	Bolton Wanderers	A	L	0–3
12 Oct	Everton	H	W	5–2
19 Oct	Leicester City	H	W	3–0
26 Oct	Grimsby Town	A	W	2–0
2 Nov	Manchester United	H	W	1–0
9 Nov	Huddersfield Town	A	D	1–1
16 Nov	Liverpool	H	L	2–3
23 Nov	Middlesbrough	A	W	3–2
30 Nov	Blackburn Rovers	H	W	3–0
7 Dec	Newcastle United	A	D	2–2
14 Dec	Sheffield United	H	W	5–1
21 Dec	West Ham United	A	L	2–5
25 Dec	Manchester City	H	L	0–2
26 Dec	Manchester City	A	W	2–1
28 Dec	Birmingham City	A	D	1–1
4 Jan	Leeds United	H	L	3–4
18 Jan	Sheffield Wednesday	A	L	0–3
1 Feb	Sunderland	A	L	1–4
5 Feb	Burnley	H	L	1–2
8 Feb	Bolton Wanderers	H	W	2–0
22 Feb	Leicester City	A	L	3–4
5 Mar	Everton	A	W	4–3
8 Mar	Manchester United	A	W	3–2
15 Mar	Huddersfield Town	H	W	5–3
22 Mar	Liverpool	A	L	0–2
29 Mar	Middlesbrough	H	W	4–2
2 Apr	Grimsby Town	H	W	4–1
5 Apr	Blackburn Rovers	A	L	0–2
12 Apr	Newcastle United	H	W	2–0
18 Apr	Portsmouth	A	W	2–1
19 Apr	Sheffield United	A	D	3–3
21 Apr	Portsmouth	H	L	0–1
26 Apr	West Ham United	H	L	2–3
3 May	Arsenal	A	W	4–2

FA Cup

11 Jan	Reading	H	W	5–1
25 Jan	Walsall	H	W	3–1
15 Feb	Blackburn Rovers	H	W	4–1
1 Mar	Huddersfield Town	H	L	1–2

SEASON 1930–1931 FOOTBALL LEAGUE (DIVISION 1)

30 Aug	Manchester United	A	W	4–3
1 Sep	Sheffield Wednesday	H	W	2–0
6 Sep	West Ham United	H	W	6–1
9 Sep	Grimsby Town	A	W	2–1
13 Sep	Bolton Wanderers	A	D	1–1
15 Sep	Grimsby Town	H	W	2–0
20 Sep	Liverpool	H	W	4–2
27 Sep	Middlesbrough	A	L	1–3
4 Oct	Huddersfield Town	H	W	6–1
11 Oct	Sunderland	A	D	1–1
18 Oct	Birmingham City	H	D	1–1
25 Oct	Leicester City	A	L	1–4
1 Nov	Blackburn Rovers	H	W	5–2
8 Nov	Arsenal	A	L	2–5
15 Nov	Derby County	H	L	4–6
22 Nov	Blackpool	A	D	2–2
3 Dec	Portsmouth	H	D	2–2
6 Dec	Sheffield United	A	W	4–3
13 Dec	Leeds United	H	W	4–3
20 Dec	Manchester City	A	L	1–3
25 Dec	Chelsea	A	W	2–0
26 Dec	Chelsea	H	D	3–3
27 Dec	Manchester United	H	W	7–0
1 Jan	Newcastle United	A	L	0–2
3 Jan	West Ham United	A	D	5–5
17 Jan	Bolton Wanderers	H	W	3–1
24 Jan	Liverpool	A	D	1–1
31 Jan	Middlesbrough	H	W	8–1
7 Feb	Huddersfield Town	A	W	6–1
18 Feb	Sunderland	H	W	4–2
21 Feb	Birmingham City	A	W	4–0
28 Feb	Leicester City	H	W	4–2
7 Mar	Blackburn Rovers	A	W	2–0

14 Mar	Arsenal	H	W	5–1
21 Mar	Derby County	A	D	1–1
28 Mar	Blackpool	H	W	4–1
4 Apr	Portsmouth	A	L	0–5
7 Apr	Newcastle United	H	W	4–3
11 Apr	Sheffield United	H	W	4–0
18 Apr	Leeds United	A	W	2–0
25 Apr	Manchester City	H	W	4–2
2 May	Sheffield Wednesday	A	L	0–3

FA Cup

10 Jan	Arsenal	A	D	2–2
14 Jan	Arsenal (R)	H	L	1–3

SEASON 1931–1932 FOOTBALL LEAGUE (DIVISION 1)

29 Aug	Leicester City	H	W	3–2
31 Aug	Huddersfield Town	A	D	1–1
5 Sep	Liverpool	A	L	0–2
12 Sep	Grimsby Town	H	W	7–0
19 Sep	Chelsea	A	W	6–3
26 Sep	West Ham United	H	W	5–2
3 Oct	Sheffield Wednesday	A	L	0–1
10 Oct	Bolton Wanderers	H	W	2–1
17 Oct	Portsmouth	A	W	3–0
24 Oct	Everton	H	L	2–3
31 Oct	Arsenal	A	D	1–1
7 Nov	Blackpool	H	W	5–1
14 Nov	West Bromwich Albion	A	L	0–3
21 Nov	Birmingham City	H	W	3–2
28 Nov	Manchester City	A	D	3–3
5 Dec	Derby County	H	W	2–0
12 Dec	Sheffield United	A	L	4–5
19 Dec	Blackburn Rovers	H	L	1–5
25 Dec	Middlesbrough	H	W	7–1
26 Dec	Middlesbrough	A	D	1–1
28 Dec	Newcastle United	H	W	3–0
1 Jan	Newcastle United	A	L	1–3
2 Jan	Leicester City	A	W	8–3
16 Jan	Liverpool	H	W	6–1
30 Jan	Chelsea	H	L	1–3
2 Feb	Grimsby Town	A	D	2–2
6 Feb	West Ham United	A	L	1–2
20 Feb	Bolton Wanderers	A	L	1–2
24 Feb	Sheffield Wednesday	H	W	3–1
27 Feb	Portsmouth	H	L	0–1
5 Mar	Everton	A	L	2–4
19 Mar	Blackpool	A	W	3–1
25 Mar	Sunderland	A	D	1–1
26 Mar	West Bromwich Albion	H	W	2–0
28 Mar	Sunderland	H	W	2–0
2 Apr	Birmingham City	A	D	1–1
9 Apr	Manchester City	H	W	2–1
16 Apr	Derby County	A	L	1–3
23 Apr	Sheffield United	H	W	5–0
25 Apr	Arsenal	H	D	1–1
30 Apr	Blackburn Rovers	A	L	0–2
7 May	Huddersfield Town	H	L	2–3

FA Cup

9 Jan	West Bromwich Albion	A	W	2–1
23 Jan	Portsmouth	A	D	1–1
27 Jan	Portsmouth (R)	H	L	0–1

SEASON 1932–1933 FOOTBALL LEAGUE (DIVISION 1)

27 Aug	Middlesbrough	A	W	2–0
29 Aug	Sunderland	H	W	1–0
3 Sep	Bolton Wanderers	H	W	6–1
7 Sep	Sunderland	A	D	1–1
10 Sep	Liverpool	A	D	0–0
17 Sep	Leicester City	H	W	4–2
24 Sep	Portsmouth	A	W	4–2
1 Oct	Chelsea	H	W	3–1
8 Oct	Huddersfield Town	A	D	0–0
15 Oct	Sheffield United	H	W	3–0
22 Oct	Birmingham City	H	W	1–0
29 Oct	West Bromwich Albion	A	L	1–3
5 Nov	Blackpool	H	W	6–2
12 Nov	Everton	A	D	3–3
19 Nov	Arsenal	H	W	5–3
26 Nov	Manchester City	A	L	2–5
3 Dec	Sheffield Wednesday	H	L	3–6
10 Dec	Leeds United	A	D	1–1
17 Dec	Blackburn Rovers	H	W	4–0

24 Dec	Derby County	A	D	0–0
26 Dec	Wolverhampton Wanderers	H	L	1–3
27 Dec	Wolverhampton Wanderers	A	W	4–2
31 Dec	Middlesbrough	H	W	3–1
7 Jan	Bolton Wanderers	A	W	1–0
21 Jan	Liverpool	H	W	5–2
4 Feb	Portsmouth	H	W	4–1
9 Feb	Leicester City	A	L	0–3
1 Feb	Chelsea	A	W	1–0
18 Feb	Huddersfield Town	H	L	0–3
8 Mar	Birmingham City	A	L	2–3
11 Mar	West Bromwich Albion	H	W	3–2
18 Mar	Blackpool	A	L	2–6
25 Mar	Everton	H	W	2–1
1 Apr	Arsenal	A	L	0–5
8 Apr	Manchester City	H	D	1–1
15 Apr	Sheffield Wednesday	A	W	2–0
17 Apr	Newcastle United	A	L	1–3
18 Apr	Newcastle United	H	W	3–0
22 Apr	Leeds United	H	D	0–0
24 Apr	Sheffield United	A	L	0–1
29 Apr	Blackburn Rovers	A	W	5–0
6 May	Derby County	H	W	2–0

FA Cup

14 Jan	Bradford City	A	D	2–2
18 Jan	Bradford City (R)	H	W	2–1
28 Jan	Sunderland	H	L	0–3

SEASON 1933–1934 FOOTBALL LEAGUE (DIVISION 1)

26 Aug	Leicester City	H	L	2–3
28 Aug	Sheffield Wednesday	A	W	2–1
2 Sep	Tottenham Hotspur	A	L	2–3
4 Sep	Sheffield Wednesday	H	W	1–0
9 Sep	Liverpool	H	W	4–2
16 Sep	Chelsea	A	L	0–1
23 Sep	Sunderland	H	W	2–1
30 Sep	Portsmouth	A	L	2–3
7 Oct	Huddersfield Town	H	W	4–3
14 Oct	Stoke City	A	D	1–1
21 Oct	Manchester City	A	L	0–1
28 Oct	Arsenal	H	L	2–3
4 Nov	Leeds United	A	W	4–2
11 Nov	Middlesbrough	H	W	3–0
18 Nov	Blackburn Rovers	A	L	1–2
25 Nov	Newcastle United	H	L	2–3
2 Dec	Birmingham City	A	D	0–0
9 Dec	Derby County	H	L	0–2
16 Dec	West Bromwich Albion	A	L	1–2
23 Dec	Everton	H	W	2–1
25 Dec	Wolverhampton Wanderers	H	W	6–2
26 Dec	Wolverhampton Wanderers	A	L	3–4
30 Dec	Leicester City	A	D	1–1
1 Jan	Sheffield United	A	D	3–3
6 Jan	Tottenham Hotspur	H	L	1–5
20 Jan	Liverpool	A	W	3–2
3 Feb	Sunderland	A	L	1–5
7 Feb	Chelsea	H	W	2–0
10 Feb	Portsmouth	H	D	1–1
21 Feb	Huddersfield Town	A	L	1–2
24 Feb	Stoke City	H	L	1–2
7 Mar	Manchester City	H	D	0–0
10 Mar	Arsenal	A	L	2–3
24 Mar	Middlesbrough	A	W	2–1
31 Mar	Blackburn Rovers	H	D	1–1
2 Apr	Sheffield United	H	W	3–0
7 Apr	Newcastle United	A	D	1–1
14 Apr	Birmingham City	H	D	1–1
21 Apr	Derby County	A	D	1–1
28 Apr	West Bromwich Albion	H	D	4–4
30 Apr	Leeds United	H	W	3–0
5 May	Everton	A	D	2–2

FA Cup

13 Jan	Chesterfield	A	D	2–2
17 Jan	Chesterfield (R)	H	W	2–0
27 Jan	Sunderland	H	W	7–2
17 Feb	Tottenham Hotspur	A	W	1–0
3 Mar	Arsenal	A	W	2–1
17 Mar	Manchester City	N	L	1–6

SEASON 1934–1935 FOOTBALL LEAGUE (DIVISION 1)

25 Aug	Birmingham City	A	L	1–2
27 Aug	Wolverhampton Wanderers	H	W	2–1
1 Sep	Derby County	H	W	3–2
3 Sep	Wolverhampton Wanderers	A	L	2–5
8 Jan	Leicester City	A	L	0–5
15 Sep	Sunderland	H	D	1–1
22 Sep	Tottenham Hotspur	A	W	2–0
29 Sep	Preston North End	H	W	4–2
6 Oct	Grimsby Town	A	L	1–5
13 Oct	Everton	H	D	2–2
20 Oct	Stoke City	A	L	1–4
27 Oct	Manchester City	H	W	4–2
3 Nov	West Bromwich Albion	A	D	2–2
10 Nov	Sheffield Wednesday	H	W	4–0
17 Nov	Arsenal	A	W	2–1
24 Nov	Portsmouth	H		abandoned
26 Nov	Portsmouth	H	W	5–4
1 Dec	Liverpool	A	L	1–3
8 Dec	Leeds United	H	D	1–1
15 Dec	Middlesbrough	A	L	1–4
22 Dec	Blackburn Rovers	H	D	1–1
25 Dec	Chelsea	A	L	0–2
26 Dec	Chelsea	H	L	0–3
29 Dec	Birmingham City	H	D	2–2
5 Jan	Derby County	A	D	1–1
19 Jan	Leicester City	H	W	5–0
2 Feb	Tottenham Hotspur	H	W	1–0
6 Feb	Sunderland	A	D	3–3
9 Feb	Preston North End	A	D	0–0
16 Feb	Grimsby Town	H	W	3–2
23 Feb	Everton	A	D	2–2
2 Mar	Stoke City	H	W	4–1
9 Mar	Manchester City	A	L	1–4
23 Mar	Sheffield Wednesday	A	L	1–2
30 Mar	Arsenal	H	L	1–3
3 Apr	West Bromwich Albion	H	L	2–3
6 Apr	Portsmouth	A	W	1–0
13 Apr	Liverpool	H	W	4–2
19 Apr	Huddersfield Town	H	D	1–1
20 Apr	Leeds United	A	D	1–1
24 Apr	Huddersfield Town	A	D	1–1
27 Apr	Middlesbrough	H	L	0–3
4 May	Blackburn Rovers	A	L	0–3

FA Cup

12 Jan	Bradford City	H	L	1–3

SEASON 1935–1936 FOOTBALL LEAGUE (DIVISION 1)

31 Aug	Sheffield Wednesday	H	L	1–2
4 Sep	Middlesbrough	A	W	2–1
7 Sep	Portsmouth	A	L	0–3
9 Sep	Middlesbrough	H	L	2–7
14 Sep	Preston North End	H	W	5–1
16 Sep	Sunderland	H	D	2–2
21 Sep	Brentford	A	W	2–1
28 Sep	Derby County	H	L	0–2
5 Oct	Everton	A	D	2–2
12 Oct	Bolton Wanderers	H	L	1–2
19 Oct	West Bromwich Albion	H	L	0–7
26 Oct	Leeds United	A	L	2–4
2 Nov	Grimsby Town	H	L	2–6
9 Nov	Liverpool	A	L	2–3
16 Nov	Chelsea	H	D	2–2
23 Nov	Birmingham City	A	D	2–2
30 Nov	Stoke City	H	W	4–0
7 Dec	Manchester City	A	L	0–5
14 Dec	Arsenal	H	L	1–7
21 Dec	Blackburn Rovers	A	L	1–5
25 Dec	Huddersfield Town	H	W	4–1
26 Dec	Huddersfield Town	A	L	1–4
28 Dec	Sheffield Wednesday	A	L	2–5
1 Jan	Sunderland	A	W	3–1
4 Jan	Portsmouth	H	W	4–2
18 Jan	Preston North End	A	L	0–3
25 Jan	Brentford	H	D	2–2
1 Feb	Derby County	A	W	3–1
8 Feb	Everton	H	D	1–1
15 Feb	Bolton Wanderers	A	L	3–4
22 Feb	West Bromwich Albion	A		abandoned
29 Feb	Liverpool	H	W	3–0
7 Mar	Stoke City	A	W	3–2
14 Mar	Leeds United	H	D	3–3
21 Mar	Chelsea	A	L	0–1

28 Mar	Birmingham City	H	W	2–1
1 Apr	West Bromwich Albion	A	W	3–0
4 Apr	Grimsby Town	A	L	1–4
10 Apr	Wolverhampton Wanderers	H	W	4–2
11 Apr	Manchester City	H	D	2–2
13 Apr	Wolverhampton Wanderers	A	D	2–2
18 Apr	Arsenal	A	L	0–1
25 Apr	Blackburn Rovers	H	L	2–4

FA Cup

11 Jan	Huddersfield Town	H	L	0–1

SEASON 1936–1937 FOOTBALL LEAGUE (DIVISION 2)

29 Aug	Swansea Town	A	W	2–1
2 Sep	Nottingham Forest	A	D	1–1
5 Sep	Southampton	H	W	4–0
7 Sep	Nottingham Forest	H	D	1–1
12 Sep	Burnley	A	W	2–1
14 Sep	Bradford City	H	W	5–1
19 Sep	Fulham	H	L	0–3
26 Sep	Doncaster Rovers	A	L	0–1
3 Oct	Coventry City	H	D	0–0
10 Oct	Plymouth Argyle	A	D	2–2
17 Oct	Bradford (Park Avenue)	A	D	3–3
24 Oct	Barnsley	H	W	4–2
31 Oct	Sheffield United	A	L	1–5
7 Nov	Tottenham Hotspur	H	D	1–1
11 Nov	Bradford City	A	D	2–2
14 Nov	Blackpool	A	W	3–2
21 Nov	Blackburn Rovers	H	D	2–2
28 Nov	Bury	A	L	1–2
5 Dec	Leicester City	H	L	1–3
12 Dec	West Ham United	A		abandoned
19 Dec	Norwich City	H	W	3–0
25 Dec	Chesterfield	A	L	0–1
26 Dec	Swansea Town	H	W	4–0
28 Dec	Chesterfield	H	W	6–2
2 Jan	Southampton	A	D	2–2
9 Jan	Burnley	H	D	0–0
23 Jan	Fulham	A	L	2–3
30 Jan	Doncaster Rovers	H	D	1–1
6 Feb	Coventry City	A	L	0–1
13 Feb	Plymouth Argyle	H	W	5–4
20 Feb	Bradford (Park Avenue)	H	W	4–1
27 Feb	Barnsley	A	W	4–0
6 Mar	Sheffield United	H	W	2–1
13 Mar	Tottenham Hotspur	A	D	2–2
20 Mar	Blackpool	H	W	4–0
26 Mar	Newcastle United	A	W	2–0
27 Mar	Blackburn Rovers	A	W	4–3
30 Mar	Newcastle United	H	L	0–2
3 Apr	Bury	H	L	0–4
10 Apr	Leicester City	A	L	0–1
17 Apr	West Ham United	H	L	0–2
24 Apr	Norwich City	A	L	1–5
26 Apr	West Ham United	A	L	1–2

FA Cup

16 Jan	Burnley	H	L	2–3

SEASON 1937–1938 FOOTBALL LEAGUE (DIVISION 2)

28 Aug	West Ham United	H	W	2–0
1 Sep	Luton Town	A	L	2–3
4 Sep	Southampton	A	D	0–0
6 Sep	Luton Town	H	W	4–1
11 Sep	Blackburn Rovers	H	W	2–1
16 Sep	Norwich City	A	L	0–1
18 Sep	Sheffield Wednesday	A	W	2–1
25 Sep	Fulham	H	W	2–0
2 Oct	Plymouth Argyle	A	W	3–0
9 Oct	Chesterfield	H	L	0–2
16 Oct	Newcastle United	H	W	2–0
23 Oct	Nottingham Forest	A	W	2–0
30 Oct	Coventry City	H	D	1–1
6 Nov	Bury	A	D	1–1
13 Nov	Burnley	H	D	0–0
20 Nov	Manchester United	A	L	1–3
27 Nov	Sheffield United	H	W	1–0
4 Dec	Tottenham Hotspur	A	L	1–2
11 Dec	Stockport County	H	W	7–1
18 Dec	Barnsley	A	W	1–0
27 Dec	Bradford (Park Avenue)	A	W	2–1
28 Dec	Barnsley	H	W	3–0
1 Jan	West Ham United	A	D	1–1

15 Jan	Southampton	H	W	3–0
27 Jan	Blackburn Rovers	A	L	0–1
29 Jan	Sheffield Wednesday	H	W	4–3
5 Feb	Fulham	A	D	1–1
19 Feb	Chesterfield	A	W	1–0
23 Feb	Plymouth Argyle	H	W	3–0
26 Feb	Newcastle United	A	L	0–2
9 Mar	Nottingham Forest	H	L	1–2
12 Mar	Coventry City	A	W	1–0
19 Mar	Bury	H	W	2–1
2 Apr	Manchester United	H	W	3–0
5 Apr	Burnley	A	L	0–3
9 Apr	Sheffield United	A	D	0–0
16 Apr	Tottenham Hotspur	H	W	2–0
18 Apr	Swansea Town	A	L	1–2
19 Apr	Swansea Town	H	W	4–0
23 Apr	Stockport County	A	W	3–1
27 Apr	Bradford (Park Avenue)	H	W	2–0
7 May	Norwich City	H	W	2–0

FA Cup

8 Jan	Norwich City	A	W	3–2
22 Jan	Blackpool	H	W	4–0
12 Feb	Charlton Athletic	A	D	1–1
16 Feb	Charlton Athletic (R)	H	D	2–2
21 Feb	Charlton Athletic (R)	N	W	4–1
5 Mar	Manchester City	H	W	3–2
26 Mar	Preston North End	N	L	1–2

SEASON 1938–1939 FOOTBALL LEAGUE (DIVISION 1)

27 Aug	Grimsby Town	A	W	2–1
31 Aug	Middlesbrough	A	D	1–1
3 Sep	Derby County	H	L	0–1
5 Sep	Everton	H	L	0–3
10 Sep	Blackpool	A	W	4–2
17 Sep	Brentford	H	W	5–0
24 Sep	Arsenal	A	D	0–0
1 Oct	Portsmouth	H	W	2–0
8 Oct	Huddersfield Town	A	D	1–1
15 Oct	Liverpool	A	L	0–3
22 Oct	Leicester City	H	L	1–2
29 Oct	Birmingham City	A	L	0–3
5 Nov	Manchester United	H	L	0–2
12 Nov	Stoke City	A	L	1–3
19 Nov	Chelsea	H	W	6–2
26 Nov	Preston North End	A	L	2–3
3 Dec	Charlton Athletic	H	W	2–0
10 Dec	Bolton Wanderers	A	W	2–1
17 Dec	Leeds United	H	W	2–1
24 Dec	Grimsby Town	H	L	0–2
26 Dec	Sunderland	A	W	5–1
27 Dec	Sunderland	H	D	1–1
31 Dec	Derby County	A	L	1–2
14 Jan	Blackpool	H	W	3–1
28 Jan	Arsenal	H	L	1–3
4 Feb	Portsmouth	A	D	0–0
8 Feb	Brentford	A	W	4–2
15 Feb	Huddersfield Town	H	W	4–0
18 Feb	Liverpool	H	W	2–0
25 Feb	Leicester City	A	D	1–1
4 Mar	Birmingham City	H	W	5–1
11 Mar	Manchester United	A	D	1–1
18 Mar	Stoke City	H	W	3–0
25 Mar	Chelsea	A	L	1–2
1 Apr	Preston North End	H	W	3–0
8 Apr	Charlton Athletic	A	L	0–1
10 Apr	Wolverhampton Wanderers	A	L	1–2
11 Apr	Wolverhampton Wanderers	H	D	2–2
15 Apr	Bolton Wanderers	H	L	1–3
22 Apr	Leeds United	A	L	0–2
29 Apr	Everton	A	L	0–3
6 May	Middlesbrough	H	D	1–1

FA Cup

7 Jan	Ipswich Town	H	D	1–1
11 Jan	Ipswich Town (R)	A	W	2–1
21 Jan	Preston North End	A	L	0–2

SEASON 1945–46 FOOTBALL LEAGUE (DIV 1 – SOUTH)

25 Aug	Luton Town	A	D	1–1
29 Aug	West Bromwich Albion	A	L	0–1
1 Sep	Luton Town	H	W	7–1
5 Sep	West Bromwich Albion	H	D	3–3
8 Sep	Swansea Town	H	W	6–3

10 Sep	West Ham United	A	W	2–1
15 Sep	Swansea Town	A	L	4–5
22 Sep	Arsenal	A	W	4–2
29 Sep	Arsenal	H	W	5–1
6 Oct	Charlton Athletic	A	D	0–0
13 Oct	Charlton Athletic	H	L	0–2
20 Oct	Fulham	H	W	3–0
27 Oct	Fulham	A	W	4–1
3 Nov	Plymouth Argyle	A	W	3–0
10 Nov	Plymouth Argyle	H	W	4–2
17 Nov	Portsmouth	H	W	3–2
24 Nov	Portsmouth	A	W	3–2
1 Dec	Nottingham Forest	H	W	3–1
8 Dec	Nottingham Forest	A	W	3–1
19 Dec	Newport County	H	W	5–2
22 Dec	Newport County	A	W	4–0
25 Dec	Wolverhampton Wanderers	A	W	2–1
26 Dec	Wolverhampton Wanderers	H	D	1–1
29 Dec	West Ham United	H	D	2–2
12 Jan	Birmingham City	H	D	2–2
19 Jan	Birmingham City	A	L	1–3
2 Feb	Tottenham Hotspur	H	W	5–1
16 Feb	Brentford	A	W	1–0
20 Feb	Tottenham Hotspur	A	L	0–3
23 Feb	Chelsea	A	D	2–2
16 Mar	Millwall	A	D	2–2
23 Mar	Southampton	A	W	5–3
27 Mar	Chelsea	H	L	0–3
30 Mar	Southampton	H	W	2–0
6 Apr	Derby County	H	W	4–1
13 Apr	Derby County	A	W	1–0
17 Apr	Brentford	H	D	1–1
20 Apr	Coventry City	H	D	0–0
22 Apr	Leicester City	H	W	3–0
23 Apr	Leicester City	A	W	1–0
27 Apr	Coventry City	A	D	2–2
1 May	Millwall	H	W	2–0

FA Cup (each tie two legs)

5 Jan	Coventry City	A	L	1–2
8 Jan	Coventry City	H	W	2–0
26 Jan	Millwall	A	W	4–2
28 Jan	Millwall	H	W	9–1
9 Feb	Chelsea	A	W	1–0
12 Feb	Chelsea	H	W	1–0
2 Mar	Derby County	H	L	3–4
9 Mar	Derby County	A	D	1–1

SEASON 1946–1947 FOOTBALL LEAGUE (DIVISION 1)

31 Aug	Middlesbrough	H	L	0–1
2 Sep	Everton	H	L	0–1
7 Sep	Derby County	A	W	2–1
11 Sep	Wolverhampton Wanderers	A	W	2–1
14 Sep	Arsenal	H	L	0–2
16 Sep	Wolverhampton Wanderers	H	W	3–0
21 Sep	Blackpool	A	L	0–1
28 Sep	Brentford	H	W	5–2
5 Oct	Blackburn Rovers	A	W	1–0
12 Oct	Portsmouth	H	D	1–1
19 Oct	Charlton Athletic	H	W	4–0
26 Oct	Preston North End	A	L	1–3
2 Nov	Manchester United	H	D	0–0
9 Nov	Stoke City	A	D	0–0
16 Nov	Bolton Wanderers	H	D	1–1
23 Nov	Chelsea	A	W	3–1
30 Nov	Sheffield United	H	L	2–3
7 Dec	Grimsby Town	A	W	3–0
14 Dec	Leeds United	H	W	2–1
21 Dec	Liverpool	A	L	1–4
25 Dec	Huddersfield Town	H	D	2–2
26 Dec	Huddersfield Town	A	L	0–1
28 Dec	Middlesbrough	A	W	2–1
1 Jan	Everton	A	L	0–2
4 Jan	Derby County	H	W	2–0
18 Jan	Arsenal	A	W	2–0
25 Jan	Blackpool	H	D	1–1
1 Feb	Brentford	A	W	2–0
15 Feb	Portsmouth	A	L	2–3
22 Feb	Charlton Athletic	A	D	1–1
8 Mar	Manchester United	A	L	1–2
15 Mar	Stoke City	H		abandoned
22 Mar	Bolton Wanderers	A	L	1–2
29 Mar	Chelsea	H	W	2–0
4 Apr	Sunderland	A	L	1–4
5 Apr	Sheffield United	A	W	2–1
8 Apr	Sunderland	H	W	4–0
12 Apr	Grimsby Town	H	D	3–3

19 Apr	Leeds United	A	D	1–1
26 Apr	Liverpool	H	L	1–2
10 May	Blackburn Rovers	H	W	2–1
17 May	Preston North End	H	W	4–2
26 May	Stoke City	H	L	0–1

FA Cup

11 Jan	Burnley	A	L	1–5

SEASON 1947–1948 FOOTBALL LEAGUE (DIVISION 1)

23 Aug	Grimsby Town	A	L	0–3
27 Aug	Sunderland	A	D	0–0
30 Aug	Manchester City	H	D	1–1
1 Sep	Sunderland	H	W	2–0
6 Sep	Blackburn Rovers	A	D	0–0
8 Sep	Everton	H	W	3–0
13 Sep	Blackpool`	H	L	0–1
17 Sep	Everton	A	L	0–3
20 Sep	Derby County	A	W	3–1
27 Sep	Huddersfield Town	H	W	2–2
4 Oct	Chelsea	A	L	2–4
11 Oct	Arsenal	A	L	0–1
18 Oct	Sheffield United	H	W	2–0
25 Oct	Manchester United	A	L	0–2
1 Nov	Preston North End	H	W	4–1
8 Nov	Portsmouth	A	W	4–2
15 Nov	Bolton Wanderers	H	W	3–1
22 Nov	Stoke City	A	W	2–1
29 Nov	Burnley	H	D	2–2
6 Dec	Liverpool	A	D	3–3
13 Dec	Middlesbrough	H	D	1–1
20 Dec	Grimsby Town	H	D	2–2
26 Dec	Wolverhampton Wanderers	H	L	1–2
27 Dec	Wolverhampton Wanderers	A	L	1–4
3 Jan	Manchester City	A	W	2–0
31 Jan	Blackpool	A	L	0–1
14 Feb	Huddersfield Town	A	W	1–0
21 Feb	Chelsea	H	W	3–0
28 Feb	Arsenal	H	W	4–2
6 Mar	Sheffield United	A	L	1–3
20 Mar	Preston North End	A	L	0–3
22 Mar	Manchester United	H	L	0–1
26 Mar	Charlton Athletic	A	D	1–1
27 Mar	Portsmouth	H	W	2–1
30 Mar	Charlton Athletic	H	W	2–1
3 Apr	Bolton Wanderers	A	L	0–1
7 Apr	Derby County	H	D	2–2
10 Apr	Stoke City	H	W	1–0
14 Apr	Blackburn Rovers	H	W	3–2
17 Apr	Burnley	A	L	0–1
24 Apr	Liverpool	H	W	2–1
1 May	Middlesbrough	A	W	3–1

FA Cup

10 Jan	Manchester United	H	L	4–6

SEASON 1948–1949 FOOTBALL LEAGUE (DIVISION 1)

21 Aug	Liverpool	H	W	2–1
25 Aug	Bolton Wanderers	A	L	0–3
28 Aug	Blackpool	A	L	0–1
30 Aug	Bolton Wanderers	H	L	2–4
4 Sep	Derby County	H	D	1–1
8 Sep	Newcastle United	A	L	1–2
11 Sep	Arsenal	A	L	1–3
13 Sep	Newcastle United	H	L	2–4
18 Sep	Huddersfield Town	H	D	3–3
25 Sep	Manchester United	A	L	1–3
2 Oct	Sheffield United	H	W	4–3
9 Oct	Portsmouth	H	D	1–1
16 Oct	Manchester City	A	L	1–4
23 Oct	Charlton Athletic	H	W	4–3
30 Oct	Stoke City	A	L	2–4
6 Nov	Burnley	H	W	3–1
13 Nov	Preston North End	A	W	1–0
20 Nov	Everton	H	L	0–1
27 Nov	Chelsea	A	L	1–2
4 Dec	Birmingham City	H	L	0–3
11 Dec	Middlesbrough	A	L	0–6
18 Dec	Liverpool	A	D	1–1
25 Dec	Wolverhampton Wanderers	A	L	0–4
27 Dec	Wolverhampton Wanderers	H	W	5–1
1 Jan	Blackpool	H	L	2–5
22 Jan	Arsenal	H	W	1–0
12 Feb	Huddersfield Town	A	W	1–0

19 Feb	Manchester United	H	W	2–1
26 Feb	Sheffield United	A	W	1–0
5 Mar	Portsmouth	A	L	0–3
12 Mar	Manchester City	H	W	1–0
19 Mar	Everton	A	W	3–1
26 Mar	Chelsea	H	D	1–1
2 Apr	Burnley	A	D	1–1
9 Apr	Preston North End	H	W	2–0
15 Apr	Sunderland	A	D	0–0
16 Apr	Charlton Athletic	A	W	2–0
19 Apr	Sunderland	H	D	1–1
23 Apr	Stoke City	H	W	2–1
27 Apr	Derby County	A	D	2–2
30 Apr	Birmingham City	A	W	1–0
7 May	Middlesbrough	H	D	1–1

FA Cup

8 Jan	Bolton Wanderers	H	D	1–1
15 Jan	Bolton Wanderers (R)	A	D	0–0
17 Jan	Bolton Wanderers (R)	H	W	2–1
29 Jan	Cardiff City	H	L	1–2

SEASON 1949–1950 FOOTBALL LEAGUE (DIVISION 1)

20 Aug	Manchester City	A	D	3–3
23 Aug	Derby County	H	D	1–1
27 Aug	Fulham	H	W	3–1
31 Aug	Derby County	A	L	2–3
3 Sep	Newcastle United	A	L	2–3
5 Sep	Portsmouth	H	W	1–0
10 Sep	Blackpool	H	D	0–0
17 Sep	Middlesbrough	A	W	2–0
24 Sep	Everton	H	D	2–2
1 Oct	Huddersfield Town	A	L	0–1
8 Oct	West Bromwich Albion	A	D	1–1
15 Oct	Manchester United	H	L	0–4
22 Oct	Chelsea	A	W	3–1
29 Oct	Stoke City	H	D	1–1
5 Nov	Burnley	A	L	0–1
12 Nov	Sunderland	H	W	2–0
19 Nov	Liverpool	A	L	1–2
26 Nov	Arsenal	H	D	1–1
3 Dec	Bolton Wanderers	A	D	1–1
10 Dec	Birmingham City	H	D	1–1
17 Dec	Manchester City	H	W	1–0
24 Dec	Fulham	A	L	0–3
26 Dec	Wolverhampton Wanderers	A	W	3–2
27 Dec	Wolverhampton Wanderers	H	L	1–4
31 Dec	Newcastle United	H	L	1–1
14 Jan	Blackpool	A	L	0–1
21 Jan	Middlesbrough	H	W	4–0
4 Feb	Everton	A	D	1–1
18 Feb	Huddersfield Town	H	W	2–1
25 Feb	West Bromwich Albion	H	W	1–0
8 Mar	Manchester United	A	L	0–7
11 Mar	Liverpool	H	W	2–0
25 Mar	Burnley	H	L	0–1
29 Mar	Arsenal	A	W	3–1
1 Apr	Sunderland	A	L	1–2
7 Apr	Charlton Athletic	A	W	4–1
8 Apr	Chelsea	H	W	4–0
11 Apr	Charlton Athletic	H	D	1–1
15 Apr	Stoke City	A	L	0–1
22 Apr	Bolton Wanderers	H	W	3–0
29 Apr	Birmingham City	A	D	2–2
6 May	Portsmouth	A	L	1–5

FA Cup

7 Jan	Middlesbrough	H	D	2–2
11 Jan	Middlesbrough (R)	A	D	0–0
16 Jan	Middlesbrough (R)	A	L	0–3

SEASON 1950–1951 FOOTBALL LEAGUE (DIVISION 1)

19 Aug	West Bromwich Albion	H	W	2–0
21 Aug	Sunderland	H	W	3–1
26 Aug	Derby County	A	L	2–4
30 Aug	Sunderland	A	D	3–3
2 Sep	Liverpool	H	D	1–1
4 Sep	Manchester United	H	L	1–3
9 Sep	Fulham	A	L	1–2
13 Sep	Manchester United	A	D	0–0
16 Sep	Bolton Wanderers	H	L	0–1
23 Sep	Blackpool	A	D	1–1
30 Sep	Tottenham Hotspur	H	L	2–3
7 Oct	Newcastle United	H	W	3–0

14 Oct	Huddersfield Town	A	L	2–4
21 Oct	Arsenal	H	D	1–1
28 Oct	Burnley	A	L	0–2
4 Nov	Middlesbrough	H	L	0–1
11 Nov	Sheffield Wednesday	A	L	2–3
18 Nov	Chelsea	H	W	4–2
25 Nov	Portsmouth	A	D	3–3
2 Dec	Everton	H	D	3–3
9 Dec	Stoke City	A	L	0–1
16 Dec	West Bromwich Albion	A	L	0–2
23 Dec	Derby County	H	D	1–1
25 Dec	Charlton Athletic	A	D	2–2
26 Dec	Charlton Athletic	H	D	0–0
13 Jan	Fulham	H	W	3–0
20 Jan	Bolton Wanderers	A	L	0–1
3 Feb	Blackpool	H	L	0–3
17 Feb	Tottenham Hotspur	A	L	2–3
3 Mar	Huddersfield Town	H	L	0–1
10 Mar	Arsenal	A	L	1–2
17 Mar	Burnley	H	W	3–2
24 Mar	Middlesbrough	A	L	1–2
26 Mar	Wolverhampton Wanderers	A	W	3–2
27 Mar	Wolverhampton Wanderers	H	W	1–0
31 Mar	Sheffield Wednesday	H	W	2–1
4 Apr	Newcastle United	A	W	1–0
7 Apr	Chelsea	A	D	1–1
14 Apr	Portsmouth	H	D	3–3
21 Apr	Everton	A	W	2–1
25 Apr	Liverpool	A	D	0–0
5 May	Stoke City	H	W	6–2

FA Cup

6 Jan	Burnley	H	W	2–0
27 Jan	Wolverhampton Wanderers	A	L	1–3

SEASON 1951–1952 FOOTBALL LEAGUE (DIVISION 1)

18 Aug	Bolton Wanderers	A	L	2–5
25 Aug	Derby County	H	W	4–1
27 Aug	Sunderland	H	W	2–1
1 Sep	Manchester City	A	D	2–2
5 Sep	Sunderland	A	W	3–1
8 Sep	Arsenal	H	W	1–0
10 Sep	Huddersfield Town	H	W	1–0
15 Sep	Blackpool	A	W	3–0
19 Sep	Huddersfield Town	A	L	1–3
22 Sep	Liverpool	H	W	2–0
29 Sep	Portsmouth	A	L	0–2
6 Oct	Stoke City	A	L	1–4
13 Oct	Manchester United	H	L	2–5
20 Oct	Tottenham Hotspur	A	L	0–2
27 Oct	Preston North End	H	W	3–2
8 Nov	Burnley	A	L	1–2
10 Nov	Charlton Athletic	H	L	0–2
17 Nov	Fulham	A	D	2–2
24 Nov	Middlesbrough	H	W	2–0
1 Dec	West Bromwich Albion	A	W	2–1
8 Dec	Newcastle United	H	D	2–2
15 Dec	Bolton Wanderers	H	D	1–1
22 Dec	Derby County	A	D	1–1
25 Dec	Wolverhampton Wanderers	H	D	3–3
26 Dec	Wolverhampton Wanderers	A	W	2–1
29 Dec	Manchester City	H	L	1–2
5 Jan	Arsenal	A	L	1–2
19 Jan	Blackpool	H	W	4–0
26 Jan	Liverpool	A	W	2–1
9 Feb	Portsmouth	H	W	2–0
16 Feb	Stoke City	H	L	2–3
1 Mar	Manchester United	A	D	1–1
8 Mar	Tottenham Hotspur	H	L	0–3
15 Mar	Preston North End	A	D	2–2
22 Mar	Burnley	H	W	4–1
5 Apr	Fulham	H	W	4–1
12 Apr	Middlesbrough	A	L	0–2
14 Apr	Chelsea	A	D	2–2
15 Apr	Chelsea	H	W	7–1
19 Apr	West Bromwich Albion	H	W	2–0
24 Apr	Charlton Athletic	A	W	1–0
26 Apr	Newcastle United	A	L	1–6

FA Cup

12 Jan	Newcastle United	A	L	2–4

SEASON 1952–1953 FOOTBALL LEAGUE (DIVISION 1)

23 Aug	Arsenal	H	L	1–2
30 Aug	Derby County	A	W	1–0
1 Sep	Sunderland	H	W	3–0
6 Sep	Blackpool	H	L	1–5
8 Sep	Wolverhampton Wanderers	A	L	1–2
13 Sep	Chelsea	A	L	0–4
15 Sep	Wolverhampton Wanderers	H	L	0–1
20 Sep	Manchester United	H	D	3–3
27 Sep	Portsmouth	A	D	1–1
4 Oct	Bolton Wanderers	H	D	1–1
11 Oct	Middlesbrough	H	W	1–0
18 Oct	Liverpool	A	W	2–0
25 Oct	Manchester City	H	D	0–0
1 Nov	Stoke City	A	W	4–1
8 Nov	Preston North End	H	W	1–0
15 Nov	Burnley	A	L	0–1
22 Nov	Tottenham Hotspur	H	L	0–3
29 Nov	Sheffield Wednesday	A	D	2–2
18 Dec	Newcastle United	A	L	1–2
20 Dec	Arsenal	A	L	1–3
26 Dec	Charlton Athletic	H	D	1–1
1 Jan	Sunderland	A	D	2–2
3 Jan	Derby County	H	W	3–0
17 Jan	Blackpool	A	D	1–1
24 Jan	Chelsea	H	D	1–1
7 Feb	Manchester United	A	L	1–3
18 Feb	Portsmouth	H	W	6–0
21 Feb	Bolton Wanderers	A	D	0–0
4 Mar	Middlesbrough	A	L	0–1
7 Mar	Liverpool	H	W	4–0
14 Mar	Manchester City	A	L	1–4
18 Mar	Charlton Athletic	A	L	1–5
25 Mar	Stoke City	H	D	1–1
28 Mar	Preston North End	A	W	3–1
4 Apr	Burnley	H	W	2–0
6 Apr	West Bromwich Albion	A	L	2–3
7 Apr	West Bromwich Albion	H	D	1–1
11 Apr	Tottenham Hotspur	A	D	1–1
18 Apr	Sheffield Wednesday	H	W	4–3
25 Apr	Cardiff City	A	W	2–1
29 Apr	Cardiff City	H	W	2–0
1 May	Newcastle United	H	L	0–1

FA Cup

10 Jan	Middlesbrough	H	W	3–1
31 Jan	Brentford	H	D	0–0
4 Feb	Brentford (R)	A	W	2–1
14 Feb	Rotherham United	A	W	3–1
28 Feb	Everton	H	L	0–1

SEASON 1953–1954 FOOTBALL LEAGUE (DIVISION 1)

19 Aug	Tottenham Hotspur	A	L	0–1
22 Aug	Cardiff City	A	L	1–2
24 Aug	Manchester City	H	W	3–0
29 Aug	Arsenal	H	W	2–1
2 Sep	Manchester City	A	W	1–0
5 Sep	Portsmouth	A	L	1–2
12 Sep	Blackpool	H	W	2–1
14 Sep	Sunderland	H	W	3–1
19 Sep	Chelsea	A	W	2–1
26 Sep	Sheffield United	H	W	4–0
3 Oct	Huddersfield Town	A	L	0–4
10 Oct	Liverpool	A	L	1–6
17 Oct	Newcastle United	H	L	1–2
24 Oct	Manchester City	A	L	0–1
31 Oct	Bolton Wanderers	H	D	2–2
7 Nov	Sheffield Wednesday	A	L	1–3
14 Nov	Middlesbrough	H	W	5–3
21 Nov	Burnley	A	L	2–3
28 Nov	Charlton Athletic	H	W	2–1
5 Dec	Preston North End	A	D	1–1
12 Dec	Tottenham Hotspur	H	L	1–2
19 Dec	Cardiff City	H	L	1–2
24 Dec	Wolverhampton Wanderers	A	W	2–1
26 Dec	Wolverhampton Wanderers	H	L	1–2
1 Jan	Sunderland	A	L	0–2
16 Jan	Portsmouth	H	D	1–1
23 Jan	Blackpool	A	L	2–3
6 Feb	Chelsea	H	D	2–2
20 Feb	Huddersfield Town	H	D	2–2
27 Feb	Liverpool	H	W	2–1
6 Mar	Newcastle United	A	W	1–0
13 Mar	Manchester United	H	D	2–2
20 Mar	Bolton Wanderers	A	L	0–3

31 Mar	Sheffield Wednesday	H	W	2–1
3 Apr	Middlesbrough	A	L	1–2
6 Apr	Arsenal	A	D	1–1
10 Apr	Burnley	H	W	5–1
17 Apr	Charlton Athletic	A	D	1–1
19 Apr	West Bromwich Albion	A	D	1–1
20 Apr	West Bromwich Albion	H	W	6–1
24 Apr	Preston North End	H	W	1–0
26 Apr	Sheffield United	A	L	1–2

FA Cup

9 Jan	Arsenal	A	L	1–5

SEASON 1954–1955 FOOTBALL LEAGUE (DIVISION 1)

21 Aug	Tottenham Hotspur	H	L	2–4
23 Aug	Sunderland	H	D	2–2
28 Aug	Sheffield Wednesday	A	L	3–6
1 Sep	Sunderland	A	D	0–0
4 Sep	Portsmouth	H	W	1–0
8 Sep	Newcastle United	A	L	3–5
11 Sep	Blackpool	A	W	1–0
13 Sep	Newcastle United	H	L	1–2
18 Sep	Charlton Athletic	H	L	1–2
25 Sep	Bolton Wanderers	A	D	3–3
2 Oct	Huddersfield Town	H	D	0–0
9 Oct	Everton	H	L	0–2
16 Oct	Manchester City	A	W	4–2
23 Oct	Arsenal	H	W	2–1
30 Oct	West Bromwich Albion	A	W	3–2
6 Nov	Leicester City	H	L	2–5
13 Nov	Burnley	A	L	0–2
20 Nov	Preston North End	H	L	1–3
27 Nov	Sheffield United	A	W	3–1
4 Dec	Cardiff City	H	L	0–2
11 Dec	Chelsea	A	L	0–4
18 Dec	Tottenham Hotspur	A	D	1–1
27 Dec	Manchester United	A	W	1–0
28 Dec	Manchester United	H	W	2–1
1 Jan	Sheffield Wednesday	H	D	0–0
22 Jan	Blackpool	H	W	3–1
5 Feb	Charlton Athletic	A	L	1–6
12 Feb	Bolton Wanderers	H	W	3–0
23 Feb	Huddersfield Town	A	W	2–1
5 Mar	Chelsea	H	W	3–2
12 Mar	Arsenal	A	L	0–2
19 Mar	West Bromwich Albion	H	W	3–0
26 Mar	Leicester City	A	L	2–4
2 Apr	Burnley	H	W	3–1
9 Apr	Cardiff City	A	W	1–0
11 Apr	Wolverhampton Wanderers	A	L	0–1
12 Apr	Wolverhampton Wanderers	H	W	4–2
16 Apr	Sheffield United	H	W	3–1
23 Apr	Preston North End	A	W	3–0
27 Apr	Portsmouth	A	D	2–2
30 Apr	Manchester City	H	W	2–0
4 May	Everton	A	W	1–0

FA Cup

8 Jan	Brighton & Hove Albion	A	D	2–2
10 Jan	Brighton & Hove Albion (R)	H	W	4–2
29 Jan	Doncaster Rovers	A	D	0–0
2 Feb	Doncaster Rovers (R)	H	D	2–2
7 Feb	Doncaster Rovers (R)	N	D	1–1
14 Feb	Doncaster Rovers (R)	N	D	0–0
19 Feb	Doncaster Rovers (R)	N	L	1–3

SEASON 1955–1956 FOOTBALL LEAGUE (DIVISION 1)

20 Aug	Manchester City	A	D	2–2
24 Aug	Sunderland	A	L	1–5
27 Aug	Cardiff City	H	W	2–0
29 Aug	Sunderland	H	L	1–4
3 Sep	Huddersfield Town	A	D	1–1
5 Sep	Birmingham City	H	D	0–0
10 Sep	Blackpool	H	D	1–1
17 Sep	Chelsea	A	D	0–0
21 Sep	Birmingham City	A	D	2–2
24 Sep	Bolton Wanderers	H	L	0–2
1 Oct	Arsenal	A	L	0–1
8 Oct	West Bromwich Albion	A	L	0–1
15 Oct	Manchester United	H	D	4–4
22 Oct	Everton	A	L	1–2
29 Oct	Newcastle United	H	W	3–0
5 Nov	Burnley	A	L	0–2
12 Nov	Luton Town	H	W	1–0

19 Nov	Charlton Athletic	A	L	1–3
26 Nov	Tottenham Hotspur	H	L	0–2
3 Dec	Sheffield United	A	D	2–2
10 Dec	Preston North End	H	W	3–2
17 Dec	Manchester City	H	L	0–3
24 Dec	Cardiff City	A	L	0–1
26 Dec	Portsmouth	H	L	1–3
27 Dec	Portsmouth	A	D	2–2
31 Dec	Huddersfield Town	H	W	3–0
14 Jan	Blackpool	A	L	0–6
21 Jan	Chelsea	H	L	1–4
11 Feb	Arsenal	H	D	1–1
18 Feb	Bolton Wanderers	A	L	0–1
25 Feb	Manchester United	A	L	0–1
3 Mar	Charlton Athletic	H	D	1–1
10 Mar	Newcastle United	A	W	3–2
19 Mar	Burnley	H	W	2–0
24 Mar	Luton Town	A	L	1–2
31 Mar	Everton	H	W	2–0
2 Apr	Wolverhampton Wanderers	A	D	0–0
3 Apr	Wolverhampton Wanderers	H	D	0–0
7 Apr	Tottenham Hotspur	A	L	3–4
14 Apr	Sheffield United	H	W	3–2
21 Apr	Preston North End	A	W	1–0
28 Apr	West Bromwich Albion	H	W	3–0

FA Cup

7 Jan	Hull City	H	D	1–1
12 Jan	Hull City (R)	A	W	2–1
28 Jan	Arsenal	A	L	1–4

SEASON 1956–1957 FOOTBALL LEAGUE (DIVISION 1)

18 Aug	Charlton Athletic	H	W	3–1
22 Aug	West Bromwich Albion	A	L	0–2
25 Aug	Manchester City	A	D	1–1
27 Aug	West Bromwich Albion	H	D	0–0
1 Sep	Blackpool	H	W	3–2
5 Sep	Luton Town	A	D	0–0
8 Sep	Everton	A	W	4–0
15 Sep	Tottenham Hotspur	H	L	2–4
22 Sep	Leeds United	A	L	0–1
29 Sep	Bolton Wanderers	H	D	0–0
6 Oct	Portsmouth	A	L	1–5
13 Oct	Newcastle United	H	W	3–1
27 Oct	Birmingham City	H	W	3–1
3 Nov	Arsenal	A	L	1–2
10 Nov	Burnley	H	W	1–0
17 Nov	Preston North End	A	D	3–3
24 Nov	Chelsea	H	D	1–1
1 Dec	Sheffield Wednesday	A	L	1–2
8 Dec	Manchester United	H	L	1–3
15 Dec	Charlton Athletic	A	W	2–0
25 Dec	Sunderland	A	L	0–1
29 Dec	Blackpool	A	D	0–0
12 Jan	Everton	H	W	5–1
19 Jan	Tottenham Hotspur	A	L	0–3
2 Feb	Leeds United	H	D	1–1
4 Feb	Manchester City	H	D	2–2
9 Feb	Bolton Wanderers	A	D	0–0
18 Feb	Portsmouth	H	D	2–2
9 Mar	Manchester United	A	D	1–1
13 Mar	Cardiff City	H	W	4–1
16 Mar	Arsenal	H	D	0–0
30 Mar	Preston North End	A	W	2–0
3 Apr	Cardiff City	A	L	0–1
6 Apr	Chelsea	A	D	1–1
8 Apr	Sunderland	H	D	2–2
10 Apr	Birmingham City	A	W	2–1
13 Apr	Sheffield Wednesday	H	W	5–0
15 Apr	Burnley	A	L	1–2
20 Apr	Newcastle United	A	W	2–1
22 Apr	Wolverhampton Wanderers	H	W	4–0
23 Apr	Wolverhampton Wanderers	A	L	0–3
27 Apr	Luton Town	H	L	1–3

FA Cup

5 Jan	Luton Town	A	D	2–2
7 Jan	Luton Town (R)	H	W	2–0
26 Jan	Middlesbrough	A	W	3–2
16 Feb	Bristol City	H	W	2–1
2 Mar	Burnley	A	D	1–1
6 Mar	Burnley (R)	H	W	2–0
23 Mar	West Bromwich Albion	N	D	2–2
28 Mar	West Bromwich Albion (R)	N	W	1–0
4 May	Manchester United (F)	N	W	2–1

SEASON 1957–1958 FOOTBALL LEAGUE (DIVISION 1)

24 Aug	Birmingham City	A	L	1–3
26 Aug	Leeds United	H	W	2–0
31 Aug	Everton	H	L	0–1
4 Sep	Leeds United	A	L	0–4
7 Sep	Sunderland	A	D	1–1
14 Sep	Luton Town	H	W	2–0
16 Sep	Wolverhampton Wanderers	A	L	1–2
21 Sep	Blackpool	A	D	1–1
23 Sep	Wolverhampton Wanderers	H	L	2–3
28 Sep	Leicester City	H	W	5–1
2 Oct	Arsenal	A	L	0–4
5 Oct	Manchester United	A	L	1–4
12 Oct	Chelsea	A	L	2–4
19 Oct	Newcastle United	H	W	4–3
26 Oct	Burnley	A	L	0–3
2 Nov	Portsmouth	H	W	2–1
9 Nov	West Bromwich Albion	A	L	2–3
16 Nov	Tottenham Hotspur	H	D	1–1
23 Nov	Nottingham Forest	A	L	1–4
30 Nov	Preston North End	H	D	2–2
7 Dec	Sheffield Wednesday	A	W	5–2
14 Dec	Manchester City	H	L	1–2
21 Dec	Birmingham City	H	L	0–2
26 Dec	Arsenal	H	W	3–0
28 Dec	Everton	A	W	2–1
11 Jan	Sunderland	H	W	5–2
18 Jan	Luton Town	A	L	0–3
1 Feb	Blackpool	H	D	1–1
8 Feb	Leicester City	A	L	1–6
22 Feb	Chelsea	H	L	1–3
1 Mar	Newcastle United	A	W	4–2
8 Mar	Burnley	H	W	3–0
15 Mar	Portsmouth	A	L	0–1
29 Mar	Tottenham Hotspur	A	L	2–6
31 Mar	Manchester United	H	W	3–2
4 Apr	Bolton Wanderers	A	L	0–4
5 Apr	West Bromwich Albion	H	W	2–1
8 Apr	Bolton Wanderers	H	W	4–0
12 Apr	Preston North End	A	D	1–1
19 Apr	Sheffield Wednesday	H	W	2–0
26 Apr	Manchester City	A	W	2–1
30 Apr	Nottingham Forest	A	D	1–1

FA Cup

4 Jan	Stoke City	A	D	1–1
8 Jan	Stoke City (R)	H	D	3–3
13 Jan	Stoke City (R)	A	L	0–2

FA Charity Shield

22 Oct	Manchester United	A	L	0–4

SEASON 1958–1959 FOOTBALL LEAGUE (DIVISION 1)

23 Aug	Birmingham City	H	D	1–1
25 Aug	Portsmouth	H	W	3–2
30 Aug	West Ham United	A	L	2–7
3 Sep	Portsmouth	A	L	2–5
6 Sep	Nottingham Forest	H	L	2–3
8 Sep	Wolverhampton Wanderers	H	L	1–3
13 Sep	Chelsea	A	L	1–2
17 Sep	Wolverhampton Wanderers	A	L	0–4
20 Sep	Blackpool	H	D	1–1
27 Sep	Blackburn Rovers	A	W	3–2
4 Oct	Newcastle United	H	W	2–1
11 Oct	West Bromwich Albion	H	L	1–4
18 Oct	Leeds United	A	D	0–0
22 Oct	Arsenal	H	L	1–2
25 Oct	Bolton Wanderers	H	W	2–1
1 Nov	Luton Town	A	L	1–2
8 Nov	Everton	H	L	2–4
15 Nov	Leicester City	A	L	3–6
22 Nov	Preston North End	H	W	2–0
29 Oct	Burnley	A	L	1–3
6 Dec	Manchester City	H	D	1–1
13 Dec	Arsenal	A	W	2–1
20 Dec	Birmingham City	A	L	1–4
26 Dec	Manchester United	A	L	1–2
27 Dec	Manchester United	H	L	0–2
3 Jan	West Ham United	H	L	1–2
31 Jan	Chelsea	H	W	3–1
7 Feb	Blackpool	A	L	1–2
18 Feb	Blackburn Rovers	H	W	1–0
21 Feb	Newcastle United	A	L	0–1

7 Mar	Leeds United	H	W	2–1
18 Mar	Bolton Wanderers	A	W	3–1
21 Mar	Luton Town	H	W	3–1
27 Mar	Tottenham Hotspur	A	L	2–3
28 Mar	Everton	A	L	1–2
30 Mar	Tottenham Hotspur	H	D	1–1
4 Apr	Leicester City	H	L	1–2
11 Apr	Preston North End	A	L	2–4
18 Apr	Burnley	H	D	0–0
20 Apr	Nottingham Forest	A	L	0–2
25 Apr	Manchester City	A	D	0–0
29 Apr	West Bromwich Albion	A	D	1–1

FA Cup

10 Jan	Rotherham United	H	W	2–1
24 Jan	Chelsea	A	W	2–1
14 Feb	Everton	A	W	4–1
28 Feb	Burnley	H	D	0–0
3 Mar	Burnley (R)	A	W	2–0
14 Mar	Nottingham Forest	N	L	0–1

SEASON 1959–1960 FOOTBALL LEAGUE (DIVISION 2)

22 Aug	Brighton & Hove Albion	A	W	2–1
26 Aug	Sunderland	A	L	0–1
29 Aug	Swansea Town	H	W	1–0
31 Aug	Sunderland	H	W	3–0
5 Sep	Bristol Rovers	A	D	1–1
9 Sep	Portsmouth	A	W	2–1
12 Sep	Ipswich Town	H	W	3–1
14 Sep	Portsmouth	H	W	5–2
19 Sep	Huddersfield Town	A	W	1–0
26 Sep	Leyton Orient	H	W	1–0
30 Sep	Stoke City	A	D	3–3
3 Oct	Lincoln City	A	D	0–0
10 Oct	Sheffield United	A	D	1–1
17 Oct	Middlesbrough	H	W	1–0
24 Oct	Derby County	A	D	2–2
31 Oct	Plymouth Argyle	H	W	2–0
7 Nov	Liverpool	A	L	1–2
14 Nov	Charlton	H	W	11–1
21 Nov	Bristol City	A	W	5–0
28 Nov	Scunthorpe United	H	W	5–0
5 Dec	Rotherham United	A	L	1–2
12 Dec	Cardiff City	H	W	2–0
19 Dec	Brighton & Hove Albion	H	W	3–1
26 Dec	Hull City	A	W	1–0
28 Dec	Hull City	H	D	1–1
2 Jan	Swansea Town	A	W	3–1
16 Jan	Bristol Rovers	H	W	4–1
23 Jan	Ipswich Town	A	L	1–2
6 Feb	Huddersfield Town	H	W	4–0
13 Feb	Leyton Orient	A	D	0–0
27 Feb	Sheffield United	H	L	1–3
1 Mar	Lincoln City	H	D	1–1
5 Mar	Middlesbrough	A	W	1–0
15 Mar	Derby County	H	W	3–2
19 Mar	Scunthorpe United	A	W	2–1
30 Mar	Liverpool	H	D	4–4
2 Apr	Charlton Athletic	A	L	0–2
9 Apr	Bristol City	H	W	2–1
16 Apr	Cardiff City	A	L	0–1
18 Apr	Stoke City	H	W	2–1
23 Apr	Rotherham United	H	W	3–0
30 Apr	Plymouth Argyle	A	L	0–3

FA Cup

9 Jan	Leeds United	H	W	2–1
30 Jan	Chelsea	A	W	2–1
20 Feb	Port Vale	A	W	2–1
12 Mar	Preston North End	H	W	2–0
26 Mar	Wolverhampton Wanderers	N	L	0–1

SEASON 1960–1961 FOOTBALL LEAGUE (DIVISION 1)

20 Aug	Chelsea	H	W	3–2
22 Aug	West Ham United	A	L	2–5
27 Aug	Blackpool	A	L	3–5
29 Aug	West Ham United	H	W	2–1
3 Sep	Everton	H	W	3–2
7 Sep	Cardiff City	A	D	1–1
10 Sep	Blackburn Rovers	A	L	1–4
12 Sep	Cardiff City	H	W	2–1
17 Sep	Manchester United	H	W	3–1
24 Sep	Tottenham Hotspur	A	L	2–6

1 Oct	Leicester City	H	L	1–3
8 Oct	Newcastle United	H	W	2–0
15 Oct	Arsenal	A	L	1–2
22 Oct	Birmingham City	H	W	6–2
29 Oct	West Bromwich Albion	A	W	2–0
5 Nov	Burnley	H	W	2–0
12 Nov	Preston North End	A	D	1–1
19 Nov	Fulham	H	W	2–1
26 Nov	Sheffield Wednesday	A	W	2–1
3 Dec	Manchester City	H	W	5–1
10 Dec	Nottingham Forest	A	L	0–2
17 Dec	Chelsea	A	W	4–2
24 Dec	Wolverhampton Wanderers	H	L	0–2
26 Dec	Wolverhampton Wanderers	A	L	2–3
31 Dec	Blackpool	H	D	2–2
21 Jan	Blackburn Rovers	H	D	2–2
4 Feb	Manchester United	A	D	1–1
11 Feb	Tottenham Hotspur	H	L	1–2
25 Feb	Newcastle United	A	L	1–2
4 Mar	Arsenal	H	D	2–2
11 Mar	Birmingham City	A	D	1–1
22 Mar	Everton	A	W	2–1
25 Mar	Burnley	A	D	1–1
28 Mar	West Bromwich Albion	H	L	0–1
1 Apr	Nottingham Forest	H	L	1–2
3 Apr	Bolton Wanderers	A	L	0–3
4 Apr	Bolton Wanderers	H	W	4–0
8 Apr	Fulham	A	D	1–1
15 Apr	Preston North End	H	W	1–0
19 Apr	Leicester City	A	L	1–3
22 Apr	Manchester City	A	L	1–4
29 Apr	Sheffield Wednesday	H	W	4–1

FA Cup

7 Jan	Bristol Rovers	A	D	1–1
9 Jan	Bristol Rovers (R)	H	W	4–0
28 Jan	Peterborough United	A	D	1–1
1 Feb	Peterborough United (R)	H	W	2–1
18 Feb	Tottenham Hotspur	H	L	0–2

League Cup

12 Oct	Huddersfield Town	H	W	4–1
15 Nov	Preston North End	A	D	3–3
23 Nov	Preston North End (R)	H	W	3–1
13 Dec	Plymouth Argyle	H	D	3–3
19 Dec	Plymouth Argyle (R)	A		abandoned
6 Feb	Plymouth Argyle (R)	A	W	5–3
22 Feb	Wrexham	H	W	3–0
10 Apr	Burnley	A	D	1–1
26 Apr	Burnley (R)	H	D	2–2
2 May	Burnley (R)	N	W	2–1
22 Aug	Rotherham United (F)	A	L	0–2
5 Sep	Rotherham United (F)	H	W	3–0

SEASON 1961–1962 FOOTBALL LEAGUE (DIVISION 1)

19 Aug	Everton	A	L	0–2
26 Aug	Chelsea	H	W	3–1
28 Aug	Wolverhampton Wanderers	A	D	2–2
2 Sep	Sheffield United	A	W	2–0
9 Sep	West Ham United	H	L	2–4
16 Sep	Blackburn Rovers	A	L	2–4
18 Sep	Manchester United	H	D	1–1
23 Sep	Blackpool	H	W	5–0
30 Sep	Tottenham Hotspur	A	L	0–1
2 Oct	Wolverhampton Wanderers	H	W	1–0
7 Oct	Fulham	A	L	1–3
16 Oct	Sheffield Wednesday	H	W	1–0
21 Oct	West Bromwich Albion	A	D	1–1
28 Oct	Birmingham City	H	L	1–3
4 Nov	Burnley	A	L	0–3
11 Nov	Arsenal	H	W	3–1
18 Nov	Bolton Wanderers	A	D	1–1
25 Nov	Manchester City	H	W	2–1
2 Dec	Leicester City	A	W	2–0
9 Dec	Ipswich Town	H	W	3–0
16 Dec	Everton	H	D	1–1
23 Dec	Chelsea	A	L	0–1
26 Dec	Cardiff City	A	L	0–1
13 Jan	Sheffield United	H	D	0–0
15 Jan	Manchester United	A	L	0–2
20 Jan	West Ham United	A	L	0–2
3 Feb	Blackburn Rovers	H	W	1–0
10 Feb	Blackpool	A	W	2–1
21 Feb	Tottenham Hotspur	H	D	0–0
24 Feb	Fulham	H	W	2–0

3 Mar	Sheffield Wednesday	A	L	0–3
14 Mar	West Bromwich Albion	H	W	1–0
17 Mar	Birmingham City	A	W	2–0
24 Mar	Burnley	H	L	0–2
31 Mar	Arsenal	A	W	5–4
7 Apr	Bolton Wanderers	H	W	3–0
14 Apr	Manchester City	A	L	0–1
21 Apr	Leicester City	H	W	8–3
23 Apr	Nottingham Forest	H	W	5–1
24 Apr	Nottingham Forest	A	L	0–2
28 Apr	Ipswich Town	A	L	0–2
1 May	Cardiff City	H	D	2–2

FA Cup

6 Jan	Crystal Palace	H	W	4–3
27 Jan	Huddersfield Town	H	W	2–1
17 Feb	Charlton Athletic	H	W	2–1
10 Mar	Tottenham Hotspur	A	L	0–2

League Cup

13 Sep	Bradford City	A	W	4–3
9 Oct	West Ham United	A	W	3–1
21 Nov	Ipswich Town	H	L	2–3

SEASON 1962–1963 FOOTBALL LEAGUE (DIVISION 1)

18 Aug	West Ham United	H	W	3–1
20 Aug	Tottenham Hotspur	H	W	2–1
25 Aug	Manchester City	A	W	2–0
29 Aug	Tottenham Hotspur	A	L	2–4
1 Sep	Blackpool	H	D	1–1
4 Sep	Arsenal	A	W	2–1
8 Sep	Blackburn Rovers	A	L	1–4
10 Sep	Arsenal	H	W	3–1
15 Sep	Sheffield United	H	L	1–2
22 Sep	Nottingham Forest	A	L	1–3
29 Sep	Ipswich Town	H	W	4–2
6 Oct	West Bromwich Albion	H	W	2–0
13 Oct	Everton	A	D	1–1
20 Oct	Leyton Orient	H	W	1–0
27 Oct	Birmingham City	A	L	2–3
3 Nov	Fulham	H	L	1–2
10 Nov	Sheffield Wednesday	A	D	0–0
17 Nov	Burnley	H	W	2–1
24 Nov	Manchester United	A	D	2–2
1 Dec	Bolton Wanderers	H	W	5–0
8 Dec	Leicester City	A	D	3–3
15 Dec	West Ham United	A	D	1–1
19 Jan	Blackburn Rovers	H	D	0–0
13 Feb	Liverpool	A	L	0–4
9 Mar	Leyton Orient	A	W	2–0
16 Mar	Birmingham City	H	W	4–0
23 Mar	Fulham	A	L	0–1
29 Mar	Blackpool	A	L	0–4
1 Apr	Everton	H	L	0–2
6 Apr	Burnley	A	L	1–3
9 Apr	Manchester United	H	L	1–2
13 Apr	Sheffield Wednesday	H	L	0–2
15 Apr	Wolverhampton Wanderers	A	L	1–3
16 Apr	Wolverhampton Wanderers	H	L	0–2
20 Apr	Bolton Wanderers	A	L	1–4
1 May	Sheffield United	A	L	1–2
4 May	Nottingham Forest	H	L	0–2
8 May	Manchester City	H	W	3–1
11 May	West Bromwich Albion	A	L	0–1
15 May	Leicester City	H	W	3–1
18 May	Liverpool	H	W	2–0
21 May	Ipswich Town	A	D	1–1

FA Cup

16 Jan	Bristol City	A	D	1–1
7 Mar	Bristol City (R)	H	W	3–2
11 Mar	Manchester United	A	L	0–1

League Cup

24 Sep	Peterborough United	H	W	6–1
17 Oct	Stoke City	H	W	3–1
12 Nov	Preston North End	H	W	6–2
3 Dec	Norwich City	H	W	4–1
12 Jan	Sunderland	A	W	3–1
22 Apr	Sunderland	H	D	0–0
23 May	Birmingham City	A	L	1–3
27 May	Birmingham City	H	D	0–0

SEASON 1963–1964 FOOTBALL LEAGUE (DIVISION 1)

24 Aug	Nottingham Forest	A	W	1–0
26 Aug	Stoke City	H	L	1–3
31 Aug	Blackburn Rovers	H	L	1–2
4 Sep	Stoke City	A	D	2–2
7 Sep	Blackpool	A	W	4–0
10 Sep	Arsenal	A	L	0–3
14 Sep	Chelsea	H	W	2–0
16 Sep	Tottenham Hotspur	H	L	2–4
21 Sep	West Ham United	A	W	1–0
28 Sep	Sheffield United	H	L	0–1
5 Oct	Liverpool	A	L	2–5
7 Oct	Everton	H	L	0–1
12 Oct	West Bromwich Albion	A	L	3–4
19 Oct	Arsenal	H	W	2–1
26 Oct	Sheffield Wednesday	A	L	0–1
2 Nov	Bolton Wanderers	H	W	3–0
9 Nov	Fulham	A	L	0–2
16 Nov	Manchester United	H	W	4–0
23 Nov	Burnley	A	L	0–2
30 Nov	Ipswich Town	H	D	0–0
7 Dec	Leicester City	A	D	0–0
14 Dec	Nottingham Forest	H	W	3–0
21 Dec	Blackburn Rovers	A	L	0–2
26 Dec	Wolverhampton Wanderers	A	D	3–3
28 Dec	Wolverhampton Wanderers	H	D	2–2
11 Jan	Blackpool	H	W	3–1
18 Jan	Chelsea	A	L	0–1
25 Jan	Tottenham Hotspur	A	L	1–3
1 Feb	West Ham United	H	D	2–2
8 Feb	Sheffield United	A	D	1–1
19 Feb	Liverpool	H	D	2–2
22 Feb	West Bromwich Albion	H	W	1–0
28 Feb	Everton	A	L	2–4
7 Mar	Sheffield Wednesday	H	D	2–2
21 Mar	Fulham	H	D	2–2
28 Mar	Bolton Wanderers	A	D	1–1
30 Mar	Birmingham City	H	L	0–3
31 Mar	Birmingham City	A	D	3–3
4 Apr	Burnley	H	W	2–0
6 Apr	Manchester United	A	L	0–1
11 Apr	Ipswich Town	A	L	3–4
18 Apr	Leicester City	H	L	1–3

FA Cup

| 4 Jan | Aldershot (3) | H | D | 0–0 |
| 8 Jan | Aldershot (R) | A | L | 1–2 |

League Cup

| 25 Sep | Barnsley | H | W | 3–1 |
| 16 Oct | West Ham United | H | L | 0–2 |

SEASON 1964–1965 FOOTBALL LEAGUE (DIVISION 1)

22 Aug	Leeds United	H	L	1–2
26 Aug	Chelsea	A	L	1–2
29 Aug	Arsenal	A	L	1–3
31 Aug	Chelsea	H	D	2–2
5 Sep	Blackburn Rovers	H	L	0–4
9 Sep	Sunderland	A	D	2–2
12 Sep	Blackpool	A	L	1–3
14 Sep	Sunderland	H	W	2–1
19 Sep	Sheffield Wednesday	H	W	2–0
26 Sep	Liverpool	A	L	1–5
5 Oct	Everton	H	L	1–2
10 Oct	West Ham United	A	L	0–3
17 Oct	West Bromwich Albion	H	L	0–1
24 Oct	Manchester United	A	L	0–7
31 Oct	Fulham	H	W	2–0
7 Nov	Nottingham Forest	A	L	2–4
14 Nov	Stoke City	H	W	3–0
21 Nov	Tottenham Hotspur	A	L	0–4
28 Nov	Burnley	H	W	1–0
5 Dec	Sheffield United	A	L	2–4
12 Dec	Leeds United	A	L	0–1
19 Dec	Arsenal	H	W	3–1
26 Dec	Wolverhampton Wanderers	A	W	1–0
2 Jan	Blackburn Rovers	A	L	1–5
16 Jan	Blackpool	H	W	3–2
6 Feb	Liverpool	H	L	0–1
13 Feb	Birmingham City	A	W	1–0
27 Feb	West Bromwich Albion	A	L	1–3
13 Mar	Everton	A	L	1–3
15 Mar	Sheffield Wednesday	A	L	1–3

20 Mar	Nottingham Forest	H	W	2–1
22 Mar	Wolverhampton Wanderers	H	W	3–2
27 Mar	Stoke City	A	L	1–2
31 Mar	West Ham United	H	L	2–3
3 Apr	Tottenham Hotspur	H	W	1–0
10 Apr	Burnley	A	D	2–2
12 Apr	Birmingham City	H	W	3–0
17 Apr	Sheffield United	H	W	2–0
19 Apr	Leicester City	A	D	1–1
20 Apr	Leicester City	H	W	1–0
24 Apr	Fulham	A	D	1–1
28 Apr	Manchester United	H	W	2–1

FA Cup

9 Jan	Coventry City	H	W	3–0
30 Jan	Sheffield United	A	W	2–0
20 Feb	Wolverhampton Wanderers	H	D	1–1
24 Feb	Wolverhampton Wanderers (R)	A	D	0–0
1 Mar	Wolverhampton Wanderers (R)	N	L	1–3

League Cup

23 Sep	Luton Town	A	W	1–0
14 Oct	Leeds United	A	W	3–2
4 Nov	Reading	H	W	3–1
23 Nov	Bradford City	H	W	7–1
20 Jan	Chelsea	H	L	2–3
10 Feb	Chelsea	A	D	1–1

SEASON 1965–1966 FOOTBALL LEAGUE (DIVISION 1)

12 Aug	Sheffield United	A	L	0–1
23 Aug	Leeds United	H	L	0–2
28 Aug	Leicester City	H	D	2–2
1 Sep	Leeds United	A	L	0–2
4 Sep	Blackburn Rovers	A	W	2–0
6 Sep	Sunderland	H	W	3–1
11 Sep	Blackpool	H	W	3–0
15 Sep	Sunderland	A	L	0–2
18 Sep	Fulham	A	W	6–3
25 Sep	Tottenham Hotspur	H	W	3–2
2 Oct	Liverpool	A	L	1–3
9 Oct	Newcastle United	A	L	0–1
16 Oct	West Bromwich Albion	H	D	1–1
23 Oct	Nottingham Forest	A	W	2–1
30 Oct	Sheffield Wednesday	H	W	2–0
6 Nov	Northampton Town	A	L	1–2
13 Nov	Stoke City	H	L	0–1
20 Nov	Burnley	A	L	1–3
27 Nov	Chelsea	H	L	2–4
4 Dec	Arsenal	A	D	3–3
11 Dec	Everton	H	W	3–2
18 Dec	West Bromwich Albion	A	abandoned	
27 Dec	West Ham United	H	abandoned	
1 Jan	Newcastle United	H	W	4–2
8 Jan	Everton	A	L	0–2
15 Jan	Nottingham Forest	H	W	3–0
29 Jan	Sheffield United	H	L	0–2
5 Feb	Leicester City	A	L	1–2
7 Feb	West Ham United	H	L	1–2
11 Feb	West Bromwich Albion	A	D	2–2
19 Feb	Blackburn Rovers	H	W	3–1
26 Feb	Blackpool	A	W	1–0
5 Mar	West Ham United	A	L	2–4
12 Mar	Fulham	H	L	2–5
19 Mar	Tottenham Hotspur	A	D	5–5
26 Mar	Liverpool	H	L	0–3
2 Apr	Northampton Town	H	L	1–2
6 Apr	Manchester United	H	D	1–1
9 Apr	Stoke City	A	L	0–2
16 Apr	Burnley	H	W	2–1
27 Apr	Sheffield Wednesday	A	L	0–2
30 Apr	Arsenal	H	W	3–0
2 May	Manchester United	A	L	1–6
16 May	Chelsea	A	W	2–0

FA Cup

| 22 Jan | Leicester City | H | L | 1–2 |

League Cup

21 Sep	Swansea Town	A	W	3–2
13 Oct	Sunderland	A	W	2–1
3 Nov	Fulham	A	D	1–1
8 Nov	Fulham (R)	H	W	2–0
17 Nov	West Bromwich Albion	A	L	1–3

SEASON 1966–1967 FOOTBALL LEAGUE (DIVISION 1)

Date	Opponent			
20 Aug	Newcastle United	H	D	1–1
22 Aug	Sheffield Wednesday	H	L	0–1
27 Aug	Arsenal	A	L	0–1
31 Aug	Sheffield Wednesday	A	L	0–2
3 Sep	Manchester City	H	W	3–0
5 Sep	Southampton	H	L	0–1
10 Sep	Blackpool	A	W	2–0
17 Sep	Chelsea	H	L	2–6
24 Sep	Leicester City	A	L	0–5
1 Oct	Liverpool	H	L	2–3
8 Oct	Leeds United	H	W	3–0
15 Oct	West Bromwich Albion	A	L	1–2
22 Oct	Sheffield United	H	D	0–0
29 Oct	Tottenham Hotspur	A	W	1–0
5 Nov	West Bromwich Albion	H	W	3–2
12 Nov	Fulham	A	L	1–5
19 Nov	Nottingham Forest	H	D	1–1
26 Nov	Burnley	A	L	2–4
3 Dec	Manchester United	H	W	2–1
10 Dec	Stoke City	A	L	1–6
17 Dec	Newcastle United	A	W	3–0
26 Dec	Sunderland	A	L	1–2
27 Dec	Sunderland	H	W	2–1
31 Dec	Arsenal	H	L	0–1
14 Jan	Blackpool	H	W	3–2
21 Jan	Chelsea	A	L	1–3
4 Feb	Leicester City	H	L	0–1
11 Feb	Liverpool	A	L	0–1
25 Feb	Leeds United	A	W	2–0
4 Mar	Tottenham Hotspur	H	D	3–3
18 Mar	Sheffield United	A	D	3–3
24 Mar	West Ham United	A	L	1–2
25 Mar	Stoke City	H	W	2–1
28 Mar	West Ham United	H	L	0–2
1 Apr	Everton	A	L	1–3
8 Apr	Fulham	H	D	1–1
15 Apr	Nottingham Forest	A	L	0–3
19 Apr	Manchester City	A	D	1–1
22 Apr	Burnley	H	L	0–1
29 Apr	Manchester United	A	L	1–3
6 May	Everton	H	L	2–4
13 May	Southampton	A	L	2–6

FA Cup

Date	Opponent			
28 Jan	Preston North End	A	W	1–0
18 Feb	Liverpool	A	L	0–1

League Cup

Date	Opponent			
14 Sep	West Bromwich Albion	A	L	1–6

SEASON 1967–1968 FOOTBALL LEAGUE (DIVISION 2)

Date	Opponent			
19 Aug	Norwich City	A	L	0–1
23 Aug	Plymouth Argyle	A	L	1–2
26 Aug	Rotherham United	H	W	3–1
28 Aug	Plymouth Argyle	H	L	0–1
2 Sep	Derby County	A	L	1–3
5 Sep	Queens Park Rangers	A	L	0–3
9 Sep	Preston North End	H	W	1–0
16 Sep	Charlton Athletic	A	L	0–3
23 Sep	Crystal Palace	H	L	0–1
30 Sep	Middlesbrough	A	D	1–1
7 Oct	Birmingham City	H	L	2–4
14 Oct	Millwall	A	W	2–1
21 Oct	Blackpool	H	W	3–2
4 Nov	Carlisle United	H	W	1–0
11 Nov	Ipswich Town	A	L	1–2
18 Nov	Hull City	H	L	2–3
25 Nov	Bolton Wanderers	A	W	3–2
2 Dec	Huddersfield Town	H	D	0–0
16 Dec	Norwich City	H	W	4–2
23 Dec	Rotherham United	A	W	2–0
26 Dec	Cardiff City	A	L	0–3
30 Dec	Cardiff City	H	W	2–1
6 Jan	Derby County	H	W	2–1
20 Jan	Charlton Athletic	H	W	4–1
3 Feb	Crystal Palace	A	W	1–0
10 Feb	Middlesbrough	H	L	0–1
24 Feb	Birmingham City	A	L	1–2
27 Feb	Bristol City	A	D	0–0
2 Mar	Millwall	H	W	3–1
13 Mar	Blackburn Rovers	A	L	1–2
16 Mar	Blackpool	A	L	0–1
18 Mar	Preston North End	A	L	1–2
23 Mar	Blackburn Rovers	H	L	1–2
30 Mar	Carlisle United	A	W	2–1
6 Apr	Ipswich Town	H	D	2–2
13 Apr	Hull City	A	L	0–3
15 Apr	Portsmouth	A	D	2–2
16 Apr	Portsmouth	H	W	1–0
20 Apr	Bolton Wanderers	H	D	1–1
27 Apr	Huddersfield Town	A	D	0–0
4 May	Bristol City	H	L	2–4
11 May	Queens Park Rangers	H	L	1–2

FA Cup

Date	Opponent			
27 Jan	Millwall	H	W	3–0
17 Feb	Rotherham United	H	L	0–1

League Cup

Date	Opponent			
13 Sep	Northampton Town	A	L	1–3

SEASON 1968–1969 FOOTBALL LEAGUE (DIVISION 2)

Date	Opponent			
10 Aug	Sheffield United	A	L	1–3
17 Aug	Fulham	H	D	1–1
19 Aug	Millwall	H	D	1–1
24 Aug	Blackburn Rovers	A	L	0–2
26 Aug	Bristol City	H	W	3–0
31 Aug	Blackpool	H	L	0–1
7 Sep	Derby County	A	L	1–3
14 Sep	Hull City	H	D	1–1
18 Sep	Bolton Wanderers	A	L	1–4
21 Sep	Birmingham City	A	L	0–4
28 Sep	Oxford United	H	W	2–0
5 Oct	Cardiff City	A	D	1–1
8 Oct	Bristol City	A	L	0–1
12 Oct	Crystal Palace	H	D	1–1
19 Oct	Norwich City	A	D	1–1
26 Oct	Carlisle United	H	D	0–0
2 Nov	Huddersfield United	A	L	1–3
9 Nov	Preston North End	H	L	0–1
16 Nov	Portsmouth	A	L	0–2
23 Nov	Middlesbrough	H	W	1–0
30 Nov	Bury	A	L	2–3
7 Dec	Charlton Athletic	H	D	0–0
14 Dec	Crystal Palace	A	L	2–4
21 Dec	Norwich City	H	W	2–1
26 Dec	Cardiff City	H	W	2–0
28 Dec	Carlisle United	A	W	1–0
11 Jan	Huddersfield Town	H	W	1–0
18 Jan	Preston North End	A	L	0–1
1 Feb	Portsmouth	H	W	2–0
8 Feb	Middlesbrough	A	abandoned	
15 Feb	Bury	H	W	1–0
22 Feb	Charlton Athletic	A	D	1–1
1 Mar	Sheffield United	H	W	3–1
4 Mar	Middlesbrough	A	D	0–0
8 Mar	Fulham	A	D	1–1
15 Mar	Blackburn Rovers	H	D	1–1
22 Mar	Blackpool	A	D	1–1
29 Mar	Derby County	H	L	0–1
4 Apr	Millwall	A	W	1–0
5 Apr	Oxford United	A	L	0–1
8 Apr	Bolton Wanderers	H	D	1–1
12 Apr	Birmingham City	H	L	2–4
19 Apr	Hull City	A	L	0–3

FA Cup

Date	Opponent			
4 Jan	Queens Park Rangers	H	W	2–1
25 Jan	Southampton	A	D	2–2
29 Jan	Southampton	H	W	2–1
12 Feb	Tottenham Hotspur	A	L	2–3

League Cup

Date	Opponent			
4 Sep	Tottenham Hotspur	H	L	1–4

SEASON 1969–1970 FOOTBALL LEAGUE (DIVISION 2)

Date	Opponent			
9 Aug	Norwich City	H	L	0–1
16 Aug	Huddersfield Town	A	L	0–2
19 Aug	Carlisle United	A	D	1–1
23 Aug	Swindon Town	H	L	0–2
27 Aug	Leicester City	H	L	0–1
30 Aug	Middlesbrough	A	L	0–1
6 Sep	Millwall	H	D	2–2
13 Sep	Watford	A	L	0–3
17 Sep	Bolton Wanderers	A	L	1–2
20 Sep	Hull City	H	W	3–2
27 Sep	Portsmouth	A	D	0–0
4 Oct	Preston North End	H	D	0–0
8 Oct	Huddersfield Town	H	W	4–1
11 Oct	Cardiff City	A	L	0–4
18 Oct	Birmingham City	H	D	0–0
25 Oct	Oxford United	A	D	2–2
1 Nov	Queens Park Rangers	H	D	1–1
8 Nov	Bristol City	A	L	0–1
12 Nov	Carlisle United	H	W	1–0
15 Nov	Blackpool	H	D	0–0
19 Nov	Bolton Wanderers	H	W	3–0
22 Nov	Sheffield United	A	L	0–5
6 Dec	Blackburn Rovers	A	L	0–1
13 Dec	Watford	H	L	0–2
26 Dec	Swindon Town	H	D	1–1
17 Jan	Portsmouth	H	L	3–5
31 Jan	Preston North End	A	D	1–1
7 Feb	Cardiff City	H	D	1–1
14 Feb	Norwich City	A	L	1–3
21 Feb	Bristol City	H	L	0–2
25 Feb	Charlton Athletic	H	W	1–0
28 Feb	Queens Park Rangers	A	L	2–4
10 Mar	Hull City	A	L	1–3
14 Mar	Charlton Athletic	A	L	0–1
16 Mar	Millwall	A	L	0–2
21 Mar	Blackburn Rovers	H	D	1–1
28 Mar	Blackpool	A	L	1–2
30 Mar	Birmingham City	A	W	2–0
31 Mar	Oxford United	H	D	0–0
4 Apr	Leicester City	A	L	0–1
8 Apr	Middlesbrough	H	W	2–0
10 Apr	Sheffield United	H	W	1–0

FA Cup

Date	Opponent			
3 Jan	Charlton Athletic	H	D	1–1
12 Jan	Charlton Athletic (R)	A	L	0–1

League Cup

Date	Opponent			
13 Aug	Chester	A	W	2–1
3 Sep	West Bromwich Albion	H	L	1–2

SEASON 1970–1971 FOOTBALL LEAGUE (DIVISION 3)

Date	Opponent			
15 Aug	Chesterfield	A	W	3–2
22 Aug	Plymouth Argyle	H	D	1–1
29 Aug	Swansea Town	A	W	2–1
31 Aug	Mansfield Town	H	L	0–1
5 Sep	Doncaster Rovers	H	W	3–2
12 Sep	Barnsley	A	D	1–1
19 Sep	Preston North End	H	W	2–0
23 Sep	Gillingham	H	W	2–1
26 Sep	Wrexham	A	W	3–2
30 Sep	Bristol Rovers	H	D	1–1
3 Oct	Brighton & Hove Albion	H	D	0–0
10 Oct	Rochdale	A	D	1–1
17 Oct	Chesterfield	H	D	0–0
19 Oct	Port Vale	A	L	0–2
24 Oct	Tranmere Rovers	H	W	1–0
31 Oct	Reading	A	W	5–3
7 Nov	Torquay United	H	L	0–1
11 Nov	Bury	H	W	1–0
14 Nov	Halifax Town	A	L	1–2
28 Nov	Fulham	A	W	2–0
5 Dec	Bradford City	H	W	1–0
19 Dec	Plymouth Argyle	A	D	1–1
26 Dec	Shrewsbury Town	H	W	2–0
2 Jan	Walsall	A	L	0–3
9 Jan	Bristol Rovers	A	W	2–1
16 Jan	Port Vale	H	W	1–0
23 Jan	Rotherham United	A	D	1–1
30 Jan	Fulham	H	W	1–0
6 Feb	Bradford City	A	L	0–1
13 Feb	Rotherham United	H	W	1–0
20 Feb	Bury	A	L	1–3
5 Mar	Tranmere Rovers	A	D	1–1
10 Mar	Gillingham	A	D	0–0
13 Mar	Halifax Town	H	D	1–1
17 Mar	Walsall	H	D	0–0
20 Mar	Torquay United	A	L	1–2
26 Mar	Doncaster Rovers	A	L	1–2
3 Apr	Swansea Town	H	W	3–0
9 Apr	Brighton & Hove Albion	A	L	0–1
10 Apr	Shrewsbury Town	A	L	1–2

12 Apr	Barnsley	H	D	0–0
17 Apr	Rochdale	H	W	1–0
24 Apr	Preston North End	A	D	0–0
26 Apr	Mansfield Town	A	L	0–2
1 May	Wrexham	H	L	3–4
4 May	Reading	H	W	2–1

FA Cup

21 Nov	Torquay United	A	L	1–3

League Cup

19 Aug	Notts County	H	W	4–0
9 Sep	Burnley	H	W	2–0
6 Oct	Northampton Town	A	D	1–1
13 Oct	Northampton Town (R)	H	W	3–0
28 Oct	Carlisle United	H	W	1–0
17 Nov	Bristol Rovers	A	D	1–1
25 Nov	Bristol Rovers (R)	H	W	1–0
16 Dec	Manchester United	A	D	1–1
23 Dec	Manchester United	H	W	2–1
27 Feb	Tottenham Hotspur (F)	N	L	0–2

SEASON 1971–1972 FOOTBALL LEAGUE (DIVISION 3)

14 Aug	Plymouth Argyle	H	W	3–1
21 Aug	Walsall	A	D	1–1
28 Aug	Rochdale	H	W	2–0
4 Sep	Bolton Wanderers	A	L	0–2
11 Sep	Brighton & Hove Albion	H	W	2–0
18 Sep	Halifax Town	A	W	1–0
22 Sep	Mansfield Town	H	L	0–1
25 Sep	Wrexham	H	W	2–0
28 Sep	Barnsley	A	W	4–0
2 Oct	Bristol Rovers	A	W	1–0
9 Oct	Rotherham United	H	L	1–2
16 Oct	Plymouth Argyle	A	L	2–3
20 Oct	Tranmere Rovers	H	W	2–0
23 Oct	Bournemouth	A	L	0–3
30 Oct	Blackburn Rovers	H	W	4–1
6 Nov	Port Vale	A	D	4–4
13 Nov	Notts County	H	W	1–0
27 Nov	Oldham Athletic	A	W	6–0
4 Dec	Bradford City	H	W	3–0
18 Dec	Bolton Wanderers	H	W	3–2
27 Dec	Swansea Town	A	W	2–1
1 Jan	Halifax Town	H	W	1–0
8 Jan	Rochdale	A	L	0–1
19 Jan	Shrewsbury Town	H	W	3–0
22 Jan	Barnsley	H	W	2–0
28 Jan	Tranmere Rovers	A	W	1–0
5 Feb	York City	H	W	1–0
12 Feb	Bournemouth	H	W	2–1
19 Feb	Blackburn Rovers	A	D	1–1
26 Feb	Port Vale	H	W	2–0
4 Mar	Notts County	A	W	3–0
11 Mar	Rotherham United	A	W	2–0
15 Mar	Shrewsbury Town	A	D	1–1
18 Mar	Walsall	H	D	0–0
25 Mar	Brighton & Hove Albion	A	L	1–2
31 Mar	Wrexham	A	W	2–0
1 Apr	Swansea Town	H	W	2–0
3 Apr	Bristol Rovers	H	W	2–1
8 Apr	York City	A	W	1–0
10 Apr	Oldham Athletic	H	W	1–0
12 Apr	Torquay United	A	L	1–2
19 Apr	Chesterfield	A	W	4–0
22 Apr	Bradford City	A	W	1–0
24 Apr	Mansfield Town	A	D	1–1
29 Apr	Torquay United	H	W	5–1
5 May	Chesterfield	H	W	1–0

FA Cup

20 Nov	Southend United	A	L	0–1

League Cup

18 Aug	Wrexham	H	D	2–2
23 Aug	Wrexham (R)	A	D	1–1
31 Aug	Wrexham (R)	N	W	4–3
8 Sep	Chesterfield	A	W	3–2
5 Oct	Crystal Palace	A	D	2–2
13 Oct	Crystal Palace (R)	H	W	2–0
26 Oct	Blackpool	A	L	1–4

SEASON 1972–1973 FOOTBALL LEAGUE (DIVISION 2)

12 Aug	Preston North End	H	W	1–0
19 Aug	Huddersfield Town	H	W	2–0
26 Aug	Burnley	A	L	1–4
29 Aug	Carlisle United	H	W	1–0
2 Sep	Brighton & Hove Albion	H	D	1–1
9 Sep	Cardiff City	A	W	2–0
16 Sep	Swindon Town	H	W	2–1
23 Sep	Nottingham Forest	A	D	1–1
27 Sep	Sunderland	H	W	2–0
30 Sep	Millwall	H	W	1–0
7 Oct	Fulham	A	L	0–2
14 Oct	Queens Park Rangers	H	L	0–1
17 Oct	Blackpool	A	D	1–1
21 Oct	Portsmouth	A	W	1–0
28 Oct	Middlesbrough	H	D	1–1
4 Nov	Sunderland	A	D	2–2
11 Nov	Blackpool	H	D	0–0
18 Nov	Luton Town	H	L	0–2
25 Nov	Oxford United	A	L	0–2
2 Dec	Hull City	H	W	2–0
16 Dec	Orient	H	W	1–0
23 Dec	Sheffield Wednesday	A	D	2–2
26 Dec	Nottingham Forest	H	D	2–2
30 Dec	Huddersfield Town	A	D	1–1
6 Jan	Burnley	H	L	0–3
20 Jan	Brighton & Hove Albion	A	W	3–1
27 Jan	Cardiff City	H	W	2–0
10 Feb	Swindon Town	A	W	3–1
17 Feb	Preston North End	H	D	1–1
24 Feb	Orient	A	L	0–4
3 Mar	Fulham	H	L	2–3
10 Mar	Queens Park Rangers	A	L	0–1
17 Mar	Portsmouth	H	W	2–0
24 Mar	Middlesbrough	A	D	1–1
27 Mar	Bristol City	A	L	0–3
31 Mar	Oxford United	H	W	2–1
7 Apr	Hull City	A	W	2–1
14 Apr	Bristol City	H	W	1–0
21 Apr	Luton Town	A	D	0–0
23 Apr	Millwall	A	D	1–1
24 Apr	Sheffield Wednesday	H	W	2–1
28 Apr	Carlisle United	A	D	2–2

FA Cup

13 Jan	Everton	A	L	2–3

League Cup

16 Aug	Hereford United	H	W	4–1
5 Sep	Nottingham Forest	A	W	1–0
5 Oct	Leeds United	H	D	1–1
11 Oct	Leeds United (R)	A	L	0–2

FA Charity Shield

5 Aug	Manchester City	H	L	0–1

SEASON 1973–1974 FOOTBALL LEAGUE (DIVISION 2)

25 Aug	Preston North End	H	W	2–0
1 Sep	Millwall	A	D	1–1
8 Sep	Oxford United	H	W	2–0
11 Sep	Crystal Palace	A	D	0–0
15 Sep	Middlesbrough	A	D	0–0
19 Sep	Fulham	H	D	1–1
22 Sep	Orient	H	D	2–2
29 Sep	Notts County	A	L	0–2
2 Oct	Fulham	A	L	0–1
6 Oct	Cardiff City	H	W	5–0
13 Oct	Bolton Wanderers	A	W	2–1
20 Oct	Bristol City	H	D	2–2
23 Oct	Crystal Palace	H	W	2–1
27 Oct	Nottingham Forest	A	W	2–1
3 Nov	Sheffield Wednesday	H	W	1–0
10 Nov	Portsmouth	A	L	0–2
17 Nov	Hull City	H	D	1–1
24 Nov	Swindon Town	A	L	0–1
8 Dec	Sunderland	A	L	0–2
15 Dec	Luton Town	A	L	0–1
22 Dec	Notts County	H	D	1–1
26 Dec	West Bromwich Albion	A	L	0–2
29 Dec	Oxford United	A	L	1–2
1 Jan	Millwall	H	D	0–0
12 Jan	Middlesbrough	H	D	1–1

SEASON 1974–1975 FOOTBALL LEAGUE (DIVISION 2)

19 Jan	Preston North End	A	D	0–0
2 Feb	Luton Town	H	L	0–1
23 Feb	Cardiff City	A	W	1–0
27 Feb	Bolton Wanderers	H	D	1–1
2 Mar	West Bromwich Albion	H	L	1–3
13 Mar	Carlisle United	H	W	2–1
16 Mar	Bristol City	A	W	1–0
23 Mar	Portsmouth	H	W	4–1
1 Apr	Sheffield Wednesday	A	W	4–2
6 Apr	Swindon Town	H	D	1–1
13 Apr	Hull City	A	D	1–1
15 Apr	Blackpool	H	L	0–1
16 Apr	Blackpool	A	L	1–2
20 Apr	Sunderland	H	L	1–2
24 Apr	Nottingham Forest	H	W	3–1
27 Apr	Carlisle United	A	L	0–2
3 May	Orient	A	D	1–1

FA Cup

5 Jan	Chester	H	W	3–1
26 Jan	Arsenal	A	D	1–1
30 Jan	Arsenal	H	W	2–0
16 Feb	Burnley	A	L	0–1

League Cup

9 Oct	York City	A	L	0–1

SEASON 1974–1975 FOOTBALL LEAGUE (DIVISION 2)

17 Aug	York City	A	D	1–1
20 Aug	Hull City	A	D	1–1
24 Aug	Norwich City	H	D	1–1
28 Aug	Hull City	H	W	6–0
31 Aug	Bolton Wanderers	A	L	0–1
7 Sep	Orient	H	W	3–1
14 Sep	Bristol Rovers	A	L	0–2
21 Sep	Millwall	H	W	3–0
28 Sep	Southampton	A	D	0–0
2 Oct	Nottingham Forest	H	W	3–0
5 Oct	Oldham Athletic	A	W	2–1
12 Oct	Blackpool	H	W	1–0
19 Oct	Sunderland	A	D	0–0
26 Oct	Sheffield Wednesday	H	W	3–1
2 Nov	Fulham	A	L	1–3
9 Nov	Notts County	H	L	0–1
16 Nov	Manchester United	A	L	1–2
23 Nov	Portsmouth	H	W	2–0
29 Nov	Oxford United	H	D	0–0
7 Dec	Bristol City	A	L	0–1
14 Dec	York City	H	W	4–0
21 Dec	West Bromwich Albion	A	L	0–2
26 Dec	Bristol Rovers	H	W	1–0
28 Dec	Cardiff City	A	L	1–3
11 Jan	Bristol City	H	W	2–0
18 Jan	Oxford United	A	W	2–1
1 Feb	Notts County	A	W	3–1
8 Feb	Fulham	H	D	1–1
18 Feb	Portsmouth	A	W	3–2
22 Feb	Manchester United	H	W	2–0
5 Mar	Bolton Wanderers	H	D	0–0
8 Mar	Nottingham Forest	A	W	3–2
15 Mar	Southampton	H	W	3–0
22 Mar	Orient	A	L	0–1
29 Mar	West Bromwich Albion	H	W	3–1
1 Apr	Millwall	H	W	3–1
9 Apr	Cardiff City	H	W	2–0
12 Apr	Oldham Athletic	H	W	5–0
19 Apr	Blackpool	A	W	3–0
23 Apr	Sheffield Wednesday	A	W	4–0
26 Apr	Sunderland	H	W	2–0
30 Apr	Norwich City (F)	A	W	4–1

FA Cup

4 Jan	Oldham Athletic	A	W	3–0
25 Jan	Sheffield United	H	W	4–1
15 Feb	Ipswich Town	A	L	2–3

League Cup

11 Sep	Everton	H	D	1–1
18 Sep	Everton (R)	A	W	3–0
9 Oct	Crewe Alexandra	A	D	2–2
16 Oct	Crewe Alexandra (R)	H	W	1–0
12 Nov	Hartlepool	A	D	1–1
25 Nov	Hartlepool (R)	H	W	6–1

3 Dec Colchester United A W 2–1
15 Jan Chester A D 2–2
22 Jan Chester H W 3–2
1 Mar Norwich City (F) N W 1–0

SEASON 1975–1976 FOOTBALL LEAGUE (DIVISION 1)

16 Aug	Leeds United	H	L	1–2
19 Aug	Queens Park Rangers	A	D	1–1
23 Aug	Norwich City	A	L	3–5
27 Aug	Manchester City	H	W	1–0
30 Aug	Coventry City	H	W	1–0
6 Sep	Newcastle United	A	L	0–3
13 Sep	Arsenal	H	W	2–0
20 Sep	Liverpool	A	L	0–3
23 Sep	Wolverhampton Wanderers	A	D	0–0
27 Sep	Birmingham City	H	W	2–1
4 Oct	Middlesbrough	A	D	0–0
11 Oct	Tottenham Hotspur	H	D	1–1
18 Oct	Everton	A	L	1–2
25 Oct	Burnley	H	D	1–1
1 Nov	Ipswich Town	H	L	0–3
8 Nov	Sheffield United	H	W	5–1
15 Nov	Manchester United	A	L	0–2
22 Nov	Everton	H	W	3–1
29 Nov	Leicester City	H	D	1–1
6 Dec	Stoke City	A	D	1–1
13 Dec	Norwich City	H	W	3–2
20 Dec	Leeds United	A	L	0–1
26 Dec	West Ham United	H	W	4–1
27 Dec	Derby County	A	L	0–2
10 Jan	Arsenal	A	D	0–0
17 Jan	Newcastle United	H	D	1–1
31 Jan	Queens Park Rangers	H	L	0–2
7 Feb	Manchester City	A	L	1–2
14 Feb	Sheffield United	A	L	1–2
21 Feb	Manchester United	H	W	2–1
24 Feb	Wolverhampton Wanderers	H	D	1–1
28 Feb	Burnley	A	D	2–2
6 Mar	Ipswich Town	H	D	0–0
13 Mar	Tottenham Hotspur	A	L	2–5
20 Mar	Leicester City	A	D	2–2
27 Mar	Stoke City	H	D	0–0
3 Apr	Birmingham City	A	L	2–3
10 Apr	Liverpool	H	D	0–0
13 Apr	Coventry City	A	D	1–1
17 Apr	West Ham United	A	D	2–2
19 Apr	Derby County	H	W	1–0
24 Apr	Middlesbrough	H	W	2–1

FA Cup

3 Jan	Southampton	A	D	1–1
7 Jan	Southampton (R)	H	L	1–2

League Cup

10 Sep	Oldham Athletic	H	W	2–0
8 Oct	Manchester United	H	L	1–2

UEFA Cup

17 Sep	Royal Antwerp	A	L	1–4
1 Oct	Royal Antwerp	H	L	0–1

SEASON 1976–1977 FOOTBALL LEAGUE (DIVISION 1)

21 Aug	West Ham United	H	W	4–0
25 Aug	Manchester City	A	L	0–2
28 Aug	Everton	A	W	2–0
4 Sep	Ipswich Town	H	W	5–2
11 Sep	Queens Park Rangers	A	L	1–2
18 Sep	Birmingham City	H	L	1–2
25 Sep	Leicester City	H	W	2–0
2 Oct	Stoke City	A	L	0–1
16 Oct	Sunderland	A	W	1–0
20 Oct	Arsenal	H	W	5–1
23 Oct	Bristol City	H	W	3–1
30 Oct	Liverpool	A	L	0–3
6 Nov	Manchester United	H	W	3–2
10 Nov	West Bromwich Albion	A	D	1–1
20 Nov	Coventry City	H	D	2–2
27 Nov	Coventry City	A	D	1–1
11 Dec	Leeds United	A	W	3–1
15 Dec	Liverpool	H	W	5–1
18 Dec	Newcastle United	H	W	2–1
27 Dec	Middlesbrough	A	L	2–3

SEASON 1977–1978 FOOTBALL LEAGUE (DIVISION 1)

20 Aug	Queens Park Rangers	A	W	2–1
24 Aug	Manchester City	H	L	1–4
27 Aug	Everton	H	L	1–2
3 Sep	Bristol City	A	D	1–1
10 Sep	Arsenal	H	W	1–0
17 Sep	Nottingham Forest	A	L	0–2
23 Sep	Wolverhampton Wanderers	H	W	2–1
1 Oct	Birmingham City	H	L	0–1
5 Oct	Leeds United	A	D	1–1
8 Oct	Leicester City	A	W	2–0
15 Oct	Norwich City	H	W	3–0
22 Oct	West Ham United	A	D	2–2
29 Oct	Manchester United	H	W	2–1
5 Nov	Liverpool	A	W	2–1
12 Nov	Middlesbrough	H	L	0–1
19 Nov	Chelsea	A	D	0–0
3 Dec	Ipswich Town	A	L	0–2
10 Dec	West Bromwich Albion	H	W	3–0
17 Dec	Middlesbrough	A	L	0–1
26 Dec	Coventry City	H	D	1–1
27 Dec	Derby County	A	W	3–0
31 Dec	Manchester City	A	L	0–2
2 Jan	Queens Park Rangers	H	D	1–1
14 Jan	Everton	A	L	0–1
21 Jan	Bristol City	H	W	1–0
4 Feb	Arsenal	A	W	1–0
25 Feb	Birmingham City	A	L	0–1
4 Mar	Leicester City	H	D	0–0
11 Mar	Norwich City	A	L	1–2
18 Mar	West Ham United	H	W	4–1
21 Mar	Coventry City	A	W	3–2
25 Mar	Derby County	H	D	0–0
29 Mar	Manchester United	A	D	1–1
1 Apr	Liverpool	H	L	0–3
5 Apr	Nottingham Forest	H	L	0–1
8 Apr	Newcastle United	A	D	1–1
15 Apr	Chelsea	H	W	2–0
17 Apr	Newcastle United	H	W	2–0
22 Apr	West Bromwich Albion	A	W	3–0
26 Apr	Leeds United	H	W	3–1
29 Apr	Ipswich Town	H	W	6–1
2 May	Wolverhampton Wanderers	A	L	1–3

FA Cup

8 Jan	Leicester City	A	W	1–0
29 Jan	West Ham United	H	W	3–0
26 Feb	Port Vale	H	W	3–0
19 Mar	Manchester United	A	L	1–2

League Cup

1 Sep	Manchester City	H	W	3–0
21 Sep	Norwich City	H	W	2–1
27 Oct	Wrexham	H	W	5–1
1 Dec	Millwall	H	W	2–0
1 Feb	Queens Park Rangers	A	D	0–0
16 Feb	Queens Park Rangers	H	D	2–2
22 Feb	Queens Park Rangers (R)	A	W	3–0
12 Mar	Everton (F)	N	D	0–0
16 Mar	Everton (FR)	N	D	1–1
13 Apr	Everton (FR)	N	W	3–2

1 Jan	Manchester United	A	L	0–2
22 Jan	West Ham United	A	W	1–0
5 Feb	Everton	H	W	2–0
12 Feb	Ipswich Town	A	L	0–1
2 Mar	Derby County	H	W	4–0
5 Mar	Leicester City	A	D	1–1
23 Mar	Sunderland	H	W	4–1
2 Apr	Bristol City	A	D	0–0
5 Apr	Middlesbrough	H	W	1–0
9 Apr	Derby County	A	L	1–2
16 Apr	Coventry City	A	W	3–2
20 Apr	Tottenham Hotspur	H	W	2–1
23 Apr	Norwich City	H	W	1–0
25 Apr	Arsenal	A	L	0–3
30 Apr	Tottenham Hotspur	A	L	1–3
4 May	Manchester City	H	D	1–1
7 May	Leeds United	H	W	2–1
10 May	Birmingham City	A	L	1–2
14 May	Newcastle United	A	L	2–3
16 May	Stoke City	H	W	1–0
20 May	Queens Park Rangers	H	D	1–1
23 May	West Bromwich Albion	H	W	4–0

FA Cup

7 Jan	Everton	A	L	1–4

League Cup

31 Aug	Exeter City	A	W	3–1
26 Oct	Queens Park Rangers	H	W	1–0
29 Nov	Nottingham Forest	A	L	2–4

UEFA Cup

14 Sep	Fenerbahce	H	W	4–0
28 Sep	Fenerbahce	A	W	2–0
19 Oct	Gornik Zabrze	H	W	2–0
2 Nov	Gornik Zabrze	A	D	1–1
23 Nov	Athletic Bilbao	H	W	2–0
7 Dec	Athletic Bilbao	A	D	1–1
1 Mar	Barcelona	H	D	2–2
15 Mar	Barcelona	A	L	1–2

SEASON 1978–1979 FOOTBALL LEAGUE (DIVISION 1)

19 Aug	Wolverhampton Wanderers	H	W	1–0
23 Aug	Tottenham Hotspur	A	W	4–1
26 Aug	Bristol City	A	L	0–1
2 Sep	Southampton	H	D	1–1
9 Sep	Ipswich Town	A	W	2–0
16 Sep	Everton	H	D	1–1
23 Sep	Queens Park Rangers	A	L	0–1
30 Sep	Nottingham Forest	H	L	1–2
7 Oct	Arsenal	A	D	1–1
14 Oct	Manchester United	H	D	2–2
21 Oct	Birmingham City	A	W	1–0
27 Oct	Middlesbrough	H	L	0–2
4 Nov	Manchester City	D	D	1–1
11 Nov	Wolverhampton Wanderers	A	W	4–0
18 Nov	Bristol City	H	W	2–0
21 Nov	Southampton	A	L	0–2
25 Nov	West Bromwich Albion	A	D	1–1
9 Dec	Chelsea	A	W	1–0
16 Dec	Norwich City	H	D	1–1
23 Dec	Derby County	A	D	0–0
26 Dec	Leeds United	H	D	2–2
31 Jan	Everton	A	D	1–1
24 Feb	Manchester United	A	D	1–1
3 Mar	Birmingham City	H	W	1–0
7 Mar	Bolton Wanderers	H	W	3–0
10 Mar	Middlesbrough	A	L	0–2
20 Mar	Queens Park Rangers	H	W	3–1
24 Mar	Tottenham Hotspur	H	L	2–3
28 Mar	Coventry City	H	D	1–1
4 Apr	Nottingham Forest	A	L	0–4
7 Apr	Coventry City	A	D	1–1
11 Apr	Derby County	H	D	3–3
14 Apr	Leeds United	A	L	0–1
16 Apr	Liverpool	H	W	3–1
21 Apr	Norwich City	A	W	2–1
25 Apr	Arsenal	H	W	5–1
28 Apr	Chelsea	H	W	2–1
2 May	Ipswich Town	H	D	2–2
5 May	Bolton Wanderers	A	D	0–0
8 May	Liverpool	A	L	0–3
11 May	West Bromwich Albion	H	L	0–1
15 May	Manchester City	A	W	3–2

FA Cup

10 Jan	Nottingham Forest	A	L	0–2

League Cup

30 Aug	Sheffield Wednesday	H	W	1–0
4 Oct	Crystal Palace	H	D	1–1
10 Oct	Crystal Palace (R)	A	D	0–0
16 Oct	Crystal Palace (R)	N	W	3–0
8 Nov	Luton Town	H	L	0–2

SEASON 1979–1980 FOOTBALL LEAGUE (DIVISION 1)

18 Aug	Bolton Wanderers	A	D	1–1
22 Aug	Brighton & Hove Albion	H	W	2–1
25 Aug	Bristol City	A	L	0–2
1 Sep	Everton	A	D	1–1
8 Sep	Manchester United	H	L	0–3
15 Sep	Crystal Palace	A	L	0–2
22 Sep	Arsenal	H	D	0–0
29 Sep	Middlesbrough	A	D	0–0

Southampton	H	W	3–0
West Bromwich Albion	H	D	0–0
Derby County	A	W	3–1
Wolverhampton Wanderers	A	D	1–1
Bolton Wanderers	H	W	3–1
Ipswich Town	A	D	0–0
Stoke City	H	W	2–1
Leeds United	H	D	0–0
Norwich City	A	D	1–1
Liverpool	H	L	1–3
Tottenham Hotspur	A	W	2–1
Coventry City	H	W	3–0
Nottingham Forest	A	L	1–2
Bristol City	A	W	3–1
Everton	H	W	2–1
Crystal Palace	H	W	2–0
Arsenal	A	L	1–3

23 Feb	West Bromwich Albion	A	W	2–1
27 Feb	Manchester City	H	D	2–2
1 Mar	Derby County	H	W	1–0
3 Mar	Brighton & Hove Albion	A	D	1–1
10 Mar	Wolverhampton Wanderers	H	L	1–3
15 Mar	Southampton	A	L	0–2
19 Mar	Middlesbrough	H	L	0–2
22 Mar	Ipswich Town	H	D	1–1
26 Mar	Norwich City	H	W	2–0
29 Mar	Stoke City	A	L	0–2
5 Apr	Nottingham Forest	H	W	3–2
7 Apr	Manchester City	A	D	1–1
19 Apr	Leeds United	A	D	0–0
23 Apr	Manchester United	A	L	1–2
26 Apr	Tottenham Hotspur	H	W	1–0
29 Apr	Coventry City	A	W	2–1
3 May	Liverpool	A	L	1–4

FA Cup

4 Jan	Bristol Rovers	A	W	2–1
26 Jan	Cambridge United	A	D	1–1
30 Jan	Cambridge United (R)	H	W	4–1
16 Feb	Blackburn Rovers	A	D	1–1
20 Feb	Blackburn Rovers (R)	H	W	1–0
8 Mar	West Ham United	A	L	0–1

League Cup

28 Aug	Colchester United	A	W	2–0
5 Sep	Colchester United	H	L	0–2 (pens)
25 Sep	Everton	H	D	0–0
9 Oct	Everton (R)	A	L	1–4

SEASON 1980–1981 FOOTBALL LEAGUE (DIVISION 1)

Opponent	V	Res	Score	Rimmer	Swain	Deacy	Williams	McNaught	Mortimer	Bremner	Shaw1	Withe	Cowans	Morley1	Sub
Leeds United	A	W	2–1	Rimmer	Swain	Deacy	Williams	McNaught	Mortimer	Bremner	Shaw1	Withe	Cowans	Morley1	
Norwich City	H	W	1–0	"	"	Gibson	Evans	"	"	"	"1	"	"	"	
Manchester City	A	D	2–2	"	"	"	"	"	"	"	"	"2	"	"	
Coventry City	H	W	1–0	"	"	"	"	"	"	"	"1	"	"	"	
Ipswich Town	A	L	0–1	"	"	"	"	"	"	"	"	"	"	"	
Everton	H	L	0–2	"	"	"	"	"	"	"	"	"	"	"	
Wolverhampton Wanderers	H	W	2–1*	"	"	"	"	"	"	"	Geddis1	"	"	"	
Crystal Palace	A	W	1–0	"	"	"	"	"	"	"	Shaw1	"	"	"1	
Sunderland	H	W	4–0	"	"	"	"2	"	"	"	"1	"	"	"1	
Manchester United	A	D	3–3	"	"	Deacy	"	"	"	"	"1	"1	"1	"	
Birmingham City	A	W	2–1	"	"	"	"1	"	"	"	"	"	"1	"	
Tottenham Hotspur	H	W	3–0	"	"	Gibson	"	"	"	"	"	"1	"	"2	
Brighton & Hove Albion	H	W	4–1	"	"	"	"	"1	"1	"2	"1	"	"		
Southampton	A	W	2–1	"	"	"	"	"	"	"	"1	"	"1		
Leicester City	H	W	2–0	"	"	Deacy	"	"	"	"	"1	"	"1	"	Williams
West Bromwich Albion	A	D	0–0	"	"	Williams	"	"	"	"	"	"	"	"	
Norwich City	A	W	3–1	"	"	"	"1	"	"	"	"2	"	"	"	
Leeds United	H	D	1–1	"	"	"	"	"	"	"	"1	"	"	"	
Liverpool	A	L	1–2	"	"	"	"1	"	"	"	"	"	"	"	
Arsenal	H	D	1–1	"	"	"	"	"	"	"	"	"	"	"1	
Middlesbrough	A	L	1–2	"	"	"	"	"	"	"	"1	Geddis	"	"	Deacy
Birmingham City	H	W	3–0	"	"	"	"	"	"	"	"1	"2	"	"	
Brighton & Hove Albion	A	L	0–1	"	"	"	"	"	"	"	"	"	"	"	Deacy
Stoke City	H	W	1–0	"	"	"	"	"	"	"	"	Withe1	"	Withe	
Nottingham Forest	A	D	2–2*	"	"	"	"	"	"	"	"1	Geddis	"	"	
Liverpool	H	W	2–0	"	"	Gibson	"	"	"1	"	"	Withe1	"	"	
Coventry City	A	W	2–1	"	"	"	"	"	"	"	"1	"	"	"1	
Manchester City	H	W	1–0	"	"	Deacy	"	"	"	"	"1	"	"	"	Geddis
Everton	A	W	3–1	"	"	Williams	"	"	"1	"	"	"	"1	"1	
Crystal Palace	H	W	2–1	"	"	"	"	"	"	"	"	"2	"	"	
Wolverhampton Wanderers	A	W	1–0	"	"	"	"	"	"	"	"	"1	"	"	
Sunderland	A	W	2–1	"	"	"	"1	"	"1	"	"	"	"	"	
Manchester United	H	D	3–3	"	"	"	"	"	"	"	"1	"2	"	"	
Tottenham Hotspur	A	L	0–2	"	"	"	"	"	"	"	"	Geddis	"	"	
Southampton	H	W	2–1	"	"	"	"	"	"	"	"	"1	"	"1	
Leicester City	A	W	4–2	"	"	"	"	"	"	"1	"	Withe2	"	"1	
West Bromwich Albion	H	W	1–0	"	"	Gibson	"	"	"	"	Geddis	"1	"	"	
Ipswich Town	H	L	1–2	"	"	"	Williams	"	"	"	Shaw1	"	"	"	
Nottingham Forest	H	W	2–0	"	"	"	"	"	"	"	"	"1	"1	"	
Stoke City	A	D	1–1	"	"	"	Evans	"	"	"	"	"1	"	"	
Middlesbrough	H	W	3–0	"	"	"	"1	"	"	"	"1	"1	"	"	
Arsenal	A	L	0–2	"	"	"	"	"	"	"	"	"	"	"	

Opponent	V	Res	Score	Rimmer	Swain	Williams	Evans	McNaught	Mortimer	Bremner	Shaw	Withe	Cowans	Morley	Geddis
Ipswich Town	A	L	0–1	Rimmer	Swain	Williams	Evans	McNaught	Mortimer	Bremner	Shaw	Withe	Cowans	Morley	Geddis

e Cup

Opponent	V	Res	Score	Rimmer	Swain	Gibson	Evans	McNaught	Mortimer	Bremner	Shaw	Withe	Cowans	Morley1	Sub
Leeds United	H	W	1–0	Rimmer	Swain	Gibson	Evans	McNaught	Mortimer	Bremner	Shaw	Withe	Cowans	Morley1	
Leeds United	A	W	3–1	"	"	"	"	"	"	"	"	"2	"1	"	Williams
Cambridge United	A	L	1–2	"	"	"	"	"	"1	"	"	Geddis	"	"1	

SEASON 1981–1982 FOOTBALL LEAGUE (DIVISION 1)

Opponent	V	Res	Score	Rimmer	Swain	Gibson	Evans	McNaught*	Mortimer	Bremner	Geddis	Withe	Cowans	Morley	Blair
Notts County	H	L	0–1	Rimmer	Swain	Gibson	Evans	McNaught*	Mortimer	Bremner	Geddis	Withe	Cowans	Morley	Blair
Sunderland	A	L	1–2	"	"	"	"	Ormsby	"	"	Donovan1	"	"	"	
Tottenham Hotspur	A	W	3–1	"	"	"	"	"	"1	"	"2	"	"		
Manchester United	H	D	1–1	"	"	"	"	"	"	"	"	"1	"		
Liverpool	A	D	0–0	"	"	"	"	McNaught	"	"	"	"	"		
Stoke City	H	D	2–2	"	"	"	"	"	"	"	"	"2	"	"	Blair
Birmingham City	H	D	0–0	"	"	"	"	Ormsby	"	"	Blair	"	"	"	
Leeds United	A	D	1–1	"	"	"	"	"	"	"	Shaw1	"	"	Blair	Morley

Date	Opponent			Score	1	2	3	4	5	6	7	8	9	10	11	12
10 Oct	Coventry City	A	D	1–1	"	"	"	"	"	"	"	*1	Geddis	"	Morley	
17 Oct	West Ham United	H	W	3–2	"	Williams	"	"	"	*1	*1	"	"	*1	"	*1 Blair
24 Oct	Wolverhampton Wanderers	A	W	3–0	"	"	"	"	"	"	"	*2	Withe	"	"	
31 Oct	Ipswich Town	H	L	0–1	"	Swain	"	"	"	"	"	"	"	"	"	
7 Nov	Arsenal	H	L	0–2	"	"	"	"	Williams	"	"	"	"	"	"	Blair
21 Nov	Middlesbrough	A	D	3–3	"	"	"	"	"	Deacy	"	*1	*1	*1	"	
28 Nov	Nottingham Forest	H	W	3–1	"	"	"	"	"	"	*2	"	*1	"	"	
5 Dec	Manchester City	A	L	0–1	"	"	"	"	"	"	"	"	"	"	"	
15 Dec	Swansea City	A	L	1–2*	"	"	"	"	"	"	"	"	Geddis	"	"	Linton
19 Dec	Everton	A	L	0–2	"	"	"	"	Blake	Bullivant	"	Donovan	"	"	"	
28 Dec	Brighton & Hove Albion	A	W	1–0	"	"	"	"	Williams	Mortimer	"	Shaw	"	"	*1	
16 Jan	Notts County	A	L	0–1	"	"	"	"	"	"	"	"	Withe	"	"	
30 Jan	Liverpool	H	L	0–3	"	"	"	"	"	"	"	Geddis	"	"	"	Blair
2 Feb	Sunderland	H	W	1–0	"	"	Blair	Ormsby	"	"	"	*1	"	"	Shelton	Bullivant
6 Feb	Manchester United	A	L	1–4	"	"	Evans	Blair	"	"	"	*1	"	"	Bullivant	
10 Feb	Southampton	H	D	1–1	"	"	Williams	"	McNaught	"	"	"	*1	"	Blair	
17 Feb	Tottenham Hotspur	H	D	1–1	"	"	"	"	"	"	"	Shaw	*1	"	Morley	
20 Feb	Birmingham City	A	W	1–0	"	"	"	"	"	"	"	"	*1	"	"	Bullivant
27 Feb	Coventry City	H	W	2–1	"	Jones	"	"	"	"	"	*!	"	*1	"	Blair
6 Mar	West Ham United	A	D	2–2	"	Swain	"	Bremner	"	"	Blair	"	*1	*1	"	
13 Mar	Wolverhampton Wanderers	H	W	3–1	"	"	"	Evans	"	"	Bremner	*1	Donovan1	"	*1	
20 Mar	Ipswich Town	A	L	1–3	"	"	"	"	*1	Bullivant	Blair	"	"	"	"	Heard
27 Mar	Arsenal	A	L	3–4	"	"	Jones	"	"	Heard1	Bullivant	*1	Withe	"	* 1	
30 Mar	West Bromwich Albion	A	W	2–1	"	"	Williams	"	"	Mortimer	Heard	*1	*1	"	"	
10 Apr	Southampton	A	W	3–0	"	"	"	"	*1	"	Bremner	"	"	"	* 1	
12 Apr	Brighton & Hove Albion	H	W	3–0	"	"	"	*1	"	"	"	Geddis2	"	"	"	Heard
17 Apr	Middlesbrough	H	W	1–0	"	"	"	*1	"	Heard	Blair	"	"	"	*t	
24 Apr	Nottingham Forest	H	D	1–1	"	"	"	"	"	Mortimer	Bremner	Shaw	"	*1	"	Blair
28 Apr	Leeds United	H	L	1–4	"	"	"	Ormsby	"	Blair	"	Geddis1	"	"	**	Walters
1 May	Manchester City	H	D	0–0	"	"	"	"	"	Heard	"	Shaw	"	"	"	
5 May	Stoke City	A	L	0–1	"	"	"	Evans	"	Mortimer	"	"	"	"	**	Blair"
8 May	West Bromwich Albion	A	W	1–0	"	"	"	"	"	"	"	"	"	"	Heard 1	
15 May	Everton	H	L	1–2	"	"	"	"	"	"	"	"	"	*1	"	Blair
21 May	Swansea City	H	W	3–0	"	"	"	"	"	"	*1	Geddis	*1	"	Morley1	Heard

FA Cup

Date	Opponent			Score	1	2	3	4	5	6	7	8	9	10	11	12
5 Jan	Notts County	A	W	6–0*	Rimmer	Swain	Gibson	Evans	Williams	Mortimer	Bremner	Shaw1	Geddis3	Cowans1	Morley	
23 Jan	Bristol City	A	W	1–0	"	"	"	"	"	"	Blair	*1	Withe	"	"	Bullivant
13 Feb	Tottenham Hotspur	A	L	0–1	"	"	Williams	"	McNaught	"	Bremner	Geddis	"	"	"	

League Cup

Date	Opponent			Score	1	2	3	4	5	6	7	8	9	10	11	12
7 Oct	Wolverhampton Wanderers	H	W	3–2	Rimmer	Swain	Gibson	Evans	Ormsby	Mortimer	Bremner1	Shaw	Withe	Cowans	Morley1	Blair 1
27 Oct	Wolverhampton Wanderers	A	W	2–1	"	Williams	"	"	"	"	"	"	"	*2	"	
11 Nov	Leicester City	A	D	0–0	"	Swain	"	"	Williams	"	"	"	"	"	"	Blair
25 Nov	Leicester City	H	W	2–0	"	"	"	"	"	Deacy	"	"	*1	*1	"	
1 Dec	Wigan Athletic	A	W	2–1	"	"	"	"	"	"	"	"	*1	*1	"	
20 Jan	West Bromwich Albion	H	L	0–1	"	"	"	"	"	Mortimer	"	"	"	"	"	Bullivant

European Cup

Date	Opponent			Score	1	2	3	4	5	6	7	8	9	10	11	12
16 Sep	Valur Reykjavik	H	W	5–0	Rimmer	Swain	Gibson	Evans	Ormsby	Mortimer	Bremner	Donovan2	Withe2	Cowans	Morley 1	
30 Sep	Valur Reykjavik	A	W	2–0	"	"	"	"	"	"	"	Shaw2	"	"	Blair	
21 Oct	Dynamo Berlin	A	W	2–1	"	Williams	"	"	"	"	"	"	"	"	Morley2	Linton
4 Nov	Dynamo Berlin	H	L	0–1	"	Swain	"	"	Williams	"	"	"	"	"	"	
3 Mar	Dynamo Kiev	A	D	0–0	"	"	Williams	Bremner	McNaught	"	Blair	"	"	"	"	
17 Mar	Dynamo Kiev	H	W	2–0	"	"	"	Evans	*1	"	Bremner	*1	"	"	"	Blair
7 Apr	Anderlecht	H	W	1–0	"	"	"	"	"	"	"	"	"	"	* 1	
21 Apr	Anderlecht	A	D	0–0	"	"	"	"	"	"	"	"	"	"	"	
26 May	Bayern Munich (F)	N	W	1–0	"	"	"	"	"	"	"	"	*1	"	"	Spink

SEASON 1982–1983 FOOTBALL LEAGUE (DIVISION 1)

Date	Opponent			Score	1	2	3	4	5	6	7	8	9	10	11	12
28 Aug	Sunderland	H	L	1–3	Rimmer	Swain	Williams	Evans	McNaught	Mortimer	Bremner	Walters	Withe	Cowans1	Morley	Heard
31 Aug	Everton	A	L	0–5	"	"	"	"	"	"	"	Shaw	Walters	"	"	Heard
4 Sep	Southampton	A	L	0–1	"	Jones	Heard	Bremner	"	"	Blair	Geddis	Withe	"	"	
8 Sep	Luton Town	H	W	4–1	"	"	"	"	"	*1	"	Shaw	*1	*2	"	Walters
11 Sep	Nottingham Forest	H	W	4–1	"	Williams	"	"	"	*1	"	"	*2	*1	"	Evans
18 Sep	Manchester City	A	W	1–0	"	Jones	Williams	Evans	"	"	Bremner	*1	"	"	"	
25 Sep	Swansea City	H	W	2–0	"	"	"	*1	"	*1	"	"	"	"	"	
2 Oct	West Bromwich Albion	A	L	0–1	"	"	"	"	"	"	"	"	"	"	"	
9 Oct	Notts County	A	L	1–4	"	"	"	"	Bremner	"	Hopkins	*1	"	"	Heard	Morley
16 Oct	Watford	H	W	3–0	"	"	Gibson	"	McNaught	"	Bremner	"	*1	"	Morley 2	
23 Oct	Norwich City	A	L	0–1	"	"	"	"	"	"	"	Geddis	"	"	"	Williams
30 Oct	Tottenham Hotspur	H	W	4–0	"	Williams	"	"	"	"	"	*1	Withe	*2	* 1	
6 Nov	Coventry City	A	D	0–0	"	Deacy	Williams	"	"	"	"	"	"	"	"	
13 Nov	Brighton & Hove Albion	H	W	1–0	"	"	"	"	"	"	"	"	*1	"	"	Walters
20 Nov	Manchester United	H	W	1–0	"	Jones	"	"	"	"	"	"	*1	*1	"	
27 Nov	Stoke City	A	W	3–0*	"	"	"	"	"	"	"	"	"	*2	"	Gibson
4 Dec	West Ham	H	W	1–0	"	"	"	"	"	"	"	"	"	*1	"	Walters
7 Dec	Arsenal	A	L	1–2	"	"	"	"	*1	Heard	"	"	"	"	"	Walters
18 Dec	Liverpool	H	L	2–4	"	"	"	"	"	Mortimer	"	"	*1	*1	Walters	
27 Dec	Birmingham City	A	L	0–3	"	"	"	"	"	"	"	"	"	"	"	

INDEX